Anonymity and Learning in Digitally Mediated Communications:

Authenticity and Trust in Cyber Education

Bobbe Baggio
La Salle University, USA

Yoany Beldarrain
La Salle University, USA

Information Science
REFERENCE

Senior Editorial Director:	Kristin Klinger
Director of Book Publications:	Julia Mosemann
Editorial Director:	Lindsay Johnston
Acquisitions Editor:	Erika Carter
Development Editor:	Julia Mosemann
Typesetters:	Julia Mosemann & Milan Vracarich, Jr.
Production Coordinator:	Jamie Snavely
Cover Design:	Nick Newcomer

Published in the United States of America by
  Information Science Reference (an imprint of IGI Global)
  701 E. Chocolate Avenue
  Hershey PA 17033
  Tel: 717-533-8845
  Fax: 717-533-8661
  E-mail: cust@igi-global.com
  Web site: http://www.igi-global.com/reference

Library of Congress Cataloging-in-Publication Data

Baggio, Bobbe.
  Anonymity and learning in digitally mediated communications : authenticity
and trust in cyber education / by Bobbe Baggio and Yoany Beldarrain.
    p. cm.
  Includes bibliographical references and index.
  Summary: "This book investigates the impact of anonymity and its effects on
online identity and learning, and reveals issues of authenticity and trust,
which are at the heart of online learning"--Provided by publisher.
  ISBN 978-1-60960-543-8 (hardcover) -- ISBN 978-1-60960-544-5 (ebook) 1.
Education--Computer network resources. 2. Internet in education. 3. Online
identities. 4. Internet--Safety measures. 5. Truthfulness and falsehood. I.
Beldarrain, Yoany. II. Title.
  LB1044.87.B42 2011
  371.33'44678--dc22
                        2010049831

British Cataloguing in Publication Data
A Cataloguing in Publication record for this book is available from the British Library.

All work contributed to this book is new, previously-unpublished material. The views expressed in
this book are those of the authors, but not necessarily of the publisher.

Table of Contents

Section 1:
What is Anonymity and Why Should You Be Concerned?

Chapter 1

Chapter 2

Section 2:
What is Identity and How Does it Impact Learning?

Section 3:
What are Some Approaches for the Future of Teaching and Learning Using Digitally Mediated Communications?

Foreword

The world of online or cyber education is approaching a cross-roads. In one direction is the openness and flexibility of a networked, connected, and user-empowered ecology and in the other, an institutionally-based set of programs that harness the power of technology and control its use and distribution. In this book, co-authored by Bobbe Baggio and Yoany Beldarrain, three critical factors associated with this approaching threshold are addressed: anonymity, identity, and authenticity.

In the first section, anonymity is approached from four different perspectives. The first chapter specifically focuses on the perennial question "who are we when we go online?" and addresses issues of collaboration, satisfaction, and learning as emergent outcomes from the level of trust of both the technology and people. The second factor considered is that of ethical behaviour in terms of our privacy, our integrity, and our right to free speech. Arguing for the responsibility of each and every stakeholder in ethical behaviour, the authors highlight the importance of understanding the environment within which we interact. The third chapter continues the focus on ethics through an analysis of intellectual property, and whether the laws are good enough (or perhaps current enough) to deal with the interchange of information that arises through social networking, connectivity, and information access. Is it a case of more stringent controls on content ownership, or recognising the added-value that networked communities can add to existing content. The fourth chapter in this initial section examines e-governance and the effectiveness of governance and management of online institutions in connected, networked environments.

The second section examines identity, highlighting another four factors that impact on the way we teach and learning within digitally-mediated educational environments. The initial examination addresses the risks inherent with data-security and profiling, which appear to align with recent political moves to monitor as much personal data as possible. For the teacher and student, the question arises as to how much information is needed, how much should be stored, and who should have access. Is this information a threat to security, or a doorway to better understanding teaching and learning? Having focused on anonymity in Section 1, the second chapter addresses community and self – what personal and social attributes might positively influence the online communities that emerge from online encounters? Whether we can have both anonymity and community is a question that remains open to debate! The third chapter addresses a very contentious issue, academic integrity. Why do students supposedly cheat and plagiarise so much? Is it the responsibility of the educator to monitor and punish, or might the educational design look to strategies and assessment where cheating becomes almost impossible. The identity section rounds out the second section, with the introduction of the pyjama effect, a valuable analysis of the blurring between work and play, and the options to study anytime, anywhere.

Section 3 of the text examines the applications of digitally-mediated teaching and learning, and the directions needed if we are to fully realise the potential of the technology. Underlying each of the four chapters is the importance of a learner-centred ethos, where the design of educational environments and resources do not focus primarily on the content, but rather on the activities the student will need to do to make sense of that content. Not only does this approach shift the power-base form teacher to learner, but also the nature of courses – from information transmission to outcome-based. The first chapter addresses this paradigm shift through an analysis of the importance of active learning, which is extended in the second chapter by a detailed exposition of what makes learning authentic and the importance of creating learning environments where students are actively engaged with problems or issues situated within the context in which they are likely to apply their learning. The final two chapters address two emerging environments in which the potential of cyber education is likely to be realised – virtual worlds and games. Rather than classrooms where the students are asked to analyse a set piece of content, the alternative is to allow students to participate and engage in interactions with a range of peers and teachers to achieve their personal learning goals.

When we reach the crossroads, we will have encountered each of the factors addressed in this diverse, yet focused text. What directional choices we make is yet to be seen. While taking account of anonymity, security, and identity, the value of cyber education is that the learning tasks can be structured to meet the individual and contextual needs of the learner, and through that, structuring the learners and teachers can engage in trustworthy, productive partnerships.

Roderick Sims
Capella University, USA
December 2010

Rod Sims has worked in the technology and education field for over 30 years. During that period, he has seen significant change in the technology we use, and has written and presented about the design of learning environments to effectively integrate that technology. Rod has worked as both a consultant in educational technology as well as designing and implementing undergraduate and postgraduate programs at the University of Technology Sydney and Southern Cross University. Over the last six years, Rod has been working as an Adjunct Professor with the US-based Capella University, with responsibilities for online teaching, course development, and PhD supervision in the field of Instructional Design for Online Learning. Currently, Rod is working with academic staff at the University of New England to enhance and revitalise a range of units through the implementation of innovative online strategies and resources.

Preface

Cyber education continues to expand globally and includes K-12, higher education, corporate training, and government programs. The topography of conventional teaching and learning is changing rapidly as educational budgets are decreasing. In the meantime, the demand for more digitally mediated forms of education is on the rise and is forever altering the silhouette of the average student and of the traditional instructor. Once confined to physical classrooms, today's learner connects globally for communication, entertainment, education, and information thus placing the individual in a new position that allows for the creation of an expanded identity (New Media Consortium, 2007). Part of the new online learner identity is influenced by the anonymity inherent in technology. Likewise, the identity of the instructor has changed, transforming the cyber educator's role from a facilitator to a member of the learning community who is part of the reciprocal exchange of knowledge. Both the medium for delivery and the pedagogy for learning are changed by technologies in the digital age. Cyber education includes all online, mobile, and digitally mediated means of communication used to connect learners and engage them in the learning process.

The increased demand for cyber education calls for a heightened sense of awareness among all stakeholders of online learning programs because digitally mediated communications afford benefits as well as constraints, especially as they relate to learning. Current literature generally discusses the benefits of such communications, yet the potential tradeoffs for learners and cyber educators are seldom explored. In this manuscript, such benefits and potential tradeoffs are discussed using the terms *online learning, cyber education,* and *digitally mediated learning* interchangeably.

Technologies for mobile learning, virtual worlds, and social software among others, are providing new opportunities and increasing the options available to instructional designers, cyber educators, and learners. New approaches to education means that concerns of anonymity, authenticity, identity, and trust will also be on the rise. In the report *Learning on Demand: Online Education in the United States, 2009* Allen and Seaman (2009) concluded that at least one in every four higher education students is taking one or more online courses. Over 4.6 million students took at least one online course during the fall 2008 term, which represents a 17 percent increase over the previous year. These numbers, however, are even higher when taking into account the increased population of K-12 online learners and the staggering increase in corporate training offered online today.

The anonymity inherent in digitally mediated communications also impacts the way learners interact in the online environment and supports the emergence of new identities. The definition of identity is no longer one-dimensional. Digitally mediated communications influence how anonymity may aid individuals to develop their online identity, and how this identity may lead to either authenticity and trust or deceit. While the sense of anonymity may free individuals to express or create a new self, the digital technologies used to enable this communication may conversely restrict free interactions and facilitate new methods of capturing, tracking, and scrutinizing data. There are legal ramifications and concerns behind this game of alter egos and emerging social mores. A close examination of the implications of anonymity in cyber education reveals how the issues of anonymity, authenticity, identity, and trust are at the center of online learning.

CHALLENGES AND THEIR IMPACT IN CYBER EDUCATION

The challenges and benefits of using digitally mediated communications for learning are explored in this manuscript through several theoretical lenses. This book focuses on the interactive and social nature of communications. While there are many other theoretical approaches and schools of thought that could be utilized to explore these issues, the authors chose those that they found to be most applicable to the discussion. Constructivism, connectivism, cognitivism, stakeholder theory, deindividuation theory, social presence theory, situated learning, situated cognitive theories, and activity theories are the key theoretical lenses used throughout the manuscript.

The "other side" to digitally mediated learning is the less discussed part of online learning that is challenged by cheating, authenticity, identity, and privacy issues. There is also a struggle with the reliability of sources, deception, and trust. Anonymity and issues of trust are interrelated. The secrecy and obscurity of faceless digitally mediated communications provides a sense of mystery and ambiguity. Anonymity is directly tied to privacy and identity. Learner authenticity, assessment reliability, and data security are issues most online establishments need to address more feverishly. But concerns are not limited to verifying the identity of the student, or making sure data is safe. Digitally mediated communications envelop dichotomies that suggest the safety of privacy and anonymity, yet capture and record each interaction.

The impact of anonymity and how it influences privacy is of global concern. Different countries have chosen contrasting approaches to regulating an individual learner's right to privacy. Regardless, Internet users leave behind a traceable trail of digital footprints and fingerprints that can be easily exploited, even in educational settings. What once was a said in casual conversation is now recorded via instant messaging, blogs, wikis, and online course rooms. Data mining is a regular practice on public servers and on the data streams connecting the Internet. Spyware is commonly used, hindering privacy by invading computer or mobile devices to collect data for marketing and profiling purposes. Enormous amounts of data are mined and sorted by companies, educational organizations, and governments alike. The problem is that the individual may never know for what purpose or whose purpose this information is collected.

Another challenge of anonymity is intellectual property rights. These include intangible rights that protect the creativity and ingenuity of the human intellect. While copy rights, trademarks, patent rights, publicity rights, moral rights, and other intellectual property rights exist, these regulations are much more difficult to enforce online. This is complicated by anonymity because digital communication has given a voice to millions of people who can share their ideas and thoughts under cover of a pseudonym or screen name. Likewise, intellectual property such as instructor created materials and student projects posted in a digital environment can unscrupulously be copied, distributed, or modified, and used as someone else's idea. Educational institutions even quarrel over who owns the instructor created materials used in a course.

The anonymity provided by communicating online, the advent of open source social software, and the fact that more individuals engage in online learning, puts academic and personal freedom in a precarious position. Questions arise regarding who owns the data and what privacy rights exist for learner and instructor. Academic freedom and liberty to explore alternative views without fear of retribution is a keystone of human rights. The ultimate question of anonymity and learning online is: can this delicate balance between anonymity, authenticity, and trust be maintained in a digitally mediated world? The definition of privacy and "time off" has also changed. The boundaries and limitations of a physical world with time and space constraints are being rapidly eroded. A community that operates 24/7, 365 has little free time. Educators and learners are both faced with a day that never ends, and where sharing details about one's personal life via social networking sites is an accepted norm.

Other perils that afflict the citizens of the cyber frontier are trolling and phishing. Trolls are individuals who intentionally post controversial or contrary messages in an on-line community with the intention of enticing users into an argumentative response. Many Internet users also fall victims to phishing, which is an attempt to criminally and fraudulently acquire sensitive information, such as usernames, passwords and credit card numbers by masquerading as a trustworthy person using digitally mediated communications. Phishing is an example of social engineering designed to manipulate the user through deceit, and is fueled by the anonymity afforded by the online environment. Cyber education is not without risks. Trolling and phishing are examples of the many cyber threats and security breaches that affect cyber education.

Digitally mediated learning also causes many institutions to struggle with evaluation and assessment, due mainly to the anonymity factor. Technology provides new ingenious methods of cheating, and the generational views on what constitutes cheating continue to evolve. Learners have easy access to a myriad of online services that provide instant answers to just about any question. Cyber educators therefore scramble to find preventative measures that safeguard academic integrity. But integrity issues do not only point to the student; integrity involves administrators and instructors. Falsifying grades and providing special favors to elite students is part of academic fraud in online learning. The prevention of plagiarism is also a subject of much attention; however, technology also makes it possible to use countermeasures that promote academic integrity. An entire industry of anti-plagiarism software now provides services to educational institutions to compare and analyze student work.

Generally there is a growing sense of awareness and frustration with the issue of academic dishonesty in online learning programs. Online assessments raise serious issues of compliance, security, and validity. Unsatisfactory methods of deterring dishonesty jeopardized the credibility in online learning. Many programs, institutions and organizations are reluctant to trust assessments other than in classroom-proctored exams because of learner anonymity. The goal is to design for authenticity, and apply newer forms of educational technologies such as avatars and virtual worlds to not only support the learning process, but to also create new forms of assessment that place the learner in a real world scenario where critical thinking skills and new concepts must be applied.

RETHINKING AND RESHAPING CYBER EDUCATION

Cyber education must be rethought and reshaped by leveraging and balancing the two sides to digitally mediated learning. Online learning programs must be grounded in trust, which in turn must be nourished and maintained in the digital environment in order for learners to be successful. It is not until a relationship is established through repeated transactions or interactions that a person will determine if the source, technological or human, is deemed reliable and trustworthy. In digitally mediated learning, it is the responsibility of cyber educators to provide a safe learning environment for students, which includes acknowledging the need for anonymity while developing trusting relationships.

Online learning is unfortunately seen by many as a way of reaching more students at a lower cost. If organizations hastily prepare the program or take financial shortcuts, quality is sacrificed. The world of cyberspace opens up a new realm of possibilities for educators; hence, a shift in perspective is needed to create a normalized set of ethical guidelines that re-focus the attention of cyber educators and other stakeholders on student learning and not on taking shortcuts. This shift requires everyone involved in the creation and support of an online learning program to accept responsibility for his or her role and how it impacts student learning.

The Internet and emerging technologies have opened up learning possibilities and have become the main way that people get information, do business, and communicate. The question of how we govern and disseminate information in the knowledge age is a challenge to all sectors of our society, and is a global concern. A closer look leads us to ponder whether or not the "e" dimension will involve changing the way individuals engage with one another to discuss pertinent issues and access information, or whether Information Technologies will simply reinforce existing power structures around the globe, including educational institutions. The interconnected globe presents a dual challenge of transparency and privacy in communication. Various international organizations have taken the lead to not only define the terminology around e-governance, but also unite e-governments around the world in their approach to governance. The future of cyber education will undoubtedly be influenced by such definitions and approaches.

The global reach of cyber education also brings about legal challenges. Legislative efforts are suddenly insufficient because traditional boundaries are quickly vanishing. Furthermore, the advent of Web-based learning has caused educational institutions to rethink intellectual property policies, which undeniably affect intellectual rights as well as the educational product that is made available to the learner. Equality of resources, access, and learner support are important issues. Materials and resources available to traditional classroom teachers and students may not always be available to those who choose an online program. Future policies must take into consideration global concerns and needs, and must be a joint effort of the global online learning community.

Ethical standards for collecting, using, and interpreting student data are also needed. The prospective benefits of data mining and tracking digital fingerprints and footprints within e-learning platforms hint at improving distance learning programs. The growing digital trail may be used to conceptualize a person's morality and ethics and used for any wrong purpose, but if used ethically within the virtual learning environment, it could be used to personalize learning in new ways. However, the privacy and the rights of the learner must always be respected.

People choose to behave in certain ways depending on the given situation, but also depending on their sense of identity and their prior experiences. Some individuals prefer higher levels of visibility and interaction while others desire more privacy. Learner preferences must be taken into account when designing online programs. In the online learning environment, synchronous as well as asynchronous technologies offer different options for cyber educators who seek to promote social presence and create learning communities. Research on the topic of identity and related phenomena has been limited to computer mediated communications (CMS). Current technology innovation, however, makes it necessary to add new categories to the list of ways in which individuals communicate. Digitally mediated communications (DMC), as discussed throughout the manuscript, include text messaging, instant messaging, emails, interactions using social software, Web 2.0 tools, and voice-to-voice interactions using Web-based applications. Any of these can be accessed not just from a computer, but also from various Web-enabled mobile devices. Cyber educators seeking to promote social presence as a way to enhance learning must consider all of these tools.

As cyber educators rethink the design of online learning programs, major pedagogical shifts are needed to move forward with teaching and learning in cyberspace. For example, the ethics and morality of the 21st century learner is impacted by technology and the anonymity many tools provide. Cheating and plagiarism are pervasive issues in face-to-face as well as online learning environments. Some see this as an indication of the decline of morals and ethics among young people today who may blatantly or otherwise inadvertently "borrow" from the repertoire of information available on the Internet. Others believe that it is more difficult to cheat if an online course is well designed. A diligent effort must be made to design for authenticity but also to create learner-centric environments that provide flexibility and choice of assessments.

The lines between right and wrong are often blurred, causing global concerns about academic fraud. Academic integrity must be maintained in order for institutions to keep their credentials. Institutions worldwide must use multiple strategies to ensure academic integrity. Pedagogical approaches and assessment techniques must be more authentic and reliable than ever before. More emphasis must be placed on prevention not only through course design, but also through assessment design. Assessments must mirror the real world, and require the learner to apply new knowledge. Traditional methods of assessment are inappropriate for cyber learning, and do not prepare learners to complete in a global marketplace that requires skills of collaboration, conceptual flexibility, and problem solving, among many others.

Technological advancements shape and re-define the way people communicate for work, leisure, or learning, and how they go about their day-to-day activities. Many praise technology for its ability to make things easier, but the other side of technology is that as it brings us closer together, it may also take away our ability to disconnect from our networks and retreat in privacy. Increased demands on our time have forced us to blend our activities in order to get things done. This, too, can affect learning. The blending of work, play, and learning is inevitable, but it can be managed.

Cyber education is also likely to be transformed by highly interactive and immersive technologies and game options. Virtual environments and avatars, for example, alter social interactions, modify human behavior, and impact current methods of delivering content. Although avatars and some types of virtual environments are recent developments, their ability to deliver learning in context is already recognized by cyber educators and researchers. The benefits of recent technologies such as avatars remain largely unexplored and untapped. The question is how to develop learning environments that apply the technical and pedagogical knowledge currently available.

A virtual environment (VE) can be immersive (IVE) or collaborative (CVE). New technologies have also allowed for the emergence of sophisticated networked collaborative virtual environments (NCVEs) that connect participants in real time via a network. A VE provides synthetic sensory information about the surroundings and the content, yet it is perceived as if it was not synthetic and thus realistic to the user (Blascovich, Loomis, Beall, Swinth, Hoyt and Bailenson, 2002). The different types of VEs hold promise for individualizing instruction in new ways never accomplished before. Avatars and other embodied agents for example, can be used to modify the learner's behavior depending on his actions, and design an individualized learning path that guides the learner toward the learning objective.

Many educators are already using new technologies to create virtual environments to foster learning through simulations and virtual games. Games today make use of strategies, simulations, role playing, sports, puzzles, inquiry, problem solving, and adventures. They have gone from single player games to Massively Multi-player Online Games (MMOGs) and Massively Multi-player Online Role Playing Games (MMORPGs). These technologies present a great opportunity for cyber educators, yet much research and empirical studies needs to be conducted to how games are and can be used to promote learning (Squire, 2003). Digital Game Based Learning (DGBL) is in essence the term used for the application of digitally mediated gaming environments for learning (Prensky, 2003). Cyber educators must continue to explore game design and acceptable pedagogy.

The global expansion of cyber education exposes the issues of trust, identity, anonymity, and authenticity. Trust is directly influenced by authenticity of learning using both synchronous and asynchronous digitally mediated communications. While it is appealing to think that technologies can provide a reliable means for delivering learning content and assessing learning, some doubts remain in the minds of the most well intentioned cyber educators. Many of these doubts are centered on the issue of assessment and the validity of results. Other doubts are related to design or pedagogy. Nonetheless, it is critical that cyber educators explore new technologies and new pedagogical approaches. The anonymity provided by the technology is quickly diminishing; therefore, future approaches to cyber education must maintain the balance between the need for anonymity and the benefits of gathering data to individualize instruction. Approaches for reshaping cyber education must maintain the learner at the center while leveraging digitally mediated technologies to support learning.

ORGANIZATION OF THE BOOK

The book is organized into three sections with a total of twelve chapters. Each section explores a theme and the implications of digitally mediated communications in cyber education. Anonymity, identity, authenticity, and trust are the main common threads throughout the manuscript, with each chapter delving deeper into concerns, benefits, legal ramifications, as well as action items and potential solutions for the future global campus. It is guided by three relevant questions:

1. What is anonymity and why should you be concerned?
2. What is identity and how does it impact learning?
3. What are the approaches for moving forward with teaching and learning in cyber space?

Section 1: What is Anonymity and Why Should You be Concerned?

Chapter 1 discusses two different types of trust: trust in the technology and trust in the humans behind the technology. This chapter explores the problems as well as the benefits associated with anonymity, and how the concealment of identities often leads to concealment of intentions that could be exploited for the purpose of deceiving others. This chapter identifies the ethical responsibilities of cyber educators as well as learners to foster trust in digitally mediated communications through repeated meaningful and trustworthy transactions and interactions.

Chapter 2 exposes current ethical codes in global learning and proposes a shift in ethical guidelines that refocus the attention of all stakeholders in online learning programs back on the learner. This chapter discusses the challenges brought about by the rapid expansion of distance learning worldwide. It redefines the roles and ethical responsibilities of stakeholders in an online learning program, including instructors, administrators, instructional designers, and Instructional Technology staff. It explores how the constraints of privacy, integrity, and freedom of speech influence these redefined roles.

Chapter 3 addresses the dynamics and challenges of escalating present day intellectual property concerns in a world of limited boundaries and digital anonymity. Not only have the geographical boundaries that traditionally supported legislative efforts been minimized by the online connection, the framework for intellectual property rights has been eroded in an avalanche of open source, collaborative sharing and freebies. In this chapter the mentality of "what is mine is yours and what is yours is mine" is explored in the context of how Web 2.0 technologies facilitate sharing in new ways, and the challenges associated with legislative efforts to protect intellectual property rights globally.

Chapter 4 explores the obstacles that educational institutions face in developing and managing a global campus. For the purpose of this discussion, the global campus includes all higher education as well as K-12 organizations that focus on online learning, whether private or public. This chapter also presents challenges to consider before embarking on e-governance reforms, approaches for the e-governance of the global campus, and suggestions for overcoming potential hurdles that could undermine success.

Section 2: What is Identity and How Does it Impact Learning?

Chapter 5 discusses key definitions and then explores the harms as well as the potential benefits of data mining, profiling, and tracking of digital fingerprints and footprints in digitally mediated communications. It analyzes how these same invasive technologies that are used to pry into private information could potentially be applied in cyber education for the purpose of improving distance learning programs.

Chapter 6 discusses computer mediated communications (CMS) and digitally mediated communications DMC as defined in the literature, however the authors propose using DMC as the revised definition to be used when exploring technologies used in cyber education today. The new definition includes synchronous and asynchronous collaborative tools and social networking. The chapter also raises awareness of how learning is affected by the different degree of deinvididuation or individuation experienced by the learner, along with each individual's interaction preferences and how technology enables the emergence of new identities.

Chapter 7 discusses ethics and morality in the age of digitally mediated communications that influence cheating, plagiarism, and falsification of records. It explores why students may cheat and what strategies may be set in motion by educators and administrators to minimize such behaviors. The authors propose strategies to deter and identify academic dishonesty, and methods for educational institutions to promote academic integrity among students, faculty, as well as administrators.

Chapter 8 reviews current trends in telecommuting, distance learning, and how technological advancements, especially mobile technologies have re-shaped the way individuals communicate, work, play, and learn using these technologies. The authors propose and define the term "pajama effect" to understand the phenomenon of successfully blending work, play and learning, and how the lines between private and professional lives continue to be erased by technology. The benefits and constraints of the pajama effect are discussed, as well as the potential dangers caused by the erosion of private time, thus the authors emphasize the need to manage the different roles cautiously. This chapter explores how the pajama effect influences our lives now, and how it may look in the future.

Section 3: What are Some Approaches for the Future of Teaching and Learning Using Digitally Mediated Communications?

Chapter 9 warns against mindsets that hinder the progress of education and highlights the importance of interaction in the virtual learning environment. It discusses the pedagogical shift needed to keep up with advancements in technology, especially taking into consideration the anonymity inherent in digitally mediated communications. This chapter also proposes strategies for creating engaging, meaningful virtual learning environments that are learner centric and meet the needs of the 21st century learner.

Chapter 10 differentiates between authentication and authenticity. The authors urge cyber educators to take proactive steps in the design and implementation of authentic assessments, and discuss approaches to designing for authenticity in both, synchronous and asynchronous digitally mediated learning environments.

Chapter 11 explores the possible implications of virtual environments (VEs) as they relate to the learner's behavior and learning. The terms VE and virtual worlds are used interchangeably throughout the discussion because virtual worlds are themselves virtual environments. Immersive (IVEs) and collaborative (CVEs) as well as networked collaborative virtual environments (NCVEs) are explored in this chapter, along with the use of avatars that can transform the social interactions experienced by learners within a virtual learning community.

Chapter 12 takes a futuristic look at digital game based learning (DGBL) and discusses its possible applications as well as challenges. The word "game" is used in this chapter to discuss games in general, including Massively Multi-player Online Games (MMOGs), Massively Multi-player Online Role Playing Games (MMORPGs) and DGBL environments that promote learning. It explores the important question facing cyber educators of how to effectively use virtual games and simulations in education.

The intention of this book is to provide cyber educators, scholars, and any stakeholder of an online program with information on key issues associated with anonymity, authenticity, and trust using digitally mediated communications in cyber education. The book raises important questions and explores their implications; thus, it provides stakeholders with building blocks for further research. The information in this book will enable stakeholders to identify areas where future decisions must be made, and areas where the impact of anonymity may be felt. This manuscript evaluates both sides of each issue and presents them in a way that helps cyber educators, instructional designers, and other stakeholders understand the social, cultural, and educational implications of anonymity.

The authors wish to raise the awareness of key issues discussed in each chapter. The depth and breadth of anonymity, authenticity, and trust using digitally mediated communications in cyber education is rarely discussed among stakeholders, yet this phenomenon affects everyone: online learners, instructional designers, online instructors, administrators, lawmakers, and the general public. By gaining an understanding of the implications of these issues and how they are shaped by digitally mediated communications, the stakeholders will be better equipped to develop creative, learner-centric solutions.

REFERENCES

Allen, I. E., & Seaman, J. (2009). *Learning on demand: Online education in the United States, 2009*. Sloan Consortium. Retrieved September 15, 2010, from http://sloanconsortium.org/publications/survey/pdf/learningondemand.pdf

Blascovich, J., Loomis, J. M., Beall, A. C., Swinth, K., Hoyt, C., & Bailenson, J. (2002). Immersive virtual environment technology as a methodological tool for social psychology. *Psychological Inquiry, 13*(2), 103–124. doi:10.1207/S15327965PLI1302_01

New Media Consortium. (2007). *The Horizon Report, 2007 edition*. Retrieved September 15, 2010, from http://www.nmc.org/pdf/2007_Horizon_Report.pdf

Prensky, M. (2003). Digital game-based learning. *ACM Computers in Entertainment, 1*(1), 2.

Squire, K. (2003). Video games in education. *International Journal of Intelligent Simulations and Gaming, 2*(1). Retrieved July 21, 2010, from http://ijigs.scit.wlv.ac.uk/ijigs41.htm

Acknowledgment

The authors would like to thank the IGI Global team for their support in completing this project, and all the cyber educators and online learners who in one form of another shared their experiences, concerns, and insights with us. Special thanks go to our friend and colleague Dr. Darin Molnar who dedicated much of his time to proofreading, formatting, and providing suggestions to enhance the content of the manuscript. Finally, we would like to thank Dr. Roderick Sims for authoring the foreword of this manuscript, and for inspiring cyber educators all over the globe to pay attention to the role of interaction in digitally mediated learning environments.

Special Thanks from Dr. Baggio

I would like to thank all my friends, family, and colleagues for their patience, support, and encouragement while we undertook this monumental task. An extra thanks to my audiences who listened to me present versions of this material all over the globe and for their precious feedback and insights. I would like to acknowledge my children: Robert, Alexa, and Victoria whose constant use of digitally mediated communication served as inspiration. Finally, Yoany, who kept reassuring me that it would happen, and it finally did.

Special Thanks from Dr. Beldarrain

First and foremost, I must acknowledge my Heavenly Father for providing me with the strength I needed when it all seemed impossible to achieve. Special thanks go to my co-author Bobbe for all the wonderful ideas and for her high-spirited friendship. My deepest gratitude and admiration goes to my family, especially my Generation Z children, Adrian and Vanessa, for being a constant source of inspiration and determination, and for their unconditional love. As digital natives and online learners, they were always ready to discuss the other side of digitally mediated communications and share their unique perspective. Lastly I would like to thank all my colleagues, awesome students and audiences for providing ideas, insight, and sharing my passion for cyber education via learning modules, training events, conference proceedings, journal articles, manuscripts, presentations, impromptu round-table discussions, and elevator speeches!

Section 1
What is Anonymity and Why Should You Be Concerned?

Chapter 1
The Other Side of Digitally Mediated Learning:
Anonymity vs. Trust

ABSTRACT

Trust is an integral part of online learning. Learners must be able to trust the technology as well as the humans behind the technology. Anonymity provides protection and other benefits that support the co-construction of knowledge, yet there are potential tradeoffs that diminish this protection and increase the risk of deception. Cyber educators are responsible for designing and creating a safe online learning environment that promotes trust, hence increasing collaboration, student satisfaction, and improving learning outcomes.

OBJECTIVES

- Describe the dichotomy of trust and anonymity existing in cyber education and the impact upon the learning community.
- Analyze the components that can be part of establishing trust in an individual and in a social community.

DOI: 10.4018/978-1-60960-543-8.ch001

- Characterize the benefits of anonymity for the cyber learner and how they enhance the learning experience.
- Recognize the potential trade-offs available in the online learning environment and how technology impacts trust.
- Discover how trust in digitally mediated environments can be enhanced through the use of solid design principles and educational methods.

INTRODUCTION

There are two sides to digitally mediated learning. On one hand it opens up the world of possibilities for learners and educators while on the other it presents challenges for cyber educators. Online learning programs must be grounded in trust. Trust must be cultivated and maintained in the digital environment in order for learners to be successful.

Two different types of trust will be discussed in this chapter: trust in the technology and trust in the humans behind the technology. When it comes to digitally mediated communications, trust is rarely taken at face value. It is natural to wonder about the trustworthiness of the source, especially during the initial contact. It is not until a relationship is established through repeated transactions or interactions that a person will determine if the source, technological or human, is deemed reliable and trustworthy. The anonymity afforded by technology provides a safe haven in which to conceal our true identities or intentions, and this anonymity is not always used for the common good; it is often used for distorting truth. In digitally mediated learning, it is the responsibility of cyber educators to provide a safe learning environment for students, which includes acknowledging the presence of anonymity while developing trusting relationships.

BACKGROUND

Psychologically speaking, humans have the innate need to seek refuge in that which is familiar and comfortable, hence trustworthy. It is no different with technology or human systems because humans add social dimensions to their interactions with technology (Nass, Steuer & Tauber, 1994; Waern & Ramberg, 1996). Humans trust a system that is reliable and will meet their needs. If the user feels safe and comfortable being dependent on a particular system, whether technological or human, he will be more willing to trust in it and return for future transactions.

Trust is generated in different ways; it must be present in order to achieve a reciprocal and successful transaction. Different degrees of trust emerge through presumptions, experience, surface inspection, and intuitions (Bailey, Gurak & Konstan, 2002). Individuals make presumptions based on their unique set of values, beliefs, and their own comfort level dealing with doubt or the absence of doubt. Their previous experience also plays a role in generating and maintaining trust. The more positive experiences an individual has trusting in a person, product or system, the more likely that individual is to trust in a new situation. Surface inspection leads to a "gut feeling" when encountering something for the first time. It may be a new product, meeting a stranger, or in the case of online learning it could be enrolling in their first online course. The learner will soon form an opinion about the course after a quick inspection of the virtual environment including interface and content, as well as the first impression of the instructor.

The decision to trust versus suspect could be based on emotions and thorough considerations or it could be based on a specific need the individual may encounter (Nikander & Karvonen, 2000). Nonetheless, trust is a matter of ascertaining a position or attitude toward a given situation. The individual's position or attitude could easily be affected by a single negative experience. Deciding to trust in cyberspace is not without risk, as anonymity protects those who are honest as well as those who intentionally deceive. Deception, however, is not present only in digitally mediated communications. According to research in the social sciences and interpersonal relationships, deception is evident in about one third of all daily communications (Buller, Burgoon, Buslig, & Roiger, 1996; Eckman, 1996).

The literature reveals different definitions of trust as it relates to technological issues and in the psychological and social realm. None are conclusive, this chapter will therefore use the description proposed by Bailey, Gurak, and Konstan (2002) which defines trust as "...the perception of the degree to which an exchange partner will fulfill their transactional obligations in situations characterized by risk or uncertainty." (p. 4).

The perspective of trust depends on the lens through which it is seen. The perspectives differ for example, from trustor to trustee, because the trustor may see trustworthiness as an attribution of the perceived trust, while the trustee may see it as more of a prevailing quality in the overall transactional obligation (Bailey, Gurak, & Konstan, 2002). A transactional obligation may be defined as the responsibility one party has to another. Regardless, the trust building process involves a certain degree of risk, as well as a reciprocal effort to sort through contextual cues to determine reliability and trustworthiness.

Cognitive style and personality may also influence the tolerance level for risk-taking on the part of both trustor and trustee. Personality elements such as sense of affiliation and hostility play a role in the development of trust (Brown, Scott Poole, & Rodgers, 2004). Trust is essential in team building and online collaborative groups. It requires that group members open up to the group and explore relationships. In a qualitative phenomenological study, Smith (2008) found that members of an online group imported individual trust concerns into the group thereby making the concerns visible to all. The group in turn adopted the concerns as being a group-wide issue, yet proceeded to evade the necessary discussion that would have helped them resolve the trust issues at hand.

In another study, Liu, Magjuka and Lee (2008) found that members of a virtual team who reportedly perceived higher levels of trust were more satisfied with the team's performance and their ability to participate in the creative decision-making process. Their findings were consistent with Sternberg's (1997) suggestion that individuals with external cognitive styles preferred to work in teams. Sternberg's findings also demonstrated that trust plays an essential role in satisfaction of teamwork.

In an earlier definition of trust, the Computer Science and Telecommunications Board implied that as long as a system performed as expected, it could be deemed reliable, secure, safe, hence trustworthy (Scheider, 1999). This definition left out the social aspects inherent in the interactions between humans and systems. On the other hand, the Board's report did include human error as one of the factors that erode trust in Networked Information Systems (NIS). Other factors include natural phenomena, environmental disruption, software errors, and attacks on the system. Technical factors that erode trust capture possible reasons why someone may stop trusting a technological system but it is important to add social factors to expand on the Board's earlier position.

Social factors are not always easily identified because the anonymity afforded by technology helps to conceal them. It is possible that after a system error the user may feel betrayed or cheated and may discontinue the use of a particular software or service. In the online learning environment, feelings of betrayal may remain undetected. For example, a student who is required to participate in a threaded discussion may have hidden intentions or may withhold from speaking his mind. There are a myriad of possible reasons why an individual may choose to partially disclose, not disclose, or completely change true information depending on how he may want to be perceived by the rest of the group or by the instructor. Anonymity provides individuals the freedom to act in private, keep their genuine thoughts to themselves, and also adopt a new persona. Privacy and anonymity are therefore closely interrelated with trust being the thread that weaves them together.

Olsen and Olsen (2003) reveal that trust in the virtual world is different from remote sites compared with those users who were in close proximity to each other. This may be explained by the feeling of detachment that has been discovered in several studies. Trust in online communications can be impacted by what the participants talk about. Researcher found that those learners who spent more time taking about non-content topics and made non-topic connections trusted their peers more than those who strictly talked about the course content. This may be because talking about non-content matters establishes an emotional connection that is different than strictly sticking to discussions about course content. These emotional connections, or affective domain connections, can be established by getting to know other learners more personally.

Research also indicates that trust may be related to the types of technologies involved. Bos, Olsen, Gergle, Olsen, and Wright (2002, as quoted in Feng, Lazar, & Preece, 2004) investigated trust in four different environments: face-to-face, video, audio, and text chat. It was found that face-to to face, video and audio combined resulted in significantly higher levels of trust than text chat alone. When combining video and audio into the conferencing groups, the trust levels were comparable with face-to-face communications. Others have found that meeting face-to-face before online encounters could help build trust even though trust generally seems to diminish during online communications (Feng, Lazar, & Preece, 2004).

The literature on the topic of trust and deception in mediated communication reveals two contending views. On one hand, when groups work at a distance, they are likely to have less trust than those who build interpersonal relationships face to face (Burgoon, Bonito, & Kam, 2002; Griffin, Patterson, & West, 2001). Conversely, deindividuation theory asserts that group identity is developed and promoted by collaboration at a distance (Tidwell & Walther, 2002). Other research guided by interpersonal deception theory and the principle of interactivity completely refute earlier views on the need for face-to-face interaction to build trust and even demonstrated that face-to-face communication was not vital for developing trust between members of a group (Burgoon, Stoner, Bonito, & Dunbar, 2003).

In the online environment, there are two identified types of deception according to Burgoon, Stoner, Bonito, and Dunbar (2003): noninteractive and interactive. Noninteractive deception takes place in covert ways. The perpetrator does not come into direct contact with the target. Well-known forms of noninteractive deception online are spoofing and identity theft; however, this form of deception could easily take place within the context of a third-party conversation or communication where a lie is interjected. Interactive deception, as the name implies, requires the perpetrator to come into direct contact with the target. This form of deception is easily modified as the situation changes, thus is dynamic in nature. The perpetrator may easily adapt and change his demeanor as well as his tone to fit his intended purpose.

Digitally mediated communications afford benefits as well as constraints, especially as they relate to learning. Typically, the literature discusses the benefits of such communications, yet the potential tradeoffs for learners and cyber educators are seldom explored. The terms *online learning, cyber education* and *digitally mediated learning* are used interchangeably throughout this book. This chapter identifies issues to consider, all of which are further explored and discussed in the remainder of this book.

A DIFFERENT PERSPECTIVE

Trust is a social phenomenon that is influenced by innumerable human issues. Face-to-face learning environments arguably present more opportunities for building trust between learner and instructor than in digitally mediated learning; however, cyber educators have learned many lessons since the early days of online education that inform current practices. Despite lessons learned, cyber educators must continue to investigate how anonymity afforded by technology influences the trust building process. Online learners should be able to trust not just the technology they use, but also the humans behind the technology.

Online learning or *digitally mediated learning* involves repeated transactions using technology to access and/or create content and communicate with the instructor as well as classmates. Each interaction is carried out with a unique and complex combination of perspectives, attitudes, preconceived notions, and biases depending on the originator's previous experience with the technology, the course, the content, the humans, or any other aspect of their environment. It is therefore important that trust is cultivated at every level of the online learning environment, thus students may be free from the constraints of deceit and have a successful learning experience.

Trusting the technology alone would render the online experience inadequate. Even when a technology system is deemed trustworthy, it is the people trusting people, not the technology that makes the difference (Friedman, Kahn, & Howe, 2000). Each time a student logs into a course, for example, she wants to know she will be able to access it without technical problems. In the same vein, she would trust that the people behind the scenes would maintain the system running properly. If any login problems occur, the negative transaction could potentially affect the student's perception of the system's reliability, therefore diminishing trust.

The complete absence of trust would bring about chaos in the online learning environment, regardless of whether it is lack of trust in the technological or human system. Deception would be rampant and could be real deception or perceived deception; nonetheless, the system would break down. Even in a Utopian environment there is risk of deception. Privacy could be compromised not by any breach of trust from an insider but from outside the organization in the form of hacking, identity theft and other security issues. It is safe to then assume that all online environments require trust in order to function properly and benefit participants.

One specific kind of trust established in online environments is "swift trust". This is a kind of trust that is established by online groups for the clear purpose of completing an assignment that has a finite end. In the online learning environment, it could be a collaborative group project or research paper. This kind of trust includes the willingness to suspend doubt of people that are unknown to accomplish the goals at hand. It has been suggested that this type of trust is what is necessary for an instructor-learner relationship online (Feng, Lazar, & Preece, 2004).

A dichotomy in trust online is revealed by people as they are in the process of getting to know each other. People want to discover things about others but may be reluctant to reveal their own information openly. By creating a zone of privacy, one can exercise control over personal information. This has far-reaching effects in trust online. Control over personal identity and identifying characteristics also allows for manipulation. The fear, and even awareness, that facts about one's identity may be manipulated can lead to lack of trust. Anonymity supports both a false sense of security and a lack of trust.

"This tension over who we were versus who we want to be is the basis for all of the friction over anonymity on the Internet. Society must find some way to balance the desire for long-term promises with the freedom of living without them. There will be those who fall on the side of commitment and permanence, and they continue to be scandalized by the fact that people online are able to do things anonymously, and there will be others who revel in the masquerade while trying to ignore the fact that hearts and wallets will be broken by scurrilous individuals escaping into namelessness" (Wayner, 1999, p.2).

Trust is also affected by social aspects in digitally mediated communications. Cyberspace is a strange and faceless environment void of space and time. *Depaysement*, an anthropological term, literally means leaving one's country and culture behind and then returning to find it to be strange and unfamiliar. Cyberspace is an opportunity to experiment with other cultures by being a different gender or race or by changing our ethnicity or sexual preference. The opportunities for depaysement in digitally mediated communications are endless. Relationships can be developed with people who will never be seen and all of this gives the participant the opportunity to alter real life and real life social constructs (Chester & Gwynne, 1998).

Since the early 1980s, social psychology has been trying to describe the environment created through digitally mediated communications. Often, the early work was based on a theory known as filtered cues. This work describes the digital world as void of the nature and status of the physical world and lacking in things like body language and verbal cues. This theory also has been used to explain the presence of unusual social behavior online. Without the normal cues for social interaction, socially prescribed interactions, and immediate feedback for violating social norms participants are free to act without inhibitions. The filtered cues position reflects the inevitability of anti-social behavior in digitally mediated communications. This leads to a lack of trust and mutual respect which is adopted by filtering cues.

A feature of digitally mediated communications is that anonymity is possible or at least the perception of anonymity is possible. People do not need to see you, know anything about you or even know you are there. This supports invisibility and many people adopt alternative personalities to visit web sites, online gaming communities and virtual worlds. It is not safe for people to assume that others are who they say they are (McGreal, 1997).

There is another downside to trust in digitally mediated communications: all communications are digital and, therefore, traceable and storable. People are lulled into believing that privacy, which they may define as solitude, represents safety from intrusion. Because huge volumes of data are collected and then stored, both political and technical limitations mean that true anonymity on the internet is very small and almost accidental. Companies like Double Click and Hitwise collect information and create profiles on consumers. Anonymity and trust are directly linked to privacy and privacy is a relative term. The balance is determined by the needs of governments and businesses to track and profile versus the right of the individual to protect information. By tracking where the user goes when online, firms can collect information that goes far beyond simple demographics and IP addresses. The lack of clear and consistent legislative policies also inhibits privacy and trust online (Gertler, 2004).

Another aspect of trust online may be empathy. Feng, Lazar, and Preece (2004) conducted a research study that focused on empathy. It discerned that both empathetic accuracy and communications style had an impact on level of trust online. Personal communication that was interpreted to be empathically accurate and supportive also increased trust. It also showed a close relationship between trust online and degree of liking. People who were well-liked in the online group were more trusted. More recently, this position has been challenged first by Joseph Walther and later by others who suggest that more intimate affiliations can be developed online through time, message exchange, and social bonding (Chester & Gwynne, 1998).

The anonymity afforded by technology is embedded in every facet of the online learning experience, including trust itself. There are benefits as well as potential tradeoffs to consider when discussing anonymity and trust in cyber education. Each potential benefit and tradeoff impacts the learning process in some way, thus possibly affecting learning outcomes. Although this chapter does not explore how benefits and tradeoffs affect learning outcomes, it is important to point out the need for further research in this area.

Benefits to Consider

The word trust can easily be associated with positive thoughts and connotations. It is no different in the online learning environment. Digitally mediated learning offers students the safety of anonymity behind which they may find safety from embarrassment or simply explore different perspectives without fear of retribution. Collaboration may flourish, changing the roles of the instructor and student.

Protected by anonymity, students in the online learning environment have the unique opportunity to initiate, reject, participate or simply observe interactions within the digital environment. This is in contrast to a live class, where the student may be pointed out or "noticed" for a particular behavior that could be labeled inappropriate. The different types of interactions that occur from student to student and instructor to student set the tone for the creation of trust and the quality of such interactions will determine the degree of the perceived trust.

While some interactions, such as threaded discussions, are more public than others, each one has the ability to transform the learning experience. A potential benefit is that the anonymity inherent in technology provides safety from embarrassment. Students who suffer from a physical, emotional or cognitive disability are free from the embarrassment of feeling different, self-conscious or inadequate. In the same vein, anonymity minimizes the chances a learner may be made to feel embarrassed because he gave the incorrect answer or cannot keep up with the group. A safe environment produces a higher level of trust that should, in turn, free the student from negative pressures and instead allow him to have a positive experience.

By perceiving a diminished risk of embarrassment and fear of retribution in the online learning environment, the student may decide to take bolder actions and experiment with different perspectives. The student may even risk sharing less popular opinions that he would otherwise keep to himself. The higher degree of risk could potentially increase the quality of the educational discourse instead of compromising it, albeit it could easily do the opposite in the absence of good intentions. A less noticeable, yet very important, benefit of anonymity in the online learning environment is when the learner feels empowered to take on a new persona. In a trusting environment, the new persona would hopefully behave in a positive, altruistic manner that would allow the learner to flourish as an individual and co-construct knowledge with peers.

Increased levels of trust may cause the student to feel more apt to be part of the group and, hence, benefit from collaborative experiences. Trust is crucial in developing relationships, but such relationships cannot be established and developed unless there is a sense of safety. Some trust issues may be less evident in digitally mediated environments than face-to-face, because of the social and psychological dynamics involved. In a face-to-face environment a person may "read" another person's non-verbal cues to determine if honesty and trust can be established. In the online environment, however, participants may rely more on intuition and trust peers based on what they say and how they say it.

Self-expression becomes more prevalent in a learning environment that emanates trust. Both learner and instructor may feel more open to participate in the academic discourse and contribute to the discussion. Anonymity protects the learner from ridicule, yet it is trust that propels him to take chances and voice opinions.

Collaboration is a key component of constructivist learning; without it, an online course would be stagnant and one-dimensional. When trust is present, members of a group are more likely to communicate in positive ways and share information freely. Members must recognize and accept each other's vulnerabilities, especially if the team is being evaluated on a group product or outcome. A benefit of collaboration is co-construction of knowledge. Peers may learn from each other but also may become mentors to one another. Roles also change for the instructor who is no longer the facilitator, but more of a partner in the learning process.

In a trusting online learning environment, the student should trust that the instructor has his best interest at heart both academically and personally. This new level of trust is likely to redefine the roles of the instructor as that of a partner in the learning process, someone who is there to cultivate knowledge, love of learning, but also to continue learning. Instructors may even surrender some of their classroom authority so students are empowered to take ownership of their learning (Smith, 2008). In a trusting environment, the instructor is also likely to learn from his students, thus the result is a symbiotic relationship where all stakeholders are continually co-constructing knowledge.

These apparent benefits to anonymity and trust in digitally mediated learning influence the overall learning experience and, potentially, the learning outcomes. A more in-depth exploration is needed in order to understand this relationship and how to capitalize on such benefits. There are, however, two sides to this discussion. Anonymity could be misused to gain protection from adverse consequences for those who have malicious intentions and rely on deception to achieve their goals.

Potential Tradeoffs

Anonymity brings about potential tradeoffs in digitally mediated learning environments. It could be used to deceive, conduct malicious activities, or inconspicuously monitor interactions for any given purpose or intention. Anonymity without trust would cause the learning process to deteriorate, thus minimizing the co-construction of knowledge.

Deception in online learning manifests itself in several different ways such as lying, withholding information, disseminating false information, disrupting communication or intentionally provoking others. Anonymity may cause some individuals to become less inhibited and act in bolder ways. Risky and unethical behavior could be hidden behind anonymous actions that could go undetected. Certain individuals may have more aggressive attitudes or biases that could result in cyber bullying or distorting truth.

Blatantly displaying biased opinions without consideration or respect of others could cause learners to withdraw emotionally from the academic discourse, hence become disengaged from the learning process. An observant instructor can easily correct this form of cyber bullying by redirecting the bully's attention to the issue discussed. Bullying and deception both break down the fiber of trust that weaves privacy and anonymity together.

The act of deception is particularly detrimental to collaborative groups. If members of a cohort feel deceived, they will be dissatisfied with the experience and will be less likely to contribute to the co-construction of knowledge. This would in turn impact the overall learning process and diminish learning outcomes. If a lack of trust permeates the learning environment, members are likely to be less productive. The organizational culture and reputation may ultimately be compromised.

An individual with ill intentions could disrupt the learning process or cause the collapse of communication by posting misleading information in threaded discussions and emails. The absence of trust makes everyone more vulnerable to negative experiences, including the instructor. Malicious activities such as spamming, spoofing and identity theft could also occur within the virtual course room. Virtual communities are especially susceptible to the malicious activities of trolls who can cause problems with authenticity and credibility of knowledge.

Most online learning organizations have in place some form of surveillance method that captures interactions within the course room. Typically used for quality assurance purposes, information gathered could be used with any intent in mind. Surveillance of digitally mediated interactions is a true tradeoff, as it diminishes the protection of anonymity and exposes to a certain degree the actions of participants. Administrators, for example, can track the digital footprints and fingerprints (see Chapter 5 for more information) of learners and the instructor to identify patterns of behavior and analyze actions taken. Opinions are formed and decisions are made based on data gathered, likely without the knowledge or consent of the individual observed.

The potential tradeoffs, although important, should not impede or discourage cyber educators from creating purposeful and trustworthy online learning environments. Cyber educators are responsible for maximizing the benefits and reducing the risk of deception perceived by learners.

Responsibilities of Cyber Educators

Cyber educators are responsible for nurturing trustworthiness with every transaction, whether it is technological or human. Cyber educators are also responsible for curtailing inappropriate or deceptive behaviors within the course room that could diminish trust among learners. Lastly, it is crucial that cyber educators provide a reliable and trustworthy technological infrastructure.

Every transaction or interaction in the online environment presents an opportunity to establish, develop and enhance trust. Interactions manifest themselves as learner-learner, learner-instructor, learner-interface, and learner-content interactions (Moore, 1989; Hillman, Willis, & Gunawardena, 1994). Students can also observe vicariously (Fulford & Zhang, 1993) the interactions of others. Cyber educators are therefore charged with providing different types of meaningful interactions for students to increase mutual trust

The learner must be able to trust the technology as well as the humans behind the technology. The technological infrastructure is not limited to the Learning Management System; it includes solid technical support, reliable software and hardware, as well as the course design and any educational resources the learner may need. If a course design is flawed, for example, the learner's experience is impacted. The overall learning experience is also impacted by malfunctioning software or hardware that may cause interruptions. The student should access the course when needed, navigate easily and be able to successfully interact with the technology as well as the content.

The design of the course must offer opportunities for collaboration that focus on increasing rapport and collegial discourse. Instructors are also responsible for lowering the affective filter to encourage participants, for instance, to express themselves freely without fear of embarrassment or retribution. Preventing and curtailing deceptive behaviors is equally important. Cyber educators are responsible for monitoring the digital environment for the purpose of keeping students safe from harm. Regular monitoring of discussion groups, emails and virtual communities will help educators identify potential bullying and deceptive actions. Although surveillance of the online learning environment diminishes the protection of anonymity, cyber educators are responsible for using data professionally and for quality assurance purposes. The intent of data mining in the online learning environment should be to enhance the learning experience for students.

In digitally mediated learning, it is the responsibility of cyber educators to provide a safe learning environment for students. This is only possible by acknowledging the need for developing trusting relationships among stakeholders. Cyber educators must understand how to recognize and diminish deceptive behavior thus augment the level of trust within the course room. The ultimate goal is to improve the learning process and promote the co-construction of knowledge, hence increase student success.

LOOKING AHEAD

The influence of trust in digitally mediated learning cannot be ignored. There are many ways to address the issue; some require less effort, yet others may require restructuring the system and reshaping the mind of the humans behind the technology to truly embrace trust. The process begins with making a deliberate effort to make the change.

Now What?

1. Cyber Educators must recognize the ongoing influence of anonymity and trust in digitally mediated communications.
2. Learning environments must be created that support trust both in the technologies and the human interactions.
3. Instructional design offers opportunities to create environments that are collaborative, supportive and encouraging thus supporting trust not only in the environment but also in the learning process.
4. Trust is absolutely necessary for learning success; therefore much research is needed to determine exactly how trust can be established in the digital world.
5. An environment that supports discourse, challenge, and new ideas with minimal risk to the participant encourages trust and authenticity.

The most critical element in developing trust is to believe that trust is not only possible, but absolutely necessary for student success. Stakeholders must make the conscientious effort to discard preconceived notions and biases based on previous experiences. They must be willing to take a risk with others and choose to believe that others will act benevolently.

Trust from within the organization will likely permeate and become evident to outsiders, hence a culture of trust is created and everyone benefits. In online learning, however, trust cannot be limited to humans. The organization must invest in the technological infrastructure and support systems that allow the learner to access their course without technical difficulties so there is no interruption to the learning process. The learner will in turn not only trust the technology, but their perception of organizational trust will also increase. When the learner feels valued, he is more likely to have a positive experience.

Instructional design is responsible for creating the type of student-centered environment that promotes trust. Course room and course design must be flexible, individualized, yet collaborative. The different types of interaction, learner-learner, learner-instructor, learner-interface and learner-content must be addressed. Designers must also be cognizant that some students prefer higher degrees of vicarious interaction, thus there should always be available interaction opportunities that are visible to the entire class.

Designing for trust demands out-of-the-box thinking. Instructional designers must have a basic understanding of the interpersonal dimensions that may influence trust, such as personality, individual preferences, cultural background, gender and cognitive style. Every opportunity for a transaction or interaction must take into consideration the dynamic relationship between trustor and trustee and how their individual characteristics influence one other, ultimately shaping the learning experience.

The technology tools needed to increase collaboration in digitally mediated learning are readily available to today's cyber educators. Building community can be achieved through the use of web conferences, wikis, blogs and other Web 2.0 tools. However, a lack of trust would be detrimental to the success of the activity. Cyber educators can increase the sense of community and increase trust by structuring online discussions in a way that allows students to get to know each other gradually. More cognitively demanding tasks may be introduced, especially those that require collaboration, once students have established a basic level of trust. Requiring students to prematurely participate in collaborative activities that demand higher order thinking may compromise trust because students may fear being rejected (Garrison, Anderson, & Archer, 2001).

Cyber educators must be careful to design collaborative activities that serve a purpose and meet the needs of their audience. The most prudent way to assess what learners need is to involve them in the design process. This, however, is a luxury in most cases, unless the instructor is also the designer. Every effort must be made to involve the learner in the design process and gain his perspective. Cyber educators are also challenged with the task of using technology to develop and establish a learning community where trust is prevalent and the co-construction of knowledge can occur.

Building Trust-Based Communities

Approaches to developing trust in the online environment should capitalize on the technological advancements available today to foster a sense of community and trust. Such approaches must also integrate what is known about the psychosocial dimensions of trust and how such trust is developed. Cyber educators must carefully balance the need for anonymity and the need for trust.

Because each individual brings their own set of values and presumptions to the online learning environment, it is important to design courses that are globally neutral with respect to content and interface. Every member of the community should feel valued and respected regardless of gender, cultural background or preferences. The content should be sensitive to diversity and the interface should be user friendly, hence minimizing frustration with usability. A course designed with trust in mind will offer various opportunities for students to interact.

A student should never be expected to adhere to a specified number or type of interactions because, in doing so, the protection of anonymity is further diminished. Learners need flexibility to choose when and how to interact, therefore gaining ownership of the learning process. Being able to refrain from interaction or from completing a transaction adds a sense of control, safety and privacy that could potentially enhance the learner's satisfaction. A person may choose to participate in those transactions that he believes will add more value to the learning experience and may disregard or vicariously interact with those which are less important.

Building a trust-based learning community requires that both interactive and noninteractive forms of deceptions be minimized. The instructor is responsible for monitoring those activities that are visible within the course room, yet system administrators are responsible for monitoring behind the scenes. Most online learning programs have an established set of netiquette rules to inform students of their roles and their responsibilities as virtual learners. Instructors and administrators will, however, often fail to properly communicate their netiquette standards to students.

Students must understand what the expected behaviors are and what the consequences are for engaging in interactive or noninteractive forms of deception within the online learning environment. Instructors must also be proactive in addressing trust issues within the course room before a small individual concern becomes a group concern. Instructors may also model behaviors that promote trust such as positive and supportive communication, especially for interactions that are visible to all members of the group.

In the case of a trust issue that is encountered by a group, the online instructor can use team-building strategies to bring cohesiveness to that group. Two helpful strategies are to refocus the group on a shared goal and re-establishing a purpose for the existence of the team. The trust issue at hand can then be identified as an obstacle that, unless dealt with, will prevent the team from achieving its shared goal. The intent is for team members to realize they should deal with the trust issue openly and honestly, allowing them to move forward. Having a purpose for the team provides a sense of group identity consistent with deindividuation theory. Identity and purpose consequently help establish and develop trust within the group.

Collegial discourse and co-construction of knowledge are more likely to occur within communities that have a higher perceived level of trust and reciprocate trust with each transactional obligation. The design of interaction opportunities should take into account how learners use cues to determine reliability and trustworthiness of the members of the group, as well as the value of resources. Interactions should be designed to allow participants to gather contextual cues embedded in text-based communications and assess the degree of risk. Interactions should also offer learners the opportunity to get to know more about each other and identify commonalities. Learners should be able to share about their preferences and interests, but also share educational resources. Each of these informal transactions helps build interpersonal relationships based on trust.

Technology advancements make it possible to create student-centered environments that promote trust through the use of social networking types of structures and other flexible environments. Yan, Krämer, Han, and Shen (2005) propose creating a trust-based community for e-learners that allows them to set up trusted connections and exchange learning resources. This approach applies the Hebbian Learning Rule to networked systems, hence placing a heavier weighted value on those relationships that are more trusted. Their idea also borrows elements from peer-to-peer systems to arrange and update buddy lists and preferences. Users are able to gain access to the e-learning platform via any mobile device or computer without the need to be connected to the server.

There are several potential advantages to this approach. Students who are already familiar with social networking will find this type of sharing to be natural. Overall, students are likely to develop a sense of identity with the buddies they have identified within the group and their level of trust will increase as they participate in more positive transactions. The peer-to-peer system gives the learner the freedom to control which relationships within the community they pursue, hence increasing ownership. The sharing of educational resources helps break the ice for those individuals who have weaker personalities and would otherwise shy away from interaction. Small, positive exchanges could lead to creating trust between these individuals.

An inherent risk, however, is the fact that any negative exchange will have an adverse effect on the creation of trust. There is also the potential of virtual "cliques" forming, in which case some individuals are likely to feel ostracized or distanced from the group. But even if all the human factors are favorable, there is always the chance that faulty technology may cause disruptions. Yan, Krämer, Han, and Shen's (2005) vision for creating a trust-based e-learner community holds promise for establishing and developing relationships within online learning environments. Regardless, this system remains to be tested and evaluated.

Cyber educators must implement strategies to build trust within online learning communities. Regardless of delivery method, a course with opportunities for different types of interaction is likely to increase satisfaction. Each opportunity for interaction brings the possibility of a positive transaction between participants that will augment perceived trust among members of the community.

Developing Trust through Knowledge Construction

Researchers and practitioners have long debated over what constitutes knowledge construction and how it occurs. In the online environment, constructivist design frameworks aim at integrating interaction to promote collaboration and co-construction of knowledge. Knowledge, however, cannot be co-constructed unless each participant first shares his perspective, eventually arriving at a mutually negotiated understanding of what the newly constructed knowledge entails.

Online discussions and other asynchronous forms of computer-mediated communications are often void of value to the learner. The designers may have indentified a purpose for a particular interaction, but this purpose may not necessarily be aligned with the needs of the learner. Online students may find themselves going through the motions to participate in a required activity but they are not truly engaged in the learning process. Lack of engagement and purpose contribute to the deterioration of trust, which is the basis for all successful interactions.

Value can be added to asynchronous communications by involving the learner in constructive, scaffolded discussions. Salmon's (2000) five-stage model for creating online debates provides cyber educators with a framework for designing tiered discussions that gradually create trust and move the learner to higher levels of critical thinking:

1. Learners gain access and explore the discussion topic.
2. Learners reflect on personal motivation and purpose for being part of the discussion.
3. Learners share information that allows participants to get to know each other.
4. The knowledge construction begins as students scrutinize their own ideas through different perspectives.
5. Learners are free to challenge and evaluate newly exposed ideas of self and others. This is the springboard for academic discourse.

This framework provides safety because it builds trust gradually with minimal risk to the participant. If deception is perceived, the learner has the ability to temporarily withdraw from the transaction until he feels it is safe again to proceed. Participants get to know one another with each small transaction, eventually identifying commonalities and traits that build a sense of identity. The group members can then fluidly exchange information and negotiate meaning, hence co-construct knowledge. Unlike face-to-face discussions where incongruent views can be immediately reconciled, asynchronous discussions will become stagnant and lose value unless the instructor facilitates the exchange of knowledge.

Cyber educators have many different options, including those presented here, to establish and develop trust in the online environment. Some may require a higher level of commitment than others; however, it is crucial that all stakeholders understand the importance of trust and how it may impact the learning process.

CONCLUSION

Digitally mediated learning opens the door of opportunities for both learners and educators, but it is not without challenges or risks. The anonymity inherent in technology provides protection to participants. They may use this protection to conceal their true identities or intentions; however, the risk of deception is always present because this anonymity is not always used for the common good. It is human nature to seek comfort in that which is familiar and trustworthy. In the online environment, cyber educators have the unique responsibility of minimizing the risk of deceit, thereby creating an environment where students feel safe to share and co-construct knowledge.

The phenomenon of trust is multi-faceted and difficult to define or explain. The perspective of trust varies depending if it is seen from the trustor or the trustee's point of view. Each individual has the responsibility to trust the other and his or her behavior will affect the outcome of the transaction or interaction. Theirs is a reciprocal relationship that is dynamic in nature. Both parties must be willing to take the risk to trust the other and sort through cues to determine reliability and trustworthiness.

In the online learning environment, is very important that learners feel supported by humans, but also by the technology system through which they access they content. Trust in the technology evolves into organizational trust and may enhance learner satisfaction. Learners should be able to access the course without technical or navigational errors and receive prompt support if such errors occur.

Anonymity is embedded in every facet of online learning. Trust is the thread that weaves anonymity and privacy together thus providing learners with a safe heaven. A sense of safety may cause learners to explore different points of view without fear of retribution or embarrassment and they may choose to initiate, withdraw from or vicariously observe interactions. This increased learner control is likely to empower and augment the feeling of ownership in the learning process.

With each transaction or interaction learners are at risk of experiencing deceit. Deceit could manifest itself in covert or overt ways. Individuals with ill intentions could disrupt the learning process unless addressed by the instructor and/or system administrator. Surveillance by the organization minimizes anonymity but should be used for the purpose of protecting learners and improving the learning experience.

Trust is necessary for student success; without it, students will not be engaged in the learning process. Cyber educators must design courses that provide various opportunities for interaction yet allow learners the flexibility to choose when and how to interact. Interaction will help build community as long as it is done in a gradual manner. Trust is gradually built, for example, if discussions are scaffolded, hence allowing students to get to know each other before engaging in discourse. Establishing a trusting relationship is a crucial step needed before learners can share, negotiate and ultimately co-construct knowledge.

There are benefits as well as potential tradeoffs to anonymity and trust in digitally mediated learning. It is therefore imperative that cyber educators understand the psychosocial dimensions of trust and how it can be promoted in the online learning environment. There is much yet to be explored, especially as this phenomenon relates to learning. A targeted, conscious effort is needed on the part of cyber educators to create a safe learning environment for all students where they can trust the technology as well as the humans behind the technology.

REFERENCES

Bailey, B. P., Gurak, L. J., & Konstan, J. A. (2002). Trust in cyberspace. In Ratner, J. (Ed.), *Human factors and Web development* (pp. 311–321). New Jersey: Lawrence Erlbaum Associates.

Brown, H. G., Scott Poole, B. N., & Rodgers, T. L. (2004). Interpersonal traits, complementarily, and trust in virtual team collaboration. *Journal of Management Information Systems*, *20*(4), 115–137.

Buller, D. B., Burgoon, J. K., Buslig, A., & Roiger, J. (1996). Testing interpersonal deception theory: The language of interpersonal deception. *Communication Theory*, *6*, 268–289. doi:10.1111/j.1468-2885.1996.tb00129.x

Burgoon, J. K., Bonito, J. A., & Kam, K. (2002). Communication and trust under face-to-face and mediated conditions: Implications for leading from a distance. In Weisband, S., & Atwater, L. (Eds.), *Leadership at a distance*. Mahwah, NJ: Erlbaum.

Burgoon, J. K., Stoner, G. M., Bonito, J. A., & Dunbar, N. E. (2003). Trust and deception in mediated communication. *Proceedings of the 36th Hawaii International Conference on System Sciences*.

Chester, A., & Gwynne, G. (1998). Online teaching: Encouraging collaboration through anonymity. *Journal of Computer-Mediated Communication*, *4*(2).

Ekman, P. (1996). Why don't we catch liars? *Social Research*, *63*, 801–818.

Feng, J., Lazar, J., & Preece, J. (2004). Empathic and predictable communications influences online interpersonal trust. *Behaviour & Information Technology, 23*(2), 97–106. doi:10.1080/01449290310001659240

Friedman, B., Kahn, P. H., & Howe, D. C. (2000). Trust online. *Communications of the ACM, 43*(12), 34–40. doi:10.1145/355112.355120

Garrison, D. R., Anderson, T., & Archer, W. (2001). Critical thinking, cognitive presence, and computer conferencing in distance education. *American Journal of Distance Education, 15*(1), 7–23. doi:10.1080/08923640109527071

Gertler, E. (2004). *Prying eyes: Protect your privacy from people who sell to you, snoop on you, and steal from you.* New York: Random House.

Griffin, M. A., Patterson, M. G., & West, M. A. (2001). Job satisfaction and teamwork: The role of supervisor support. *Journal of Organizational Behavior, 22,* 537–550. doi:10.1002/job.101

Hillman, D. C. A., Willis, D. J., & Gunawardena, C. N. (1994). Learner-interface interaction in distance education: An extension of contemporary models and strategies for practitioners. *American Journal of Distance Education, 8*(2), 30–41. doi:10.1080/08923649409526853

Liu, X., Magjuka, R. J., & Lee, S. (2008). The effects of cognitive thinking styles, trust, conflict management on online students' learning and virtual team performance. *British Journal of Educational Technology, 39*(5), 829–846. doi:10.1111/j.1467-8535.2007.00775.x

McGreal, R. (1997). The Internet: A learning environment. *New Directions for Teaching and Learning, 71,* 19–26.

Moore, M. G. (1989). Three types of interaction. *American Journal of Distance Education, 3,* 1–6. doi:10.1080/08923648909526659

Nass, C., Steuer, J., & Tauber, E. R. (1994). Computer are social actors. *Proceedings of ACM Conference on Human Factors and Computing Systems.*

Nikander, P., & Karvonen, K. (2000). Users and trust in cyberspace. *Proceedings of the Cambridge 2000 Workshop on Security Protocols,* 2000. Retrieved November 1, 2010, from http://www.tml.tkk.fi/~pnr/publications/cam2000.pdf

Olsen, G., & Olsen, J. (2003). Human computer interaction: Psychological aspects of human use of computing. *Annual Review of Psychology, 54*(1), 491–516. doi:10.1146/annurev.psych.54.101601.145044

Salmon, G. (2000). *E-moderating: The key to teaching and learning online.* London: Kogan Page.

Schneider, F. B. (1999). *Trust in cyberspace. Committee on Information Systems Trustworthiness, Computer Science and Telecommunications Board, National Research Council.* Washington, D.C.: National Academy Press.

Smith, R. O. (2008). The paradox of trust in online collaborative groups. *Distance Education, 29*(3), 325–340. doi:10.1080/01587910802395839

Sternberg, R. J. (1997). *Thinking styles.* New York: Cambridge University Press. doi:10.1017/CBO9780511584152

Tidwell, L. C., & Walther, J. B. (2002). Computer-mediated communication effects on disclosure, impressions, and interpersonal evaluations: Getting to know one another a bit at a time. *Human Communication Research, 28,* 317–348. doi:10.1111/j.1468-2958.2002.tb00811.x

Waern, Y., & Ramberg, R. (1996). People's perception of human and computer advice. *Computers in Human Behavior, 12*(1), 17–27. doi:10.1016/0747-5632(95)00016-X

Wayner, P. (1999). Technology for anonymity: Names by other nyms. *The Information Society, 15*(1), 91–97. doi:10.1080/019722499128556

Yan, F., Krämer, B. J., Han, P., & Shen, R. (2005). Exploiting the construction of e-learner communities from a trust connectionist point of view. *Journal of Integrated Design and Process Science, 9*(2), 1–11.

Chapter 2
A Code of Ethical Conduct for Global Learning

ABSTRACT

Cyberspace is host to conflicting views of cyberethics. National boundaries and traditional social values are distorted by the influence of globalized values that are linked to technology. The inevitable change prompted by technology calls for a code of ethical conduct for the global online learning community where all stakeholders ultimately share the responsibility for student success.

OBJECTIVES

- Define constraints for ethical behavior in cyberspace including code, market, and norms.
- Identify the roles and the collective responsibility for the quality of the online learning program and the ultimate desired outcome, which is student learning.

DOI: 10.4018/978-1-60960-543-8.ch002

- Discuss the ethical and theoretical framework used in online learning, and why cyber educators must remain focused on student learning.
- Analyze global learning and the necessity to re-evaluate its existence and refocus on the purpose behind education.
- Evaluate the need for the educational community to come up with new approaches in the areas of course design, pedagogy, and learner activities and assessment.

INTRODUCTION

Educators generally share the calling of helping students learn. This is not true, unfortunately, of all stakeholders in educational systems. Many see online learning as a way of reaching more students for less money than would otherwise be needed with a physical infrastructure. Organizations often hastily prepare online learning programs or take financial shortcuts, thus sacrificing quality. Valuable lessons can be learned from the early days of distance education, especially when it comes to the ethical responsibility of those involved in the design, implementation and delivery of programs.

The world of cyberspace opens up a new realm of possibilities for educators; hence, a shift in perspective is needed to create a normalized set of ethical guidelines that re-focus the attention of cyber educators and other stakeholders on student learning. This shift would require everyone involved in making an online learning program function to accept responsibility for his or her role and how it impacts student learning. This chapter redefines the roles and ethical responsibilities of stakeholders in an online learning program, including instructors, administrators, instructional designers, and Instructional Technology staff and explores how the constraints of privacy, integrity, and freedom of speech influence these redefined roles.

BACKGROUND

Innate in each human being is the desire to be free from harm and to flourish. Universal values promoting well-being transcend cultural, ethnic and social barriers, as well as time. Technology provides an environment where these values also transcend cyberspace. Connectivity enables the emergence of new values that impact every facet of learning, including the ethical roles and responsibilities of cyber educators, learners, as well as everyone involved in the design, implementation, and delivery of online learning programs.

Ethics in cyberspace, often referred to as *cyberethics*, include all of the behaviors typically be associated with any other type of environment. In cyberspace, however, anonymity protects the individual from the possible consequences of their misbehavior. This leads to concerns regarding the roles and responsibilities of those involved in online learning programs, especially when such programs have a global reach. Global learning implies global concerns, thereby calling for a comprehensive approach to developing and implementing a code of ethical conduct that takes into account the changing roles and responsibilities of stakeholders while providing a safe environment for learners from different backgrounds.

Universal in application, ethical behavior is set into action when an individual makes a conscious decision between what is right and wrong (Adamson & Mietus, 2000). Morality, on the other hand, is infused with cultural and societal norms. Such norms, or values, define the attitudes within a society regarding what is right and wrong (Brown, 1998). Because global learning encompasses many norms, a code of conduct that crosses multiple boundaries is more difficult to establish. Justice therefore becomes an ambiguous term that is subject to interpretation. Justice is a term that can vary so widely that it is intentionally left out of many legal books.

When a code of ethics is typically discussed, it is usually within the framework of fairness. The quandary here is that the term *fair* is subject to interpretation. The idea of fairness includes both process and product, but is highly dependent upon interpretation. Regardless of the difficulty of interpretation, the need to establish a code of ethics to underpin the expansion of global learning has never been greater.

This code of conduct should rely on projecting more confidence, engaging in less deception, as well as reveling in truth and in the fundamental underlying belief that because truthfulness in others is indeed the norm, they can be trusted even in a computer mediated environment (Boyle, Kacmar, & George, 2008). There are restrictions that are imposed by different elements of cyberspace. Individual behavior may be influenced, conditioned or even controlled by these restrictions.

The constraints on ethical behavior in cyberspace are, according to Lessig (1999), laws, codes, market, and norms. Laws would include any limitations set by governmental agencies, usually enforced after violations have occurred. Code refers to the technology that is in place to either enforce such laws or to influence certain behaviors in cyberspace. A code, for instance, can be a firewall, software applications, or Internet protocols that require specific action on the part of the user. The market enforces its rules before the customer can obtain the goods, such as paying tuition before accessing an online course. Finally, norms provide both covert and visible rules for acceptable behavior among members of a group. The self-identity of members is usually tied to these social norms. The use of social networking tools is a good example of a cyber group where new norms emerge. Lessig (1999) combines all these elements to create the architecture for governing cyberspace, which he admits could be dangerous if government uses them to exercise too much control.

There is evidence around the globe to suggest that governments have different views regarding the regulation of cyberethics. In China and Saudi Arabia, for example, government has imposed far more control, limiting the privacy, anonymity, and freedom of speech of individuals. Other countries such as Germany and France have focused on regulating certain aspects of cyberethics, such as flaming speech. Germany, along with other European Union countries, has also focused on enacting laws that protect privacy. In 1970, the German state of Hesse was the first governmental entity in the world to protect privacy. This proactive approach led to the Federal Data Protection Act of 1977 and several subsequent legislative efforts to provide individuals the right of owning their personal data and controlling who has access to it.

In the United States, a different stance is evident when it comes to regulating cyberethics. Instead of the government imposing rules, self-regulation is the prevalent philosophy, thereby allowing the private sector to decide how it will regulate itself and protect consumers. Privacy advocates have generally been in the minority, except when it comes to protecting children. The dispute over how much control the government should exercise was substantiated by the demise of the Communications Decency Act of 1996, which then shifted the attention to the Children's Internet Protection Act of 2001. Freedom of speech and censorship continue to be cited as the primary reasons for challenging legislative efforts to regulate cyberethics in the United States.

In the business world, concerns during the 1990s triggered a flurry of policies centered on a global information infrastructure and electronic commerce. Penalties were established for failure to meet these guidelines and civil and criminal punishments were established. Unethical behavior on the part of commerce led to the Sarbanes-Oxley Act of 2002, which required businesses to demonstrate through their annual reports compliance with a code of conduct to protect consumers. The underpinning of this kind of regulation was the assumption that businesses should create a code of ethics and then operate according to that code. Likewise, cyber educators must operate under a code of ethical conduct that is in the best interest of students. Most would agree that a code of conduct implies the adherence to a set of conditions that are ethical, moral and ensure justice for all.

The literature reveals different frameworks that may be applied to draw conclusions about ethics and justice. Several constructs, including Utilitarianism, Contractarianism, Natural Rights and Pluralism impact cyberethics. Table 1 provides a definition of each of these frameworks along with examples of ethical applications. Challenges arise when the global learning community expands. A global learning

Table 1. Ethical framework examples

Ethical Framework	Definition	Example of Ethical Application in Western Culture
Utilitarianism	Bringing about the greatest amount of good for the greatest number. Actions are desirable that promote the general good for all. Group good over good for the individual.	Providing eLearning that is supported by Broadband/VOIP despite the fact that there are a few learners that still have 56K dial up.
Contractarianism	Both a political and moral theory that claims that government must be derived from the consent of the governed. Based on the idea that an individual has contract right or a claim to something.	Making the Internet available to all student of the public school system in support of their right to a free education until the age of 20.
Pluralism	Based on Kant's perspective referred to as pluralism, this holds that the right of the individual should not be violated despite good intentions of others. Morality under this model is based on categorical imperative not prudential considerations.	Collecting and using information from other people's computers without their knowledge or permission should be avoided. Giving credit to the creator for ideas such as intellectual property.
Natural Rights	Adheres to the fundament rights of mankind are grounded in the common nature of humans. These rights should be protected regardless of the elected governance.	Unwanted adds and spamming on the internet interferes with our natural right to reach our fullest potential and our right to privacy.

community is composed of members from different cultural backgrounds, ensuring that safety and justice are crucial.

The examples in Table 1 indicate that each of the frameworks is indeed valid and applicable to cyber education. Each framework serves as an ethical lens through which the particular issue is viewed. But how does one know which is the best ethical lens to use? The best approach to determining which framework is the best choice is to view the same issue through each ethical lens. A comparison of possible scenarios will lead to the emergence of one option that provides the most benefits to the learner, which would ethically be considered the best option.

Regardless of which ethical and theoretical framework is used, cyber educators must remain focused on student learning. Part of the challenge is the communication of expectations to promote ethical teaching and learning practices at every level. Operationalizing the values of corporations and institutions of higher learning is only a part of the puzzle. Behaviors must be established in the educational community that supports these values and minimizes risk (Passoff, 2004). This is in direct opposition to much of the teaching and learning that has been practiced for centuries.

Morality in cyberspace has become exceptionally challenging because of the technical venue and the speed at which it has changed lives, yet humans remain intrinsically good. Connectivity has hastened the merging of cultures and ethnicities, creating new globally accepted values that influence behavior. Justice is often used as the umbrella term to cover the concepts of ethics, morality and fairness, but because justice is in the eye of the beholder, it is quite subjective. Globalized learning must use a code of ethical conduct that is global, yet just for all members.

ETHICAL CONDUCT IN THE FACE OF INEVITABLE CHANGE

Cyberspace facilitates the evolution of social mores and is fertile ground for conceiving new ethical principles. National boundaries and ethnic traditions are distorted by the influence of globalized values that are brought about by technology. Moral values affect every facet of online learning hence a relevant code of ethical conduct for global learning is needed to ensure the viability of cyber education. New roles are emerging for learners as well as other stakeholders in the educational process; these continue to be molded by the more obvious constraints of privacy, integrity and freedom of speech.

Boards, consortiums and other associated national and international bodies increasingly scrutinize and monitor the quality of online teaching and learning. The complexities of ethical practice in the field of education are now compounded with the expansion of global e-learning. Only when ethics are internalized and become part of the collective consciousness of a community of practice do they become effective. Implementation of philosophically complex concepts into a global community is infinitely intricate and must include a consideration of the reality of multiple conflicting and competing perspectives, codes of conduct, ideals and principles (Campbell, 2001). A concern for doing what is right has always been an underpinning of the educational process. Now that this process extends to a global online community, the inadequacy of current practices has become evident.

New information available in a connected world is increasing exponentially. With knowledge doubling daily and expertise in a subject changing rapidly, expectations for both cyber instructor and online learner are being challenged. Disseminating knowledge can only be managed through a global transfer of this knowledge and understanding the changing roles of stakeholders.

Redefining Roles and Responsibilities

Inherent in this new information revolution are opportunities and challenges brought about by the feasibility of globally networked learning, freedom from the constraints of distance, and by placing control back in the hands of the learner who navigates according to individual vision and purpose. Information is transformed into knowledge once the learner takes ownership and control of learning and makes a commitment to choose both purpose and interest. Educators are at the threshold of reaching students in unprecedented ways, but they must first understand how roles are redefined by technology and how ethics influence roles and behaviors.

Global connectivity has prompted the entry into an age of knowledge, which not only requires access to information but the transformation of this information into insights through the synthesis of multiple perspectives. Educators are no longer purveyors of information but facilitators of knowledge. The learner must take more responsibility for the direction and assimilation of information. This begins by distinguishing between the relevant and irrelevant. This involves a tremendous amount of risk on the parts of the learner and the teacher (Dreyfus, 1999).

The risk taken by both learner and educator is likely to be the result of each individual reaching a functional level within their own reality and what is considered important. Dreyfus (1999) expanded on Søren Kierkegaard's idea that before a beginner in any domain can become competent, he must develop a perspective that allows him to distinguish between what is relevant and what is irrelevant. Kierkegaard, a 19th century Danish theologian and philosopher, favored individual uniqueness over mass appeal, which is the very essence of individualized instruction. The detached follower perspective of the novice learner must be replaced by an interactive stance, and this interactive stance must include a degree of risk and an acceptance of responsibility for acquisition of knowledge. A different scenario begins to unfold for the novice learner, however, when immersed in cyberspace.

Decision-making on the Internet is usually fairly simple and often free from penalty. This freedom can lead to a breakdown in commitment and the ethical sphere, according to Dreyfus (1999). When choices can be made and revised rapidly without risk of consequences, they become meaningless and arbitrary. Anonymity serves to remove the limits normally placed on our roles either social or personal and enhances the range of possible actions.

Ethics tend to break down because the power to make and change commitments interferes with discerning what is important. Rather than taking each event seriously, the perspective becomes one of experimentation because the self can, at any moment, change and start all over again. The increased connectivity and the ease of decision-making on the Web is a factor that could, influence risk-taking behaviors in the global online environment. The value of risk-taking, therefore, becomes globalized as a result of technology.

When individual online identities become intermingled with the perceived identity of the community, ethics may deteriorate as a result of racism, sexism, or almost any other "ism." Often, in the wilderness of Web 2.0, individuals who do not consider themselves sexist or racist unknowingly establish unintended "isms" or partake of the group consciousness. Such events are strikingly damaging and significantly impact people's lives. Covert "isms" are far more difficult to correct and unmold than blatant displays of unethical behavior. Based on fear and propagated by anonymity and lack of understanding of the diversity of individuals, groups or properties based on gender, sexual orientation, race, disability, ethnicity or national origin can lead to intolerance and fear (Kurubacak, 2008). A more accurate picture of isms in the online world forces an emphasis on multiculturalism.

A code of ethics requires exploring how a community focuses to generate social justice and make sense of social experiences. Online learning with its proclivity for blogs, wikis, discussion boards and chats help promote the exchange of discussions that could influence the ethical decisions of a culturally diverse global society. The intersection of culturally diverse globalization and increasing reliance on technology influences notions, perceptions, roles and responsibilities in cyber education. More and more individuals are drawing meaning from multimedia and the Internet, for example. Teachers in a virtual environment serve as facilitators by providing synchronous and asynchronous learning opportunities to permit the learner to have the flexibility of learning anywhere and almost any time. With increased freedom, though, comes increased responsibility.

Today's learners demand different methods of teaching and learning; they are increasingly connected and understand how to navigate the cyber jungle to obtain information quickly. Today's learners also demand relevant information that helps them get what they want. It is no longer the role of the instructor to provide knowledge but to help learners find meaningful information and guide learners through the construction and application of knowledge. The global marketplace requires that workers are not only able to collaborate with colleagues around the world, but also be able to generate solutions, synthesize ideas and be risk-takers. These are skills that traditional education never provided. In cyberspace, the ultimate responsibility of learning rests with the student, who is encouraged to take ownership of learning. The instructor is more than a facilitator, he is a partner who shares expertise and guides the learner toward success. This partnership is reciprocal between the learner and the instructor, thus challenging learners to become reflective, critical thinkers (Beldarrain, 2006) and demanding that cyber educators keep pace with technology as well as the andragogy of teaching online.

Other stakeholders in cyber education share the ethical responsibility for the learning process. Success is ultimately a human responsibility (Russell. 2006), as each stakeholder contributes his part. Instructors, administrators, curriculum developers, instructional designers and Information Technology (IT) personnel, among others, have important roles to play in the success of the online learner. Together, these individuals must create and uphold a statement of ethical conduct that assures the best interest of the learner. The changing nature of teaching and learning in online environments has facilitated an opportunity to reflect on how traditional paradigms of education may or may not be effective. Limitations of the old way of thinking, teaching and learning have given way to new techniques, processes, and methods of implementation. The shared responsibility of stakeholders also includes a legal and moral duty to promote quality learning. Cyber educators and the educational community at large are the gatekeepers of ethics in learning.

Implementing and monitoring a code of ethical conduct for global learning is not a simple task; it is a complex endeavor, especially if the customer and learner are not seen as the same entity. It becomes dangerous when organizations sacrifice learning over profits and place emphasis on the organization serving itself instead of the learner. Often in the IT industry, technologies are adapted from the business world and deployed before the true impact of their effect on learning is asserted. The rapid changes faced by online learning create the attitude that everything is experimental until proven worthy. While this modus operandi allows for much needed flexibility to learn from trial and error, it remains imperative that decisions are made in the best interest of the learner who indeed is the customer.

Another ethical concern is that, in some cases, stakeholders do not accept or shy away from responsibility for the final product. Human nature indicates that when something goes well, there is someone ready to take credit; however, humans are too quick to play the blame game if something goes wrong. In order to truly focus on the success of the learner, stakeholders must acknowledge the individual and collective ethical responsibilities that come with their role. They must be aware of their responsibility to society, their ability to meet social needs, and their responsibility to avoid physical or mental harm to the customer.

There are certain moral values that are considered universal, while others vary from one social or cultural group to another. It is the ethical responsibility of cyber educators and stakeholders in the learning process to create online learning environments that take into consideration these varying norms. While blatant infractions like plagiarism, dishonesty or lying may be easier to identify universally, other forms of unethical conduct, such as misrepresentation of gender roles or minority groups, can remain hidden until a product is marketed overseas. Such events would trigger harmful consequences for the user. Good and harm can be more clearly understood in light of John Stewart Mill's theory on Utilitarianism. Utilitarianism supports the idea that those in IT who are involved in the creation or design of a product can be seen as committing a morally offensive act if the product contributes to unhappiness.

The real key to moral and ethical aptitude is the knowledge of potential harm. In the cyber world, some individuals have no knowledge of potential harm because, with technology, too often the link between cause and effect is blurred. Obscured by anonymity and the Internet, the responsibility of individuals behind the technology can be difficult to identify and measure. This is further skewed by the motive to make a profit; after all, the responsibility of the corporate executive is to make money (Russell, 2006).

The craving to make a profit brings forth ethical concerns related to cultural sensitivity and language barriers. Currently, English is predominantly the language of choice for most online courses and learning opportunities globally. This is being supplemented somewhat in Spanish; however, there are clear disadvantages to working online in a non-native language when students have to contribute to discussion boards, chats and collaborative assignments. Language is not the only issue. Many online courses come with foreign social and cultural contexts (Bates, 2001). Examples of writing style and even instructional style may vary greatly across cultures. The open and friendly style of encouraging the free flow of ideas is intrinsically a Western cultural influence. In many cultures, teachers are to be revered and respected at any cost and challenging or openly arguing a point with a teacher is not acceptable. To what extent is it ethical to impose culturally diverse approaches on the learner? Cyber educators must ponder if the global learning community has the ethical right to impress these values of critical thinking, debate, discussion, and questioning on a culturally diverse population.

A code of global ethics for the learning community must reflect all participants. There must be a distinction between the code that supports virtues like honesty, loyalty, and discretion and one that supports professional evaluation for the purpose of improving learning for students. A code of ethics may define the difference between professional and non-professional behaviors; it must move beyond generally accepted standards. Too often, the terms standards and ethics are used interchangeably. Normative ethical behaviors or standards are not the same as the underlying ethical principle. In essence, "the central objective of ethics is to determine what is good, or right, or what one ought to do" (Gross, 1999, p. 202 as quoted in Campbell 2001, p. 397). A code of ethics should advance clearly underlying moral virtues such as honesty, integrity and social justice.

In his book *Five Minds for the Future*, Gardner (2007) includes the disciplined, synthesizing and creative minds, as well as the respectful and ethical minds. The respectful mind responds to differences between individuals or groups constructively and with compassion. An individual's ethical point of reference, which depends upon their home environment according to Gardner, later transfers to schools and the workplace. The ethical mind acknowledges the role at work and the role of the individual as a citizen and then chooses to act consistently with the expectations of each role.

The essential concern for developing these five minds for the future has globalization at the core. Gardner (2007) assumes the continuous expansion of cyberspace, movement across cultural borders, movement of human beings around the globe, and the instantaneous movement of capital, all of which will be influenced by the five minds. Although this is a good place to start when conceptualizing an approach to global learning, what needs to be added is the effect of global learning itself on the entire process of cultivating the five minds. The spread of global education can alter or at least influence the means and the methods in which globalization takes place (Pava, 2008).

Constraints that Influence the Role of Cyber Educators

The constraints of privacy, integrity and freedom of speech influence the role of cyber educators and their ethical responsibilities. All of these constraints affect the learning process and the overall experience for the learner.

Privacy issues are often categorized into access issues, data mining and information brokering. Information brokering is the collecting and selling of information, which has permeated the digital world. As the rich e-learning environment explodes, so does the sea of data that underpins it. Information about people has become a valuable commodity. Organizations supply the service of collecting information and passing it along. There are several global initiatives that focus on the integration of information (Bressan & Lee, 1997) but what remains ethically strained is the lack of knowledge of the individual about whom the information is collected and distributed. Because issues about data privacy remain largely misunderstood, it is important that cyber educators prepare learners for safeguarding their privacy, as well as educate them about their rights.

A disconnect exists between using digitally mediated communication and understanding the flow of data behind it. As Turow (2003, p.16) puts it, "the great majority of adults who go online at home reject the general proposition that their information is a currency for commercial barter." The flow, extraction, manipulation, and use of data to make money from advertising elude the average user. Certainly, a combination of education, legislation, and a code of ethics must govern issues such as privacy policy and data flow in global learning. While technologies are becoming more complex and their ability to extract and manipulate information about the individual even greater, a code of ethics compels us to develop both a more straightforward and more wide-reaching approach.

Integrity is pivotal for ethical behavior in the online learning environment. Nonetheless, cyber educators continue to fight plagiarism and cheating just as they did in traditional face-to-face classrooms. Because the anonymity afforded by technology creates a veil behind which unethical behavior is more difficult to identify, the role of cyber educators has been redefined to include policing of academic integrity. Ethically speaking, cyber educators are responsible for upholding integrity. One mistake may mar the organization's reputation, not to mention the educator's career.

The responsibility for maintaining academic integrity does not rest solely in the hands of the instructor; however, it is the collective liability of all stakeholders.. Instructional designers, for example, have the individual responsibility of designing for authenticity, hence minimizing potential academic integrity infractions. On the other hand, administrators are responsible for providing training and support for instructors, as well as students, so they may recognize and prevent infractions. IT is in turn responsible for maintaining the infrastructure needed to deliver the course in the most efficient manner, yet be able to trace pertinent information that may be helpful in identifying infractions and those who committed them.

Cyber educators must nurture the element of trust in order to create a safe environment where learners may exercise their rights to freedom of speech without fear of retribution. Likewise, online instructors should have the freedom to engage their students in collegial discourse without censorship from administration. Unfortunately, the prized freedom of speech may become compromised if the reader misinterprets the learner's intent, whether it is a blog, discussion posting, or written assignment. The written product of the online learner will be judged not only by whatever evaluation rubric is in place, but also based on the evaluator's own biases and perceptions.

Cyber educators are ethically and morally responsible for removing any biased lens through which they are likely to view student work. Their role is to be impartial, opening up a world of equal learning opportunities for individuals regardless of background. Inside the course room, all interactions are traceable. As more Web 2.0 tools are used in cyber education, it is crucial that stakeholders maintain freedom of speech as a core value. Unlike traceable footprints in the course room, Web 2.0 tools offer more anonymity to the learner. Whether it is a teacher created or student created blog or wiki, learners who are savvy using these digitally mediated forms of communication are probably more likely to feel "at ease" speaking their mind They may prefer to do so behind the protection afforded by anonymity. It is the responsibility of cyber educators to respect each learner's comfort level by providing different options for sharing views.

Faced with the dilemma of having to enforce antiquated rules in a world that has changed, the typical educator is likely to shun student created content that is not favorable to the particular school or system. Traditionally, the courts will side with the school system if the student has disrupted the classroom by publicly displaying rebellious content on school-sponsored publications. If the content is published on a personal student Web site or blog, for instance, the courts will consider the student's actions protected under the First Amendment as long as it does not involve violence or becomes a threat to the safety of others. This may represent a philosophical shift for educators who are still grappling with the influence of technology in education. For the most part, the role of the cyber educator includes the ethical responsibility of protecting the rights of students when it comes to self-expression, as well as educating them in how to properly express their opinions without the use of violence or endangerment.

A code of ethical conduct that serves global learning must be all-inclusive, taking into account the varying ways in which technology continues to redefine the roles and ethical responsibilities. Educators must also understand how the constraints brought about by technology influence their roles. The types of constraints will likely continue to evolve as will the extension of global values that blur national and cultural lines.

LOOKING AHEAD

Future trends point toward the need for distance learning organizations to devise a global code of ethical conduct not just for cyber educators and learners, but also for all stakeholders in the educational process. This can only be accomplished by refocusing on the purpose of education.

Learning platforms, Web 2.0 tools, and mobile technologies will continue to evolve and, hence, create new challenges that will continually shape the roles and ethical responsibilities of stakeholders.

Now What?

1. Cyber educators are responsible for developing a code of ethics which takes into account the changing roles and responsibilities of stakeholders.
2. This code of ethics must focus on student learning first and foremost, but it must also aim at minimizing deception.
3. All stakeholders must take responsibility for implementing and monitoring an ethical code that supports universal moral values and focus on education.
4. Academic integrity must be supported by trust and by removing the biased lens from which educators are likely to view student work in the online environment.

5. All stakeholders must face the fact that the rules have changed and will continue to do so. It is necessary to develop a common vision to unite the global learning community in both intent and purpose.

A code of global ethics for learning must insure the elimination of duality. It must strive to preserve integrity and prevent moral trauma or harm. Cartesian duality, where the end justifies the means, is no more appropriate in a global learning community than in traditional education. Philosophers like John Dewey have long argued that the processes cannot be separated from the objectives. The challenges for a global community united through cyber education can be seen in terms of separation, effacement of identity, anonymity and distance. The more disengaged the community, the easier it is to justify duality. When a face is hidden or masked, it is much easier to make that face the enemy. The unseen is easier to condemn than the seen. Global learning must therefore re-evaluate its existence and refocus on the purpose behind education.

Having a common vision for global learning will ensure that cyber educators remain vigilant of potential hazards brought about by technology yet be savvy enough to exploit these technologies for the benefit of education. Although ethical behavior is a universal expectation, each group or culture may define it differently. A common vision in e-learning will unite the global learning community in both intent and purpose, therefore developing an acceptable definition of ethical behavior in the online environment.

Globalization of learning is far more than IT and the Internet. Globally extended communications will affect the evolution of human lives. For years there has been an obsession in learning with content. The term "content is king" has echoed through the halls of e-learning; however, this is not entirely true. A great deal more attention must be paid to the environment and hidden side effects of globalization of learning.

Global learning must take into account ethical considerations to ensure fairness, authenticity and justice. In order to consider accountability, there must be a defined code of ethics and conduct that is measurable and quantifiable. Higher levels of accountability are necessary for all stakeholders, including learners.

The answer may lie in changing the way we do things. Long gone are the days of rote memorization; however, poorly designed online courses encourage just that, opening the door to academic integrity infractions. Authentic learning strategies, combined with formative and summative assessments that require the student to synthesize learning and create their own content is perhaps a good insurance for integrity. Open-ended approaches to learning and assessment might also make it possible for a learner to update and expand their knowledge. Without a conflict of ethics or morals, perhaps assessment might be an event that can add to the learning while the event is going on (Anderson, 2005).

If the online world of global learning is to be one that is healthy, strong and respectable it must go even a step further, it must foster learner identities that are credible and meaningful to the learner. Learners must feel safe and have a sense of purpose before they become active members of the online community. They will need to be involved citizens of a collective enterprise and have the skills needed to develop and use this new knowledge effectively. The goal of the global learning community is and should be more than just the acquisition of information. It should be as Aristotle said, to develop practical knowledge (Dreyfus, 1999).

Many would argue that unethical behaviors are enhanced by anonymity and online education. Some may even suggest that students act less ethically because of the opportunities presented by technology and the anonymity it affords. The financial crisis of 2008 serves as a recent reminder that moral distancing and an ethical collapse.. What might be presented to us is an opportunity to change the way things are done in education. Current systems do not call for the typical pendulum swing, but instead the reinvention of education via the opportunities granted by technology. The educational community might just be able to transgress the way it has always operated and come up with new approaches in the areas of course design, pedagogy and learner activities and assessment (Sharma & Maleyeff, 2003).

CONCLUSION

Online learning programs will continue to expand and the community of those involved in cyber education will continue to increase. A new code of ethical conduct for global learning is needed to bind this international community together for the purpose of focusing on what is best for the learner.

While some basic moral values are shared across cultures, other norms vary from one social group to another. Increased connectivity has brought about the globalization of certain values, such as risk-taking behaviors that in turn impact learning. There is concern for not only the ethical behavior of students, but also of all stakeholders involved in online learning programs. It is crucial to develop a code of ethical conduct that takes into consideration the changing roles of each stakeholder, including the role of the student.

Privacy, integrity and freedom of speech are constraints that shape the roles and responsibilities of stakeholders. Instructors, administrators, curriculum developers, instructional designers and IT personnel, among others, each play an important role in the success of the learner. Stakeholders ethically share the collective responsibility for the quality of the online learning program and the ultimate desired outcome: student learning.

Careful attention must be given to how the members of learning communities interact, and how these communities generate social justice and interpret social experiences in a manner that does not undermine the rights of its members. The stakeholders involved in the design, implementation and delivery of online learning programs are responsible for ensuring that all participants are safe and protected from harm.

Regardless of ethical framework used, a code of ethical conduct in global learning must be grounded on what is best for the student. Educational institutions and companies with distance training programs must acknowledge that the learner is indeed the customer, thus the urge to make a profit must be put aside for the sake of focusing on student learning. When all stakeholders in an online learning program collectively take ethical responsibility for student success, everyone wins.

REFERENCES

Adamson, J., & Mietus, N. (2000). *Law for business and personal use* (15th ed.). New York: Southwestern.

Anderson, R. (2005). Traditional classroom testing for online courses. Allied Academics International Conference, Las Vegas. *Proceedings of the Academy of Educational Leadership, 10*(2), 1–5.

Bates, T. (2001). International distance education: Cultural and ethical issues. *Distance Education, 22*(1), 122–136. doi:10.1080/0158791010220107

Beldarrain, Y. (2006). Distance education trends: Integrating new technologies to foster student interaction and collaboration. *Distance Education, 27*(2), 139–153. doi:10.1080/01587910600789498

Boyle, R., Kacmar, C., & George, J. (2008). Distributed deception: An investigation of the effectiveness of deceptive communication in a computer-mediated environment. *International Journal of e-Collaboration, 4*(3), 14–25. doi:10.4018/jec.2008070102

Bressan, S., & Lee, T. (1997). *Information brokering on the World Wide Web*. Webnet 97 World Conference. The Sloan School of Management, Massachusetts Institute of Technology, Cambridge, MA.

Campbell, E. (2001). Let right be done: Trying to put ethical standards into practice. *Journal of Education Policy, 16*(5), 395–411. doi:10.1080/02680930110071011

Committee on the Internet in the Evolving Information Infrastructure. (2001). *The Internet's coming of age*. National Academy Press.

Dreyfus, H. (1999). Anonymity versus commitment: The dangers of education on the Internet. *Ethics and Information Technology, 1*(1), 15. doi:10.1023/A:1010010325208

Gardner, H. (2007). *Five minds for the future*. Boston: Harvard Business School Press.

Kumar, R., & Mitchell, C. (2004). What happens to educational administration when organization trumps ethics. *McGill Journal of Education, 39*(2), 127–135.

Kurubacak, G. (2008). Online identity: Guidelines for discerning racism in blogs. *International Journal of eLearning. Education Module, 7*(3), 403–426.

Lessig, L. (1999). *Code and other values of cyberspace*. New York: Basic Books.

Paskoff, S. (2004, September 29). ELI (R) releases online workplace ethics programs. *PR Newswire*. New York. Retrieved October 17, 2010, from http://www.thefreelibrary.com/ELI(R)+Releases+Online+Workplace+Ethics+Programs.-a0122624992

Pava, M. (2008). Loving the distance between them: Thinking beyond Howard Gardner's Five Minds for the Future. *Journal of Business Ethics, 83*, 285–296.. doi:10.1007/s10551-007-9619-6

Russell, G. (2006). Globalization, responsibility and virtual schools. *Australian Journal of Education, 50*(2), 140–154.

Turow, J. (2003). *Americans & online privacy: The system is broken*. A report from the Annenberg Public Policy Center of the University of Pennsylvania, Retrieved October 17, 2010, from http://www.asc.upenn.edu/usr/jturow/internet-privacy-report/36-page-turow-version-9.pdf

Chapter 3
Intellectual Property in an Age of Open Source and Anonymity

ABSTRACT

Current intellectual property (IP) laws are under scrutiny. The increased connectivity and sharing capabilities afforded by social networking Web 2.0 tools have added new dimensions and challenges to different sectors of society, including businesses and educational systems alike. This chapter explores why current laws do not meet the needs of a changing global community and probes into options afforded by Open Educational Resources (OER).

OBJECTIVES

- Define intellectual property in the digital age.
- Identify global policy makers and legal boundaries for intellectual property in cyber space.
- Discuss the ramifications of intellectual property breaches in a global community that is connected and shares just about everything.
- Discuss the potential and constraints of Open Educational Resources (OER) and the impact of new technologies on intellectual property.

DOI: 10.4018/978-1-60960-543-8.ch003

- Characterize learner equity online and the challenges of collaboration and connectivity.

INTRODUCTION

The United States Constitution contains an Intellectual Property clause that guarantees the exclusive rights to the writings, ideas and discoveries of authors and inventors for a limited period of time. The anonymity afforded by the technologies available in the digital age has challenged these rights. Technology facilitates copy and transfer without permission or knowledge of the parties involved and makes it effortless to multiply and distribute content at little or no cost.

As is evidenced in the world of music, products belonging to other people are being passed around the world without permission and without royalties. Many laws that were designed for a world of printing and publishing seem out of sorts in a digital age. There are the problems of boundaries and legislative reach because we are living in a world where boundaries are quickly disappearing. Furthermore, the advent of virtual learning has caused educational institutions to rethink intellectual property policies, which undeniably affect the ownership rights as well as the educational product. The issue of equity is also involved, since materials and resources available to traditional classroom teachers and students may not be available to those who choose an online program.

This chapter addresses the dynamics and challenges of escalating present day intellectual property concerns in a world of limited boundaries and digital anonymity. Not only have the geographical boundaries that traditionally supported legislative efforts been minimized by the online connection, the framework for intellectual property rights has been eroded in an avalanche of open source, collaborative sharing and freebies. Sharing is Web 2.0; what is mine is yours and what is yours is mine.

BACKGROUND

Intellectual property can be defined as an original work that is created in a tangible medium of expression. Often referred to as ideas or collections of ideas, intellectual property is the result of cognitive processes and is characterized by nonphysical properties (Moore, 2004). Generally thought to include trademarks, patents and copyrights, intellectual property protects the rights of the inventor or author to their work.

Trademarks can be a slogan, symbol or a mark that a business uses to identify and distinguish their products or operations, hence making it part of their branding strategy. It can be a graphic, logo, name, word or other means. Once a trademark is established, it is exclusive to the owners and others cannot use or imitate it. Many well-known trademarks conjure up images instantly. Trademarks are vitally important to companies and their effort to brand their products and maintain brand loyalty. When the Nike® trademark is envisioned, the "swoosh" instantly comes to mind. When the Golden Arches are mentioned, McDonald's® is visualized and for Morton® Salt it is the little girl with the umbrella that is conjured up. Trademarks are good for 10 years and may be renewed in 10-year increments (Brown & Sukys, 1998). Trademarks online are especially powerful because they provide visual familiarity. Traditionally regulated by both state and federal laws, trademarks are registered in the United States Patent and Trademark Office. The ® symbol indicates that a trademark is registered in the United States.

Inventions can be produced and sold only under exclusive patents. Inventors can patent processes, articles of manufacturing or a composition of matter like a pharmaceutical or drug from being copied or manufactured by another company. To receive a patent, the device or process must be new and previously unknown. It must also be useful and not obvious to ordinary people in the business. Patents are good for 17 years.

Creative works by artists, photographers, musicians or writers have to be copyrighted in order for the artists to publish and sell their work exclusively. Copyrights are protected for the life of the author plus 50 years. Copyrights generally apply to literary works, dramatic works, musical works, choreographed works, pictorial, graphic or sculptured works, motion pictures or videos, audios works and sound recordings. In 1989, the use of the © to indicate copyrighting was made optional; in the past it had been a requirement (Brown & Sukys, 1998). The intent of the copyright law is to limit reproduction of the work without permission of the copyright holder.

In the United States, there is one exception to a copyright breach and that is the fair use doctrine. Fair use allows for limited reproduction of the work for use in scholarship or review, for example, without the permission of the copyright holder. If the four-part balancing test is met under U.S. Code Title 17, 107, the work may be used without the permission of the copyright holder (United States Copyright Office, 2009) when:

"...The purpose and character of the use, including whether such use is of a commercial nature or is for nonprofit educational purposes; the nature of the copyrighted work; the amount and substantiality of the portion used in relation to the copyrighted work as a whole; and the effect of the use upon the potential market for or value of the copyrighted work..."

United States common law was the first to incorporate fair use, but it has also been adopted by the United Kingdom and Israel. A similar concept called fair dealing is also in use in common law countries like Canada (Brown & Sukys, 1998). Nevertheless, these laws are complex, especially in a global society connected through technology. The manner in which people communicate and exchange information through technology has affected views on intellectual property.

Complexities of Intellectual Property and Cyber Law

Copyright laws in the United States and around the globe are far from simple. Several trade agreements and treaties have tried to address the issue of global copyright protection. The Uruguay Round Agreement (URAA) the General Agreement on Tariffs and Trade (GATT) and Trade-Related Aspects of Intellectual Property (TRIPS) Agreement are a few of such efforts to unite the international community.

Since the 19th century and the Berne Convention, people have been thinking about how to address and enforce global copyright issues. The World Intellectual Property Organization (WIPO) was created but had no binding jurisdiction. The TRIPS agreement is the most effective method of enforcement because it incorporates international trade and offers retaliatory tools like tariffs (Bromberg & Underwood, 2005). This agreement, which tries to fashion international copyright legislation after Western law, holds promise for the protection of intellectual property rights internationally (Moore, 2004).

Intellectual property has always had skeptics who felt its limitations. The law in the United States itself is limited. It is the only grant of power that requires Congress to pursue a narrow goal and it also balances the power of Congress to achieve that goal. In a letter from James Madison to Thomas Jefferson, Madison reflects that government granted monopolies are a nuisance. Jefferson shared his contempt for government power and was concerned about inherent abuse. The founding fathers realized a need to encourage artists and inventors, but were unwilling to give unrestricted rights to issue copyrights and patents. Jefferson was particularly ahead of his time. He recognized that creativity had the economic property of ideas which are non-adversarial, so they can be used by multiple individuals and not be exhausted or consumed. Jefferson understood open source in the 1700s (Bromberg & Underwood, 2005).

There is another field of thought which implies that not much is actually all new, but that both scientific works and literature build on the past. Many new inventions and works of literature are but reinventions or derivatives of older ideas. Novels become plays, plays become novels, names and faces change, but the plots remain uncannily similar. Even Isaac Newton realized that progress is made by standing on the shoulders of giants. Creativity is sparked by the availability of great scientific and literary works. This open source, or idea anarchy, is supported by the Web 2.0 cyber community. The open availability of ideas clears the way for the argument to demand access to all types of information. This is also being echoed in developed and underdeveloped countries alike where access to information is not only considered a social right but an economic one. The result has been a dislodging of the copyright system and an explosion of violations and piracy (Moore, 2004).

Orphan works are another example of the complexities of copyright laws. Orphan works are older and people may be reluctant to publish or use them because the original authors are unknown. The United States Copyright Office recommends not publishing orphan works unless a diligent search was conducted to find and compensate the original authors. This, however, falls apart because many of these works are published and available in some form digitally. The Copyright Office also requests that if these works exist in nonprofit institutions online, they might be exempt; however, if the original owner contacts a library, institution or museum and asks that they discontinue using the work, it should be discontinued immediately to avoid being fined.

On one hand, intellectual property is protected for the benefit of the originator of the idea, while on the other this protection may limit the benefits to society at large. Every industry, including educational institutions, continues to grapple with the concept of intellectual property versus open source. This is likely to be an ongoing concern until more balanced international laws are enacted.

CHANGING TIMES AND FAR REACHING IMPACT

The impact of technology has caused society to rethink its position on intellectual property. The views of each generation influence societal perspectives and, eventually, the laws.

Generation We or Millennials (those who were born between 1978-2000), for example, are the largest generation in American history. Ninety-five million strong, this generation grew up around computers and quickly learned how to easily access and reproduce Web content. The generation that follows, sometimes called Generation Z or V (virtual), is truly a phenomenon. This generation of digital natives is growing up immersed in technology, which they use to not just access and reproduce Web content, but also to create and share content in virtual communities. How their use of content affects societal views of intellectual property remains to be seen. Their full impact is yet to come. In the meantime, the international community continues to collaborate in the enactment of international laws and treaties. The coalition's efforts are aimed at curtailing ethical issues such as cyber-crimes and creating cyber-jurisdictions.

In matters of economy, logic says that the originator of an idea would want to be able to profit from his/her idea, which would require making it known to a large audience. But with technology, there is a delicate balance between equitable economics and intellectual property, as everything is easily reproduced. Digital capacities to easily reproduce have heightened the free rider issue, among others. The free rider problem says that easy reproduction may drive down the price and therefore prevent the author from making enough money. The real fear is that without some protection against reproduction, the author may not be able to recuperate the costs of creating the product or concept. Intellectual property has always taken into account two different interests: granting exclusive rights and limiting the duration of those rights (Bromberg & Underwood, 2005).

Many developments have challenged the laws relating to intellectual property in the last decade. The world of cyber-law is emerging and beginning to come into its own. As it matures, it is attempting to define cyber-crimes, cyber-jurisdictions and cyber-communities and it is even creating places to resolve disputes. Cyber-terrorism, cyber-stalkers and cyber-theft are all too real. The change is taking place on an almost daily basis. Web sites like CyberSettle are attempting to supplement civil courts. For the most part, the laws are based on U.S. Common law and the U.S. Constitution (McNamara, Ropp, & Lowenstein, 2008).

Other Web sites are springing up with intellectual property right information available to the international community. Google™ boasts over 16 million hits for intellectual property rights. Sites like the World Intellectual Property Organization (WIPO), have taken on the ominous task of protecting intellectual property worldwide. This organization concerns itself with how authors are to make living and shares information about laws, treaties and just about anything else that pertains to the worldwide intellectual property challenge. WIPO has also dedicated publications to educate individual nations in regards to their intellectual property rights (World Intellectual Property Organization, 2009). This is just one of many global resources.

The United States government sponsors a training data base for intellectual property issues because such issues are so far reaching and complex. This site is focused on training international officials about United States copyright laws so they have a better chance of meeting the obligations of the World Trade Organization (WTO) and complying with Trade Related Aspects of Intellectual Property (TRIPS) mentioned earlier. The training data base also helps United States officials learn about the laws in other countries (IPR Training Data Base, 2008).

Another law enacted to address the ever growing issue of unauthorized sharing of protected intellectual property was the Digital Media Copyrights Act of 1996 (DMCA). The DMCA, which was unanimously passed in the United States Senate in 1998 under President Clinton, attempts to bring into enforceable law two treaties set forth by WIPO. It makes it a criminal offense to sell or distribute technologies, services or devices that compromise Digital Rights Management (DRM) access to copyrighted works whether or not a violation in the copyright has occurred. DMCA also creates more stringent penalties for violation of the copyright laws on the Internet (Moore, 2004).

Unauthorized sharing may be as innocent as purchasing a pirated movie or downloading a copy of the same movie from the Internet that someone filmed with their camcorder at the movie theater. The Millennials come to mind when it comes to accessing and sharing media through the Internet, as Greenberg and Weber (2008) explain:

Millennials assume they have unlimited and free (or virtually free) access to information. For them, the Internet has the effect of obliterating the boundaries between what can and cannot be known. For many, it even demolishes the boundary between what is and is not possible. (p.95)

The issue is of global magnitude. Internationalization of copyright and ownership has put added pressure on the third world countries, especially those on the African continent. Developed countries expect underdeveloped countries to adhere to the international standards of copyright legislation. Countries in Africa are struggling to meet the very basic requirements of the TRIPS agreement (Nicholson, 2007). Part of the challenge is that the European Union, Australia and the United States all have different terms.

The far-reaching effects of intellectual property laws in the digital age have also affected education on a global scale. The increasing demand for online learning is causing government agencies and the educational community at large to rethink the copyright laws to enable schools and universities to use the same content and materials online as in the classroom. To accomplish this, changes to the policies and procedures need to address traditional copyright exceptions. Issues like showing videos to learners that are physically present in a face-to-face classroom versus virtually presenting them in a classroom are ambiguous. This can also be expanded to include the recording of on-demand communications, webinars, chats and other broadcasts. Two questions that come to mind are: (a) Who owns these resources? and (b) Who can access them and when?

There is no doubt the status of ownership in cyberspace is changing the way we think about intellectual property. In online education, many schools have tried to develop an approach that both encourages faculty to go online and protects their intellectual property rights. Many schools have begun to give pay incentives to faculty as well as rewards and limited rights to their intellectual property. This is given in exchange for letting the universities retain some copyright ownership of the courses and utilization rights (Campus-Information Systems, 2001).

The phenomenon of anonymity adds to the issues at stake. How can a school or teacher be sure that what is sent to learners in a distance education mode is only being used by those learners? Anonymity prohibits the sender from knowing with certainty the receiver's intent, distribution and authenticity. This is exemplified by situations like photocopying pages from printed works and distributing them. Every segment of society and culture is being affected more and more by the influence of copyright laws and the implications of those laws for music, games, sports and education.

CHANGING TECHNOLOGIES, CHANGING IDEOLOGIES

Long before the advent of ripping software, copyright protection advocates had concerns with technologies that copied and or reproduced the works of artist, writers and inventors. Player piano roles, audio tapes and VHS all had issues with copying and reproduction using disruptive technologies. Digital mass market technologies have heightened concerns because of the ease with which digital items can be re-produced and distributed (Coyle, 2003). Systems for Digital Rights Management (DRM) have been developed to remove the anonymity inherent in the copying and transfer of digital mass media.

Distributing information in digital form raises the concern that digital content can be reproduced and distributed without the owners knowing. The anonymity provided by the Internet can and often does, lead to unauthorized distribution, forgery and defacement of the information. DRM systems attempt to manage the distribution of digital content to those individuals or organizations that have paid for it or have an affiliation that allows them to have access to the information (Damiani & Fugazza, 2006).

DRM systems also attempt to take the anonymity out of the distribution of materials. Most DRM technologies rely upon four elements to protect the owner's rights: permissions, rights holders, constraints and obligations. Permissions are what having the right to use the material allow the person accessing this material to do, while rights holders are those who are entitled to use these permissions. Constraints are restrictions to these permissions and obligations are what must be done to exercise such rights. Research is needed in this area, as the evolution of technologies that support the concept of DRM continue to be developed. Currently, only a very limited version of this concept is applied in the online environment (Damiani & Fugazza, 2006).

The Ownership of Knowing

Intellectual property, by definition, may imply something that is very difficult to protect, thus raising a controversy around the very idea of the ownership of *knowing*. There are many definitions of intellect but most imply "the power of knowing or understanding" (Simonson, 2006, p. 68). Property is easier to come to grips with and usually implies something tangible. The controversy arises when the words are combined. Intellectual property rights deal with those creations that are protected under copyrights, trademarks, and patents among other forms of protection, whether they are abstract or concrete symbols or creations (Miller & Davis, 2000).

Instead of looking at intellectual property as a legal battle, it might serve everyone more to look at it as an academic issue. In a society where each person is looking for self-protection and remuneration, balancing individual rights with the philosophy behind open source may prove to be an ongoing challenge. Academically speaking, proponents of open source, especially for educational purposes, believe in sharing for the common good.

Open Educational Resources

From its inception, the Internet has been about access to information and reaching people. More and more traditional institutions are harnessing the Internet to educate and share digital resources at no cost. This sharing of digital resources without charge is called Open Educational Resources (OER). The volume of OER is growing. Many schools, including the Massachusetts Institute of Technology, have made volumes of educational materials available to anyone with Internet access. Globally, the sharing of these resources helps to promote the development of educational and economic systems around the world.

The Center for Educational Research and Innovation (CERI), which is sponsored by the Organization for Economic Cooperation and Development (OECD), strongly suggests that a lot of knowledge will be available for free online. In their publication *Giving Knowledge for Free: The Emergence of Open Educational Resources*, OER is defined as "digitized materials offered freely and openly for educators, students and self learners to use and re-use for teaching, learning and research" (OECD, 2007, p. 11). OECD's focus is on improving the global economy by empowering through education and technology. The impact of OER may be better seen in underdeveloped, financially strapped countries, which would otherwise not be able to purchase quality educational resources for its youth, thus perpetuating the socio-economic implications that come with lack of education.

While the benefits of OER are being expounded, there is another side to this challenge. OER is confronting the same laws and regulations stemming from traditional intellectual property rights. However, the world has changed and those laws that governed the reuse and distribution of materials have become obsolete in cyberspace. Yet, legal restrictions that governed a world where the primary source of distribution was printing and publishing do not address these concerns. Because these laws are being applied to OER, educators and researchers are frustrated by adherence to laws that slow down progress.

Innovative licensing may help to bridge the gap between the needs of OER and intellectual copyright law. Organizations like the Creative Commons group are attempting to introduce moderation in an open source world. By creating new business models, copyright agreements, and licensing that is innovative might provide some protection and help for authors, educators, scientists and artists (Hylén & Schuller, 2007).

In some cases organizations providing OER repositories to educators allow the creator of the content to say how they prefer their material should be used. The content is then licensed accordingly. Others, such as TeacherTube.com, explicitly say that the content creator retains all ownership rights, yet users must agree to Creative Commons Attribution-Share Alike licensing. This licensing states that users may share someone else's work if they give credit to its originator and they may adapt a piece of content but must distribute the new version only "under the same, similar or a compatible license" (TeacherTube, 2009, para. 8).

In order for OERs to be effective, someone has to insure the quality of the materials being offered. Many of the sites will remove questionable content, but they may not necessarily be looking at the quality of the content. Organizations and even countries must get involved with the idea of lifelong learning and create copyright laws that bolster the sharing of knowledge while protecting authorship and ownership. Strong and innovative government policies should be created that support the distribution of digital resources (Hylén & Schuller, 2007).

IP Disengagement in Online Teaching

The increasing use of technologies is impacting education in an unforeseen way. Policies that have been in place for generations are no longer applicable or doing what they were intended to do. Most of these policies formulated for a face-to-face context no longer apply in an online environment. Higher education, specifically, is a sector that is experiencing an onslaught of change with regard to both existing policies and the creation of new policies. Many categories, including teacher workload, grading and evaluation, privacy and records, the rights to third party materials and use, as well as ownership, are being challenged. The demand for online learning programs has prompted administrators to reconsider old practices, yet meaningful change has yet to be seen.

Although there are many categories covered by this disconnect, there are two major areas where universities are being challenged: academic policies and administrative policies are in dire need of attention. Despite the growth of technologies, most policies in higher education still reflect an on campus population (Wallace, 2007). In universities, both academic and administrative policies struggle with the issues of intellectual property and anonymity.

Academic policies usually include the responsibilities of staff, their interactions with learners and assessment and evaluation. They may also be concerned with learner privacy, academic integrity and any type of appeals process for infringements. It is clear that in many cases copyright laws are just not on the radar screen. Teachers, professors and learners remain inattentive to and not educated on intellectual property laws. Although there is no shortage of materials and information available on this subject, the parties involved could easily become oblivious. There are many Web sites available that familiarize educators with the laws, but this does not make them more likely to adhere to them if they think they are not going to be challenged or sued (Starkman, 2008). What educators may not realize is that a simple incident like a learner plagiarizing could potentially affect the entire institution if this work is placed on a blog, wiki or e-portfolio.

Administration policies often do not take into account the online environment. Privacy and disclosure policies are developed as if the learners were all in a face-to-face environment. The phenomenon of anonymity in the digital environment is requiring universities to develop permission forms for retaining and releasing online contributions, use of discussions by third parties and those who have access to the course, discussions and web tools. It is these release policies that begin to bump up against copyright issues.

Online ownership and copyrights have become controversial points for universities, mostly because of outdated policies. Faculty members were sometimes thought to be exempt from typical employer-employee ownership laws. The creation of online courses has, in some cases, challenged this concept. Universities have taken to paying the faculty separately either in the forms of bonuses or incentives to develop courses for the online environment. Learning objects, repositioning of the content and reproducibility are all concerns. Changing policies that have been in place for many years is a balancing act between the needs of the institution, the faculty and the needs of the learners (Wallace, 2007).

These facts are an indication that higher education moves at a glacial pace. While the government continually cuts funding and support, a new learner has emerged demanding integration of the Internet and new technologies. These are forces at work which challenge higher education as the purveyor of knowledge. Far reaching, they affect the institution financially, structurally and culturally. The adult learner has different demands than the traditional undergraduate student and more choices have become available to this population. It is generally well accepted that learning is a lifelong process. The pace of change in our world causes high school and post-secondary graduates to constantly update their skills. This emphasis on continual reeducation has created a new group of learners, the adult learner (Folkers, 2005).

Colleges and universities are not generally run like a business. Traditionally, geographical constraints protected regional institutions from competition. Now, competition can come from anywhere in the world. Faculty members have been hesitant to make the leap to online education for a number of reasons. One is certainly increased visibility. The cloak of privacy afforded a faculty member, where course creation is a solo occupation, is being challenged. New support staff and instructional design professionals are often involved in the creation of online courses. This raises the question of who really owns the course (Wallace, 2007).

The legal question of ownership is covered by the United States Constitution and copyright law. Although the law provides for and is intended to protect, the creator of works with this protection, there is an exception and that is the situation of "work for hire". Work for hire is when work is created by an employee in the scope of employment. Faculty members have been immune to this in most instances and have usually owned the course, content and syllabus. Online brings two major and conflicting concerns: (a) Will faculty be required to alter the content because it is controversial or commercially infeasible? and (b) Will the original course be kept up to date? Different organizations have handled this in different ways. Currently, there is no one policy for ownership of faculty materials in distance learning or online environments.

Under work for hire, if an employee creates something for an employer, the copyright belongs to the employer. Online course materials were never subject to patents, which many universities typically own, but fell under copyright law, which usually gave the rights to the intellectual property to faculty. *Publish or perish* is the mantra of academic faculty, it is an expectation for tenure, awards, and promotions. As the lines of ownership are further blurred, the world of academia may also have to rethink its definition of original publication.

It is clear, however, that intellectual property is one of the issues that has caused faculty to shy away from developing online courses. Part of the challenge is the line where technology ends and content begins. Until this is defined, faculty will remain reluctant about committing to online education as long as the copyright issues remain unresolved (Folkers, 2005). One way to begin this process is for administration to acknowledge the existing gap and take steps to protect the faculty. Because educational funding is not what it used to be, even large research universities are scrambling to reinvent themselves. In an effort to meet the needs of a new clientele and remain competitive, higher education institutions create schools of continuing and professional studies, and create certificate programs as well as non-degree programs to address the evolution of job descriptions.

As academic institutions continue to grapple with the concept of intellectual property and copyright laws, the demand for online learning programs is likely to increase. It would be in the best interest of all stakeholders to move swiftly toward the common goal of redefining policies that will ultimately increase the quality of education thus benefitting learners.

LOOKING AHEAD

The digital age has brought about its share of ethical confrontations around the globe. Illegal use of intellectual property is so common that some organizations hire hackers to assess vulnerability. It is estimated that American companies are losing in excess of one trillion dollars annually from theft of intellectual property. In the educational arena, equity seems to be another issue. Distance educators should have access to the same resources that face-to-face educators are allowed to use in their classrooms.

Now What?

1. Individual organizations as well as the international community must act upon the idea of lifelong learning and create copyright laws that bolster the sharing of knowledge while protecting authorship and ownership.
2. All stakeholders must move toward a common goal of redefining laws and polices to increase the quality of education for a global community.
3. Organizations, institutions, and particularly higher education need to academic policies and administrative policies that reflect the growth and integration of technologies in learning.
4. Much discussion and additional research is needed, as society rethinks its position on intellectual property.
5. Ongoing collaborative efforts between government, organizations and educational institutions must support both, the individual and the needs of the global learning community.

The Economic Espionage Act of 1997 (EEA) was enacted to prevent the theft of trade secrets. Prior to this act, no legislation dealt directly with the theft of commercially valuable trade secrets. This act protects "all forms and types of financial, business, scientific, technical, economic or engineering information" (Albert, Sanders, & Mazzaro, 2005, p. 631). The law covers tangible and intangible trade secrets no matter where or how they are stored. Controversies have been raised as to what constitutes a violation. Under EEA, even search engine keywords have been challenged. Global results from cases undertaken by Google™ and Yahoo® have brought mixed results in North America and Europe. Currently, it remains under the auspices of the trademark owners to monitor how third parties are using their marks in advertisements, Web sites, search engine results and other forms (Klein & Huffnagle, 2007).

Changes to copyright laws have removed the economic gain restriction for copyrights and made it a federal offense to illegally reproduce and distribute protected materials. The copyright laws now include those who act to harm another or attempt to do so for commercial gain. Under this legislation, the government has the burden of proof of a valid copyright, infringement of the copyright, willfulness and either purpose of commercial advantage or reproduction and distribution of a copyrighted work valued at more than $1,000. There are areas where this law is vulnerable, however. For example, reverse engineering has been found to be fair use if it is the only route to access ideas and elements when there is a legitimate reason to take such action. Additionally, databases are offered minimal protection under the EEA.

Two areas that have been tested with the famous Napster case is the concept of first sale and intent, as well as financial gain by distribution. In 1991, Napster, the first file sharing technology, began to charge individuals for songs after many long and lengthy battles. Shortly thereafter, other file sharing technologies filled in the gaps (Moore, 2004). The distribution of music through Napster was found to be in violation of fair use. The first sale doctrine had been undermined and Napster was found in violation of the copyright provisions (Albert, Sanders, & Mazzaro, 2005).

Learner Equity in Cyber Learning

While copyright legislation restricts distribution, online educators are crying for equal rights. As distance learning becomes more available and widespread, it is raising serious questions about the fairness of copyrights and fairness of access. Distribution of materials for online education is raising more questions than answers. With limited funding for education, it would seem appropriate to somehow relieve educators from the burden of having to adhere to current copyright laws. Change is definitely needed.

Current laws do not address the world in which technologies are changing daily. A great deal of controversy is being created between the owners of copyrights and the online educational community. Currently, the burden falls upon the educator to be wary of copyright violations and judicious in the use and distribution of copyrighted materials. Educators are asking the United States Copyright Office to amend the scope of works and make available to distance education the same exclusions allowed in a face-to-face classroom (D'Amico Juettner, & Girasa, 2001, p.109).

The real problem is in digitizing copyrighted works, whether printed, audio or visuals because it opens up the works to manipulation. Similarly, downloading and copying works can lead to a significant revenue loss. It is not practical to ask educators and owners to sign permissions for use of these works; the volume is just too high.

The debate rages with educators indicating that licensing fees increase educational costs and copyright owners pleading a case for licensing fees. Although government intervention does not seem to be working well, another alternative has not yet presented itself. Unless copyright protection is to be eliminated altogether, either an unabated breach of copyright use will continue or materials will not be made equitably available to distance learners (D'Amico Juettner & Girasa, 2001).

Challenges of Collaboration and Connectivity

Future trends indicate that Web 2.0 technology tools will continue to influence societal views of intellectual property rights, open source and what constitutes appropriate sharing. Social networking sites, while they offer undeniable benefits of collaboration, also bring about challenges related to what is shared and how it is shared, as well as identifying the original proprietor of the content.

The challenge that Web 2.0 presents is less a legal challenge and more a fundamental change in the way people view and share information and the ethics behind it. This shift is far reaching and has been initiated by the prevalence of the Internet. The protection afforded by anonymity is diminished on sites such as Facebook® and MySpace®, among others. These sites include third-party applications that will use the user's information as well as information from the user's contacts to promote their services and widgets. Users must be savvy in protecting themselves by limiting visibility and withholding certain private information. When it comes to sharing user-created content, users must understand that anyone who sees their content can easily copy it, redistribute it or change it.

Significant innovations are no longer coming from leaders in the industry such as Microsoft®, IBM®, university research departments or think tanks of our world, but from small highly motivated startups and individual entrepreneurs. Innovation has gone grassroots and mash-ups and open source are fundamental parts of the Web 2.0 culture. Although the opportunities offered by collaborating via blogs, wikis and social networks are exciting, their source is less established and secure.

A wide variety of legal issues have sprung up regarding control and responsibilities. Web 2.0 takes the information out of its three dimensional context and takes away hierarchy and territory. Information is available without the traditional seals of approval and applied credibility of corporate seals or academic prowess. Malcolm Gladwell (2005) in his book *Blink: The Power of Thinking Without Thinking* describes this as a form of rapid cognition where we instantly make a decision and intuitively determine the trustworthiness. Where is the protection for authorship in open source? Where does the responsibility of the organization belong? This raises the risk of authorship, something that the intellectual property laws were designed to protect. Innovation is different for the organization than it has been in the past. It has a new role, one that reaches far beyond developing and providing intellectual property.

Most importantly, this has and will continue to expand the rate of innovation and change. With the traditional barriers to ownership and protection diminished or dismissed, the pace of change will continue to accelerate. Social networks, virtual worlds, tools and initiatives are being thrust upon us at a rate that is difficult to assimilate. Integrating these new tools into an existing culture can be challenging. First, there is the ominous task of selecting and evaluating these choices; next, there is the task of immersion. All of these technologies come with nuisances and affordances which give way to concerns. Anonymity and trust are directly linked to authorship and authenticity. Traditional intellectual property publication paths provided these handrails, but the emerging world of Web. 2.0 is taking them away.

The concern remains, however, about how to protect information beyond the availability to the primary learner. Social software and Web 2.0 have not made this any easier. One approach to posting intended to reduce anxiety and apprehension is to provide students with pseudonyms and allow them to post anonymously, or ask them to use abbreviations like DA for devil's advocate or VOD for voice of dissention/dissent. Nonetheless, this is often not without risk since learners may feel empowered to post and act without inappropriately. This still does not control the distribution and use issues of items distributed online.

While Web 2.0 offers opportunities for networking and collaboration, it is also causing concern regarding intellectual property. Open source development, networking and open communications are being applauded by the technology community, but user-generated content, open source systems and sharing all challenge traditional models of intellectual property and ownership. Change and innovation are inescapable. A paradigm shift must occur in order for policies and regulations to be aligned with current and future methods of communicating and sharing information. Societal views on this topic will continue to evolve and be challenged.

CONCLUSION

The digital age has thrust upon writers, publishers, educators and every technology user a challenge that has never before been faced. What is needed is a sweeping approach to intellectual property laws and a whole new structure to support it. The entire position of publishing and sharing information needs to be rethought. Intellectual property law has to be enforceable, yet be applied in the best interests of all stakeholders. Intellectual property laws must ensure that information is equally accessible and ideas are conveyed. Technologies will continue to evolve and bring about both constraints and freedoms. Experts emphasize the urgent need for a new paradigm that is structured in generalities and not based on technologies that will become obsolete in time (Williams, 2008).

The increased connectivity and sharing capabilities afforded by social networking tools have affected the way the global community accesses and shares information; it has also impacted the level of accountability and anonymity offered to the user. Furthermore, the manner in which Millennials and Generation Vs use these tools will, in time, influence societal views on intellectual property laws and open source. Individual countries, as well as global organizations, must proactively work together to ensure both protection and equal access to resources, thus promoting the sustainability of economic and educational systems worldwide.

REFERENCES

Albert, S., Sanders, J., & Mazzaro, J. (2005). Intellectual property crimes. *The American Criminal Law Review*, *42*(2), 631–677.

Bromberg, D., & Underwood, S. (2005). Constitutional limits on copyrights. *Intellectual Property & Technology Law Journal*, *17*(2), 1.

Brown, G., & Sukys, P. (1998). *Understanding business and personal law. Mission Hills, CA*. Glencoe: McGraw Hill.

Campus Information Systems. (2001). Intellectual property policy for online education. *Campus Information Systems*, *18*(2), 52–60.

Coyle, K. (2003). *The technology of rights: Digital rights management*. Based on a talk originally given at the Library of Congress, November 19, 2003. Retrieved November 10, 2009, from http://www.kcoyle.net/drm_basics.pdf

D'Amico Juettner, D., & Girasa, R. J. (2001). Copyright issues for the distance learning professor. *International Journal of Value-Based Management*, *14*(2), 109–130. doi:10.1023/A:1011158613992

Damiani, E., & Fugazza, C. (2007). Toward semantics-aware management of intellectual property rights. *Online Information Review*, *31*(1), 59–72. doi:10.1108/14684520710731038

Folkers, D. (2005). Competing in the marketspace: Incorporating online education into high education-an organizational perspective. *Information Resources Management Journal, 18*(1), 61–77. doi:10.4018/irmj.2005010105

Gladwell, M. (2005). *Blink: The power of thinking without thinking.* New York: Little, Brown and Company.

Greenberg, E., & Weber, K. (2008). *Generation we: How millennial youth are taking over America and changing our world forever.* Emeryville, CA: Pachatusan.

Hylén, J., & Schuller, T. (2007). Giving knowledge for free. Organization for Economic Cooperation and Development. *The OCED Observer, 263,* 21. Retrieved September 22, 2010, from http://www.oecd.org/dataoecd/35/7/38654317.pdf

Klein, S., & Huffnagle, H. (2007). Split decisions: The issue of use in the context of search engine keyword-triggered advertising. *Intellectual Property & Technology Law Journal, 19*(12), 1.

McNamara, B., Ropp, D., & Lowenstein, H. (2008). Property rights in cyberia; A study of intent and bad faith. *Journal of International Academy for Case Studies, 14*(7), 41.

Miller, A. R., & Davis, M. H. (2000). *Intellectual property: Patents, trademarks, and copyright* (3rd ed.). New York: West/Wadsworth.

Moore, A. (2004). *Intellectual property and information control: Philosophic foundations and contemporary issues.* Piscataway, NJ: Transaction Publishers.

Nicholson, D. R. (2006). Intellectual property: Benefit or burden for Africa. *International Federation of Library Associations and Institutions (IFLA). Journal, 32*(4), 310–334.

Organization for Economic Cooperation and Development. (2007). *Giving knowledge for free: The emergence of open educational resources.* Retrieved October 10, 2010, from http://www.oecd.org/dataoecd/35/7/38654317.pdf

Simonson, M. R. (2006). If it is intellectual, can it be property? *Distance Learning, 3*(2), 68.

Starkman, N. (2008). Do the (copyright) thing. *T.H.E. Journal, 35*(3), 22.

TeacherTube. (2009). Terms of use. Retrieved October 10, 2010, from http://www.teachertube.com/terms.php

United States Copyright Office. (2009). *Title 17, 107.* Retrieved November 10, 2010, from http://www.copyright.gov/title17/92chap1.html#107

Wallace, L. (2007). Online teaching and university policy: Investigating the disconnect. *Journal of Distance Education, 22*(1), 87–100.

Williams, P. (2008). Industry's IP struggle in a digital age. *Information World Review,* 245.

World Intellectual Property Organization. (2009). *World intellectual property guide.* Retrieved September 10, 2010, from http://www.wipo.int/about-ip/en/ipworldwide/

Chapter 4
E–Governance on a Global Campus

ABSTRACT

Nations around the world are eager to harness the power of the Internet to accomplish their agendas. Globalized efforts to define and implement a one-size fits all approach to e-governance has in turn influenced local government and the e-governance of the global campus. A customer-centric approach is needed to ensure the needs of the learner are addressed as new meta-trends are identified and new needs emerge. Visionary leadership is needed to diminish the doublethink issues exposed by technology and globalization of online learning.

OBJECTIVES

- Define e-government versus e-governance.
- Identify stakeholder theory as an approach to the e-governance of government, public and private institutions.
- Discuss effective e-governance of the global campus using a customer-centric approach.

DOI: 10.4018/978-1-60960-543-8.ch004

- Discuss the current global approaches to e-governance, including laws to protect privacy, and how these laws affect education.
- Analyze how globalization influences the global campus of online learning.
- Identify examples of doublethink in education.
- Expose the dangers of the Internet if used as a weapon.
- Identify potential challenges and approaches in moving forward, such as meta-trends in K-12 and higher education.

INTRODUCTION

The Internet and emerging technologies have opened up learning possibilities and have become the main way that people get information, do business, and communicate. Traditionally, higher education has not kept up with these changes quickly enough. This chapter explores the obstacles that educational institutions face in developing and managing a global campus. For the purpose of this discussion, the global campus includes all higher education as well as K-12 organizations that focus on online learning, whether private or public. This chapter also presents challenges to consider before embarking on e-governance reforms, approaches for the e-governance of the global campus, and suggestions for overcoming potential hurdles that could undermine success.

The question of how we govern and disseminate information in the knowledge age is a challenge to all sectors of our society. The answers are evolving and emerging as the Internet continues to thrive and influence how we communicate. The initial quagmire revolves around the organization's structure. A closer look leads us to ponder whether or not the "e" dimension will involve changing the way individuals engage with one another to discuss pertinent issues and access information or whether information technologies will simply reinforce existing power structures. The interconnected globe has presented a dual challenge of transparency and privacy in communication. Web sites offer services and convenience, as well as engagement and literacy (Mitchinson & Ratner, 2004). Information technology has become part of the infrastructure of organizations and institutions. The current methods used to manage global visions have gone under scrutiny as various international organizations have taken the lead to not only define the terminology, but also unite e-governments around the world in their approach to e-governance.

BACKGROUND

The terms e-government and e-governance are some times used interchangeably in some circles yet they are distinctively different. Definitions available, although general in scope, all focus on using technology to distribute information and connect to citizens. Governance is a larger terminology that envelops government. Governance includes both the formal and informal processes and procedures that guide the activities of the institution (Saxena, 2005).

An important distinction should be drawn between the terms government and governance. Government, according to Saxena (2005, p. 449) "…is the institution itself where as governance is the broader concept describing forms of governing which are not necessarily in the hands of the formal government," government therefore influence governance. Higher education governance can be defined as being the internal mechanisms in place that provide for accountability to the stakeholders and share public policy. The government of the campus may include organizational hierarchy that influences policymaking. Characterized by long-term outcomes, policies and programs, governance is the process. Governance focuses on the objectives rather than the means for achieving it. This distinction is critical in understanding that outcomes and outputs are not the same. E-governance has evolved in the knowledge age to encompass the potentiality of the incorporation of information and communication technologies.

If e-government is deemed as the institution that provides services and information to businesses and citizens, e-governance is conversely using information communication and technology (ICT) to provide digital exchange (Rocheleau, 2007). The reach of both is global and the impact significant. The E-Government Act of 2002 created guidelines for government agencies in the United States for the purpose of improving the process through which government organizes, preserves, and provides access to information to the public, including via the Internet (National Archives, 2010). Likewise, the European Union adopted its i2010 eGovernment Action Plan (Commission of the European Communities, 2006) to ensure that all its citizens would have reliable, trustworthy and easy access to services, information, and the democratic process.

E-governance is generally seen as the specific, deliberate actions taken by a government to connect with its citizens. UNESCO has taken the definition of e-governance a step further. Its worldwide projects aim at helping countries set up infrastructures that also promote participation by citizens in the decision-making process, as a way of making government more effective, and providing transparency and accountability while building capacity (UNESCO, 2010). UNESCO also differentiates between e-government and e-governance by emphasizing how e-governance can impact the way citizens and governments interact with one another. There are three areas of concern for e-governance, according to UNESCO (2005):

1. **e-administration:** which focuses on enhancing the processes used by government and how these processes interact with the public sector.
2. **e-services:** which focus on improving how public services are delivered to citizens.
3. **e-democracy:** which focuses on promoting active participation in government on the part of citizens.

It is the third component, e-democracy, which affects education the most. Because the goal of e-democracy is to raise consciousness about the democratic process and share information about the government instead of solely providing services, it is considered to be the lowest level of e-governance and relies on education to keep the public informed (The Commonwealth Network of Information Technology for Development Foundation, 2000). It is therefore through education that e-democracy is propagated.

In the 2000 global survey on e-governance conducted by The Commonwealth Network of Information Technology for Development Foundation (COMNET-IT) it was revealed that 89 percent of the 62 respondents, made up of 39 developing and 23 industrialized nations, acknowledged having e-governance initiatives. Universities accounted for 46 percent of entities involved in e-governance endeavors according to the survey, compared to 90% of government and 60% of private entities involved. Meanwhile there was only a two percent difference between the involvement of universities in developing (45%) versus industrialized nations (43%).

Understanding the term e-governance requires exploration in a variety of contexts. Although Vint Cerft and Bob Kahn first coined the term Internet in 1974, the Internet is a relatively new phenomenon compared to institutions of higher education and governments. Government has always been at the forefront of developing new technologies. It was precisely the need to be and remain connected that prompted the U.S. Air Force back in the early 1960's to seek ways to build an electronic infrastructure through which command center could maintain communication, hence the packet switched network was born, later to be reinvented as the Internet. Therefore, it is not surprising that governments around the globe desire to swiftly harness the power of the modern Internet to accomplish their goals. For democratic governments the main goal would be to perpetuate democracy, while for others like communist China, it may be something completely different. The ideal model for e-governance according to Garson (2006) is one that provides a one-stop portal, which connects private, public, and governmental entities to citizens.

To talk about e-governance while ignoring the structure of institutions that have been around for a long time is to ignore many factors that influence the application of the technologies to the existing foundation (Rose, 2005, a). Most organizations have gone beyond the initial stage of Internet presence and are incorporating interactions that create enhanced value. This interim provides the user with increased reflexivity and the institution the challenge of managing it. The future of e-government on a global university campus is not what it was on a local campus or even branched physical campuses in the recent past.

The allocation of resources must go beyond bricks and mortar. How an institution allocates these resources gives clues to the focus of either a learner centric or an organization centric viewpoint. The Internet has affected both the government and the governance of institutions (Marche & McNiven, 2003). E-governance involves the use of information and communication technologies to transact the business of the organization (Saxena, 2005). Getting the benefits from global reach has not been as easy as expected for a variety of reasons. It is often a challenge for the organizations to get beyond the focus on technologies. It is also difficult to change the mindset of institutions that have been around for a long time.

GOING GLOBAL

The multiple definitions and perspectives in regards to e-governance make it difficult at the present time to develop optimum applications of the concept. History has entered warp speed and the technological changes are unpredictable and rapid. This leads to uncertainty as to the impact of these new developments and the effects that they will have on our lives (Streib & Willoughby, 2005).

Going global is both a function of the supply of IT services and the demand for global connectivity and governance. Going global requires modern resources and Internet connectivity. Although some early players have established themselves as international leaders in the e-education revolution, a diffusion of new technologies has leveled the playing field. (Rose, 2005,b). In a world shaped by connectivity, limitations are quickly disappearing because technology has managed to eliminate the geographical boundaries that once separated people. The evolution of a new form of e-governance extends over physical and intellectual borders and unites society in a new way.

Empowered by interconnected networks and digital media, the new governance is less about control and more about engagement. This brings up emerging issues like security, community and regulation both academic and governmental (Roy, 2005). Debates continue to rage over the optimum configuration of strengths in an organization and how much power the organization has to utilize the strengths of its stakeholders. Governance suggests that stakeholders not only share a desire for self-actualization, they should also be cherished as partners in the system, which is a striking departure for many institutions (Lim, Tan, & Pan, 2009).

Stakeholder Theory

E-governance is more than the implementation of information technologies. In 2000, Bolt and Crawford published the Digital Divide and purported a chasm between the haves and have not's as society sprinted to get globally connected. This work unearthed the social implications of a connected world where disparities in race, sex, religion, ethnicity, and income exist. The concerned echoed across the globe as it became evident that few governments had engaged their citizens electronically in the democratic process (The Commonwealth Network of Information Technology for Development Foundation, 2000). Corporations, government agencies and educational institutions all find themselves at the crossroads of two different approaches, one using the traditional focus on profit, or a new approach that focuses on the stakeholders. Stakeholder theory offers an alternative to traditional business management models, which only focused on a small group of individuals who were considered to have the most interest or influence over profit. Stakeholder theory broadens the perspective of organizations, thus by paying attention to those affected by decisions made by the organization, a win-win situation is created.

As a strategy, the stakeholder approach is inclusive, thus acknowledging the need to involve other individuals and groups that are also stakeholders, and identifies the interests of those stakeholders. This is the "who" and "what," according to Freeman's (1984) original discussion. An inclusive model would then account for the needs and interests of members belonging to different social economic groups, thus closing the digital divide and promoting democracy through open and connected e-governance. The global campus, including K-12 as well as higher education institutions, are affected by e-governance and will benefit from the stakeholder approach. The win-win situation is created as stakeholders feel acknowledged and affirmed, thus customer service is enhanced. This give and take relationship creates a thriving environment for business, government or educational institutions, where mutual trust and respect are projected.

Far from sounding Utopian, this type of model is only a step toward progress and forward thinking. Governance is often defined as the processes, regulations, and behaviors that affect the way an institution is administered. The twenty first century will undoubtedly place a stronger emphasis on technology and should support more collaborative structure and stakeholder networks (Wong, Fearon, & Philip, 2007). Governance will require new interactions with internal and external stakeholders.

In the global campus, e-communities will underpin the existence of both learner-to-learner connections and relationships within the institution.

Many online interactions involve policy, commerce or behavior (Thomas & Streib, 2005) but other types of interactions are needed that promote trust and information literacy. Information literacy is more that mere computer literacy and knowledge. Skills are needed to find information, evaluate it and then apply it to real problems. "Trust" is an important factor in evaluating the credibility of online information. Because of the anonymity afforded by technologies that attach and disconnect individuals at the same time, for "trust" to be established there has to be total faith not only in the infrastructure of the institution but also in the intent of governance (Sridhar, 2005, p.258).

Inherent in the emerging networks is the development of stakeholder theory. Collective responsibility is a central tenant when decisions regarding the interests of the stakeholders are involved. The movement toward replacing the current form of government with the stakeholder model is being fueled by the inclusion of collective information, collection, dissemination, and integration of collective responsibility and decision-making.

Advances in technologies also often complicate institutional governance. Power sharing, resource allocation and decision-making can be impacted. Innovative leadership style, adaptive management and definition of purpose are often challenged. Suddenly, educational institutions are being challenged to align their purpose and approach in order to leverage technologies to strategically inform, manage, and support stakeholders. If this is not accomplished, educational institutions will fail to secure a competitive advantage in the ever-evolving global campus.

Whether it is the private or the public sector, integration of technologies is reforming the institutions and placing an emphasis on external stakeholders (Lim, Tan, & Pan, 2009). This will offer researchers an excellent opportunity to evaluate the tactics deployed in adaption of stakeholder theory to governance in a global campus setting. Today the need for research in regards to e-governance and e-government of the global campus is not limited to institutions of higher education. It also includes providers of K-12 online learning, which continue to exponentially increase each year. Table 1 below highlights the four dimensions of transformation, as discussed by Pablo and Pan (2002), which present challenges for change in e-governance and e-governments alike.

As depicted in the table above, technologies bring about challenges to government that require careful attention. The effects of a well thought out approach are far-reaching and potentially highly beneficial. The principles of governance are enhanced through communication, participation, integrity, and transparency. The functions of government and the interactions between government and the governed

Table 1. Pablo and Pan's four dimensions of transformation

Transformation	Effect
In the operational principles of governance	Enhanced communication, participation, integrity, and transparency
Internal functions of government	By automating public transactions, administration processes
Interactions between government and citizens	Interactions between government and citizens are changed
In society itself	Creating and sustaining networks of social relationships through electronic networks

are transformed. Social networks established though technologies are created and sustained.

The debate continues over aligning the purpose of governance with business objectives or stakeholder objectives. What is clear is that effective e-governance on a global level translates into improved operational efficiencies. These operational gains turn into profits and relational rewards and more intimate connections with the stakeholders. Theorists are still divided about the approach, but the benefits cannot be ignored.

Some institutions have taken solace in the satisfaction that administrative records, financial transactions, and administrative duties have been globalized and transferred online. Too often little has been done to adapt the underlying mechanism that supports bureaucracy. The use of the Internet and communication technologies, rather than supporting better governance, is often avoided (Wong, Fearon, & Philip, 2007). Greater research is needed to understand effective governance and particularly for global universities. Understanding the role of the stakeholder, relationships, commitment and engagement might help institutions as they go forward with developing stronger strategies for globalization. The first step toward this goal is to understand what legal approaches governments have already taken, and how they affect the e-governance of not only the local community, but also the global community at large.

Global Legal Approaches

Internet technologies have facilitated the transformation of organizations and institutions in North America and in Europe alike, with Asian-Pacific nations currently following suit. Ignited by the incentive of European based research and fueled by the desire to coordinate and control knowledge on behalf of its citizens, the European Union has set specific objectives for e-governance. Likewise, the United

States has defined goals and purpose. However, because of the global implications of e-governance, there is a push toward a global consensus in regards to definition, purpose, and approach. As national governments take a lesser role in determining and regulating, there will likely be a shift in the level and type of involvement that e-governments will have with the public and private sector, hence a secondary level of governance may emerge.

Educational institutions, whether private or public, are usually among the first type of organizations that are impacted by governmental changes, including e-governance. There are a myriad of rules, which are in part setting up a centralized approach to e-governance for educational institutions. These rules are often directly or indirectly associated with technologies and can be at a transactional level. Early in the development of a centralized approach to governing educational institutions were the ideas of accreditation and ranking. It is difficult to determine how e-governance will affect the accreditation or ranking of educational institutions, however, if stakeholder theory is applied, it can be speculated that stakeholders would be more involved in this process.

The shift to a globalized e-governance has caused local governments to exert a lesser amount of power over rules and regulations. Rather than the local governments reducing the deregulation of universities, which would entail less regulation, there has actually been a significant change in the type of rules and the type of rule structure; thus reregulating with more rules influenced by the global approach. According to Hedmo and Wedling (2006), European higher education has undergone and will continue to experience changes in organizational structure and be reregulated.

Both, the institutional framework and the Web architecture form constraints that must be considered when prescribing policy. The Internet is so vastly different than traditional media that comparisons are inept. The sheer volume of data, indeterminate terrain, and encryption supported anonymity make traditional regulation impossible. The controversy of self-regulation versus government regulation continues as the approaches used by the United States and European Union differ in philosophy and implementation. Harmful content such as the exposure of youth to pornography has lead to attempts at regulation. On one hand, regulation and policy must account for the technical standards set forth by the IT industry, and on the other hand it must consider how much self-regulation it is actually encouraging or expecting.

While the United States has taken a much more prophetic approach to privacy laws and how personal information is collected and shared on the Internet, European Union nations have jointly passed legislation. Lead by the United Kingdom, laws have been passed to establish standards and purposes for the collection and dissemination of personal data from the Internet; however, the laws limiting explicit Web content are more lenient. Violation of privacy laws can be a costly proposition with heavy fines and restitution to the victims. Governance of the Web is only a part of the challenge of governance of a global university. It is not just about creating standard based and organizational policies for accessibility and standards compliance, but also these policies then have to be monitored, and assured (Musthaler & Musthaler, 2008).

Web governance alone can involve crawling through the multitude of pages of a Web site and looking for signs of trouble. There is more than adherence to policy and quality control at stake; Web governance should be a part of the overall vision of a global university. The Data Protection Act of 1998 (United Kingdom Office of Public Sector Information, 1998) established the groundwork of the legislation for the European Union, with Sweden and Japan later also implementing laws involving accessibilities and public Web sites.

European Union commissioners have argued that there is an inclination for search engine sites to store as much information as possible on individuals and that this tendency needs to be curtailed. The issue has been accelerated by the influx of social software that retains information indefinitely. Cases of employers and universities checking up on Facebook® have repeatedly made the news both in the Europe and the United States. In a 2008 survey, ten percent of 500 top colleges in the United States admitted to searching for information on social networking sites before making a decision on an applicant (Hechinger, 2008). Surprisingly, 38% of those searches accounted for a negative impression of the applicant. Many people are innocently putting their personal information online, therefore risking phishing, and identity theft. Regulation of the data storage and data mining industry is only the latest in a long line of formidable challenges in managing of online interactions.

Search engines like Google™ pose a huge threat to anonymity and privacy in the online environment. Little regulation currently exists that limits the capacity of search engines to hold and store information. There is a substantial lack of knowledge about what and how long this information is stored or used. What appears to be developing is a two-sided sword where government mandates are used as an excuse to keep large amount of data that can then be analyzed for trends and sales data and corporations act as private spies for the government (Finkelstein, 2007). The threat to anonymity and privacy in the online environment is a global concern. As evidenced in the Google™ versus China crisis of early 2010, those governments, which do not desire to involve its citizens in a democratic process, are finding innumerable ways to use technology to subject their citizens to censorship and governmental control.

In the United States a complex and disjointed group of guidelines and laws have impacted Web sites including Section 508 of the American for Disabilities Act (Federal Register, 2000), The World Wide Web Consortium [W3C] (2010) Web Content Accessibility Guidelines (World Wide Web Consortium (1999). These laws and guidelines have been implemented by many government agencies across the globe with the intention of standardizing their approach. For example, the idea that Web sites should be accessible to individuals with disabilities has been globally accepted and implemented by government, public, and private entities. Lawsuit after lawsuit attests to the fact that regulation in the battle of Internet privacy is at best difficult. As already stated, social networking has again come to the forefront with sites like MySpace® and Xanga® being sued for collecting information on underage minors without parental consent. According to the Federal Trade Commission, in 2006 Xanga® was ordered to pay a $1 million dollar fine in violation of the Children's Online Privacy Protection Act [COPPA] of 1998. The concerns go on and on, the World Wide Web is laden with anti-privacy minefields that can only be deactivated one at time. The challenge remains to find existing dangers while preventing the development of new ones.

A common challenge is the misunderstanding of privacy policies throughout the United States. United States law is lacking in policy concerning the extraction, sharing, and manipulation of data about individuals and their online activities. Privacy policies for the most part, do not protect the public. There are exceptions such as the Health Insurance Portability and Accountability Act [HIPPA] (United States Department of Health and Human Services, 2010), the Family Rights and Privacy Act [FERPA] (United States Department of Education, 2010), and other policies protecting financial information and health care regulations.

Online companies otherwise virtually have free reign on information they take, utilize, and share. With more transparent reactions many are appalled at the ramifications of laws like the

Uniting and Strengthening America by Providing Appropriate Tools Required to Intercept and Obstruct Terrorism [USA PATRIOT ACT] Act of 2001 (United States Senate, 2001) and its influence on dissention and academic freedom. The European Union on the other hand, has rather stringent prohibitions against using data in ways for which it was not intended. In the United States no such broad rules apply, although more attention is being given to regulation of personal data. The dilemma for educational institutions, especially those in cyber education, develops when a global presence includes faculty and learners from multiple regions of the globe and their transactions are taking place on the public highways of the Internet.

The commercial world has set up a "safe haven" approach with the European Union. As a result, American companies wanting to use the personal information of European citizens in the United States have had to recognize that the two approaches in policy differ. The United States has taken an approach that online privacy is more a technological issue and should be dealt with by private enterprise. Although, many years down the pike, there is still a widespread absence of technological solutions.

One of the most distressing illusions is the idea that American citizens are aware and protected by the privacy agreements posted on Web sites. However, as a result of COPPA, some restrictions were mandated for those under the age of 13. The rest of the American population is subjected to online privacy policies and agreements that are confusing and in some cases intentionally misleading. The ambiguity of terms such as "affiliates" and warnings that the site's privacy policy can change at anytime, are cause of concern and confusion (Turow, 2003). Challenged by confusing laws and guidelines, educational institutions are faced with harsh realities. The push toward a globalized approach of e-governance by e-governments around the world is likely to rapidly change the global campus as we know it.

LOOKING AHEAD

Managing a global university campus requires more than merely implementing information technologies and computer connectivity. The roles of the learners, teachers and school administrators are challenged and changed when governing a global campus. Many universities, especially those with distance learning programs, are still in the early stages of development. Traditional educational institutions may for the first time be facing competition that was not a problem when location provided a type of geographical monopoly. Others such as those in the K-12 field are experiencing a dramatic change as they are expected to adapt to rapidly changing times and include online learning options for students. Technologies and globalization may have helped many universities stream line bureaucratic mechanisms through the process of e-governance, however, the focus on learning must be at the center of all policies.

Now What?

1. New methods of e-governance, on a global scale must be established to improve efficiency, global competiveness, and innovation.
2. Visionary leadership is needed to create customer-oriented programs using technology, thus providing students with the skills necessary to compete and be productive global citizens.
3. New attitudes and initiatives must be developed to deliver services, content, and media in ways that reach a global audience but protects citizens.
4. Government legislation must address the governance of data collected, categorized, analyzed, interpreted, sold, and used for whatever purpose.
5. Government legislation must be balanced, not exercising too much control, but addressing the implications of data collection and how it impacts personal privacy.

The future of the global campus demands forward thinking leadership that can make the best of political, social, and social contradictions while implementing customer-centric policies that promote democracy. Education will continue to play a role in the propagation of an open, democratic e-government, especially during times when closed regimes in countries such as China seek ways to use technology as a weapon against its own citizens and against the rest of democratic societies around the world.

Doublethinking Education: Living with Contradictions

Globalization via technology has undoubtedly set up a world of contradictions. One hand we have privacy and anonymity and on the other hand we live in a world where our every action is tracked and recorded. According to Bloom (2002)*doublethink* is a term invented by George Orwell (1949, p. 32) in his novel "1984" and means the power of holding two contradictory beliefs in one's mind simultaneously." Interestingly, the term doublethink, which has come about in the last twenty years, has been spread easily by globalization. Doublethink has changed our perspective on education and in many ways skewed our sense of fairness. At a quick glance, one easily finds examples of doublethink in the global campus.

Although education has always been an international concern, higher education specifically has never been on the global agenda except in very general terms. The contradiction of believing in the importance of higher education but neglecting to place it on the global agenda created a dichotomy that was only partially bridged via the recent use of technology. The process of globalization has placed an emphasis on higher education and heightened its significance for prosperity. While this is undoubtedly a positive change, learners who obtain a degree from newer educational institutions that provide online learning programs however, are at risk of becoming victims of the validation effect. Other learners still lack the opportunity to pursue a higher education due to financial constraints in the global economic downturn.

The demand for cyber education continues to skyrocket. Many traditional universities quickly transfer entire degree programs online and poise themselves for competition. Others still hold on to the traditional systems in place for years. The competition however, is made up of rapidly growing private online universities and colleges such as University of Phoenix Online, Capella University, Penn Foster, Walden University, the Open University, among many others globally. Although these programs will continue to expand, graduates from these programs may fall short in the eyes of employers looking at resumes from candidates who may have graduated from a similar program at a traditional university's new online or traditional degree program.

The validation effect takes place as the employer recognizes the name of the traditional university and places more value on the applicant who attended there, based on the organization's past reputation thus assuming that applicant is more apt for the job. The employer does not really know if that applicant from the better known college or university is indeed better prepared for the job, but the fact that the person attended such a school may automatically imply in his mind that this applicant must have done something right. The applicant who graduated from a lesser known college or university however, may have partaken in an educational online program that promoted real-world problem solving skills, thus better preparing the applicant for the position. The doublethinking here relates to the importance of technology and the validity of online learning. On one hand globalization promotes online learning and the use of technology as the way of the future, but on the other hand it continues to validate and promulgate traditional systems of education.

This same globalization exerts pressures on the online universities and colleges that were not prevalent before. These pressures may well result in a transformation of policy and dogma. Higher education is no longer a luxury and is especially essential to the developing world. If underdeveloped countries are to prosper and excel in the future it is critical that the global reach of higher education also include them. If developed nations around the globe wish to maintain their status and propel their society forward, they too must place more emphasis on higher education. One challenge in making this happen is affordability of education in hard financial times. The technology however, makes it possible to deliver content to large groups of individuals anywhere in the globe without having to spend money on a large physical infrastructure. The savings if wisely invested in the right technology tools, can translate into a large return on investment for the organization and a more educated, and better prepared workforce.

This expansion will also cause the reform of the system as a whole and many individual institutions in particular. The luxury of being dysfunctional is one that cannot be afforded with the pressures of globalization. Many more resources will need to be dedicated to the formal and informal educational sectors. Finally, good ideas for globalization and e-governance in cyber education are not enough, action is necessary to follow through and carry out policy.

Another challenge of globalization is the need for leadership at the highest levels. Leaders with vision to exercise and carry out changes within the organization are critical to the e-governance of higher and K-12 education, whether private and public. Never before in history has there been as strong a need for as dramatic a change in the way that learners and these educational institutions interact. Drastic changes are also needed in terms of what we teach and how we teach it. Visionary leadership is needed to facilitate the changes on our interactions with each other and with the way we work and learn. The doublethink for leadership is the fact that most talk the talk, discussing the issue of change, yet very few actually take steps to make any changes because they may be costly or difficult. Part doublethink, part hypocrisy, this type of leadership keeps learners in an educational program that is outdated. Visionary leadership is needed to walk the walk necessary to move education from its outdated form into a system that immerses learners in real-world problem solving through the use of technology, hence preparing them for the global job market.

A proactive stance by university presidents, provosts, and other leading administrators is also needed on issues like digital rights and intellectual property, access, online identity, and security. Higher education needs to ignite its faculty and address issues of stagnation, tenure, promotion and reward because certainly these issues are not going to be handled well without visionary leadership (New Media Consortium, 2007). Likewise, K-12 education is in dire need of visionary leadership that will admonish against the sporadic use of technology and will push teachers and administrators to bring the world of connectivity into the classroom.

The K-12 dilemma brings about another doublethink example. The words "no child left behind" (United States Department of Education, 2010) have echoed in the minds of educators, parents and legislators alike since the inception of the act in 2001. In essence, the purpose behind the act was to push education reform across the United States that would raise the reading and math scores of students, while providing more choice of schools to parents. Many funding mechanisms were put in place to create programs that would help students learn and succeed. The dichotomy is that while the goal was to provide educational opportunities for all children, there was no importance given to vocational programs for high schoolers who find themselves with no choice but to drop out of school due to the mere lack of options.

Federal money continues to be poured into federal programs tied to No Child Left Behind, yet high drop out rates continue to afflict low-income communities as well as middle class America. Wilma Stephenson, a forward-thinking teacher at Frankford High School in Northeast Philadelphia, recognized the need to provide her low-income culinary arts students with real world skills they could take to the marketplace (Julian, 2009). She formed partnerships with culinary career advocates and provided students with relevant knowledge they could apply on the job and also helped them get scholarships in their vocational field.

Stories such as the one from Frankford High School are testament to the fact that the reason students are being left behind is because the educational system has not created enough options for them. Not all students fit in the world of academia and many others are not willing to partake in the world of higher education, therefore it is the responsibility of educators to provide more options for students to learn a skill that will help them obtain gainful employment.

Doublethinking in education presents a hindrance to providing all learners with educational opportunities that are truly fair. Future approaches to the e-governance of the global campus must include customer-centric initiatives that remove double-think altogether. In looking ahead, it will take visionary leadership to create such programs using technology, thus students will have the skills necessary to compete with others around the globe and be productive citizens.

Geocaching Meta-Trends in Cyber Education

Effective e-governance of a global campus will involve a closing of the gap and adherence to application of seven significant meta-trends for higher education (New Media Consortium, 2008). A meta-trend according to Snyder (2005, p.1) is "a system-wide development arising from the simultaneous occurrence of a number of independent demographic, economic and technologic trends." According to The Horizon Report of 2008 (New Media Consortium, 2008, p.7), higher education institutions must focus on:

1. adapting to the evolving approaches to communications between man and devices
2. promote collective sharing and generating of knowledge
3. computing in three dimensions
4. connecting people via the network
5. games as pedagogical platforms
6. shifting of content production to users
7. embracing and adapting to the evolution of a ubiquitous platform

Globalization presents the pressure to deliver services, content and media in new ways. Cellular devices and mobile learning are still in their infancy. The expectation of anywhere and anytime learning has increased, and higher education is pressed to use these mobile devices for learning. But if e-governance of the global campus is going to take place, several obstacles will have to be overcome. Faculty attitudes and abilities to go global must be addressed. Although students now view online education as just as good of better than a face to face experience, only 33% of the academic leadership surveyed by The Sloan Consortium in 2007 reported that their faculty accept the legitimacy and value of learning online. This has changed little in since 2002, when only 28% of faculty accepted the online movement. This suggests a challenge in moving a group of slow adaptor to an environment where innovation and quick evolution prevail (Allen & Seaman, 2007).

The gap between the technological perceptions and skills of students and faculty continues to widen according to the Horizon 2008 report. Therefore faculty training is yet another area that is affected by the increased application of technology. If effective online learning programs are to be designed and deployed, then faculty training must be paralleled in quality. Very few cyber educators are trained on the use of media, visual, and technological literacy.

The adoption of several best practices may also help in the movement toward effective e-governance of the global campus. Some of these include leveraging private and university partnerships, promoting the use of digital technologies, establishing university wide and system wide think tanks, investing in infrastructure, providing intellectual property protection, and committing to an open regime and delivery of services over the Internet (Asia Pacific E-Learning Alliance, 2002).

The physical borders that limited learners and teachers have become invisible. Global dissemination of information and influence has changed the way we work, live interact, and learn. A global university online can encompass a collaborative community, multinational staffing, distributed campus and multimedia all because of the connectivity provided by enhanced and emerging technologies. This connectivity is challenging existing methods of governance and on a global scale it is improving efficiency, global competiveness, and innovation (Sridhar, 2005). Despite the challenges, cyber educators must keep up with meta-trends and focus on helping students learn.

Using the Internet as a Weapon

The Internet is a powerful tool. In the wrong hands, it can easily be used as a weapon. Much has been discussed about the contradictions of technology, whereas it has the ability to provide the safe haven of anonymity, as well as the ability to track and monitor an individual's every move. Those who value intellectual exchange without fear of retribution cherish the rights to free speech and academic freedom, but even in societies where democracy is prevalent, these rights are in danger of being compromised by ignorant lawmakers who rather leave the issue of privacy to the hands of the private IT industry. In other governments where such rights are obscure, repressed or non-existent, the Internet becomes a dangerous weapon that can be used to oppress citizens.

Leaving the issue of anonymity up to the IT industry in hopes of self-regulation implies that government is not overly concerned with the violation of individual's privacy. A person's private and personal information can circumnavigate the earth in a nanoseconds' time. It can be collected, categorized, analyzed, interpreted, sold, and used for whatever purpose the private or government entity wishes. The ease with which datum is manipulated is enough to alarm even the most careful Web surfer.

The thought of not being able to express yourself is highly anti-American, and anti-democratic. Recent events in China have unlocked Pandora's box, as the entire world is witness to unprecedented decisions on the part of technology moguls who finally get in touch with technological morality. In early 2010 Google™ announced that it would stop censoring Internet searches within China after it was hacked, along with other code-writing companies, by Chinese insiders who collected private information about human rights activists and targeted them.

This bold move inspired other private American companies such as GoDaddy.com to review its business practices with China, and captured the interest of lawmakers in the United States who believe that government should play a more active role in protecting American Internet companies in countries such as China (MacMillan, 2010). According to an editorial from the Washington Post (2010) online, "China aims not just at eliminating the free speech and virtual free assembly inherent to the Internet but at turning it into a weapon that can be used against democrats and democratic societies."

In looking ahead, there is danger of governments such as China's to continue using the Internet as tools of oppression. China is likely to forge ahead with domestic companies such as Baidu to conduct search services and build their own infrastructure so the services of American Internet companies will no longer be needed. American lawmakers and leaders across the free world need to collaborate with global Internet companies to ensure that they are not being used as vehicles through which such governments can violate human rights.

Considered to be the most important speech by a United States official on Internet policy, Senator Hillary Clinton's speech to China in early 2010 struck a chord with supporters of free speech everywhere:

"We stand for a single Internet where all of humanity has equal access to knowledge and ideas. And we recognize that the world's information infrastructure will become what we and others make of it. Now, this challenge may be new, but our responsibility to help ensure the free exchange of ideas goes back to the birth of our republic."

Google™ has pulled out of the Chinese market and has moved its main servers to outside of China. Speculators disagree over the benefits of pulling out; stating that maintaining its presence would indeed continue promoting free speech. By pulling out it opens to doors to Chinese national companies to emerge. The Global Internet Freedom Consortium (GIFC), an organization determined to fight censorship around the world, is also likely to have a stronger presence in the near future. Support for GIFC by politicians such as Senator Clinton would help finance their Internet-freedom initiatives for projects such as developing firewall busting software (Washington Post, 2010).

The Internet offers many possibilities. In the case of China and other governments, which seek to oppress their citizens by withdrawing their rights of free expression and exchange of ideas, the Internet becomes a powerful weapon with which to coerce citizens. The free world has awakened to a new reality, one that exposes the dangers of technology if used for the wrong reasons.

CONCLUSION

The Internet has been heralded as having influence on all aspects of society including education. As such it is not merely a change in the way communications are carried out, but a fundamental change in the practice and organization that affects and is affected by social order or political agendas. Much research is needed to determine the effects of these changes. Currently they can take the form of George Orwell's Big Brother or the Habermasian cybercafé and neither is totally acceptable. E-governments are eager to harness the power of the Internet to achieve their goals through deliberate e-governance. Because education is the vehicle through which e-governments promote their schema to citizens, cyber educators must be aware of the impact of e-governance on educational institutions and ultimately on learners.

Contradictory views emerge on the role of technology and globalization. On one hand, enhanced government control, data mining and information collecting is increasing the control of central powers and limiting all kinds of freedoms, including academic. On the other hand, the Internet is considered the purveyor of democracy and promotes open and democratic exchange and collective intelligence. Regardless of the take, it is obvious that the Internet has far reaching implications for our understanding of global communications and organizational power (Ainsworth, Hardy, & Hardy, 2005).

Few doubt that the Internet is changing people's interactions and relationships with institutions and government. Along with a change in the communication patterns comes a change in the relationship with the institution. E-governance of the global campus must take into account these challenges in order to reposition itself as a necessity for societal and governmental progress.

The future challenges for K-12 and higher education stem from the emergence of e-governance at a local and global scale. The pressure to be transparent and more efficient presents educational institutions as well as other sectors with the opportunity to involve stakeholders in the decision-making process. This should be seen as a positive challenge. By applying stakeholder theory to e-governance, governments around the globe may effectively go beyond the dissemination of information to involving citizens in the democratic process.

Effective e-governance of educational institutions is also expected, as educational institutions in the global campus are required to disseminate knowledge but also capture, manage, and apply it around the globe. The globalized approach to e-governance, as evidenced in laws passed in the United States as well as the European Union, has in some ways minimized the power of local governments. There has been an increase of re-regulation of universities in European Union nations, and the same is likely to occur in other countries. There is little understanding of how these actions truly impact the learner who is the ultimate stakeholder.

E-learning which has been slow to catch on in higher education after a multitude of stops and starts over the last ten years, has now evolved into a global necessity. The same future lies ahead for K-12 education, which is also under constant scrutiny. Technological literacy is no longer a wish but a need. K-12 educators must rapidly embrace the benefits of online learning as another option to help students succeed in a global community.

Challenges and trends continue to grow for higher education and cannot and will not be addressed without forward thinking visionary leadership to meet the challenges of a global environment. The expectations on higher education and K-12 online learning are rising. The gap is growing between the old and the new. Innovation is needed at all levels of the academy including learners, faculty, and administration (New Media Consortium, 2008).

Meta-trends such as using mobile devices for e-learning, connecting people via the network, and using open source e-learning platforms pose challenges for IT specialists.

However it is the other meta-trends that require pedagogical shifts such as using games for learning, allowing learners to produce content, and allowing the co-construction and sharing of knowledge that must be embraced quickly. Delaying this shift in pedagogy risks stalling the advancement of education for yet another decade.

All the while, e-governments across the globe exploit the power of the Internet. The Internet can be a friend or foe, depending who is controlling it. In the case of communist-authoritarian governments such as China, the Internet can be used as a powerful weapon of oppression. Inherent in technology are tools to liberate or coerce. Behind the superficial purpose of providing citizens with easy access to information, and creating a transparent e-government, the democratic world seeks to use technology to propagate the ideals of democracy. In the next few years we are likely to witness an increase in international laws and regulations to further the purpose of democratic e-governments.

The effects of e-governance on the global campus remain to be explored. It can be extrapolated from current events that cyber educators must remain vigilant, as many more rapid changes are to be expected. Only by taking an informed, proactive approach will the e-governance of the global campus be effective and purposeful.

REFERENCES

Ainsworth, S., Hardy, C., & Harley, B. (2005). Online Consultation: e-democracy and e-resistance in the case of the development gateway. *Management Communication Quarterly, 19*(1), 120–145. doi:10.1177/0893318905276562

Allen, E., & Seaman, J. (2007). *Online nation: Five years of growth in online learning*. Report to the Sloan Consortium. Retrieved October 11, 2010, from http://www.sloan-c.org/publications /survey/pdf/online_nation.pdf

Asia Pacific, E.-Learning Alliance. (2002). *A report on e-learning and best practices*. Retrieved October 11, 2010, from http://unpan1.un.org/intradoc/groups /public/ documents/APCITY/UNPAN011272.pdf

Bloom, D. E. (2002, September 19). *Mastering globalization: From ideas to action in higher education reform*. (Speech at Harvard University, September 19, 2002). Retrieved September 12, 2010 from http://www.bi.ulaval.ca/Globalisation-Universities/pages/ actes/BloomDavid.pdf

Bolt, D., & Crawford, R. (2000). *Digital divide: Computers and our children's future*. New York: TV Books.

Cerf, V. G., & Kahn, R. E. (1974). A protocol for packet network intercommunication. *IEEE Transactions in Communication, 22*(5), 637-648. Retrieved May 6, 2010, from http://www.cs.princeton.edu/courses /archive/fall06/cos561/papers/cerf74.pdf

Commission of the European Communities. (2006, April 25). i2010 eGovernment action plan: Accelerating eGovernment in Europe for the benefit of all. *Communication from the commission to the council, the European parliament, the European economic and social committee and the committee of the regions*, Brussels. Retrieved October 26, 2010, from http://www.csae.map.es/csi/pdf /COM_2008_798_final_eID_eSign.pdf

Federal Register. (2000, December). *Electronic and information technology accessibility standards (Section 508)*. Retrieved October 12, 2010, from http://www.access-board.gov/508.htm

Federal Trade Commission. (2006, September 7). *Xanga.com to pay $1 million for violating children's online privacy protection rule*. News release on September 7, 2006. Retrieved October 31, 2010, from http://www.ftc.gov/opa/2006/09/xanga.shtm

Federal Trade Commission. (2010). *Children's Online Privacy Protection Act [COPPA] of 1998*. Retrieved May 12, 2010, from http://www.ftc.gov/ogc/coppa1.htm

Finkelstein, S. (2007, June 21). Is Google just the tip of the iceberg of concerns about online privacy? *The Guardian* (online). Retrieved October 31, 2010, from http://www.guardian.co.uk/ technology/2007/jun/21/digitalmedia.media

Freeman, R. E. (1984). *Strategic management: A stakeholder approach*. Boston: Pitman.

Garson, D. G. (2006). *Public information and e-governance: Managing the virtual state*. Sudbury, MA: Jones & Barlett.

Hechinger, J. (2008). College applicants, beware: Your Facebook page is showing. *The Wall Street Journal* (online). Retrieved October 27, 2010, from http://online. wsj.com/article /SB122170459104151023.html

Hedmo, T., & Wedlin, L. (2008). New modes of governance: The re-regulation of European higher education and research. In Mazza, C., Quattrone, P., & Riccabon, A. (Eds.), *European universities in transition: Issues, models and cases*. Cheltenham, UK: Edgard Elgar Publishing.

Julian, L. (2009, August). Learning for a living. In defense of vocational ed. *Doublethink Online*. Retrieved October 25, 2010, from http://americasfuture.org/ doublethink/2009/08/learning-for-a-living

Lim, E. T. K., Tan, C., & Pan, S. (2009). E-government implementation: Balancing collaboration and control in stakeholder management. In Khosrow-Pour, M. (Ed.), *E-government diffusion, policy, and impact: Advanced issues and practices* (pp. 60–88). Hershey, PA: Information Science Reference. doi:10.4018/978-1-60566-130-8.ch005

MacMillan, D. (2010, March 25). Google's quixotic China challenge. *Business Week*. Retrieved May 15, 2010, from http://www.businessweek.com/technology / content/mar2010/tc20100324_284005.htm

Marche, S., & McNiven, J. (2003). E-government and e-governance: The future isn't what is used to be. *Canadian Journal of Administrative Sciences*, *20*(1), 74–86. doi:10.1111/j.1936-4490.2003.tb00306.x

Mitchinson, T., & Ratner, M. (2004). Promoting transparency through the electronic dissemination of information. In Oliver, E. L., & Sanders, L. (Eds.), *E-government reconsidered: Renewal of governance for the knowledge age* (pp. 89–106). Saskatchewan, Canada: Saskatchewan Institute of Public Policy.

Musthaler, L., & Musthaler, B. (2008, July 28). Web governance monitors Web sites for trouble signs. Web governance helps to ensure standardization, control and compliance with privacy and accessibility regulations. *Network World* (online). Retrieved October 31, 2010 from http://www.networkworld.com

National Archives. (2010). *E-government act of 2002*. Retrieved October 26, 2010, from http://www.archives.gov/about /laws/egov-act-section-207.html

Orwell, G. (1949). *Nineteen eighty-four*. London: Martin Secker & Warburg Ltd.

Pablo, Z. D., & Pan, S. L. (2002). A multi-disciplinary analysis of e-governance: Where do we start? In *Proceedings of the 6th Pacific Conference on Information Systems* (PACIS 2002), Tokyo, Japan.

Rocheleau. (2007). Whither e-government? *Public Administration Review, 67*(3), 584-588.

Rose, R. (2005a). Introduction: The Internet and governance in a global context. *Journal of Public Policy, 25*(1), 1–3. doi:10.1017/S0143814X05000267

Rose, R. (2005b). A global diffusion model of e-governance. *Journal of Public Policy, 25*(1), 5–27. doi:10.1017/S0143814X05000279

Roy, J. (2005). E-governance and international relations: A reconsideration of newly emerging capacities in a multi-level world. *Journal of Electronic Commerce Research, 6*(1), 44–56.

Saxena, K. (2005). Towards excellence in e-governance. *International Journal of Public Sector Management, 18*(6/7), 498–513. doi:10.1108/09513550510616733

Snyder, D. P. (2004, July/August). Five meta-trends that are changing our world. *The Futurist Magazine*. Retrieved October 21, 2010, from http://www.the-futurist. com/five-meta- trends_that_are_changing_our_world.htm

Sridhar, S. (2005). E-government, a proactive participant for e-learning in higher education. *Journal of American Academy Business, 7*(1), 258–268.

Streib, G., & Willoughby, K. (2005). Local government as e-governments: Meeting the implementation challenge. *Public Administration Quarterly, 29*(1/2), 77-112.

The Commonwealth Network of Information Technology for Development Foundation. (2000, December). *Global survey on on-line governance. Final report*. United Nations Educational, Scientific and Cultural Organization, Paris, December 2000. Retrieved October 31, 2010, from http://unesdoc.unesco.org/images/0012/001220/122040e.pdf

The New Media Consortium. (2007). *Horizon Report, 2007 edition*. Retrieved October 31, 2010, from http://www.nmc.org/pdf/2007_Horizon_Report.pdf

The New Media Consortium. (2008). *Horizon Report, 2008 edition*. Retrieved October 31, 2010, from http://www.nmc.org/pdf/2008-Horizon-Report.pdf

Thomas, J. C., & Streib, G. (2005). E-democracy, e-commerce, and e-research: Examining the electronic ties between citizens and governments. *Administration & Society, 37*(3), 259–280. doi:10.1177/0095399704273212

Turow, J. (2003). Family boundaries, commercialism, and the Internet: A framework for research. In Turow, J., & Kavanaugh, A. (Eds.), *The wired homestead: An MIT press sourcebook on the Internet and the family* (pp. 25–44). Cambridge, MA: MIT Press.

UNESCO. (2005). *Defining e-governance*. Retrieved October 26, 2010, from http://portal.unesco.org

UNESCO. (2010). *E-governance*. Retrieved October 6, 2010, from http://portal.unesco.org

United Kingdom Office of Public Sector Information. (1998). *Data Protection Act of 1998*. Retrieved October 12, 2010, from http://www.opsi.gov.uk/acts /acts1998/ukpga_19980029_en_1

United States Department of Education. (2010). *Family Educational Rights and Privacy Act (FERPA)*. Retrieved October 21, 2010, from http://www2.ed.gov/policy/gen/guid/fpco/ferpa/index.html

United States Department of Education. (2010). *No Child Left Behind Act of 2001*. Retrieved May 15, 2010, from http://www2.ed.gov/legislation/ESEA02

United States Department of Health and Human Services. (2010). *The Health Insurance Portability and Accountability Act of 1996*. Retrieved October 21, 2010, from http://www.hhs.gov/ocr/privacy

United States Senate. (2001). *Uniting and Strengthening America by Providing Appropriate Tools Required to Intercept and Obstruct Terrorism [USA PATRIOT ACT] Act of 2001*. Retrieved May 12, 2010, from http://epic.org/privacy/terrorism/hr3162.html

Washington Post. (2010, January 14). Google vs. China. *Washington Post* (online). Retrieved October 25, 2010, from http://www.washingtonpost.com

Wong, K., Fearon, C., & Philip, G. (2007). Understanding e-government and e-governance: Stakeholders, partnerships and CSR. *International Journal of Reliability Management, 24*(9), 927–943. doi:10.1108/02656710710826199

World Wide Web Consortium. (1999.) *Web content accessibility guidelines*. Retrieved October 27, 2010, from http://www.w3.org/TR/WCAG10

World Wide Web Consortium. (2010). *Standards*. Retrieved October 27, 2010, from http://www.w3.org/standards

Section 2
What is Identity and How Does it Impact Learning?

Chapter 5
How Safe is Your Identity?
Security Threats, Data Mining, & Digital Fingerprints/Footprints

ABSTRACT

Digitally mediated communications offer ease and flexibility to exchange informa-tion across a networked global community. All interactions could potentially be captured however, using different invasive technologies for spoofing, phishing, data mining, profiling, and tracking an individual's digital fingerprints and footprints. Ultimately, the exposure of private information not only compromises an indi-vidual's identity, security, and privacy, but also the security of organizations and governments. Nonetheless, these same technologies present unique opportunities for cyber educators to track and monitor, within e-learning platforms, the activities of students with the goal of using this data to improve the learning experience for the benefit of all learners.

OBJECTIVES

- Describe data mining, profiling, spoofing, phishing, digital fingerprinting, digital footprints and other terms unique to privacy and anonymity concerns in the online environment.

DOI: 10.4018/978-1-60960-543-8.ch005

- Analyze the detrimental and potentially positive effects of the digital trails learners leave in online learning.
- Identify the diametrically opposing positions of FERPA and the USA PATRIOT Act
- Recognize the variety of threats that may be present to learner privacy and identity in the online environment.
- Discuss security trends, threats, and safeguards that affect e-learning.

INTRODUCTION

Privacy and anonymity co-exist in the realm of digitally mediated communications. Increased connectivity increases the risks of security threats to individuals as well as organizations and governments. Besides the well known threats posed by worms, viruses, Trojans and the like, other dangers may come in the form of email spoofing and phishing or in the form of tracking an individual's whereabouts. Lack of awareness of these threats often results in breaches that affect individuals as well as organizations.

With every click, a person's digital trail is captured. These data can be gathered and analyzed for any particular intent or purpose. Aside from compromising a person's identity, the visibility brought about by social networking tools diminishes the protection that would otherwise be offered by anonymity. Anyone, including employers, collection agencies, friend or foe, could locate information about an individual and make inferences about their preferences, personality, and character. The growing digital trail may be used to conceptualize a person's morality and ethics.

These same invasive technologies that are used to pry into private information could potentially be applied to cyber education. Although the danger of misusing learner information remains a concern, the prospective benefits of data mining and tracking digital fingerprints and footprints within e-learning platforms hint at improving distance learning programs. This chapter discusses key definitions and then explores the harms as well as the potential benefits of data mining, profiling and tracking of digital fingerprints and footprints.

BACKGROUND

Privacy and anonymity are inextricably mixed. Anonymity may be defined as the absence of identity and privacy as the ability to be apart from and unidentified by, others. The right to private communications and freedom of speech is guaranteed in the United States Constitution, yet digital privacy and true anonymity remain both misleading and elusive. Donald Kerr, Deputy Director of National Intelligence in the United States tells us "privacy no longer can mean anonymity" (Bradner, 2007, p.26). Privacy is now subject to a new interpretation according to Kerr, which has impelled government and business agencies to make attempts at safeguarding our private communications. Digitally mediated communications, whether used for business, personal or educational purposes, open the door to security threats such as spoofing, phishing, data mining and the capture of digital fingerprints and footprints. There is promise that these invasive technologies may be used to capture information about the individual learner. If used properly, these same technologies may help cyber educators not only personalize the learning experience, but also focus on student achievement.

Fear, misconduct and improper use of technologies surface occasionally only to be suppressed by the mesmerizing appeal of communicating online. An overwhelming 60% of Internet users in the United States do not necessarily worry about how much of their personal information is available online (Madden, Fox, Smith, & Vitak, 2007). This lack of concern affects not only individuals, but also eventually impacts organizations and institutions. With the increased use of social networking sites, especially by the Millennials (those born between 1980 and 2000), it would be expected that it is the younger generation that is not concerned about protecting their online identity. Surprisingly, the opposite is true. According to the Pew Internet Project, 55% of teens have an online profile, which they manage in some way; this is in contrast to 20% of adults who use social networking tools (Madden, Fox, Smith, & Vitak, 2007).

Virus software, firewalls, polices and procedures, passwords and proxy servers are not enough to keep an organization safe. While 73% of malicious attacks come in the form of viruses, about 47% were attributed to insider issues and abuse. Lack of security awareness accounts for most of today's security issues and may be handled without the need for more sophisticated security technologies (Gordon, Loeb, Lucyshyn, & Richardson, 2005).

The threat of spoofing, phishing, Trojans, data mining and profiling are also very real in cyber education. Even the most sophisticated firewalls and anti-virus packages can be rendered useless by a lack of understanding or awareness of risk. Security has generally been a major concern of many organizations that have an e-commerce component, but even in cyber education stakeholders have become aware that viruses, worms, denial-of-service attacks, stolen passwords, social engineering, authority and authenticity violations can be a result of lack of security awareness. The educational community can no longer remain still. Proactive steps must be taken not only to protect the educational community from harm, but also to tap the power of these technologies to create solutions intended to help promote student success.

The distance learning community became even more aware of cyber threats when Family Educations Rights and Privacy Act (FERPA) and the controversial USA PATRIOT Act (Uniting and Strengthening America by Providing Appropriate Tools Required to Intercept and Obstruct Terrorism) set anonymity and privacy at diametrically opposing positions. Institutions began to recognize their firewall was not enough. Web 2.0 had ushered in an era of open communications, blogs, wikis and shared video, but the community was committing risky acts that were giving their Information Technology departments reasons for concern. Not only were academic freedom, self-expression and discourse being challenged, but also the traditional infrastructure. The last few years have brought a keen awareness of perilous acts, deterrence, prevention and recovery. In certain cases, institutions may have some control of these acts, whether initiated internally or externally. Most threats, however, come from carelessness, negligence and lack of awareness (Chen, Shaw, & Yang, 2006).

Beyond the limitations to security and anonymity imposed by digitally mediated communications, there appears to be the potential for using these technologies for actually improving education. Data mining, for example, although it may sometimes have a detrimental effect, can also provide the learning community with insights and vision for improving the conditions for the individual learner. Profiling, like so many other attributes of the online environment, has both pros and cons. Digital fingerprints of learner identities are being sprinkled everywhere they click and usually with the learner being totally oblivious to the fact that they are being monitored.

There is a shocking lack of awareness among cyber educators of the impending threats and challenges facing the learning community. If the words virus, hacker or spammer are mentioned, it may trigger an uncomfortable awareness of the underworld of digitally mediated communications. However, most learners go blissfully along the Internet highway having no thoughts about the implications of the digital trail they are leaving behind. Lawsuits, international scandals and trials have sparked court cases and online privacy and safety concerns. Cyber educators have the opportunity to learn from these key lessons thus not only protecting themselves, but also their students from harm. If this opportunity is thoughtfully pursued, cyber educators are also in a unique position to harness the power of invasive technologies to ultimately improve the online learning experience.

SECURITY THREATS

The more education relies on digital forms of communications, the more security threats find their way into every day lives of digital learners. Two of the main threats are spoofing and phishing; they are relatively easy to perpetrate and many people are unaware of such threats. Both spoofing and phishing are by-products of the inherent anonymity in digitally mediated communications.

Spoofing is the forgery of an email header to get the recipient to open an email that appears to have originated from someone or somewhere other than the real source. Spoofed emails are often used for phishing. Phishing is an email that attempts to trick the user into surrendering personal and confidential information that might be used for identity theft. These security threats can take many forms but all basically have the same result: a user receives an email that appears to be from one source but is actually from another and is tricked into revealing personal or sensitive information such as social security number or passwords (Kruck & Kruck, 2006).

Spoofing is possible because of the anonymity offered in the online environment. It is possible to send an email or chat message that appears to be anyone or from anywhere, saying whatever the sender wishes it to say, hence obscuring the real identity of the sender. Spoofing and spamming, in their various forms, have already been made illegal in many states such as Washington, Maryland, Illinois, and Florida. In new legislation enacted in 2008, Florida even made caller ID spoofing punishable, although a stream of lawsuits from private companies may force the state to reconsider. There are generally two main varieties of spoofing with many subsets. The first type of spoofing is traditional email spoofing where an email is intentionally made to look like it came from someone else.

The second type of spoofing relies on supplying false information either on a Web site or over digital communications that makes the user think it is someone or something other than what it really is. A common example of typical email spoofing is reversing identities where an individual who is responsible for spoofing is in between two senders, intercepts data and then switches it. An example of identity spoofing, on the other hand, is placing articles or false information on a Web site and claiming it is copyrighted to another.

While there are really no obvious beneficial applications of spoofing and phishing to e-learning, it is important for cyber educators to be aware of potential threats. It is incumbent upon cyber educators to alert their students and show them not just how to recognize the dangers posed by spoofing and phishing, but also show them how to protect themselves from compromising their identity, privacy and security.

DATA MINING AND PROFILING

An extraordinary amount of data is continually collected on each and every individual both over the Internet and via their organization's intranet. How this data is used depends on the intent of the gatherer. There are many reasons why information are collected; the data may be used to promote or sell a product, learn about user habits or gather demographics, among other reasons. Nonetheless, data mining and profiling go hand-in-hand, especially at a time when K-20 distance education programs and corporate e-learning training programs continue to expand. Learner profiling, though not fully exploited, opens the door to customizing cyber education to truly meet the needs of individual learners.

Private and public sectors alike have made investments in technologies to support this expansion of e-learning and reap the financial rewards that come with it. Data mining and profiling are central to this purpose. The more an organization or company knows about its customers, the more it can target their needs and make a profit.

The predominant reason that data mining has attracted so much attention in recent years is the vast amount of information that is stored and available. Along with this comes a burning desire to turn this information into something useful. A by-product of technological evolution, data mining evolved from data collection, storage, retrieval and processing to warehousing and data mining. Different types of databases and a variety of data architectures have morphed into data repositories capable of housing a wide variety of data sources organized under a single schema at a single site. All this information can be analyzed to support management decision-making using a variety of in-depth analysis techniques (Hanna, 2004).

Data mining involves determining relevance from vast amounts of information. This is done by creating rules, which are applied to discover and extract latent knowledge (Palace, 1996). These rules are used to further identify correlations and patterns. Although the term "data mining" was developed relatively recently, the use of computer technology to scan large amounts of data for meaning has been in place for several decades. As the use of technology increases and the processing and storage capabilities of computers become more robust, the cost of analyzing data is diminished. The accuracy of the results, however, appears to be improving thus making data mining and profiling more attractive than ever.

Application of latent knowledge ranges from usage patterns to behavior patterns and demographic trends (Pahl, 2004). Data mining is also used in a wide variety of ways, including the support of systems, analysis and knowledge construction. The concept of constructing latent knowledge from data is based on the ability to discern and extract from the volumes of information discoveries that prove to be useful and relevant.

Data mining techniques exist to support the extraction of knowledge from data. Several types of evaluations can fall under the area called data mining including; usage statistics, classifications, clustering, association, time series and sequential patterns. Increasingly sophisticated levels of abstraction of knowledge and languages to express knowledge are crucial to data mining success.

Generally in Web mining, the database is the access log created by the server. Web mining usually consists of activities and in that way is different from content data mining. Creating meaning out of low-level data requires classification and interpretation of patterns. The implementation of data mining techniques takes data through a variety of stages such as cleaning or scrubbing, classification and interpretation (Pahl, 2004).

In cyber education, data are typically housed in learning management systems (LMS) or learning content management systems (LCMS). Data mining software has been developed to discern relationships, create profiles and to analyze learner behavior. Some software even has the capability to track and predict learning outcomes. Data mining software examines learning and helps analysts identify ways to enhance satisfaction of the customer; in this case, the learner. Furthermore, analysts use measures and metrics to establish relationships and meaning (Hanna, 2004). This would not only enhance the learning experience, but also potentially increase retention rates hence augmenting profits for distance learning programs.

Mining e-learning data may be done on the Web, within the LMS or LCMS or via email. It has the potential to be quite beneficial and useful. It can involve information from the Web page itself, structures of linked pages, usage and demographics. Many Web content mining techniques have centered on summarizing the information found. A typical example is keyword summarization and search in Google™. Search engines retrieve relevant information based on keyword-search and retrieval algorithm (Hanna, 2004).

The anonymity provided by Internet technologies combined with the attribute of ubiquity has enabled the emergence of new data mining techniques and applications for analyzing user behaviors. Data mining has already proven to be a powerful tool in the construction of superior Web site structures and e-commerce buying behaviors. Data mining remains largely untapped in the educational realm and stands to offer exciting opportunities for analyzing learner interactions and engagement (Pahl, 2004).

Technologies and techniques currently used for commercial data mining and profiling customers can be assets to cyber educators. The question remains whether they are prepared to use this data to customize learning and improve courses, thus increasing retention rates and making e-learning relevant to all learners. More often than not, educators remain light-years behind commercial systems due to lack of appropriate funding. The future is now and cyber educators cannot afford to wait for government to provide resources. It will require creativeness on their part.

DIGITAL FINGERPRINTS AND FOOTPRINTS

The thought of leaving a trail of fingerprints and footprints in a digital environment may evoke thoughts of a science fiction novel, but they are far too real and have implications beyond the imagination. As each person's activity on the Internet is captured and their information is published for the world to see, the sense of anonymity is compromised. That person's privacy and reputation could potentially be affected. Conversely, the ability to use tracking technologies in cyber education could help educators unleash true individualized instruction, as well as properly manage student progress. This is, of course, if cyber educators can keep "Big Brother" at bay and focus on the noble pursuit of student learning.

Digital fingerprints are the string of coded binary digits that are deeply embedded in a document's structure. This metadata is unique to each document and most of it is hidden from regular view. While simple information is easily seen under a document's properties, it would take a special program to reveal the hidden fingerprints, which would show information about every edit, version, person who edited the document, the computer it came from and much more. In an attempt to counteract fingerprinting technology, programs that help users wipe out a document's digital fingerprints have been developed, but, in most cases, are considered inadequate.

Hiding data from prying eyes is the goal of techniques such as cryptology, which is still the preferred method. It is common knowledge among experts that the protocols and algorithms used for encrypting data today will not provide strong protection forever. Encryption remains a widely debated topic, especially as it relates to free speech. The United States and European Union nations have over the years revised their policies to allow individuals the right to use encryption software to scramble their private messages without fear of government surveillance (Spinello, 2003).

Another technique used for hiding data is called steganology, which "keeps the host media perceptually unchanged after hiding the secret information" (Si & Chang-Tsun, 2006, p. 3). Governments may now favor steganology when it comes to securing their digitally mediated communications and protecting national security. This technique, however, also has its pitfalls. It can be used to detect hidden data through steganalysis thus potentially compromising security. Governments may combine the use of cryptology and steganology techniques to protect against security breaches and safeguard their citizens' privacy and anonymity.

Digital fingerprints are embedded in a document or file. Digital footprints on the other hand, could be thought of as the trail that is created by our online presence, whether it was something the individual posted or that someone else shared about the individual or even Internet searches. Digital footprints may either be active or passive. More people are becoming aware of their footprints. Forty-seven percent of all Internet users in 2007 searched for information about themselves online, up from 22% in 2002 (Madden, Fox, Smith, & Vitak, 2007). Being aware of one's digital footprints is the first step toward managing one's online presence, privacy and anonymity.

Passive footprints are created gradually with each search or Web page visited. These actions are stored in databases and may be analyzed for different purposes. In some instances, the IP address is also recorded as part of the footprint, thus tracking the origin of the "hit". Corporate and educational institutions may use passive digital footprints stored in the hard drive's local temporary files to track the activity on a particular computer, but the originator of the footprint is not revealed. Passive footprints are also created when organizations and entities upload information about an individual. According to the Pew Internet and American Life Project report (Madden, Fox, Smith, & Vitak, 2007):

These are the data points uploaded to the Internet as a matter of course, along with other public records like home sales, court records and newspaper accounts. Layered on top of these publicly available sources are proprietary databases containing information such as cell phone numbers and political affiliations. (p. 3, para. 5)

The proverbial "cookies" are used for monitoring the actions of a Web visitor. Third-party cookies are more sophisticated than the common cookie, having the ability to track the movements of the visitor within a network of related sites. A cookie is a small data file sent to a computer by a Web site. Cookies make it easier to search and remember Internet sites. They appear in the browser's bookmarks or favorites lists and allow for the customization of the Web. There is a dark side to cookies, however, particularly if they are not solicited or go undetected. The cookies deposited on the computer leave a data trail that reveals a great deal about the learner's habits. Though most data can be traced to an IP address or computer and not an individual, it is still considered to be anonymous. The difference maker in the anonymity debate is the inclusion of personally identifiable information such as the person's address, social security number or anything that would facilitate a connection to an individual (Roha, 2000).

Advertisers use every trick to monitor the whereabouts of potential customers and their methods continue to be more covert and more threatening to privacy. A less talked about yet more concealed surveillance tool is the "Web bug". Web bugs come in different forms and levels of complexity, including small graphic images on a Web page or in HTML code. They are ideal for scrutinizing and determining if and when the email was read or forwarded and from what computer the action was taken. These are just some of the invasive technologies used to capture, track and monitor an individual's digital footprints.

In contrast to passive digital footprints, the user, when uploading online content, usually initiates active digital footprints. Active digital footprints are triggered and stored each time the person logs into a social networking site, for example and posts or edits an item. Another way for a user to create an active digital footprint is if the network administrator is using keylogger technology. Keylogging is in essence a way of capturing, recording and storing every keystroke the user makes, including passwords. In most situations, a user may not be aware that their company is using a keylogger to monitor productivity. Active digital footprints captured by a keylogger reveal not only the actions taken on the computer, but also identifies who took each action.

A recent phenomenon that adds to the trail of footprints is the use of "mashup" social software, which can be defined as the combination of data or functionality from several related or unrelated sources to create a new, integrated tool. Mashups have led to controversy around creating profiles of individuals from seemingly unrelated sources. This brings up the inevitable question of who really owns the trail of digital footprints. The ownership of the transaction interactions of individuals currently rests with the organization. However, the implications to individual privacy and anonymity are staggering. Many feel that the ownership of a digital persona should rest with the individual. Profiles created by the digital trail should be in support of and in the control of, the individual, not just the organization (Basu, 2005).

Several lawsuits, including one against the advertising firm DoubleClick, Inc. in 2002, have pushed the boundaries of online privacy. DoubleClick® created profiles of hundreds of thousands of Web surfers without their knowledge or consent; it accomplished this by depositing cookies on the computers of visitors to a Web site via advertisements on a page. The outcome of this lawsuit has prompted many Web sites to initiate privacy policies and the passage of legislation in the United States is beginning to surface. One of the real challenges is designing enforceable standards at the national and international level. Self-regulation by organizations and businesses and placing the responsibility for anonymity on the individual has not worked. The guidelines are difficult to follow and convenience too often wins because the veil of anonymity covers the digital trail (Roha, 2000).

Nowhere did anonymity become more tragic and apparent than in the incident involving Yahoo® and Chinese prisoners in 2007. Two Chinese journalists had anonymously posted information that went against the Chinese political establishment. These journalists and their families accused Yahoo® of turning over emails, digital records and personal information to the Chinese government, hence unmasking the digital trail and incriminating them for dissention. One journalist, Wang Xiaoning, was arrested and jailed in 2002. Another. Shi Tao, was arrested in 2004. Like Xiaoning, Shi thought he was operating in privacy and with privacy protection, but he was not (Milbank, 2007). Both were sentenced to ten years in prison for instigating anti-government sentiments. Xiaoning and his wife sued in a United States court under the Alien Tort Claims Act and the Torture Victims Protection Act. Yahoo® finally settled on behalf of both journalists and their families but it was not without raising the eyebrows of the Human Rights community. This landmark case was the first of its kind filed against an Internet company with business operations in communist China. Although the United States government intervened and eventually gained the release of the prisoners, the real issue of anonymity and digital communications remains unaddressed.

Data mining, as defined earlier, is only possible because of the extensive trail of data left behind by digital communications over the Internet. By virtue of the fact that the communications are digital, it is feasible to monitor and record all of it. This capability translates easily into cyber education. Monitoring inside the online course room is already common practice. E-learning platforms currently allow the recording and monitoring of information. In an effort at tracking student activity for the sake of evaluation, "Big Brother" is indeed watching over learners too. Data mining and profiling, however, do have a place in cyber education if used ethically and conscientiously for the purpose of improving learning.

This type of monitoring has both positive and negative effects on e-learning. By watching closely the amount of time spent on the Internet, a paradox of productivity has developed around the new technologies. Employees may easily spend work time online emailing friends, text messaging, searching information on topics of personal interest, or shopping. Rather than fight the tide, many K-20 institutions, as well as corporate organizations, have begun to strengthen their e-learning initiative.

In order to win the war for time and productivity organizations are integrating social networking tools as part of the e-learning experience. Cyber educators continue to experiment with social networking tools and explore pedagogically appropriate uses. Social software, chats and other sharing tools also increase the number of ones and zeros in the digital trail. The more interactions learners have online, the more the extensive the digital trail grows.

Cyber educators currently look at the most obvious digital fingerprint for the purpose of ascertaining the identity of the content creator. Many unsuspecting young e-learners have been discovered submitting someone else's work. But it would take a more focused effort on the part of educational institutions and corporate training departments to provide cyber instructors with the proper tools and training needed to uncover deeper hidden information.

Digital footprints, on the other hand, are widely used in cyber education to track where and how students navigate within the course room, how much time they spend logged in and from which IP address they logged in. Administrators also collect digital footprints of online instructors to assess their efficiency, thus using this data for evaluation purposes.

Data mining, profiling and tracking digital fingerprints and footprints may each be thought of as a double agent. On one hand, they interfere with our privacy and diminish our anonymity; on the other, the invasive technologies used to perpetrate these activities may offer cyber educators unconventional solutions to pressing issues. These potential solutions will be explored in the section of this chapter titled *Looking Ahead.*

Safeguarding Against Spoofing and Phishing

Safeguarding against spoofing and phishing takes some effort, but it is not impossible. There are steps that can be taken by individuals either at their workplace or within the virtual course room to protect themselves. It begins with awareness of how spoofing is disseminated. There are also browser extensions that can be used to store and track personal information before it is redirected to a Web site.

Hackers from outside the organization not only propagate spoofing, it can also be an inside job. Spoofers and phishers come from all walks of life and all corners of the globe. As many as 80%, of all computer attacks are reported to be inside jobs (Kruck & Kruck, 2006). Intrusion detection systems (IDSs) are often ineffective because the employee or learner was given the email. As spoofing and phishing schemes are on the rise, email education and awareness become even more critical. Training and education on email and spoofing and phishing scams, along with the awareness that no email is really that secure, is essential. Table 1. offers a look at the top ten strategies to protect against spoofing (Baggio & Beldarrain, 2009).

Phishing remains an immediate concern for everyone. Policy and law require confidentiality of personal information. In most organizations, the guidelines are stricter than legislation requires, but the breakdown usually occurs due to a lack of awareness. Personally identifiable information includes names, addresses, emails, social security numbers and personal characteristics. Anything that makes the identity of the individual easily traceable is personally identifiable information. Spoofed emails and phishing schemes are not easy to detect. Anonymity provides the perfect smoke screen and lack of attention and awareness the spark. Simple things like leaving a browser open on a desktop and walking away may lead to trouble. Storing confidential information on your desktop or sending it via an email is also prevalent.

Innocently clicking on an email attachment can inadvertently launch malicious phishing schemes. Another way phish that has surfaced is the collection of personal information by using pseudo-sites or aliases and can result in the loss of confidence or identity theft (O'Sullivan, 2003). Phishing is still an online threat with some 25,000 attacks reported each month according to the Anti-Phishing Working Group, (Goldsborough, 2008). By using Web addresses that are similar to real URLs, cyber criminals are tricking innocent people into giving up personal information.

Table 1. Top ten strategies to protect against email spoofing

Strategy
1. Give out your email address judiciously.
2. Create one for educational purposes, one for family and friends and another for Internet purposes (e.g. discussion boards).
3. The email for non-internet purposes should be from a trustworthy source that does not resell email information.
4. Do not subscribe to spam lists as it confirms your email address.
5. Never divulge financial or personal information in email forms or emails-linked to Web pages.
6. Never put your email on a Web page in machine-readable format.
7. Learn how to spot a spoofed address.
8. Keep your anti virus file up to date.
9. Watch for undeliverable email that you never sent.
10. Check for the locked padlock on the browser's status bar indicating a secure connection.

New anti-phishing strategies are emerging. For online education, it is a question of awareness and implementation.

Awareness is the most important weapon of protection the online learner has against phishing, spoofing and other forms of identity theft. Some simple strategies and basic rules can help protect the online learner. A simple strategy such as being aware of bogus phone numbers in emails and phony Web addresses is helpful. If an email uses a phone number to request information, the learners should be sure to look up the phone number themselves. Web addresses that use the @ sign should always be suspect as should any email that asks the learner to click an image (Goldsborough, 2008). Installing and keeping a security application up to date will reduce the likelihood of a phishing attack. Be consciously aware that it is never, ever a good idea to click on a link in an email that asks for any kind of personal information. Updating personal information should only be done by going directly to the Web site by either typing in the URL or using a favorites or bookmark link.

Browser extensions like AntiPhish may offer further protection. These browser extensions keep track of sensitive information and offer the online learner the possibility of awareness. AntiPhish is based on the premise that software is less likely to be fooled than an unsophisticated user. This application keeps stores of personal information and prevents the passing of information to a Web site. Several browsers such as Mozilla Firefox® and Microsoft Internet Explorer® have integrated this tool. A master password protects the content and AntiPhish tracks where the content is being sent using domain names instead of Web site addresses because Web sites can span multiple servers. Besides passwords, AntiPhish relies on the user to determine what is considered sensitive information. The vulnerability, however, stems from the flexibility given to the user who has the ability to install or not install the application with these browsers (Kirda & Krugel, 2006). Regardless, the benefits of anti-phishing features are undeniable. Popular browsers such as Microsoft Internet Explorer®, Mozilla Firefox® and Opera® have recently added anti-phishing features to their new versions.

Another approach for combating phishing attacks comes in the form of visual similarity assessment. This anti-phishing strategy requires site owners to register their true URLs and keywords with a system called WebSiteWatcher. WebSiteWatcher runs on mail servers, since emails are still the number one way that phishing attacks occur. By comparing keywords, the application determines if the email is suspicious. Although many anti-phishing approaches use tool bars in Web browsers to determine the validity of a site, it does not always work. Similar to detecting fraudulent documents or plagiarism, instead of focusing on text-based features, this approach focuses on visual similarities. Full pages are analyzed for visual similarities, which is a more effective way of determining phony phishing sites because phishing pages may use similar and/or exact visual effects to mimic the authentic pages (Lui, Deng, & Fu, 2006). Any site that asks the learner to submit information into a form can be suspected as a phishing possibility.

Individuals should be aware of the different strategies to safeguard against spoofing and phishing. Cyber educators are charged with ensuring that e-learners know how to recognize these threats and protect themselves both inside the course room and with their private digitally mediated communications.

LOOKING AHEAD

The future of cyber security as it relates to private lives, corporations or educational institutions may be seen through either the half-empty or half-full glass approach. For the sake of humankind, it is best to pursue the half-full version. The connectivity afforded by technology has made the world a smaller place indeed, but there are likely more good guys than bad guys. As cyber criminals work in the shadows of anonymity to create malicious attacks, legitimate software companies work hard at creating patches faster and developing proactive measures to prevent attacks.

Now What?

1. The educational community must become aware of the impending threats and challenges brought about by digital communications.
2. Cyber educators should look to harness the power of invasive technologies to ultimately improve the online learning experience.

3. Educational organizations must find ways to use the technologies and techniques of data mining and digital fingerprints/footprints to customize learning and improve courses, evaluate and assess learner behavior, thus increasing transfer of knowledge and retention rates.
4. An informed and proactive approach is needed to safeguard privacy and anonymity.

Looking ahead may be easier said than done; however, it is critical that educators become aware of cyber threat trends and learn from past mistakes. Threats will continue to be prevalent in education, especially as more social networking tools are used for pedagogical purposes. Nonetheless, there are golden opportunities at the end of the rainbow. Individualized instruction and assessment, for example, could become a reality through the application of data mining and learner profiling techniques. Learners would benefit from a customized learning experience that meets their needs. An added potential benefit would be increased revenues for both K-20 e-learning as well as corporate Web based training programs.

Cyber Threats on the Rise

The future of Internet security certainly includes a rise in cyber threats. Cyber threats are predicted to rapidly increase in 2009 in the form of malware, botnets, attacks on mobile devices, VoIP services and even cyber warfare (Ahamad, et al., 2008). Perpetrators will rely on social networking sites and digitally mediated communications to penetrate more inconspicuously and cause more extensive damage than with previous methods.

Experts estimate that the number of malware items will increase by 10 percent in 2009 and will be designed to deceive the end receiver into following links that come from a trusted sender and appear legitimate (Ahamad, et al., 2008). Once the person clicks on the apparently safe link or site, the malware will be downloaded. Malware, which is intended to gain access to a computer, will also be key in creating botnets.

Botnets are created when one computer is infected with malware. This malware may be in the form of a "bot", which is a malicious code that, once installed, will create its own command center from the host computer, update itself and send commands to other computers. The result is a botnet. The worse news is that even the most savvy computer user will not realize they are downloading a bot. These bots may be hiding under the cover of legitimate Web sites, links and emails. Because bots use http protocols, not even firewalls can protect the user. The end results are botnets that cannot be traced back to the bot master because their identity remains hidden behind the host computer, which is the secret command center (Ahamad, et al., 2008).

Variations of malware will continue to increase in sophistication and number. By the end of 2007 alone, over a half million new types of malware were detected (Orr, 2008). Microsoft, in 2008, reported that in the first six months of the year, malware removal was up 55% over the same time period a year earlier (McMillan, 2008).

Phishing is likely to increase as is spamming. The main purpose of cyber threats, including attacks on mobile devices, according to security expert George Heron, is to gain access to personal and financial data (Ahamad, et al., 2008). Mobile devices are easy targets for malware. Botnets will be easier to create as more individuals use smart phones and service providers barely keep up with network security.

Attacks on VoIP networks are also expected to be on the rise, hence increasing voice phishing to steal personal data. Voice phishing uses voice response telephone systems to prompt individuals to "punch in" personal and financial data such as social security, credit card information and bank account numbers. Consumer watchdogs continually warn consumers about bank scams. Malware could also easily interfere with normal functions of the network by jamming it and disrupting communication.

Cyber criminals will likely rely on social engineering and creature habits for tricking individuals into surrendering data by using the technology behind social networking tools to hide the malware (Ahamad, Amster, Barret, Cross, Heron, Jackson, et al. 2008). Social networking sites are expected to be a preferred method of spreading infectious code. Membership with MySpace®, Facebook® and similar sites continues to grow exponentially. MySpace® alone boasted 106 million accounts in September 2006 (Wikipedia, 2009). Some sources estimate Facebook membership to be around 500 million as of this writing. It is understood that if malicious code is embedded into these social networking sites it would spread rapidly, hence present tremendous problems (Grinberg, 2008) to individuals and organizations.

Cyber warfare, on the other hand, is by nature more serious than any other threat. Wikipedia lists several kinds of activities linked to cyber warfare, including cyber espionage, Web vandalism, distributing propaganda, gathering classified data to facilitate espionage, disrupting functions of military equipment, attacking critical infrastructures such as water, fuel, transportation and food supplies, denial of service (DoS) attacks and setting up hardware that functions as a bot. These activities are certain to conjure images of an action thriller, but unfortunately, many of these tactics have already been employed for cyber warfare.

Cyber warfare was used as recent as the summer of 2008 when Russia launched a multi-faceted war against Georgia. According to reports, Russia was blamed for hacking Georgian networks then hijacking, defacing and posting false propaganda on legitimate Web sites including government sites. A barrage of DoS attacks were aimed at paralyzing Georgian infrastructure (Swaine, 2008). The United States government is by no means ignoring cyber warfare. Earlier in 2008, the Department of Homeland Security led a nation-wide exercise called "Cyber Storm II", which was aimed at forming partnerships between federal, public and private stakeholders to collaborate in strengthening the country's defense against cyber warfare via simulated scenarios (Bain, 2008).

Software companies are desperately trying to keep up with cyber criminals. More comprehensive security initiatives are needed to address cyber threats, but it can only happen if all stakeholders come together in a multi-layered approach; this includes manufacturers, software developers and awareness from the end user. Cyber criminals can easily access and purchase software and platforms for the specific purpose of launching attacks. Malware is now a profitable market.

New and more sophisticated approaches to entice users to give up personal information will continue to surface. Malware, unlike phishing, relies on stealth to steal crucial software code at the browser. Trojans and worms lie in wait watching for useful coding strings until some interesting trigger is discovered. Once inside the software on the site, this devious malware can create false transactions and steal information. The only good news is that as quickly as it is being developed, anti-malware is, too. Applications with quick reaction time and reporting capabilities are finding ways to reach enterprises, gateways and even mobile devices. As quickly as the bad guys develop malware companies are combating it with new security applications. Nevertheless, the stakes continue to grow and an end to the war is not currently in sight. The future for spoofing, phishing and malware looks all too bright. Awareness that these types of attacks are going on is the first step to avoiding falling prey to some of the above incidences (Goldsborough, 2008).

Harnessing the Power of Data Mining and User Profiling to Benefit Cyber Education

There is a positive side to the future of data mining and profiling that may very well serve the e-learning community. Data mining as applied to the Web combined with the big business of K-20 education provides the incentive for perhaps integrating data mining into the e-learning platform. This holds promises for evaluation and assessment of behavior and interactions that were previously unavailable.

Because data mining is non-intrusive and is supported by anonymity, it holds the power for evaluating learner interactions and educational content. In digitally based learning environments, it is important to analyze interactivity (Sims, 1997). Interactivity in support of learning environments relates to the learner interactions with the content, other learners, the instructor and the interface. Although a great deal of research is needed to determine specifics, it is generally accepted that interactions are supportive in creating well-designed learning environments. The challenge for instructional designers and cyber educators is to design interactive environments that support teaching and learning.

The promise of digitally mediated learning environments includes individualized and formative assessments delivered to and tailored for the learner, custom developed multimedia environments customized in support of preferred learning styles and goals and creation of novel forms teaching and learning that have not always traditionally been understood. In order to design these environments instructional designers need to have answers to some fundamental questions regarding learner interactions and learning.

This is accelerated by the anonymity offered by the Web-based environment because often learner interactions cannot be directly observed. Digital footprints, however, help track the learner's whereabouts and increase the knowledge about their actions. Analysis of the large amounts of data available from digitally mediated learning environments might prove to be invaluable in determining learner interactions and effective learning (Pahl, 2004).

Higher education has become a huge business with significant investments in technologies in support of online learning. This awareness has been propelled by a shift in paradigm that supports life-long learning and a knowledge economy. Millions of adults have returned to school and more are doing so, a great many online. Although it is more familiar to the government and corporate sector, data mining and profiling in e-learning is a relatively new phenomenon. Not only does it have the potential identify from a multitude of data from potential customers, it has the ability to potentially enhance the effectiveness of the learning process.

Most universities, for example, have massive learning management systems (LMS), content management systems (CMS) or learning content management systems (LCMS). All of these systems offer basic features that would enable the organization to pursue data mining. Data may be gathered for example, from student registration, tracking, course room interactions, grades and any other source of value to the organization. Depending on the vision of the institution, e-learning information could support the mission in a variety of positive ways (Hanna, 2004).

The search engine technology capable of searching Web pages and tracking Web activity has been available for some time and could also hold promise for cyber educators. Some search engines rely on keywords, while others rely on concept hierarchies and sophisticated algorithms that analyze the links between Web pages. The tools to do the searching can be simple and broad or complex and individualized. These tools include intelligent search engines, information filtering and personalized agent-based software that aid in mining content. Whatever the case, the information is usually summarized into some type of useful format.

Personalization is key to developing unique pages, like Dashboards, designed to the specific needs of the user. It is this personalization that has the potential to create e-learning systems that can automatically be adapted to the interests and levels of the learner. Complete with customizable feedback and stored levels of expertise and preferences, these individually customized environments could indeed provide a revolutionary way to provide education in a world that supports learning for a lifetime (Li & Chang, 2005).

User profiling holds the promise of unleashing this potential nirvana where constructivists claim learning occurs: with the individual learner. User profiling has the potential to put an end to "one size fits all" education and allocate learning resources based on preferences, interests and expertise level. Personalized search engines could construct learner profiles based on history and background. They could also capture and track a student's progress through their individual courses as well as their academic career with the particular institution. The continuous process of life long learning and tracking may sound like Orwell's 1984, but does hold potential if used auspiciously.

Many common approaches to user profiling currently rely on the user for input. Information fusion coupled with multiple feedback streams offers a way to harvest more complete and accurate learner information. Profiling can be accomplished by adaptive methods that are dynamic in origin and application. Probabilistic modeling techniques can provide for optimization based on data gathered (Nokelainen, Tirri, Miettinen, Silander, & Kurhila, 2002).

Data mining provides the possibility of learner profiling. Learner profiling therefore allows educators to create intelligently tailored and individualized learning environments that support the learner. From adaptive questionnaires to backend data gathering, customizable learning holds the promise of being better than the blanket approach that has been deployed for a long time. The diversity of learners using digitally mediated devices certainly presents challenges, but it also abounds with opportunity. User profiling is a promising approach to personalization of learning environments both big and small (Li & Change, 2005).

Personalization offers more than just "personalized" learning. Personalization offers the possibility of personalized selling. Advertisements could be sent to potential customers (learners) and target individuals to perhaps purchase or enroll in a course they may not have otherwise thought about. Unlike common commercial targeting, personalization is about enticement through a one-on-one relationship and marketing a desirable learning product to the individual with her name embedded right on the page. Education is a multi-trillion dollar endeavor that begins not long after birth and lasts a lifetime. Organization-wide services that integrate standards, customized applications and local needs with learner preferences and needs in mind are more likely to gain a better return on their investment.

Extracting the power of e-learning will depend on the ability of cyber educators to harvest the tremendous amounts of data available and turn it into knowledge. Many techniques and proposals look at the possibility of personalization and adaption of the learning environment to the individual. Data mining tools provide a key to uncovering knowledge through analysis of patterns, knowledge bases and research. By empowering the learner and the learning providers with knowledge that influences outcomes, it may be possible to impact how we learn, hence delivering on the promise of e-learning (Hanna, 2004).

CONCLUSION

Technology is here to stay. The advent of Web 2.0 has opened up the world of opportunity for friend and foe alike and has diminished the level of anonymity originally offered by technology. There is no question that threats to security on the Web are increasing. The forecasted rise in sophisticated malware will lead to more phishing, spoofing and botnets involving not just computers, but also mobile devices and VoIP lines. While software companies scramble to develop solutions and preventative applications, the first step in safeguarding against these attacks is awareness.

The use of social networking tools for work, play and educational purposes also continues to increase. The participatory Web has enabled the tracking, monitoring and storing of active as well as passive digital footprints of individuals, yet most Internet users do not necessarily manage their digital profile (Madden, Fox, Smith, & Vitak, 2007). As more social networking software finds its way into formal and informal educational practices, the stakes get higher. As membership in social networks continues to grow, so do the threats to security aimed at collecting personal and financial information.

Data mining and profiling both have their dark sides if used unscrupulously, but if the same invasive technologies are used to capture specific student data within e-learning platforms, then the potential benefits to learners and distance learning programs are beyond limits. True customization of learning is indeed possible and would move e-learning to the next level.

The future of e-learning will be affected by security trends in cyber space. Cyber educators must remain aware of potential threats to keep themselves and their students from harm. Radical changes are necessary to safeguard privacy and anonymity, but to also use available technologies to improve e-learning.

REFERENCES

Ahamad, M., Amster, D., Barrett, M., Cross, T., Heron, G., Jackson, D., et al. (2008, October). *Emerging cyber threats report for 2009.* Georgia Tech Information Security Center. Retrieved October 10, 2010, from http://www.gtisc.gatech.edu/pdf/CyberThreatsReport2009.pdf

Baggio, B., & Beldarrain, Y. (2009). *Anonymity in cyber education: Should you be concerned?* Presented at the eLearning Guild 2009 Annual Gathering, Preparing You for the Next Evolution of Learning, March 11-13, Orlando, Florida. Retrieved October 10, 2010, from http://www.elearningguild.com/showFile.cfm?id=3267

Bain, B. (2008, February). Cyber storm II stirring. *Federal Computing Week.* Retrieved January 27, 2009, from http://fcw.com/Articles/2008/02/29/Cyber-Storm-II-stirring.aspx

Basu, S. C. (2005). On computer crimes, online security and legal resources. *Journal of Information Privacy & Security, 1*(4), 1.

Bradner, S. (2007, November 13). Anonymity as a thing of the past. *The Insider Newsletter, Network World, 24*(45), 26. Retrieved October 18, 2010, from http://www.networkworld.com/columnists/2007/111307-bradner.html?fsrc=rss-columns

Chen, C. C., Shaw, R. S., & Yang, S. C. (2006). Mitigating information security risks by increasing user security awareness: A case study of an information security awareness system. *Information Technology, Learning and Performance Journal, 24*(1), 1–14.

Goldsborough, R. (2004). Don't get phished out of cyber space. *Black Issues in Higher Education, 21*(21), 37–40.

Gordon, L. A., Loeb, M. P., Lucyshyn, W., & Richardson, R. (2005). *FBI computer crime and security survey 2005.* Computer Security Institute. Retrieved July 10, 2010, from http://www.cpppe.umd.edu/Bookstore/Documents/2005CSISurvey.pdf

Grinberg, M. (2008). Hackers hijack MySpace music page. *Risk Management, 55*(1), 11.

Hanna, M. (2004). Data mining in the e-learning domain. *Campus-Wide Information Systems, 21*(1), 29–36. doi:10.1108/10650740410512301

Kirda, E., & Kruegel, C. (2006). Protecting users against phishing attacks. *The Computer Journal, 49*(5). doi:10.1093/comjnl/bxh169

Kruck, G., & Kruck, S. (2006). Spoofing: A look at an evolving threat. *Journal of Computer Information Systems, 47*(1), 95.

Li, X., & Chang, S. (2005). *A personalized e-learning system based on user profile constructed using information fusion.* Paper presented at the eleventh International Conference on Distributed Multimedia Systems (DMS'05), Banff, Canada, (pp. 109-114). Retrieved October 10, 2010, from http://www.cs.pitt.edu/~flying/File/DMS05-LC.pdf

Liu, W., Deng, X., Husang, G., & Fu, A. (2006). An antiphishing strategy based on visual similarity assessment. *IEEE Computer Society, 10*(2), 1089–1801.

Madden, M., Fox, S., Smith, A., & Vitak, J. (2007, December). *Digital footprints.* Washington, DC: Pew Internet & American Life Project, December 16, 2007. Retrieved October 10, 2010, from http://www.pewinternet.org/pdfs/PIP_Digital_Footprints.pdf

McMillan, R. (2008). Microsoft starts show Web attacks taking off. *PC World, 26*(7), 55.

Milbank, D. (2007, November 7). Searching for an explanation: No results found. *The Washington Post.* Washington, DC.

Nokelain, P. Tirri, H., Miettinen, M. Silander, T. & Kurhila, J. (2002). Optimizing and profiling users online with Bayesian probabilistic modeling. *Proceedings of the NL 2002 Conference*, Berlin, Germany.

O'Sullivan, O. (2003). Gone phishing. *American Bankers Association: ABA Journal, 95*(5), 7–8.

Orr, B. (2008). Security 2.0: Not just a new kettle of phish. *American Bankers Association: ABA Journal, 100*(2), 54.

Pahl, C. (2004). Data mining technology for the evolution of learning content interaction. *International Journal on E-Learning, 3*(4), 47–55.

Roha, R. (2000, August). Prying eyes. *Kiplinger's Personal Financial Magazine*, 119-124.

Si, H., & Chang-Tsun, L. (2006). Maintaining information security in e-government through steganology. In Anttiroiko, A. V., & Mälkiä, M. (Eds.), *Encyclopedia of digital government* (3rd ed., pp. 1180–1184). doi:10.4018/9781591407898.ch178

Sims, R. (1997). Interactivity: A forgotten art? *Computers in Human Behavior, 13*(2), 57–180. doi:10.1016/S0747-5632(97)00004-6

Spinello, R. A. (2003). *Cyberethics: Morality and law in cyberspace* (2nd ed.). Sudbury, MA: Jones & Bartlett.

Swaine, J. (2008, August). Georgia: Russia conducting cyber war. *Telegraph*. Retrieved October 10, 2010, from http://www.telegraph.co.uk/news/worldnews/europe/georgia/2539157/Georgia-Russia-conducting-cyber-war.html

Chapter 6
Emergence of a
New Identity

ABSTRACT

Online learning communities are created and sustained by a collective sense of we-ness. There are many factors however, that influence the development of the community. Cyber educators may use digitally mediated communications (DMC) that are synchronous or asynchronous to promote social presence and connectedness within the online environment. The identity of the self as well as the identity of the group must be developed in order for knowledge to be co-constructed by the group and for trust to be established. Often times, however, a new self identity emerges as part of the process.

OBJECTIVES

- Recognize the meaning of identity and social self.
- Distinguish between deindividuation, depersonalization and the SIDE model.
- Describe the impact of identity on virtual communities.

DOI: 10.4018/978-1-60960-543-8.ch006

INTRODUCTION

People choose to behave in certain ways depending on the given situation, but also depending on their sense of identity and their prior experiences. Some prefer higher levels of visibility and interaction. In the online learning environment, synchronous as well as asynchronous technologies offer different options for cyber educators who seek to promote social presence and create learning communities.

Research on the topic of identity and related phenomena has been limited to computer mediated communications (CMS). Current technology innovation however, makes it necessary to add new categories to the list of ways in which individuals communicate. Digitally mediated communications (DMC) as discussed in this chapter includes text messaging, instant messaging, emails, interactions using social software, Web 2.0 tools, and voice-to-voice interactions. Any of these can be accessed not just from a computer, but also from various mobile devices. This chapter discusses CMS and DMC as two separate definitions; however DMC is the proposed revised definition to be used in cyber education.

BACKGROUND

The concept of identity formation can be traced back to the psychosocial work of Erick Erikson, Sigmund Freud and others. Erickson (1968) coined the term "identity crisis" and explored how one's feelings about the self and about one's origins were reflected in character, goals and ability to handle life's changes. Although it has become a common term in our vocabulary, the actual meaning of identity is still difficult to pin point. Most definitions of identity though, will show that it is comprised of two parts: personal identity and social identity. Personal identity is a set of beliefs and rules for action that a person holds about him or herself. This term is also akin to individuation, which is a Jungian term that refers to the development of the self. Personal identity is sometimes used to describe the characteristics of the individual. Social identity on the other hand, is derived from membership in a group. Social identity attaches value and emotions to membership.

Social identity is formed when people see themselves as part of the group. In the context of digitally mediated communications, technology tools such as social software offers learners the opportunity to establish a social identity online (Meng, 2005). Below are few of the most commonly recognized definitions of identity as cited by Meng:

"...a subjective sense as well as an observable quality of personal sameness and continuity, paired with some belief in the sameness and continuity of some shared world image..." (Erikson, 1970).

"Social identity is the individual's knowledge that he belongs to certain social groups together with some emotional and value significance to him of this group membership." (Tajfel 1981, p. 255).

"Self is construed in 3 levels: individual level, interpersonal level and group level. Individual level identity is the "...differentiated and individuated self-concepts..." interpersonal self is "...the self-concept derived from connections and role relationships with significant others..." and collective self "...corresponds to the concept of social identity..."(Brewer and Gardner 1996. p. 84).

"The individual's self-appraisal of a variety of attributes along the dimensions of physical and cognitive abilities, personal traits and motives and the multiplicity of social roles including worker, family member and community citizen." (Whitbourne & Connolly, 1999. p.28).

"Identity refers to either (a) a social category, defined by membership rules and (alleged) characteristic attributes or expected behaviors or (b) socially distinguishing features

that a person takes a special pride in or views as unchangeable but socially consequential or (a) and (b) at once." (Fearon 1999, p.1.)

Cyber education re-defines and morphs the roles and identities traditionally associated with face-to-face education. Understanding the environment that virtual education provides is a prerequisite in understanding the roles of the participants. E-facilitators are faceless and play a different role than the traditional classroom instructor. E-facilitators who establish and share their identity with learners are likely to develop trusting relationships with their students. The "guide on the side" (Salmon, 2000, p.99) has a different identity that that of expert or *sage on the stage*. Digitally Mediated Communications (DMC) have opened the doors to a variety of techniques and pedagogy thus shifting the roles and identities of both the facilitator and the learner. The facilitator becomes the pillar which supports open-ended interactions and experiences to promote the co-construction of knowledge, while the learner becomes a teacher to his peers. The learning process is therefore reciprocal, with both, instructor and student learning from and with each other.

The literature suggests that virtual communities and social presence are key elements in online learning. Social presence theory has been discussed for nearly three decades yet it was within the last decade that social presence was identified as a crucial element in online learning. Online environments support a constructivist epistemology and recognize learning as a constructive practice. This approach to learning combines the mental processes of individuals with widely distributed social activities, thus fusing individual insights and developing group consensus for meaning. Through engagement and active learning, these environments support the construction of knowledge through interactive activities and experiences.

The social presence is reflected in relational aspects within the online community, including how the individuals perceive themselves and other group members. Social presence is the sense of awareness of the person with whom we are interacting. Social presence in online line learning is dynamic and the roles and functions of the learner and facilitator are related to a variety of factors including the context in which the communications occur. Because there is a focus on the tangibility and proximity of communications as well as the degree of affective connection (Kehrwald, 2008), it is important for cyber educators to promote social presence in a positive context. More on this topic is discussed in the *Looking Ahead* section of this chapter.

Participation in online communities reflects the theory of social psychology of participation. Outcomes of this online participation include the development of social identity, community interactions and a collective consciousness by contextualizing learner engagement in a technological context (Siddiquee & Kagan, 2006). Web 2.0 tools are examples of technological venues utilized to promote the development of social identity.

The recognition of identity within a virtual community leaves clues in regards to a person's identity. From the spammers to the trolls, there are all too many cases of identity deception in virtual communities. Misinformation can be very costly to the information-seeking learner. If members of a community perceive the presence of deceptive identities within the group, they may be discouraged from participating in community activities.

There are many reasons why a person may choose to present an alter ego in a virtual environment. The person may use an alter ego to gain access to a group, increase their sense of safety or simply play a trick. For most learners in a virtual community though, trust and reputation and inextricably mixed. Learners work to establish their own identities and to discern at face value another's credibility. After many dubious postings, others may start to wonder about a person's reputation or social awareness. Identity can also play a significant role in motivation and participation. Reputation is established by contributions that are admired or accepted by the group. Identity is also central for providing support and affiliation. Trust in the motivations and beliefs of other participants or the social identity of the group is essential to forming virtual communities (Donath, 1998).

Developing the Individual and Social Self

Learning communities are built around common information or the collective identity that is derived from *we-ness*. A community though is not fully realized without the concept of self. A person is influenced by belonging to the group and their individual identity is changed because of this sense of belonging. This supports the idea that one's true identity is stronger because of the bonds that unite us to others. Communities are therefore defined by how self is defined. Self-categorization theory asserts that the self-perception of an individual is interchangeable with that of other in-group members and that eventually the self will internalize and identify with the attributes of the group, hence self-stereotyping (Turner, et al., 1997). The quest to discover how the method of communication affects the community is paramount.

Does DMC therefore constrain our efforts to communicate or does it free us from the repression of traditional constraints? Technology supports pursuing individual interest and self-expression and through anonymity, it masks the typical cues that would otherwise give away a person's intent; as McLuhan (1964, p.32) put it: "The content of a medium is like the juicy piece of meat carried by the burglar to distract the watch dog of the mind." All of the users although interconnected by the computer network are still somewhat isolated by the same technology unless conscientious efforts are made to increase social presence and share information safely.

The self is not all that exists in the realm of DMC, the ego is also present. This ego can be seen on the walls of Facebook®, MySpace® and throughout Web 2.0 tools as people advertise themselves via photos, videos and status updates among others. Connectivity has the potential to redefine both personal and communal identity. The connection between the two may be so influential that the personal and the communal identity merge. There is a consistent oscillation between openness and closeness which requires the communicator to exert self control and be discriminating and selective about what information is revealed to others and what is revealed bout the self (Foster, 1996). The degree of social presence could potentially affect a person's online behavior, including how the ego chooses to display itself. Some online behaviors include social loafing, social facilitation and deindividuation.

Some see social loafing, social facilitation and deindividuation as behaviors that can be manipulated by changing personal or social identity, difficulty of a task or by changing the personal degree of presence within the group. Social loafing implies that people work less in a group because the ability to be identified is diminished and usually the method of evaluation of performance is based on a group goal. Regardless of task difficulty and expectations, social loafing eventually affects the learning community if left unchecked. Social facilitation on the other hand, implies that people working alone who are closely supervised, do better on simple tasks or when there is a sense of competition. Other important factors include individual effort and whether or not there are distractions.

Deindividuation, Depersonalization and SIDE Model

Deindividuation theory originally presented a different perspective of groups, asserting that people in groups produce more defiant and anti normative behaviors. This however, was refuted by Postmes and Spears (1998) whose meta-analysis demonstrated that members of a crowd did not lose their sense of self identity. Instead it was anonymity and a minimized awareness of self that increased sensitivity to group norms. Deindividuation can be effected by personal and group identity, group behaviors, accountability and evaluation as well as anonymity. There is evidence of an association perhaps between social loafing and social facilitation, but none with deindividuation (Guerin, 1999). Guerin suggested that there may be a link between social loafing and deindividuation but one of the challenges in measuring these phenomena is that they are all too often looked at in different frameworks. Very seldom are they discussed even in the same chapters of textbooks. More research is needed to look at these in terms of either social identity or social consequences frameworks because related to the same basic processes. The structuring of group interactions will then become clearer and social and cultural consequences be better understood.

Deindividuation is regarded as "a psychological state where inner restraints are lost when individuals are not seen or paid attention to as individuals" (Festinger et al., 1952, p. 382). Studies of deindividuation in Northern Ireland showed that disguised offenders were more likely to commit more violent acts, attack more people and inflict more injury that those that did not were masks. In this study, significant positive relationships emerged between the ability to be disguised and several measures of aggression (Silke, 2003). Another study that looked at deindividuation and impression management for adolescents' sexual self disclosure on the Internet looked at 1,347 adolescents. The results showed that the greater the anonymity the greater the intent for self disclosure (Chiou, 2006). Deindividuation is affected by the sense of anonymity, even in group settings. Anonymity can either support social or antisocial behavior depending on the norms of the group and the behaviors that the group accepts and maintains. Behavior outside of the group, however, still shows evidence that people may be more willing to engage in deviant behaviors because of the anonymity provided by the Internet (Demetriou & Silke, 2003).

The effects of belonging to a group as well as the psychological processes it may contribute to the loss of normal behavioral restraints. Some reasons can be anonymity, loss of the sense of responsibility, arousal of interest, lack of structure among other factors. Deindividuation is different than depersonalization, which is responsible for the process of changing individuals into members of a group. Their behavior however, is regulated according to the norms of the group. An individual may operate within in-group norms but is still responsible for his or her own behaviors. Depersonalization also causes the out-group members to have more stereotypical perceptions of the group, according to self-categorization theory (Turner et al., 1987).

The Social Identity Model of Deindividuation Effects (SIDE) developed by Reicher, Spears and Postmes (1995) speculates that there may be strategic reasons in some groups for individuals to act out. There may also be reasons why some group members to follow group norms in the presence of an audience. It may be to gain acceptance in the group or to avoid punishment. This may also facilitate acceptance by the group and allow individuals a chance to assert their identity. The effects of identity and seclusion on behaviors have interested researchers for many years and much research has been centered on the hypothesis that communications via computers are somehow changed because of anonymity. The SIDE model has been modified over the years to include in-group as well as out-of-group members. Research supports the hypothesis that language used with in-group member tends to be stereotypical of the group, which explains why expression of group norms and views is typically shared with in-group audiences (Douglas & McGarty, 2001).

The original SIDE model assumes that impressions formed reflect the underlying application of social categorization processes. The DMC members become part of a group and their group identity is stronger than their individual identity. The results can be strong and positive feelings toward another and an intensified sense of similar attributes unless the conditions accentuate a negative feeling. Social Information Processing (SIP) theory (Walther, 1992, 2002) challenged the SIDE perspective on another concern, the development of social impressions over time. SIP asserts that computer mediated communication delays the rate at which interpersonal relationships develop when compared to face-to-face interactions. Over time, impressions that might be very vague and incomplete at first develop because the communicators seek out information about each other. Walther proposes that it takes longer because individuals need time to develop their own ways of filtering and interpreting cues. Originally developed for computer mediated communications, SIP theory should be extended to include all forms of digitally mediated communications, including mobile technology and smart devices.

Walther (1996) produced the hyperpersonal model which combines the attributes of computer mediated communications (CMC) with an extended version of the SIDE model and the attributes of social information processing theory. He later modified the hyperpersonal model to include several processes including cognitive, behavioral and experimental that might produce interpersonal impressions via CMC that are more intense rather than less intense (Hancock & Dunham, 2001).

Hyperpersonal communications indicate that relationships develop over time and that there are no negative effects from CMC compared to traditional face-to-face communications. On one hand CMC has a liberating facility that frees the individual from social influences and inequalities. At best the interpretation of CMC is a bit paradoxical. The SIDE model can be seen as explaining behavior in terms of group norms. These norms emerge from interactions in specific contexts and can give way to group conformity. An example is the consumption of music online is both supportive of normative behavior in tribal communities and anti-normative behavior in file sharing and downloading (Penz, 2007). Research on the effects of perceived authority in instant messaging revealed that learners perceived informal authority when the instructor used instant messenger and a decreased presence of the instructor. Results on the perceived authority of the instructor were mixed and students in the study did not show an increase in self indulgent behavior (Tremayne, Chen, Figur & Huang, 2008). Future research should include all digitally mediated communications (DMC), not just those communications mediated via computers.

The social sciences are becoming increasingly interested in understanding the intricacies of all digitally mediated communications. Interaction in cyber education is paramount for learning. DMC supports users in constructing knowledge by keeping them interconnected for a purpose as they develop their own identity and group identity. In DMC the context serves as a link between cognition and interaction. Communication is not so much about the delivery of information but the activation of a relationship in which interrelated conditions support the construction of reality (Riva & Galimberti, 1998).

Positive relationships within the online learning environment help create the learning community. The sense of community is essential for collaborative groups to be effective in cyber education. Social software widely available today continues to influence the social structure of communities and the behaviors of its members.

BUILDING THE VIRTUAL COMMUNITY

A virtual community is group of people that communicate in cyberspace, develop relationships and create a social structure. A great deal of attention has been focused upon virtual communities in support of cyber education because a strong community base is associated with the success (Meng, 2005). Building online learning communities to promote the co-construction of knowledge is an important function of cyber education. Communication is enhanced through the use of social software, hence increasing social presence. Communication transactions however, are interpreted based on the receiver's framework of reference and previous experiences. Identity in cyberspace emerges as individuals behave in certain ways and leave a trail of cues.

The types of online communities created using technology tend to follow two models: consumption and community. The consumption model involves searching for ad-retrieving information, usually at a price and relies heavily on "anonymity, reliability, speed and visual appeal" (Adria, 2007, p.37). In this model communication is very limited because it comes at a price. In contrast, the community model is all about associations. These associations are usually not economic in nature but are in support of the group's norms, values and meaning. Social software is a combination of these two models. Because of the speed of delivery and the structure of interactive episodes, interactions are carried out instantly rather than evolving over time. Social software is used to build communities, however it is also used for consumption. YouTube®, Facebook® and even Second Life® can involve consumption, production and sales. Social software has enhanced what can be created online by supporting interaction-centric designs (Floyd, Jones, Rathi, & Twidale, 2007).

Social software are applications that encompass conversational interactions between people and groups, social feedback, social networks and a bottom-up approach that enables people to organize themselves based on their own preferences (Baggio, 2008). Social software is a technology that is delivered over the Internet and supports at least three of the forms of digitally mediated communications: one-to-one, one-to many or many-to-many. This communication allows for the formation of online communities and evolves based on the way the technologies are used by the individual or the group.

Social software has evolved to support people interacting both online and offline. Social software is termed "social" because of the connections it makes between people. The Internet is now seen as an important avenue for social and cultural exchange. By increasing the ability to communicate with neighbors and friends and communicate with people around the globe, social software is a culture of connectivity. Social software creates its own feedback loop by building tools that allow people to come together and exchange ideas and suggestions, new ideas for more collaboration, cooperation and conversation emerge. (Tepper, 2003). Social software facilitates the evolution of new interactions, understanding and learning by supporting individual and social interactions and experiences.

Facebook® stands as an example of social software with well over 500 million users as of this writing (Facebook, 2010). The mode of communication is like a linked personal bulletin board, where an individual posts photos, videos, messages and conversations that are then linked to other bulletin boards that already exist. These are not the first technologies to do this, but Facebook® and its facsimiles are a more visionary version of their predecessors. As far back as 1970, Marshall McLuhan, who birthed the concept of a "global village," identified the power of these technologies even before they ever existed. Theorists have since then argued that media can create social and psychological environments that support changes in the behaviors of individuals and/or groups. These changes are not directly caused by the technologies but are rather a function of the new environment because the new environment supports social preferences and norms that are unique to the community. The changes that occur could be at the individual level, but there are also intergenerational changes that take place within the community or social sphere (Adria, 2007).

Human perception is profoundly influenced by technologies and the speed of technological development (Virilio, 2006). Users of social software have unprecedented speed to conduct their interactions and transactions. Long gone are the days when people in different continents had to wait for a piece of mail to make the transatlantic journey before it reached its final destination. DMC makes communication instantaneous, hence adding the element of universality. Social software allows people to develop a relationship without the constraints of time and space.

Skype™ is an example of a technology tool that removes the constraints of time and space, as well as geographical boundaries. Within one application, participants can talk in real time, exchange files and even conference call regardless of geographical location. The ability to connect at the click of the mouse is liberating, it increases the perception of proximity which helps to build relationships. The effects of the physical distance are therefore greatly reduced thus increasing the perception of social presence and enhancing the interaction experience. Although participants see each other on the screen, the synchronicity of Skype™ adds a dimension of connectedness unparalleled to asynchronous technologies. Synchronicity allows the self to become more apparent through visual, auditory and non-verbal cues much like face-to-face interactions. The perceived identity eventually mirrors the revealed self, consequently augmenting the sense of *we-ness*.

The removal of the constraints of time, space and geographical boundaries, opens up the opportunity for the symbolic accumulation of resources. This means that having more connections on LinkedIn for instance, may be of more value socially, even if the people you are connected to may not be of interest to you. Social software however, also lends itself to the misrepresentation of self and propaganda. Propaganda defined not in the traditional sense but in the sense of identity. Propaganda in the online social context may be rational because it provides facts, but may be in an incomplete or misleading context (Adria, 2007).

The exact way that technology influences the formation of and sustainability of virtual communities is not clear. Some, like Facebook® and MySpace® are highly successful, while others wither away because of lack of participation. MSN.com reported that over 91.2% of the virtual communities established have less than 25 member and fewer than twenty posts (Meng, 2005, p.3). In the end, psychological and social approaches seem to be the only way to describe the sustainability of a social gathering. Virtual communities seem to be intricately linked to the concept of identity.

An important question is whether the ability to connect with growing numbers of likeminded people is indeed empowering. Communication and community are linked at the very root word and although related, both concepts are different. It is very possible to communicate without community but it is not possible to have a community without communication. People across the globe are connected via the Internet, which provides a technological structure for digitally mediated communications. Without the restrictions of time and space, the Internet provides a place for the exchange of individual's digital communications. It is this exchange and the establishment of a virtual "co-presence" that creates what is commonly called a virtual community (Foster, 1996, 24). Howard Rheingold called virtual communities places on the Net where community happens if enough people carry on enough conversation long enough. Even Rheingold added that to create community a certain amount of feeling and relationship must be established.

The virtual nature though of virtual communities makes it a difficult existence to characterize. Common elements attributed to community, such as commitment, have a different meaning in cyber space. Observers of DMC have wrestled with defining and categorizing what makes up a virtual community. Although approaches can differ greatly an interesting insight can be found in Anderson's (1991, p.6) *Imagined Communities:*

All communities larger than primordial villages of face-to-face contact (and perhaps even these) are imagines. Communities are to be distinguished, not by their falsity or genuineness, but by the style in which they are imagined...

The digital world with its inherent anonymity warrants emphasis on the imagination. Both public and private exchanges get mixed in online communication. The sense of virtual community is influenced by which is more dominant, the *I-ness* or the *we-ness*. A strong community binds people together who share some sense of commonality. Virtual communities are what emerges from a shared interest, involvement and respect or shared responsibility (Foster, 1996). Communities are built from sharing we-information. Social software has emerged as a mechanism to do more sharing and potentially build stronger communities.

Social Software is also providing new ways for students to communicate self-expression and collaboration. Social software has expanded the communications to include expressing opinions, collaborating with other learners and sharing knowledge (Bryant, 2006). Simple social software has expanded to include multidimensional networks, therefore broadening the reach of the virtual community. Social software networks have been developed to include multiple media, graphical systems and virtual environments. Dedicated networks that support the individual like Friendster, Ryze and LinkedIn have inspired industry giants like Google™ to create Orkut®, its own social software network (Baggio, 2008).

Social software, as any technology, offers benefits as well as well as drawbacks. On one hand anonymity offers protection, but on the other the technology makes almost everything traceable as long as there is someone willing to follow digital footprints and fingerprints (as discussed in Chapter 5). The next section explores the relationship between identity and anonymity in the online learning environment in terms of how people filter cues in digitally mediated communications and determine the other person's identity.

Are You Who You Say You Are?

Empowerment and identity are important aspects of the online learning community. A variety of factors such as ethnicity, socioeconomic status and gender may influence a person's sense of identity in both, face-to-face and online environments. The web can provide a safe haven for developing new identities and offer a place for alternative discourse and forums. It can provide a safe space where conventional stereo types are less evident. In online environments the importance of geography as an identifying factor is suddenly minimized and those who are marginalized have a place to redefine and express a new identity. The web empowers individuals because it provides ease of access to vast amounts of information therefore augmenting opportunities for learning and for communication.

Participation in a community can also be empowering if the conditions for participation within the community support personal or group improvement. The social process of learning characterized by dialogue and participation enables the individual to develop understanding (Siddiquee & Kagan, 2006). Identity is at the heart of the virtual community. Knowing the identity of those in the community that you are communicating with is essential to understanding and evaluating interactions. Members of a group are less likely to interact if they do not "know" the rest of the members. Identity online though can be ambiguous. In a virtual world many of the clues to identity and social presence that we take for granted are missing. Identity in virtual communities is established differently than in a face-to-face environment and the conditions that exist in a virtual world can lead to identity deception.

The online learning environment is void of three-dimensional attributes available to us in face-to-face interactions. The lack of non-verbal cues potentially increases the chances for identity deception or misunderstanding the other person's projected identity. Aware of this potential, the self may conveniently project a compelling vision that may be far from the true self.

Though the intricacies of the self may change over time, the body provides a stabilizing norm: "one body, one identity" (Donath, 1998, p.1). The virtual world is composed of information, not of visible non-verbal cues based on the physical realm; hence the clues that identify members of the virtual communities are greatly diffused and are subject to interpretation. Identities can be created online for different purposes; it depends on how the person wants to be perceived.

The assessment of the reliability of each identity depends on the perception of the receiver. In cyberspace, it is the person receiving the message who decides if the sender's identity is trustworthy and the content reliable. Identity is very important to trust and reliability of information in the virtual environment and in the creation of learning communities. Although there are fewer identity clues in the cyberspace, they do still exist.

The end receiver filters an array of cues using his own framework of reference that is based on his prior experiences and previous transactions with the sender. In the absence of non-verbal and typical contextual cues, the receiver may focus on different aspects of the message or make a decision based on the overall first impression. It is difficult to determine how individuals may go about gathering and filtering cues because the literature on the subject is scarce. The Hyperpersonal Model and Social Information Processing Model theories provide a point of reference yet more research is needed in this area.

Research in this domain has been limited to computer mediated communications (CMC) however; the rapid advancement of technology prompts the need to add new categories to the list of ways in which individuals communicate. Digitally mediated communications (DMC) include text messaging, instant messaging, emails and interactions using social software and Web 2.0 tools, voice-to-voice interactions using web-based applications. Any of these can be accessed not just from a computer, but also from various web-enabled mobile devices.

Technology has influenced the way people communicate. The advent of web-enabled mobile devices has increased the speed at which people access, process and respond to information received. This could potentially affect how they filter cues from the sender. Although Walther (1992, 2002) proposes that people build relationships over time in CMC because they need more time to filter cues, the opposite is evident in the way people use their web-enabled devices. Upon closer examination, it is apparent that people feel a sense of attachment to their web-enabled mobile device and find themselves checking emails and text messages often. Web-enabled mobile devices also allow the user to quickly log into their favorite social networking site or use instant messaging services. The receiver finds himself reading, processing and responding instantly. These processes are likely to occur at a slower pace with text-based CMC, but with instant access to the message, these processes happen simultaneously when using web-enabled mobile devices, unless the receiver makes the conscious decision to respond later.

The speed at which people communicate using such devices does not give them time to filter many cues but instead users may perceive the message as a package, including emoticons and initialisms such as LOL (laughing out loud) among others. The response is likely to come from the receiver's gut feeling or level of pre-established trust in the sender. One major factor that may influence why people readily reply to the sender from their mobile device is that they may already have a sense of established identity and social presence. Regardless of the speed to filter cues or process the "package," people who communicate digitally using web-enabled mobile devices are also actively building relationships through their interactions. There is an immediate need to explore this phenomenon as e-learning platforms move toward the development and implementation of mobile learning applications.

The types of cues filtered in digitally mediated communications may vary depending on the technology used to communicate. For example, in text messaging or instant messaging, the receiver may filter through more emoticons, initialisms or Internet slang to determine the temper and mood of the sender and the meaning of the content than in an email message where these types of cues are less prevalent. Internet slang is considered to include abbreviations, keyboard symbols and shortened words used to save time with keystrokes. Email messages on the other hand, lend themselves for more text-based cues based on the language used, tone and voice. Cues can also be gathered from the structure and organization of the written message. Because the receiver interprets communications via DMC, misinterpretations could lead to erroneous inferences and conclusions about the sender's intent or identity.

Impressions formed in digitally mediated communications (DMC) are different than those formed in a face-to-face encounter. As human being our interactions with other humans usually reflect some general impressions about the person's characteristics and disposition. When forming impression, we take into account not only information, but also autonomous cues such as physical appearance, personality traits and behaviors. We then sort through this input and develop impressions based on a series of strategies and heuristics. A unifying theme among much early research conducted around computer mediated communication (CMC), was that there was a reduction in many social and nonverbal clues and therefore depersonalized communications and a decreased awareness of others. An expanding body of research shows that behavior on the internet can be different than behavior in a three dimensional environment. These behaviors may be positive or negative for the online community. Social deviance in cyberspace for instance, is a real phenomenon as evidenced in the behavior of not only hackers and malware writers but also in more innocent behaviors such as posing to be someone else.

Maintaining social networks has been a primary function of online social networks and is a primary function of instant messaging. In a research study focusing on the use of instant messenger by young people, it was found that the use of instant messenger enhanced their perceived social status. Instant message technology makes it easy for users to pose as someone else. Accounts are easy to create with a bogus email address that could lead the end receiver to think the person is someone else. The poser might try to change their identity and be a different gender or a different person all together. Because the physical body is not present, instant messenger users have a greater opportunity to hide their own identities and monitor the interactions of others. Many young people take pleasure in occasionally posing and see it as play parody and performance (Lewis & Fabos, 2005).

Disinhibition Effect

Another effect of computer mediated communications is the disinhibition effect, which explains why some people act more openly and self disclose more easily online than in a face-to-face environment (Suler, 2004). According to Suler, this lack of inhibition leads to either benign disinhibition or toxic disinhibition. Benign disinhibition occurs when people share more openly therefore revealing feelings, thoughts and emotions or showing unusual acts of kindness or generosity. Conversely, toxic disinhibition are those behaviors that are rude, threatening or lead the participant to interface with elements of society, such as pornography, that they would not do in person. The distinction can be complex and ambiguous.

At least six factors can produce this disinhibition effect: dissociative anonymity, invisibility, asynchronicity, solipsistic introjection, dissociative imagination and the minimization of status and authority. Table 1. describes the factors and their definitions as proposed by Suler (2004). Anonymity is the most obvious of the disinhibition factors. As the definition implies, anonymity is the ability to remain nameless and faceless. People might even be able to convince themselves that online line behaviors are not really associated with them because they feel like they do not have to own their behaviors. Invisibility gives people the freedom to move around in stealth mode. The opportunity to move around invisibly amplifies the disinhibition effect. Although on Facebook many people many have exposed a great deal of personally identifying information, the ability to check on what someone has posted without their awareness is different than just enjoying anonymity.

Asynchronicity gives people the ability to suspend time and disrupts the continuous feedback loop of conversation. A continuous feedback loop gives people and behaviors reinforcement and can powerfully shape the flow of self disclosure and expression. Lack of real time gives the person the option to escape and return to the conversation at ones will. Solipsistic introjection allows the person to role

Table 1. Suler's disinhibition factors

Factors Contributing to Disinhibition	Definition
Dissociative Anonymity	Hiding all of some of their identity online
Invisibility	Ability to unseen or remain undetected while visiting a website or chat area
Asynchronicity	Not having to cope with another immediate reaction, not interacting in real time.
Solipsistic Introjection	Assigning a voice in one's psyche to text communication and the absence of face-to- face cues
Dissociative Imagination	Splitting or dissociating online fiction from offline reality. Creating and imagined world or reality from the online environment.
Minimization of Status and Authority	Lack of cues of authority, status and power online, establishment of a false peer relationship

Adapted from Suler (2004).

play in one's head the interactions with the other person online. The typed conversation becomes a voice in the head of the interpreter; the conversation can be experienced as talking to one's self which is safer than talking to others.

The dissociate imagination can magnify the disinheriting process by combining the ability to escape with the creation of imaginary characters according to Suler (2004). They create a make believe play world online and do not associate it with real life behaviors. Finally, the lack of authority and freedom to share equally which has been a part of the Internet since the beginning, takes away the threat of power and authority. It creates a sense of peer to peer communication and false equality. Although the temptation exists to read into to these factors the sense of true needs and emotion because of the release of inhibitions, this is not necessarily the case. Personal and cultural values along with the inter psyche contribute heavily to determining the true aspects of one's identity (Suler, 2004).

Disinhibition is just one of the effects of anonymity in online environments. More research is needed in this area to understand how it affects not just the average Internet user, but also online learners. The importance of building online learning communities that promote the co-construction of knowledge is paramount. Social software applications provide the infrastructure for connections and communications. How these communication transactions are interpreted depend largely on the receiver's framework of reference and previous experiences. It is not known exactly how receivers of digitally mediated communications sort and filter cues embedded in a transaction. Future research should also aim at understanding this phenomenon.

LOOKING AHEAD

Social presence and identity may be increased through intentional course design. Increased social presence through the use of technology provides a heightened sense of connectedness between members of the learning community. Today's online learners not only experience more and different ways of communicating, they are also exposed to different pedagogical practices that are influenced by the availability of digitally mediated communications and the instructor's online presence. Although some instructors are inclined to use the same old techniques that have worked in the classroom, generally methods that work in the classroom are not transferable to the online environment.

Now What?

1. Digital natives should be given the opportunity to express themselves and develop a healthy sense of identity through pedagogically appropriate uses of Web 2.0 tools and social software that may bring out the positive effects of disinhibition.
2. Cyber educators should make use of open-ended interactions and experiences to enhance the co-construction of knowledge.
3. Learners should be given, whenever possible, control over the degree of anonymity they can maintain.
4. Cyber educators should focus on ending each learner-instructor interaction it in a positive manner, therefore increasing social presence.

The instructor's self identity as a facilitator, leader or guide may influence the pedagogical approach he uses. Both the identity of the instructor and the learner can be altered in the online course room. The absence of visual clues in the learning environment is just one of the many challenges to implementing effective instructional practices. Distance and lack of interaction will lead learners to feel more isolated. Frustration from technical glitches and delayed feedback or lack of guidance can cause added uncertainty (Shieh, Gummer & Niess, 2008). Many instructors and learners have challenges with their new online identities, particularly when it comes to interacting online. They may have a low perception of social presence and this psychological distance can play roles that affect both the instructor and the learner's identity.

Although the arrival of Web 2.0 and the social software revolution has been well trumpeted, the revelation that it has changed teaching and learning online was only widely acknowledged until recently. What has emerged is a sophisticated learning community which stresses the importance of constructivism as a pedagogical approach. Didactical methods are giving way to what Daniel Pink termed "a whole new mind" both for the instructor and the learner (Conrad, 2008). Twenty first century e-learning discussions revolve around communities, reflection, socialization, knowledge transfer and social presence. Blogs, wikis and Personal Learning Environments (PLE's) are leading the way according to Conrad. The use of these Web 2.0 tools and social software may be used to bring out the benign effects of disinhibition. Disinhibition can be re-directed to influence the degree of self-disclosure among members of the group so they are comfortable sharing information and collaborating.

The renewed relevance of online interaction overrides old models and schemas of online learning. The four types of interactions; learner-instructor, learner-learner, learner-content and learner-interface (Moore, 1989; Hillman, Willis, & Gunawardena, 1994) seems ancient when learners have options like YouTube, Facebook and Hulu among other social networking technologies. Futurist and gamer extraordinaire Marc Prensky (2007) invokes visionary scenarios where students are passionate about learning, express themselves through creativity and belong to a community. He calls for a new community-centered learning culture that supports self expression and identity.

Today's learners respond to social and external stimuli and sometimes, given the chance they can and will create multiple online selves (Conrad, 2008). The Millennial generation wants to be heard and wants to be seen. These digital natives readily use social software such as YouTube, Facebook, MySpace and the like; they seek to assert themselves within the community yet maintain a sense of integration. Their sense of identity, according to Prensky (2007) is attached to their own personal goals; therefore importance is only given to information and resources that support those goals.

The new generation of online learners is likely to prefer higher levels of exposure and self-promotion. Already used to sharing photos, media, as well as opinions through Web 2.0 and social networking tools, they transfer these preferences to the online learning environment. The online instructor or e-facilitator is responsible engaging learners by providing open-ended interactions and experiences that promote the co-construction of knowledge. Ample opportunities should be given for learners to share insight yet maintain their preferred degree of anonymity. Those learners who would like more visibility should be able to experiment with the role of facilitator, thus removing the perception of positional authority from the instructor and reciprocating the learning process.

The increased tangibility and proximity of communications, as well as the degree of affective connection between the instructor and the learner is foundational in building a learning community. Instructors can increase their own social presence by revealing more about themselves and exposing the self. Students who feel they "know" their instructor at a more personal level are likely to feel more connected and may have an enhanced sense of trust. A positive relationship between instructor and learner can only be a win-win. Instructors may reveal more of themselves through their feedback, course emails, announcements, public or individual postings, among other methods. Every interaction with a learner should be seen as an opportunity to increase social presence and complete a positive transaction.

The development of the individual self as an online learner is influenced by what the learner experiences within the online learning environment. The instructor must understand that individual responses may reflect the influences of the group upon the individual. Participation in online communities reflects the theory of social psychology of participation. The collective consciousness of the group may become evident especially in collaborative projects. To minimize loafing however, e-facilitators may ask members to break down difficult tasks into more manageable tasks that can be assigned to individual group members. This would increase everyone's social presence and allow for up-close evaluation of each participant's contribution to the group.

It is also important that instructors allow individuals to assert their own identity within the group, especially if they are strategically complying with group norms just to be accepted or for fear of punishment or embarrassment. Increased interaction provides opportunities for learners to build relationships over time, as proposed by Walther (1992, 2002) therefore a sustained effort must be made to provide different types of interaction using various technological venues, including Web 2.0 tools to promote the development of social identity within the online learning community.

Cyber educators have different options for increasing social presence and enhancing both, the personal and social identity of online learners. Thoughtful course design should plan for increased interactions that take advantage of the benefits afforded by technology tools available today as well as those yet to be created. E-facilitators must understand their own roles and how the identity of learners is influenced by the community, therefore intentional steps must be taken to increase the sense of *we-ness* that enables learners to co-construct knowledge within the learning community. Cyber educators must find ways to empower students regardless of gender, ethnicity or background so they may feel safe in this learning community. An increased sense of belonging is likely to promote satisfaction and impact academic success.

One proposed method to increase a sense of belonging and increase the level of self-expression is to balance the use of asynchronous and synchronous communications in the online learning environment. Because the feedback loop in synchronous communications is continuous, it can be intentionally used to reinforce positive behaviors within the group and increase social presence as learners get to know one another. The instructor's authority should not be minimized, but instead it should be used to affirm and guide learners through their learning experience. Cyber educators are responsible for designing the structure around which the learning activities will take place.

Future approaches to building learning communities should include methods that enhance the learning experience, but also promote a healthy identity. Learners who have a positive self identity as well as a positive social identity are likely to have a beneficial influence on the learning community and an increased sense of connectedness.

CONCLUSION

A radical pedagogical shift is needed to move cyber education into the future. In moving forward, cyber educators and researchers must expand the definition of computer mediated communications (CMC) to digitally mediated communications (DMC) to include those communications using mobile technologies and smart devices, not just computers. Mobile learning, although not fully explored, is already a reality. Social software and Web 2.0 tools provide options for cyber educators who want to promote social presence within the virtual learning community. The roles of the educator and the learner continue to be redefined by the use of technology and it is more important than ever to be cognizant of how technology can be used to enhance the learning experience.

The cyber educator is a facilitator within the learning environment. He is the pillar which supports open-ended interactions and experiences designed to promote the co-construction of knowledge. The learner becomes a teacher to his peers and also to the instructor, therefore making the learning process reciprocal among members of the community. It is very important to promote relationship building among members of the community, as it will also promote social presence and group identity.

Through the use of social software and Web 2.0 tools cyber educators will be able to balance the use of synchronous and asynchronous interactions to enhance the learning experience and bring out the positive effects of disinhibition. Benign disinhibition will allow members of the community to communicate freely and self-disclose more openly, thus increase the opportunities for the co-construction of knowledge. Interaction is an influential force in the development of online learning communities. Course design must take into consideration the varying levels of preferred interaction and visibility. Students will have different preferences based on experience, gender, cultural or ethnic background. It is imperative that cyber educators remain sensitive to these needs.

Future research endeavors should extend Social Information Processing theory to include all forms of digitally mediated communications available today, including mobile technology and smart devices that connect people digitally. Special attention should be given to the ways in which people process, filter and interpret cues and how relationships are built using the different types of technologies. Synchronous technologies for example, may allow the self to become more visible and augment the sense of *we-ness* more so than when using asynchronous technologies.

Identity is a crucial component of trust and in the development of social presence. Increased social presence is in turn necessary for the creation and sustainability of a learning community. Through engagement and active learning, members of the community exchange information and co-construct new knowledge. Approaches to going forward must include methods to support learners in the creation of healthy personal and social identities that will positively influence the online learning community.

REFERENCES

Adria, M. (2007). The ontology of Facebook: Popular culture and Canadian identity. *Canadian Issues, 36.*

Anderson, B. (1991). *Imagined communities: A reflection on the origin and spread of nationalism.* London: Verso.

Baggio, B. (2008). *Integrating social software into blended-learning courses: A delphi study of instructional design processes.* Proquest Information Learning Company. (UMI No. 3297938).

Brewer, M. B., & Gardner, W. (1996). Who is this we? Levels of collective identity and self-representation. *Journal of Personality and Social Psychology, 71*(1), 83–93. doi:10.1037/0022-3514.71.1.83

Bryant, T. (2006). *Social software in academia.* Retrieved September 15, 2006, from http://www.educause.edu/apps/eq/eqm06/eqm062.asp

Chiou, W. (2006). Adolescents' sexual self-disclosure on the Internet: Deindividuation and impression management. *Adolescence, 41*(163), 547–561.

Conrad, D. (2008). Reflecting on strategies for a new learning culture: Can we do it? *Journal of Distance Education, 22*(3), 157–162.

Demetriou, C., & Silke, A. (2003). A criminological internet sting. *The British Journal of Criminology, 43*(1), 213–222. doi:10.1093/bjc/43.1.213

Donath, J. (1998). Identity and deception in the virtual community. In Kollack, P., & Smith, M. (Eds.), *Communities in cyberspace.* London: Routledge.

Douglas, K., & McGarty, C. (2001). Identifiability and self presentation: Computer-mediated communication and inter group interaction. *The British Journal of Social Psychology, 40*(1), 399–416. doi:10.1348/014466601164894

Erikson, E. H. (1968). *Identity: Youth and crisis.* New York: Norton.

Erikson, E. H. (1970). Reflections on the dissent of contemporary youth. *The International Journal of Psycho-Analysis, 51*, 11–22.

Facebook. (2010). *Statistics.* Retrieved October 20, 2010, from http://www.facebook.com/press/info.php?statistics

Fearon, J. (1999). *What's identity (as we now use the word)? Political Science Department.* Stanford, CA: Stanford University.

Festinger, L., Pepitone, A., & Newcomb, T. (1952). Some consequences of deindividualtion in a group. *Journal of Abnormal and Social Psychology, 47*, 382–389. doi:10.1037/h0057906

Foster, D. (1996). Community and identity in the electronic village. In Porter, D. (Ed.), *Internet culture* (pp. 23–37). New York: Routledge.

Guerin, B. (1999). Social behaviors as determined by different arrangements of social consequences: Social loafing, social facilitation, deindividuation and a modified social loafing. *Psychological Reports, 49*(1), 565–578.

Hancock, J., & Dunham, P. (2001). Impression formation in computer-mediated communication revisited. *Communication Research, 28*(3), 325–347. doi:10.1177/009365001028003004

Hillman, D. C. A., Willis, D. J., & Gunawardena, C. N. (1994). Learner-interface interaction in distance education: An extension of contemporary models and strategies for practitioners. *American Journal of Distance Education, 8*(2), 30–41. doi:10.1080/08923649409526853

Kehrwald, B. (2008). Understanding social presence in text-based online learning environments. *Distance Education, 29*(1), 89–106. doi:10.1080/01587910802004860

Lewis, C., & Fabos, B. (2005). Instant messaging, illiteracies and social identities. *Reading Research Quarterly, 40*(4), 470–501. doi:10.1598/RRQ.40.4.5

McLuhan, M. (1964). *Understanding media: The extensions of man* (1st ed.). New York: McGraw Hill.

Meng, M. (2005). IT design for sustaining virtual communities and identity based approach. Unpublished doctoral dissertation. Retrieved October 26, 2010, from http://drum.lib.umd.edu/bitstream/ 1903/2833/1/umi-umd-2830.pdf

Moore, M. G. (1989). Three types of interaction. *American Journal of Distance Education, 3,* 1–6. doi:10.1080/08923648909526659

Penz, E. (2007). Paradoxical effects of the Internet from a consumer behavior perspective. *Emerald Business, 3*(4), 364–380.

Postmes, T., & Spears, R. (1998). Deindividuation and anti-normative behavior: A meta-analysis. *Psychological Bulletin, 123,* 238–259. doi:10.1037/0033-2909.123.3.238

Prensky, M. (2007). New issues, new answers: Changing paradigms. *Educational Technology, 47*(4), 64.

Reicher, S., Spears, R., & Postmes, T. (1995). A social identity model of deindividuation phenomena. *European Review of Social Psychology, 6,* 161–198. doi:10.1080/14792779443000049

Riva, G., & Galimberti, C. (1998). Computer-mediated communications: Identity and social interaction in an electronic environment. *Genetic, Social, and General Psychology Monographs, 124*(1), 434–464.

Salmon, G. (2000). E-moderating: The key to teaching and learning online. *Journal of Distance Education, 15*(1), 99–101.

Shieh, R., Gummer, E., & Niess, M. (2008). *The quality of a Web-based course: Perspectives of the instructor and the students.* Boston: Springer.

Siddiquee, A., & Kagan, C. (2006). The Internet, empowerment and identity: An exploration of participation by refugee women in a community internet project (CIP) in the United Kingdom. *Journal of Community & Applied Social Psychology, 16*(3), 189–206. doi:10.1002/casp.855

Silke, A. (2003). Deindividuation, anonymity and violence: Findings from Northern Ireland. *The Journal of Social Psychology, 143*(4), 493–499. doi:10.1080/00224540309598458

Suler, J. (2004). The online disinhibition effect. *Cyberpsychology & Behavior, 7*(3), 321–326. doi:10.1089/1094931041291295

Tajfel, H. (1981). *Human groups and social categories.* Cambridge, MA: Cambridge University Press.

Tremayne, M., Chen, X., Figur, N., & Huang, S. (2008). Perceived authority and communication channel: Experiments with instant messaging. *Social Science Computer Review, 26*(2), 178–189. doi:10.1177/0894439307301895

Turner, J. C., Hogg, M. A., Oakes, P. J., Reicher, S. D., & Wetherell, M. (1987). *Rediscovering the social group: A self-categorization theory.* Oxford: Basil Blackwell.

Virilio, P. (2006). *Speed and politics.* Boston: MIT Press.

Walther, J. B. (1992). Interpersonal effects in computer-mediated interaction: A relational perspective. *Communication Research, 19,* 52–90. doi:10.1177/009365092019001003

Walther, J. B. (1996). Computer-mediated communication: Impersonal, interpersonal and hyperpersonal interaction. *Communication Research, 23,* 3–43. doi:10.1177/009365096023001001

Walther, J. B., & Parks, M. (2002). *Cues filtered out, cues filtered in. Handbook of Interpersonal Communication.* Thousand Oaks, CA: Sage Publications.

Whitbourne, S. K., & Connolly, L. A. (1999). The developing self in midlife. In Willis, S. L., & Reid, J. D. (Eds.), *Life in the middle: Psychological and social development in middle age* (pp. 25–45). San Diego, CA: Academic Press.

Chapter 7

Academic Integrity:
Ethics and Morality in the 21st Century

ABSTRACT

Academic dishonesty is rampant and statistically rising. Academic integrity in online learning programs is of global concern. Individuals who commit academic fraud rationalize their behavior in different ways. Educators must constantly be aware of what students are doing. In the past, too many educators remained oblivious to technologies that students were using to cheat or plagiarize. Promoting academic integrity requires faculty training and then the adherence of that faculty to certain principles and policies. Some schools and institutions have developed honor codes to deter cheating incidents. Most importantly, academic integrity requires a culture of trust and honesty, which can have the strongest influence over morality and ethical behaviors. Academic integrity begins with the individual educator and must permeate the entire organization.

OBJECTIVES

- Define academic integrity as it applies to digitally mediated communications.
- Discuss online learning and the challenges of plagiarism and cheating in the digital environment.

DOI: 10.4018/978-1-60960-543-8.ch007

- Discuss the roles that faculty and students play in establishing and adhering to academic quality assurance policies.
- Identify ways in which technologies may present challenges to academic integrity.
- Evaluate strategies for discouraging cheating and encouraging academic integrity when using digitally mediated communication.

INTRODUCTION

The ethics and morality of the 21st century learner is impacted by technology and the anonymity many tools provide. Academic integrity concerns have always existed since the early history of academia. Today's learners may have more tools at their fingertips to facilitate plagiarism and cheating, but educators are also using new strategies and software technology to deter such behaviors. While some academic integrity breaches occur due to lack of knowledge on the part of the student, others are intentional.

Cheating and plagiarism are pervasive issues in face-to-face as well as online learning environments. These concerns are heightened in a cyber environment and a global community that relies on Web-based courses and training to reach a large portion of its constituents. Many see this as an indication of the decline of morals and ethics among young people today who may blatantly or otherwise inadvertently "borrow" from the repertoire of information available on the Internet. Others believe that it is more difficult to cheat if an online course is well designed. The lines between right and wrong are often blurred, causing global concerns about academic fraud.

Academic integrity must be maintained in order for institutions to keep their credentials.

Institutions worldwide have established academic integrity policies with the aim of curtailing incidents. Some like Clemson University and Duke University have created special centers for academic integrity that educate and train students and faculty. Yet globalization and internalization of higher education trends according to a UNESCO report indicate that morality is uncertain not just with students, but also with many professors and even administrators accepting bribes for favoring students (Hallack & Poisson, 2005).

Although the tactics might be different, the possibilities for cheating and plagiarizing have not diminished over the years. Online resources may have replaced crib notes and answer services such as ChaCha™ may have replaced cheating from other students, even so it is clear that where there is a will there is too often a way. Instructors no longer have the luxury of analyzing handwriting or changes in ink color but they can find other strategies to detect fraud. It might appear that insuring integrity in online assessment is impossibility, but that is not exactly true. New approaches to ensuring honesty in assessment online have developed through trial and error. Changes in pedagogy and application of assessment techniques are not only creating viable assessments but in some cases more authentic and reliable than what had been traditionally done.

The stakes are high for institutions to curtail plagiarism and cheating, as well as other forms of academic integrity breaches such as bribery and falsification of data. This chapter will discuss mainly why students may cheat and what strategies can be set in motion by educators and administrators to minimize such behaviors. It is doubtful that any given institution will ever be able to eradicate all cheating and plagiarism, but the pursuit of academic integrity should never be relinquished.

BACKGROUND

Humans have dealt with deceit and fraud since the beginning of time. As cheating, plagiarism and other types of academic fraud evolve with technology and take on new forms, educators also develop new methods to counteract it. Researchers have discussed at length the issue of dishonesty in academia but not in the context of online learning (Lanier, 2006). A combination of research-based and practice-proven strategies will help ensure academic integrity in online learning programs worldwide.

The phenomenon of academic dishonesty has attracted much interest over the years. In a meta-analysis of 107 such studies, Whitley (1998) reported that as much as 70% of college students admitted cheating, mainly by plagiarizing. None of these studies however included online learning (Lanier, 2006) because these programs were in their infancy. Lanier's literature review also exposed gender as a predictor of cheating. The author consistently found that males are more likely to cheat than their female counterparts (Brown & Emmett 2001; McCabe & Bowers, 1994), as so are students who are not doing well academically (Brown & Emmett 2001; Finn & Frone, 2004). In a similar synthesis of ten years of research, McCabe, Treviño, and Butterfield (2001) expounded on the increasing prevalence of cheating in traditional academic settings. They found that the most influential factor in cheating was how a student perceived a peer's behavior. The authors asserted that honor code systems are an effective method of influencing "good" behavior and offered suggestions that will be reviewed in other sections of this chapter.

Research on the topic of cheating and plagiarism in online learning remains limited, but current findings mirror what is known about cheating in the traditional face-to-face setting. In a study of online college students versus those in a traditional classroom Lanier (2006) compared the number of self-reported cheaters and their perceptions. Overall, 58.9% of the students said they never cheated in their online courses, while 41.1% admitted to some form of cheating. Those taking the traditional courses, 78.7% self-reported they never cheated, versus 4.4% who said either sometimes or often cheated. Concurrent with previous studies of cheating in traditional school settings, Lanier found that males also were more likely to cheat than females, with 43.7% of male online students and 38.7% of females cheating. Furthermore, findings supported previous research stipulating that a low grade point average, being younger, or being single are all predictors of cheating.

Academic integrity in online learning programs is of global concern. Emerging trends in the last five years indicate that there is an global increase in academic corruption involving faculty and administrators who accept bribes for falsifying grades, obtaining fake certifications and degrees, granting access to exams, or giving special considerations to students (Hallack & Poisson, 2005). This increase in corruption is attributed to the sharp rise in the number of students who enroll in programs outside of their own country. For this reason, the European Consortium for Accreditation in higher education (ECA, 2010) was created in 2003. In the United States, the American Consortium of Universities (ACU, 2010) serves a more limited function because it involves a small number of member institutions that focus on international programs and the transfer of international students.

While in Europe the goal is to centralize accreditation in order to standardize the accreditation process and the degrees awarded. The United States follows a more autonomous approach by allowing each state to regulate its university system and each university to accept transfer credits or not. In general, there is no centralized control system in the United States because there is no Federal Ministry of Education (U.S. Department of Education, 2010). Instead, regional boards accredit higher education institutions. The result is many types of educational programs that vary in quality and philosophical and ontological approach. To say one system is more efficient than the other in addressing academic fraud and dishonesty issues is debatable. In either system the professionalism and honesty of faculty and administration is key to ensuring academic integrity.

Other types of online misbehaviors of students have also captured the attention of researchers. For example, in a study of undergraduate students in the United Kingdom, Selwyn (2008) found that an overwhelming 93.9% of students self-reported online misbehavior that included at least one type such as plagiarism, misrepresentation of self, unauthorized access to someone else's account, unauthorized downloading of music or films, or using pornography. Just as demonstrated in a myriad of other investigations, Selwyn's study also points to gender as a contributing factor to all types of online misbehaviors with the exception of unauthorized access to some else's account, where there was a small difference showing that 5% more females than males participated in this activity. The implications to online learning are tremendous, as anonymity inherent in technology tools makes it imperative that cyber educators are prepared not only to identify and counteract online misbehavior, but prevent it altogether.

More research needs to be conducted to understand the phenomena of academic dishonesty in online learning programs. Some researchers propose that online learners may actually cheat less than their face-to-face counter parts because there are just as many ways to see who is cheating as there are ways to cheat (Kaczmarczyk, 2001; Rowe, 2004) while others such as Lanier (2006) have found opposite results. The limited knowledge renders any conclusion too premature at this time. According to Rowe (2004), earlier studies of online cheating mainly involved smarter and more professional students who were attracted to technology and would not typically cheat, however, as online learning becomes more popular and attracts different types of students, the author posits that the issue of academic dishonesty will be more severe and challenging.

Trusting in the results of assessments is critical to determining the success or failure of a learning program. Staggering statistics give rise to the concern of the validity and reliability of testing. An increase of cheating with age until at least the age of 25 adds additional concern about adult learners cheating (Rowe, 2004). This could potentially make online learning even more susceptible to cheating because the emotional, verbal and physical cues of information following from learner to assessor are obscured by the anonymity of digitally mediated communications. Since the learner cannot be seen and the assessment is not always constrained by time, critics would argue that it is easier to cheat online. The temptation to cheat may also accelerated if learners are more technologically savvy than their instructors who for reasons of money, time or mere convenience, may be willing to turn a blind eye to the problem. This however would certainly place the program at risk; risk administrators are likely not to allow for obvious reasons. Teacher training is therefore paramount, so they are always prepared to recognize and address academic integrity issues.

Cyber educators often discuss the ease of cheating, yet opinions frequently diverge. Proponents of using course design as a means to prevent and discourage academic dishonesty insist that it is more difficult to cheat online. If the course activities, discussions, and assessments are all inter-connected, it becomes harder for surrogate students to complete part or all of the course, yet easier for instructors to identify cheating because the related assignments provide insight into the student's writing style as well as their capabilities (Heberling, 2002). The fact that many academic institutions use anti-plagiarism software may also serve as a deterrent. In an exploratory study of the attitudes of students toward using Turnitin it was found that only those students who had apprehension on their ability to cite and quote properly had a negative attitude toward the software (Dahl, 2007). All other users remained positive.

Despite the positive attitudes toward using plagiarism detection software as cited by Dahl (2007), earlier results of surveys on beliefs and attitudes toward plagiarism are still cause for concern. In a survey of beliefs and attitudes toward Internet plagiarism, Szabo and Underwood (2004) discovered that 50% of the 291 science students surveyed at a large university in the United Kingdom openly admitted they accepted such dishonest behaviors. The researchers also found that just as predicted based on previous investigations on the topic of academic dishonesty, males and younger students had more liberal views than female students or those who where in their third year of study.

To the dismay of many, the attitudes toward academic dishonesty continue to worsen even among high schoolers. The decline in academic morality among youth is well documented (Bushweller, 1999; McCabe & Treviño, 1996; McCabe, Treviño, & Butterfield, 2001). Results from a longitudinal survey of *Who's Who Among American High School Students* indicated that 80% of respondents in 1998 confessed to cheating on an exam; ten points higher than results from 15 years earlier (Bushweller, 1999). Cheating however, has certainly become more high tech since then, especially as morality seems to be on the decline as captured in recent youth surveys.

Every two years the Josephson Institute for Youth Ethics, based in Los Angeles, conducts a comprehensive survey of ethics and morality among youth. The 2008 version, *Report Card on the Ethics of American Youth* (Josephson Institute of Ethics, 2009), surveyed 29,760 students from 100 random private and public high schools across the nation. To everyone's concern, the findings showed that cheating on exams among high school students had risen 4% in just two years, from 60% in 2006 to 64% in 2008. Thirty-six percent also admitted to using the Internet to plagiarize, an increase from 33% in 2006. Dishonesty involving stealing and lying was also as a major concern, with 30% of students admitting they had stolen something from a store in the past year, and 83% having lied to a parent about something important. Furthermore, an overwhelming 93% of students still concluded that they were content with their personal ethics. The original press release issued by the Josephson Institute pointed out clearly that the lack of ethics is far worse than even the survey results showed, because 26% of students had acknowledged that they had lied in at least two survey questions.

If the aforementioned survey is alarming, more so are the 2009 results of the survey titled *A Study of Values and Behavior Concerning Integrity: The Impact of Age, Cynicism and High School Character* also by the Josephson Institute for Youth Ethics. In this large-scale survey of almost 7,000 adults, researchers found a definite correlation between the behaviors and attitudes of "cynics" as called in the report, when they were of high school age, and their attitudes and behaviors later on in adulthood. According to the results, cheating and lying as a youth are predictors of the very same unethical behaviors, especially when those behaviors are seen as "necessary" to succeed in life. The unethical behaviors of these individuals were displayed in both, their private and professional lives.

The impact of dishonesty therefore impacts every facet of life. The economic future relies on honest decision-makers and leaders. Efforts on the part of educators to teach ethics, citizenship, and morality are wasted if young children do not experience it also at home. As discussed before, often times youth are more savvy with technology than their parents or other adults around them. Common Sense Media (2009), a non-for-profit organization dedicated to educating families about the impact of media in their lives, conducts regular surveys and polls on a wide range of technology topics and uses the information to develop educational resources for teachers and parents. In their 2009 poll of cell phone use and cheating in the classroom, it was discovered that 35% of middle and high school students admitted to using a cell phone to cheat in class, while 52% admitted to using the Internet to cheat or plagiarize.

Furthermore, 41% of teenagers reported that using a cell phone to store cheat notes for a test was unethical, while 23% thought this act did not constitute cheating. Others (20%) did not see anything wrong with using text messaging to contact friends and get help on an exam and did not even believe that plagiarism was a form of cheating. Perhaps more dumbfounding is the fact that parents seem to be oblivious to the notion that their children cheat, 76% of them reported they were aware of unethical behavior involving cell phones in school but only a mere 3% of parents acknowledged that their own child would be using a cell phone to cheat. Teachers do not even see when students are using their cell phones, otherwise students would not be sending an average of 440 text messages per week, or about 110 text messages during class time, as reported by Common Sense Media. The findings make it urgent for educators, parents and the community to join forces and address these issues in an effort to mend the moral fibers of our society for generations to come. Stakeholders in morality; parents, students, educators, and the community, each have a key role to play in the quest toward renewed academic and moral integrity.

The stakes are high for cyber educators. Ethics and morality in online learning are directly influenced by what is happening in the physical world and in the every day lives of learners. The attitude of each individual toward integrity versus dishonesty can in turn be somewhat shaped by their life experiences. Cyber educators cannot erase those past experiences but can provide new, enriching opportunities that will help learners become confident with their new knowledge and minimize the potential for academic dishonesty. Cyber educators must also refrain from using a policing approach and should instead use an approach using multiple strategies to ensure academic integrity. The section below discusses potential challenges as well as strategies for quality assurance in online learning environments.

CHALLENGES AND STRATEGIES FOR QUALITY ASSURANCE

Rampant academic dishonesty is everyone's concern. The first step toward quality assurance is to understand why and what would cause a person to act dishonestly. Only then can strategies be employed to curtail such behaviors. Cheating and plagiarism occur across all sectors of the population. Strategies must therefore be multi-dimensional, addressing the human need to succeed. Cyber educators cannot rely any one single strategy, but rather should employ a multi-strategy approach. It is the combination of research-proven and practice-proven strategies that is likely to make a greater impact.

"The Devil Made Me Do It" and Other Lame Excuses

There are many possible reasons as to why someone would commit academic fraud. Some are indicative of laziness, poor time management, fear of failure; others perhaps are truly defiant behaviors. Yet many other reasons why students cheat or plagiarize provide a window into how they perceive their educational experience, thus these reasons serve as a tool to evaluate instruction.

As demonstrated in surveys cited in the previous section, those committing academic integrity infractions rarely believe they are doing anything wrong, and in many cases they may show no shame or regret of their actions. Those are the most difficult situations to deal with, because morality is not something that can be taught in one course, instead it develops over an individual's lifetime. The reasons for cheating and plagiarizing are various.

In the case of high schoolers, educators realize that students are constantly under pressure to do more. Pressure from parents is disguised behind sports, extra-curricular activities, and expectations to achieve. High schoolers are often expected to get a part time job to help pay for their car, gas money, and insurance. Very few have parents who expect them to only go to school and study. Competition to get in a good college program also raises their anxiety level, even for honor students. Cheating then becomes a risky but easy proposition if it can lead to a higher GPA, or passing the last class for graduation.

In an Associated Press (2008) article, which discussed the results of the Josephson Institute of Youth Ethics (2009) survey *Report Card on the Ethics of American Youth*, several administrators interviewed agreed that educators are partly responsible for cheating incidents. They concurred that not only are students being bombarded with activities and expectations, but that schools currently emphasize getting the correct answer instead of focusing on the learning process. The result is a generation that uses high tech tricks to gain access to the answers they need, because in their mind, the end justifies the means.

College students cheat on exams and participate in unauthorized collaboration for the very same reasons as high school students. A combination of being too busy and having poor time management skills could cause someone to be unprepared thus cheat on an exam. Furthermore, college level students or those adults participating in a training program may be under pressure to complete their program quickly so they can care for a family or get the job advancement opportunity they seek. Others cannot afford high tuition and failing a course is not an option. Regardless of the "reason," academic dishonesty is always wrong.

Beyond the "devil made me do it" excuses there are always individuals who exhibit dubious behaviors. Their limited or selective morality may lead them to defy authority and social norms. If it is easy to cheat, then these individuals seize the moment because they can, and because no one is looking. Others may be tempted to cheat or plagiarize because they know other classmates are doing it, thus academic dishonesty becomes accepted among peers. One particularly comical type of cheating is the collaboration excuse. In the old days the dog ate the homework or a smarter sister wrote the essay, but today students are reaching out to more than just one source. Unauthorized collaboration on quizzes, projects, and other forms of assessments is commonplace in face-to-face as well as online courses. If students know that academic dishonesty is easy to perpetrate without getting caught, the problem will not only persist, but it will increase as evidenced in the literature.

It has also been discussed in the literature that too many instructors are not identifying academic dishonesty, and those who notice do not necessarily report what they find (Kaczmarczyk, 2001; McCabe & Pavela, 2004). In a survey of over 2,5000 faculty members, less than two thirds added information on academic integrity in their syllabi, and 44% said they had turned a blind eye to "at least one suspected cheating incident" (McCabe & Pavela, p. 13). Likewise, teachers of middle and high school students do not notice that students are using their cell phones to text questions and answers during exams (Common Sense Media, 2009). Furthermore, students do no have a reason to stop cheating if parents and educators are not even noticing there is a problem. Overwhelmingly, the data collected over the years suggests that parents and educators must "talk the talk" but also "walk the walk." Even when policies and procedures are in place to deter infractions, parents and educators must be willing to follow up on the incidents and enforce strict but fair consequences.

Plagiarism is also rampant among middle schoolers, high schoolers, as well as adult learners. Reasons for plagiarizing range from the innocent to once again, the deliberate. Widely recognized reasons for not crediting sources include lack of note taking skills, not knowing how to cite properly, misunderstanding the difference between paraphrasing and plagiarism, misunderstanding the difference between intellectual property and public domain information, or simply choosing to plagiarize for the same reasons others would cheat on a test. If students do not have proper note taking skills, they are more likely to forget to put quotation marks around other people's words and accidentally include them as their own.

Citing properly is a very common problem, especially with undergraduates who were never taught how to do so in high school. Moreover, they may be confused about using the different citation formats available. Others may prefer to ignore proper citations because it takes time to check references and cite properly. Paraphrasing is another common mishap. If the student does understand the technical terminology used in a source, and fails to cite the source correctly while trying to paraphrase, they may inadvertently plagiarize (Roig, 1999; Jackson, 2006) because they are not able to synthesize the information and form their own conclusions. The student may also accidentally plagiarize if they do not know a particular source is not public domain and is protected by intellectual property laws.

Most cyber educators agree that the anonymity provided by modern technology tools plays a role in cheating and plagiarism. No longer is it necessary to pass cheat notes in class, lean over to look at a classmate's exam, or write notes on the wrist. It is not even necessary to steal the test from the teacher's desk. Instead, postmodern cheaters can send a quick text message to question and answer sites such as ChaCha. com. ChaCha™ was launched in 2008 and already counts with 10 million "unique US visitors" each month, surpassing Google™ as the top SMS search service in the United States according to Nielsen Mobile market reports (ChaCha, 2010). In a 2008 interview, ChaCha's officials denied that using ChaCha's search services for cheating was a widespread problem, and insisted that the service was not created to help with homework but instead as a resource for people needing information (Snyder, 2008).

Two years later, ChaCha™ continues to grow rapidly, and it is well known among students as a place for quick answers. Educators on the other hand, are generally unaware. ChaCha™ may be the leading SMS search service, but Google™ provides a similar SMS service, followed by other Web-based answer services such as MrWhy. com (2010). It can only be projected that such sites will continue to proliferate and be used by learners.

I Spy a Cheater

The problems of academic dishonesty are compounded when instructors do not notice what is happening, as stated earlier. This is true of face-to-face as well as online learning environments. It is a concern that permeates all levels of education. Detecting academic fraud must be a top priority, as it cannot be deterred if educators do not know what to look for, or how to look for it. The first rule of thumb is to always expect the unexpected. Learners of all ages use ingenious methods to commit academic fraud.

To detect plagiarism, the first line of defense for educators should always be running the paper through plagiarism detection software such as Turnitin® or SafeAssign™. There is also WriteCheck™, a more cost effective solution created by Turnitin® that can be used by smaller schools or even students. To do this, they will need an electronic copy of the paper, not the hard copy. Educators must make it a habit to look at reports that raise a red flag and use their judgment in determining what is acceptable in terms of citations and what constitutes plagiarism.

Anti-plagiarism software relies on the Overall Similarity index to calculate what percentage of the text in the paper is a match to Web sources and publications or in some cases, to sources within the institution's database. For example, if University A uses Turnitin® services, administrators are able to compile a database of all the papers submitted to the Turnitin® system by their users. This is quite helpful because each submission can then be checked against the Web sources and publications, but also against the institution's database. Any match will be highlighted in the report, even if the student cited properly.

Often times catching plagiarized work is simple, especially if the cheater is in-experienced. More naïve students may copy from a Web source and directly paste on their paper and forget to change the font style, color, or size. Others may have a non-formatted layout or embedded hyperlinks in the text they copied. Hints can also be derived from the reference list. For example, the paper may be missing citations for quotations used, or maybe the sources are old.

There are many details that provide the instructor with information about the real author of the paper. Instructors should pay attention to the writing style of students, their usual tone of voice, vocabulary level, their grammar skills, and ability to summarize and synthesize the material to arrive at conclusions. Work that is written for paper mills or plagiarized from either one or multiple sources will be easier to detect if instructors already have an understanding of the individual student's abilities.

Countless Websites offer desperate individuals help on writing essays, term papers, research papers, and even thesis papers for a fee. The so called "paper mills" generally publish a disclaimer on their Websites saying that their papers are to be used as models for those who need a paper. Sites such as essaysonline.com (2010), claim their papers will be custom written to the student's requirements and will be 100% original. Other sites such as scribd.com (2010) make use of social networking to collect works from its members. More of a social publishing service, scribd.com encourages members to share their work with global readers. All of the files can be conveniently downloaded to a mobile device or simply downloaded to a computer.

The idea of "sharing" information appeals to Millenials who are more apt to use social networking tools and have a broader interpretation of academic integrity. The potential for plagiarism is further increased by sites such as freeonlineresearchpapers.

com (2010), which lures members in by promising to provide them with access to the site's database if they in turn share one of their own papers.

Cheating on quizzes and exams during a face-to-face class should be obvious to the instructor if students are using a cell phone or other mobile device. In the old days the instructor may have paced back and forth around rows of desks, but in overcrowded classrooms or auditorium-style rooms the instructor is one person against many. Devious cheating behaviors often go unnoticed because the instructor simply has one set of eyes. Detection of face-to-face cheating can be enhanced if more proctors are made available for the examination, and by using practice-proven strategies such as multiple forms of the exam, and asking higher order questions that require the student to demonstrate a deeper understanding of the subject.

Likewise, assessment in online learning requires careful design but also careful observation on the part of the instructor. Red flags in the online environment are raised if a student reports repeated computer crashes and asks for the test to be reset, or if the student cannot verbalize concepts from the exam during class discussions. More on assessing the iGeneration, those who were born digital natives, is discussed in the *Looking Ahead* section of this chapter. That section will explore strategies for proactively deterring academic dishonesty. But first, educators must learn from past mistakes that have influenced the increase in academic dishonesty.

In the past, much effort was given to policing academic integrity, instead of teaching students how to make use of resources, or even establish a clear definition of academic integrity. Academic integrity policies might be developed jointly between instructor and learner where a clear definition of what is not acceptable is established. Often collaboration on out of class assignments and plagiarism are not clearly understood. Collaborating on the definition and jointly creating guidelines for falsifying information or fabricating references establish a mutual contract.

These policies should be publicized on the web, in handbooks, help areas, and course materials. Faculty should also rely on a variety of evaluation methods and give plenty of opportunity for learner-to-learner and faculty to learner interactions. Our ability to use technology to aid in the assessment process, like giving pop quizzes in chat rooms and searching databases for similar papers might just lead to better assessment standards.

Strategies like smaller, more frequent assignments make it very difficult for the learner to ascertain assistance through out the course, and assignments and require cooperation and collaboration among students may also make it more difficult to cheat. Assessment should take into account long-term transfer. A big problem of assessment in distance learning is it is very difficult to assure that all learns take the assessment at the same time. Assessment software provide random selection possibilities, question pools and other alternatives in a effort to increase reliability. Technologies are also becoming available to assist the cheaters. Products like "sniffers" that decipher message packets make it easy for those that want to cheat (Rowe, 2004; McClure, Scambray, & Kurtz, 2001). Computer forensic tools also aide in this process and learners who have intent can find ways, without being computer geniuses, to get information that was supposedly deleted or downloaded.

Then there is the problem that all learners do not take the quiz or test at the same time so that answers can be sent via text or IM to other learners. Many online assessments allow the learner to take it multiple times, which just compounds the issue. Probably the most serious threat to online trust is the issue of anonymity in learner identity. Even in a synchronous environment with a web cam there is no sure fire method for determining if the person on the other end is really who they say they are. This is more less the reasoning behind using honor codes. Honor codes place the responsibility of academic integrity in the hands of the students.

Honor codes give the learner the opportunity to rise to the occasion and be proud of their accomplishments without having to resort to cheating. Students also have the opportunity to self-police. With honor codes, students sign a pledge of integrity. Likewise, faculty should also pledge to abide by the honor codes. Traditional honor codes are rooted in the philosophy that stakeholders will co-create a culture of mutual respect, responsibility, integrity, and trust (Dodd, 2010). Educators in the United States have used honor codes for over 100 years, yet the majority of US institutions of higher education do not have honor codes as a method of discouraging academic dishonesty today (McCabe, Treviño, & Butterfield, 2001). After analyzing a decade of research, McCabe, Treviño, and Butterfield concluded that the use of honor codes directly caused lower levels of cheating. Most importantly, they concluded that it is the culture of trust and honesty that has a stronger influence and not the mere fact of having honor codes.

A strong academic integrity policy would benefit from using elements of traditional honor codes, or modified honor codes. Timothy Dodd (2010), Executive Director of the Center for Academic Integrity at Clemson University, suggests that the ideal code or policy should capture the consensus of institutional values, be enforceable, culturally appropriate, and allow the learners to educate peers. Dodd also insists on using fair and consistent due process, and an efficient record keeping system that combines academic as well as non-academic infractions in one single file for disciplinary purposes.

Promoting academic integrity requires that faculty abide by certain principles and policies. Training is paramount; faculty cannot enforce policies they do not themselves understand. McCabe and Pavela (2004, p.10-15) propose ten basic principles of academic integrity to empower faculty to foster academic integrity:

1. Recognize and affirm academic integrity as a core institutional value.
2. Foster a lifelong commitment to learning.

3.   Affirm the role of the teacher as guide and mentor.
4.   Help students understand the potential of the Internet and how that potential can be lost if resources are used for fraud, theft, and deception.
5.   Encourage student responsibility for academic integrity.
6.   Clarify expectations for students.
7.   Develop fair and creative forms of assessment.
8.   Reduce opportunities to engage in academic dishonesty.
9.   Respond to academic dishonesty when it occurs.
10. Help define and support campus-wide academic integrity standards.

Administrators must also support the focus on faculty principles and proper training. A top down approach is necessary to ensure that administrators are creating such training programs and collecting data about reported incidents. Milliron and Sandoe (2008) adamantly call out for more enforcement on the part of administrators who may acknowledge there is a cheating problem but choose to ignore it. Milliron and Sandoe add their voices to the concerns of other researchers whom they identified in their exposé: (1) administrators are motivated to ignore academic fraud because announcing any statistics will impact funding for their programs (Callahan, 2007); (2) faculty prefer not to spend time addressing or promoting academic integrity because it is not rewarded by administration or contribute to their career goals (Sperber, 2005); (3) many campuses have a very poorly written academic integrity policy that is haphazardly enforced (Bok, 2006).

Individuals who commit academic fraud may rationalize their behavior in different ways. Whether it is to get ahead quickly, or because they are under pressure to succeed, every reason is an unethical excuse. Countless methods of cheating and plagiarizing can be counteracted with different strategies that help discourage and detect infractions. Educators however, must be properly trained, and count with the support of administrators.

LOOKING AHEAD

Educators must constantly be aware of what students are doing. In the past too many educators remained oblivious to technology tools that students were using to cheat or plagiarize. Many others lacked training on the subject. Sadly, some are still unprepared and untrained, thus contributing to more academic fraud. It is unacceptable for any educator to be unaware of academic integrity policies for the institution, or to not promote academic integrity within their own course. Furthermore, those who notice something is wrong but do not anything about it are themselves committing academic fraud. Academic integrity begins with the individual educator and must permeate the entire organization.

Now What?

1. Institutions should strive to eliminate cheating and plagiarism, and pursue of academic integrity.
2. All the stakeholders in morality: parents, students, educators, and the community, must each take and active role in the quest toward renewed academic and moral integrity.
3. Cyber educators should employ a multi-strategy approach using research-proven and practice-proven strategies that is likely to make a greater impact.
4. Educators must take the initiative to once and for all address student identity verification.
5. Assessment should be planned and designed with utmost care, using authentic and appropriate approaches that math the learning objectives and environment.

Assessing the iGeneration

Strategies for discouraging cheating and plagiarism are as varied as the reasons why learners commit such infractions. First and foremost, the organization must have set guidelines, definitions, and consequences for academic integrity and must advertise them to students, not as a "we are watching" warning, but as part of academic and ethical expectations. It is the role of the educational institution and of individual educators to model those expectations and to provide students with the resources necessary to successfully complete their program.

Many institutions have a resource library and tutorials for students to learn about academic integrity, and how to cite properly. Others have writing labs with real tutors. Every instructor must include academic integrity policies as part of their syllabi, in cooperation with the school, to project a unified front to students. It is only when students suspect that no one is watching, or that only some educators are watching, that they may be willing to blatantly cheat and tell others about their success not getting caught.

Institutions must also have set consequences for those who are caught, and should make students aware through student groups, student newspapers, and implicit as well as explicit methods, that administrators and instructors know about new cheating methods and tools used by students. The unified message must be sent across the virtual or physical campus that academic dishonesty will not be tolerated. If academic integrity is handled as a public relations campaign, students are made aware of the school's seriousness in deterring fraud. Those thinking of cheating or purposefully plagiarizing may think twice. Consequences for committing academic fraud must be thoroughly advertised, but consistently and fairly enforced.

The literature exposes many ideas for minimizing online cheating and plagiarism. Honesty can be modeled and encouraged by instructors by implementing strategies during design, instruction, as well as assessment. Large projects should be broken into smaller tasks that can be monitored. For example, instructors may require that students provide an outline, followed by brainstorming notes or a thesis statement before submitting each subsequent draft of a research paper. Even if it is a product-based project, the instructor should be able to follow the development of ideas that show comprehension of difficult topics.

Collaborative projects should be tied to other assignments in the course where the instructor has had the opportunity to "see" each contributor's writing style or abilities. Requiring students to write a synopsis of their project is another method to detect and deter plagiarism. If the student plagiarized he will be less able to intelligently summarize the contents without having gone through the thought process associated with writing original work. An alternate method of checking the originality of written work is to integrate the plagiarism detection software with the learning management system. Some institutions set it up in a way that specific assignments are automatically run through the software. A powerful yet less used method is to allow students to submit the work themselves, thus they receive the report and have the opportunity to learn from their mistakes. In this manner, students are empowered to check their work, make corrections, and resubmit.

Another possible method is to require students to include notes or other assignments previously submitted in the course to "add" to the new project. This way the student cannot rely on plagiarized work to match their previous assignments. Whenever possible, instructors should incorporate product-based assessments, but should focus on the though process behind the product, not just the product itself. Formative assessment and assignments should be varied, using a combination of perspectives, observations, reports, interviews, and proposals.

Instructors must be careful and change assessments and activities often to minimize students sharing information from year to year. Ideally, the course design should be flexible enough to update assessments and activities each semester. Learner-learner and learner-instructor interaction may also help deter cheating because a surrogate person is less likely to maintain contact with the other students and the instructor, or attend synchronous sessions. Surrogates will also be less likely to agree to academic fraud if the course requires different levels of discussions and high commitment.

Assessment should be planned and designed with utmost care. High stakes exams are not the best method of evaluating the online learner because it would be too simple to have a surrogate test-taker for that one time exam. Cyber educators must accept the fact that learners have access to more resources than any other generation. Friends are resources, as so are books and Internet sites. The online learner can easily right click on their favorite Web browser and open a new tab, and leaving the course tab open. Assessments in online learning should therefore be designed with the understanding that if able, learners will look up any answer.

Traditional educators have fretted over the concept of open book testing for decades. The fact is that 21st century learners do not learn, research, or do things the same way as previous generations. Therefore they cannot be assessed in the same manner. Formative and summative assessments are to be designed in ways that hamper cheating, and with the mindset that students have many resources available to them. Olt (2002) agrees that instructors have no control over the use of unauthorized resources while a student is taking an online assessment, and that assessments should therefore be designed with pre-determined goals and instructions that would be shared with the student.

One method to discourage cheating is to take the time to create robust test banks. Each student would get randomly selected questions from the test bank, and even if the test has to be reset due to a reported computer "crash," or if the student claims he got disconnected from the Internet, or experienced a power outage, the student will get a completely different version of the test. Many institutions require that students also obtain a password from the instructor, or set a time limit for tests. Passwords would need to be changed often or created randomly for each learner.

If the password option is used, instructors must determine what criteria the student must meet in order to obtain it. For example, the instructor may require that the student first be able to verbally discuss key concepts in the unit. This would be time consuming, but would provide the instructor with a hands-on approach that not only promotes academic integrity, but also builds personal relationships between the student and instructor. By talking with the student, the instructor has a unique opportunity to remediate students who may have difficulties, and demonstrate an honest concern for student success.

Test design cannot rely solely on traditional formats such as multiple choice and matching. Tests for online learners should include higher-level questions that demonstrate the thought process behind the answer. Scenarios and situational questions are good options. Chiesl (2007) suggests that online exams should have a low point value, and that multiple attempts should be allowed. The author notes that if the exam is open all week, and students are allowed to retake it as often as they wish, then the students are actually learning from the repetition. The key however, is to randomize all questions. Chiesl's point holds merit because educators should be focusing on the learning process, and not on producing the correct answer one time. Furthermore, the author insists that there should be a good number of these exams embedded throughout the course. The objective is to conduct formative assessment that is less likely to promote cheating, even if a surrogate test taker agrees to do it once, he or she may not want to provide help ten times, according to Chiesl.

Many common knowledge strategies for promoting integrity in face-to-face learning environments are also applicable to the virtual learning space. If the instructor takes the time to personally get to know the students, then he or she will more likely understand if the student is facing any particular challenges that may cause cheating. Maintaining security of assessment is also a basic step. In traditional environments the instructor would keep the examination papers in a secure location, but in the online learning environment the instructor cannot do it alone. The cooperation of the Information Technology department, as well as administrators, is needed to develop and implement security measures that authenticate learner log ins. Finally, if an instructor has the ability to proctor exams in traditional settings, the same should be made available in the virtual course room. While proctoring each test taker is impossible in cyber education, there are some strategies that could help curtail cheating.

Cheating could be discouraged by randomly proctoring summative assessments. If random proctoring is practiced, it should be part of the institution's academic integrity policy; therefore every student is aware that they could be randomly selected at any time. Psychologically speaking, students would always be wondering if they are next. To randomly proctor, the school needs to create a network of approved proctors. A downside of this strategy is that the school would have to designate funds for the program. The more globally dispersed the students are, the more challenging the strategy becomes. There are two possible ways in which this idea could be implemented. First method is to have the student take the exam at a physical location, and second, to enable the technology to assist human proctors at monitoring the student at a distance. Either way, high tech cheating must be counteracted with high tech solutions.

In looking ahead, cyber educators are confronted with a difficult decision; how to be certain that the student taking the test is the real student enrolled in the course. Castagnera (2009) points out that options for physical proctoring are not only expensive, but are temporary measures. After consulting with industry experts and educators, the author suggests that technology should be used to verify student identity in more than one way. For example, the first step could be to require students to answer a set of challenge questions based on public information, very much the same as some corporations and credit card companies already use. Once the student is successfully logged in to take the assessment, a web cam could be used for the teacher to visually see the student. The visual of the student would be compared to a previously recorded picture of the student.

Using already existing verification technologies such as biometrics for iris recognition, digital fingerprinting, or voice recognition are options that, according to

Castagnera, are not being utilized by educators due to cost constraints. The funding problem has plagued the education sector since always, therefore Castagnera blames the Department of Education for not taking proactive measures to prescribe solutions and fund them. As online learning continues to surpass the growth rate of the total college student population (Castagnera), somehow, educators and politicians must take the initiative to once and for all address student identity verification and implement plausible solutions.

Assessing the iGeneration will entail collaboration on the part of stakeholders. The design and implementation of assessments and activities must take into account the fact that learners have the world as their oyster, but also as their endless source of information. Employing proactive strategies that focus on the learning process and not on finding the right answer can discourage cheating and plagiarizing. Instructors will also be more likely to detect academic dishonesty if they get to know their students. Moreover, action is needed on the part of stakeholders, including government agencies, to find feasible solutions using biometric technology to aide cyber educators deter and detect academic dishonesty.

CONCLUSION

Academic dishonesty is identified as being rampant and statistically rising. Addressing academic dishonesty in the 21st century will require the collaborative efforts of educators, parents, the community at large, and the students themselves. The shared responsibility must be acknowledged and solutions must be pursued.

The phenomena of academic dishonesty has been extensively explored, but not in the context of online learning. The continued increase of online learning programs make it imperative that more comprehensive research is conducted expeditiously. Current knowledge of online cheating and plagiarism concurs with previous research of face-to-face learning environments. The literature consistently reveals that males are more likely to cheat than females, and that younger student also more likely to cheat. More research is necessary to understand which approaches to deterring academic dishonesty are more effective. Studies on the effectiveness of honor codes indicate that the success of honor codes is not based on having a code or not, but on the creation of a culture which values integrity and trust (McCabe, Treviño, & Butterfield, 2001).

Academic fraud is a global concern, especially as more online programs are created and student enrollment crosses national boundaries. Global fraud involves not just students, but also administrators and faculty. Without clear and comprehensive academic integrity policies in place, educational institutions cannot expect students to simply do the right thing. Moreover, these policies should be developed in conjunction with the student body, and enforced in a fair but consistent manner. Giving ownership of academic integrity to the students empowers them to self-police. Educators however, must always be prepared to detect infractions and prevent new ones. Administrators must support faculty by providing proper training in how to nurture academic integrity, and must be open in their pursuit of academic integrity. Integrity must be modeled and nurtured at all levels of the organization.

Educators must understand the basic causes of cheating, and acknowledge the fact that learners have access to unlimited resources. Some reasons for plagiarizing are obviously deviant behaviors, while unintentional incidents could be prevented through modeling and by creating resources and tutorials that will help students learn to avoid plagiarizing. There are a myriad of strategies for detecting cheating and plagiarism in online learning, from focusing on design of assessments, to randomly proctoring students or following up with a verbal discussion before providing a password. Educators must be familiar with the high tech tools that students use to cheat, and combat cheating and plagiarism with high tech solutions themselves. Student identity must also be verified as a first step in preventing academic fraud. The use of available biometric technology can prove helpful if further implemented and explored across virtual campuses.

Technology however, should never be seen as the only approach to solving the academic dishonesty riddle. Educators should not just use the technology but also basic human contact. Getting to know students is the most important factor in deterring and detecting dishonesty. Educators who know the writing style, cognitive ability, and tendencies of a learner will more than likely be able to identify discrepancies in the work submitted.

Academic dishonesty has always been around. The fact that technology provides safety in anonymity makes it more tempting for today's learners to cheat. As evidenced in surveys of youth cited earlier in this chapter, morality in the 21st century is ambiguous for many individuals and it continues to deteriorate. These individuals are the future leaders of the world, and their ethical views and moral values will influence each succeeding generation. All stakeholders therefore share the responsibility of academic integrity.

REFERENCES

American Consortium of Universities. (2010). *Statistics*. Retrieved July 10, 2010, from http://www.americanuniversities.org/

Associated Press. (2008, November 30). Students cheat, steal, but say they're good. *USA Today*. Retrieved July 15, 2010, from http://www.usatoday.com

Bok, D. C. (2006). *Our underachieving colleges*. Princeton, NJ: Princeton University Press.

Brown, B. S., & Emmett, D. (2001). Explaining variations in the level of academic dishonestly in studies of college students: Some new evidence. *College Student Journal, 35*(4), 529–539.

Bushweller, K. (1999). Generation of cheaters. *The American School Board Journal, 186*(4), 24-30. (ERIC EJ583645).

Callahan, D. (2007). Epilogue: Moving an integrity agenda. In Anderman, E., & Murdock, T. (Eds.), *Psychology of academic cheating* (pp. 313–317). Burlington, MA: Elsevier Academic Press. doi:10.1016/B978-012372541-7/50017-6

Castagnera, J. (2009, November). Student identity verification moves to center stage. *Today's Campus*. Retrieved July 17, 2010, from http://www.todayscampus.com/articles/ load.aspx?art=1921mber

ChaCha. (2010). *Company profile*. Retrieved July 16, 2010, from http://www.chacha.com/

Chiesl, N. (2007). Pragmatic methods to reduce dishonesty in Web-based courses. *The Quarterly Review of Distance Education, 8*(3), 203-211. (ERIC EJ875060).

Common Sense Media. (2009). *35% of teens admit to using cell phones to cheat*. Press Release, June 18, 2009. Retrieved July 14, 2010, from http://www.commonsensemedia.org/ about-us/press-room/hi-tech-cheating-poll

Dahl, S. (2007). Turnitin®: The student perspective on using plagiarism detection software. *Active Learning in Higher Education, 8*, 173–191. doi:10.1177/1469787407074110

Dodd, T. M. (2010). *Honor Code 101: An introduction to the elements of traditional honor codes, modified honor codes and academic integrity policies*. Center for Academic Integrity, Clemson University. Retrieved July 17, 2010, from http://www.academicintegrity.org/ educational_resources/honor_code_101.php

Essays-online. (2010). *Home page*. Retrieved July 16, 2010, from http://essays-online.com

European Consortium for Accreditation. (2010). *Statistics*. Retrieved July 10, 2010, from http:www. ecaconsortium.net

Finn, K. V., & Frone, M. R. (2004). Academic performance and cheating: Moderating role of school identification and self-efficacy. *The Journal of Educational Research, 97*(3), 115–123. doi:10.3200/JOER.97.3.115-121

Free Online Research Papers. (2010). *Home page*. Retrieved July 16, 2010, from http://www.freeonlineresearchpapers.com

Hallack, J., & Poisson, M. (2005). *Academic fraud and quality assurance: Facing the challenges of internalisation of higher education*. Report for the International Institute for Educational Planning, UNEŞCO. Retrieved July 7, 2010, from http://www.iiep.unesco.org

Heberling, M. (2002). Maintaining academic integrity in online education. *Journal of Distance Learning Administration, 5*(1). Retrieved July 13, 2010, from http://www.westga.edu/~distance/ ojdla/spring51/heberling51.html

Jackson, P. A. (2006). Plagiarism instruction online: Assessing undergraduate students' ability to avoid plagiarism. *Plagiarism Instruction Online, 67*(5), 418-428. Retrieved July 15, 2010, from http://crl.acrl.org/content/67/5/418.full.pdf

Josephson Institute Center for Youth Ethics. (2009). *Report card on the ethics of American youth*. Retrieved July 14, 2010, from http://josephsoninstitute.org/surveys/index.html

Kaczmarczyk, L. (2001). Accreditation and student assessment in distance education. Why we all need to pay attention. *Proceedings of the 6ᵗʰ Conference on Innovation and Technology in Computer Science Education*, Canterbury, UK, (pp. 113-116). New York: ACM.

Lanier, M. M. (2006). Academic integrity and distance learning. *Journal of Criminal Justice Education, 17*(2), 244–261. doi:10.1080/10511250600866166

McCabe, D. L., & Bowers, W. J. (1994). Academic dishonesty among males in college: A thirty year perspective. *Journal of College Student Development, 35*, 5–10.

McCabe, D. L., & Pavela, G. (2004). Principles of academic integrity. *Change, 36*(3), 10–15. doi:10.1080/00091380409605574

McCabe, D. L., & Treviño, L. K. (1996). What we know about cheating in college: Longitudinal trends and recent developments. *Change, 28*(1), 28–33.

McCabe, D. L., Treviño, L. K., & Butterfield, K. D. (2001). Cheating in academic institutions: A decade of research. *Ethics & Behavior, 11*(3), 219–232. doi:10.1207/S15327019EB1103_2

McClure, S., Scambray, J., & Kurtz, G. (2001). *Hacking exposed: Network security secrets and solutions* (3rd ed.). New York: McGraw-Hill Osborne Media.

Milliron, V., & Sandoe, K. (2008). The net generation cheating challenge. *Innovate, 4*(6). Retrieved July 17, 2010, from http://innovateonline.info/pdf/vol4_issue6/The__Net_Generation_Cheating_Challenge.pdf

MrWhy. (2010). *Home page*. Retrieved July 16, 2010, from http://answers.mrwhy.com

Olt, M. (2002). Ethics and distance education: Strategies for minimizing academic dishonesty in online assessment. *Online Journal of distance Learning Administration, 5*(3). Retrieved July 17, 2010, from http://www.westga.edu/~distance/ojdla/fall53/olt53.html

Plagiarism.com. (2010). *Plagiarism self-detection test*. Retrieved July 16, 2010, from http://www.plagiarism.com/self.detect.htm

Roig, M. (1999). When college students' attempts at paraphrasing become instances of potential plagiarism. *Psychological Reports, 84*, 973–982. doi:10.2466/PR0.84.3.973-982

Rowe, N. (2004). Cheating in online student assessment: Beyond plagiarism. *Online Journal of Distance Learning Administration, 7*(2), 1–8.

Scribd. (2010). *Home page*. Retrieved July 16, 2010, from http://www.scribd.com/

Selwyn, N. (2008). A safe haven for misbehaving? An investigation of online misbehavior among university students. *Social Science Computer Review, 26*(4), 446–465. doi:10.1177/0894439307313515

Snyder, S. (2008, September 10). ChaCha service raises fears of cheating via cell phone. *The Philadelphia Inquirer*. Retrieved July 22, 2010, from http://www.philly.com/inquirer

Sperber, M. (2005). How undergraduate education became college lite. In Hersh, R., & Merrow, J. (Eds.), *Declining by degrees* (pp. 131–144). New York: Palgrave MacMillan.

Szabo, A., & Underwood, J. (2004). Cybercheats: Is information and communication technology fuelling academic dishonesty? *Active Learning in Higher Education, 5*(2), 180–199. doi:10.1177/1469787404043815

U.S. Department of Education. (2010). College accreditation in the United States. Retrieved July 10, 2010, from http://www2.ed.gov/admins/finaid/ accred/accreditation_pg2.html#U.S.

Whitley, B. E. (1998). Factors associated with cheating among college students: A review. *Research in Higher Education, 39*(3), 235–274. doi:10.1023/A:1018724900565

Chapter 8

The Blending of Work, Play & Learning Online:
The Pajama Effect

ABSTRACT

Increased connectivity through digitally mediated communications has brought about a radical change in the way people interact and communicate, thus blurring the lines between different facets of life. The pajama effect helps to explain how individuals in an increasingly connected society are able to blend online work, play and learning while remaining productive. Shifts in pedagogy include constructivism and connectivism as the preferred theories for developing m-Learning applications and platforms. Faster and smarter technologies will enable virtual teams, learners, and educators to better collaborate and remain connected.

OBJECTIVES

- Propose a new term called "the pajama effect" for the purpose of better understanding the phenomenon of how members of a fast-paced, digitally connected society are able to blend the different facets of their lives and still get things done.
- Define the pajama effect.

DOI: 10.4018/978-1-60960-543-8.ch008

- Identify and discuss current trends in telecommuting and mobile learning.
- Identify and discuss how technology tools aide in the blending of work, play, and learning, thus changing the way people communicate and collaborate.
- Explore constructivism as pedagogy for work, play, and learning online.
- Identify and discuss the future of work, play, and learning, as technology continues to evolve and impact our lives.

INTRODUCTION

Technological advancements shape and re-shape the way people communicate for work, leisure or learning and how they go about their day-to-day activities. Many praise technology for its ability to make things easier, but the other side of technology is that as it brings us closer together, it may also take away our ability to disconnect from our networks and relax. Increased demands on our time have forced us to blend our activities in order to get things done.

In this chapter the blending of work, play and learning are explored through the lens of the pajama effect. The term "pajama effect" is proposed by the authors of this chapter as a means of understanding the blending phenomenon. For the purpose of this discussion, the pajama effect will be defined as:

The pajama effect is the ability of those connected via digitally mediated communications, such as telecommuters and online learners, to blend their private and public lives while remaining highly productive as they work, play and learn online, hence thriving in a flexible environment that is physically detached and where distractions and interruptions abound. Such individuals may work in a more relaxed environment yet they are vulnerable to isolation and other challenges that emerge from being detached from the physical work, play, or learning space.

Despite the challenges of remaining connected and increased demands by employers and educational institutions, users crave increased mobility, higher network speeds and more flexibility. Companies around the globe continue to opt for telecommuting as a means to save, but also to increase productivity. The increase in telecommuting translates into more virtual teaming and extensive requirements for collaborating and communicating using technology.

Education continues to be affected by technological advancements as well. Whether for professional development, specialized training, K-12 online learning or higher education, the blending of learning and playing is more evident with technology. The same is for work, with more professions than ever before relying on virtual reality games for training purposes. Mobile learning technologies will play a key role in the future of learning and sophisticated collaboration tools will enable virtual teams to focus on outcomes. The blending of work, play and learning is inevitable, but manageable. This chapter explores how it influences our lives now and how it may look in the future.

BACKGROUND

There is no question that the Internet has blurred the boundaries of time, space and place over the last decade. Offices are becoming homes and homes are becoming offices. Interspersed throughout the workday are tweets, text messages and instant messages that keep us connected with family members and friends but are also often distractions. Bosses can reach from around the globe anytime of the day or night. Online teachers and students can stay in touch any time, anywhere. This also means it is more difficult to call it a day and getting away from work or school. The nine to five is no longer applicable and neither is the school day. Instead of computers becoming human, like the droids in science fiction, humans are becoming computerized. Trends indicate the increase of telecommuters for all industries and point to the rapid expansion of mobile learning for training and education. Others who work or study in a traditional physical space may find themselves working during personal time or simply playing during work time.

More and more people have their offices in their homes. Companies, large and small are realizing the financial benefits of employees to working from home. Employees are also quick to see all the perks associated with telecommuting however, many fail to understand how their lives will be changed. Telecommuting replaces the physical commute to a work location with virtual communication and interaction.

Jack Nilles (1976) first coined the term telecommuting while he worked for NASA. The original definition included geographical location as a variable and communication as the focus. Nille's updated definition, published online by the consulting firm he founded (JALA, 2010) defines telecommuting as:

Periodic work out of the principal office, one or more days per week, either at home, a client's site or in a telework center; the partial or total substitution of information technologies for the commute to work. The emphasis here is on reduction or elimination of the daily commute to and from the workplace. Telecommuting is a form of teleworking.

AT&T, an early adopter of telecommuting, reported that from 1991 to 1998 it had saved $550 million dollars by allowing employees to work remotely (Apgar, 1998). After years of proving that telecommuting can improve the bottom line of many companies, it is no surprise that today it remains a favorable option. In a comprehensive survey, WorldatWork (2009) reported trends that point toward the rise of telecommuting.

The WorldatWork survey results illustrate a sharp increase in the number of workers in the United States who worked from home or an alternate location at least once per month. Over the period of two years, from 2006 to 2008, there was a 39 percent increase, from approximately 12.4 million to 17.2 million of telecommuters. The report also indicates that the total number of teleworkers, regardless of trade, who telecommute at least once per month has risen by 43 percent in five years, from 23.5 million in 2003 to 33.7 million in 2008.

Telecommuting or not, remaining connected for work or play is simple enough thanks to technology. There are PDAs, smart phones, netbooks and laptops to mention only a few of the gizmos and gadgets that connect us to the workplace and each other constantly. Newer and more sophisticated gadgets such as the Apple® iPad help blend work and play. Phone applications put us in touch with YouTube™, Facebook®, Plaxo™ and a host of other social software that keep us going nonstop. No longer is the physical commute to work a time for reflection or peace, now it is a time to log on and respond to "tweets" IM's, and emails, which often happen while driving.

Historically speaking, working remotely became possible as computer conferencing and emailing became available in the business world in the 1980's, but on large computers and in a limited way. The Internet made it possible in 1983 to communicate via networked personal computers and in 1990 Tim Berner-Lee's creation of the World Wide Web opened up the information superhighway. It was with the advent of the World Wide Web that personal computers became personal communication devices. Progressively our communications have moved from hardwired to wireless and from stationary to mobile.

Tools for communicating in both work and play are limited only by the imagination of the users. At its infancy, computer communication was coded in a language called ASCII (American Standard Code for Information Interchange) which used 128 characters and mostly used English. Many other languages around the world entered the arena and the need to broaden the languages of communications increased with the expansion of the digital age. The impact of these technologies has had ramifications on culture and ideology around the globe. Simple customs like the way dates are represented become questionable when information is global. In America the date is traditionally month, day, year, while in Europe the date is day, month year. Selection of a date format makes a cultural statement as well as representing a mere field of data (Baron, 2005). Informal digital communication however, has evolved into a global language represented by emoticons, Internet slang and other forms of quick visuals that convey a feeling or thought.

The blending of work, play, and learning is not limited to telecommuters. It takes place in office buildings, schools and out in the field. It is a phenomenon that is becoming accepted as part of a technologically connected society. The blending of work and play affects every facet of life, personal, professional and educational.

Using Digital Communication for Working, Playing and Learning

The globalization of technologies has brought about a change in the way we communicate and the explosion of cell phones and mobile devices throughout the last two decades has accelerated connectivity and mobility. Most importantly is the way mobile computer mediated communications has influenced thinking about time and about which facets of one's personal life should be kept out of cyberspace. Smart mobile devices are used to coordinate personal, educational and professional everyday activities. By relying on mobile devices, users have softened the time barrier and created direct links between human beings (Baron, 2005).

Mobility by definition implies unlimited locations. Technology has removed the time barrier from the concept of location, thus enabling access around the clock to friends, relatives and co-workers. The business world quickly adapted to the convenience of having constant access to workers, but education was slower to see the potential benefits.

Mobile learning has always been around, according Kress and Pachler (2007), because learners have always had the opportunity to learn outside of the classroom. Whether taking a field trip or taking a walk to observe nature, learners have always been in a mobile environment. They point out that in the modern world, mobility is just another "feature of the contemporary social, political, economic and technological world" (p. 27). Mobile learning in the contemporary world is therefore not exclusive to technology.

Mobile learning is on the rise, making headway in corporate training and in all levels of educational programs. Software companies and phone companies are catering to the trend by developing applications and tools that facilitate learning on the go. Hall (2009) ranked mobile learning as the number one trend in 2009. Companies are maximizing their training budget by delivering content to cell phones and other mobile devices. For example, Microsoft has reduced training costs by using its own Academy Mobile application (Hall). Also known as mLearning, mobile learning continues to advance in 2010. It is a main focus for mobile devices worldwide, with unprecedented development of software and learning management systems that will enable users to access content seamlessly (Woodill, 2010).

According to the ongoing cell phone count sponsored by EyeMags.com (2010), a heaven for amateur and professional cell phone application writers, there will be a cell phone for each person in the planet in about two years. This is concurrent with Woodill's (2010) report, which shows that the demand for mLearning applications continues to increase in all continents, especially those with higher connectivity and bandwidth such as North America and Europe.

Digital communications are part of a connected society but they are causing distractions at work, play, and at school. The discussion of what constitutes appropriate use is seldom heard. Users tend to gravitate toward their device and multitask, simultaneously checking in on a friend and listening to a business presentation. Hiding the Blackberry® under the conference room table to write a message has become a common human reflex just like automatically saying "bless you" when someone sneezes. A similar scenario plays out in restaurants and social gatherings. Messaging a work colleague from your son's baseball game, checking business email while at a dinner date with a spouse, or answering the phone because the client is calling late in the evening, are all indications that technology could potentially endanger our ability to enjoy special moments in life or have quality "down time." The same is true for school. The number of children carrying cell phones continues to increase. Parents like the fact that they can locate and keep contact with their child, anytime. But schools quickly realized that teachers were competing with cell phones and other mobile gadgets for the student's attention.

Digital communications such as text and instant messaging is infiltrated with a degree of anonymity that lends itself toward new ways of playful exchange. This might be attributed to the fact that digital communication is more interactive than traditional writing and therefore lends itself to a more playful slant. Because of the anonymity factor, early critics argued that computer-mediated communications (CMC) lacked the emotional quality and sometimes the authority of paper based communications. However, technological advancements now make it possible to attach a certain level of emotion to a digital message, such as using emoticons, pictures and other digital representations of an emotion, or representing oneself under the pseudonym of an avatar, or an assumed identity.

The preference and tone of digital communications used for personal and business purposes are different between cultures. These tones and preferences are transferred online, and can be confusing. The emergence of a need for globally accepted forms of digitally mediated communications brings about the concern of adapting English as the language of the Internet. This may facilitate communication, however, it potentially negates the unique traits of other cultures that could enrich communication. Already prevalent in business communications globally, English has become the pervasive online language for global Web communications. This tendency is also evident in current Internet slang.

Various communication methods have emerged over the last decade, Internet slang using acronyms such as LOL (laughing outloud) or ROFL (rolling on floor laughing) are prevalent in CMC's thus adding a new emotional dimension. There are also different ways to write a message, for example, writing a message in all capital letters implies someone shouting. Although this type of communication is accepted in the world of digital communication, it is not much different than when acronyms such as TGIF (Thank God it's Friday) where used years ago either verbally or in an under the table note to a colleague during a boring Friday meeting. In business however, many managers would deem Internet slang unprofessional. The global expectation is that correct grammar is used for business and for school.

Digital communications have evolved tremendously, as so has the public's perception of what is real in the virtual world. Until recent times, the virtual space lacked the structure and authority of a more rigid physical environment, and the digital format did not seem as credible as the tangible source. In today's Internet, digital content of a newspaper or journal is equally credible as a paper copy. The Internet allows users all over the globe to access the online version national and international newspapers, hence increasing access and exchange of information. As a result, there is the perception that Internet communication is essentially democratizing.

Some digital communications in cyber space may also be perceived as amateurish yet democratic because of the instant exchange of ideas via forums, blogs, wikis and other spaces. The transfer of newspapers and journals online offer credibility of what is posted in the virtual space. The danger it seems, is that because everything is posted online, one must navigate through much more information in order to decipher was is credible or not, hence making it a huge distraction when searching for information. Technology enables anyone of any age to create Web content with no previous experience necessary. With blogging and other content producing technologies reaching epidemic proportions, it is not always easy to discern between the serious, professional post and the mischievous one. Some individuals create content as part of their work, while others create it to play. Either way, it adds to the repertoire of information available.

Technology has made it impossible to get away to our hypothetical private island. The global marketplace for business and online education is eroding personal time. This has happened so fast that the expectations of workers and employers are also blurred. Mobile technology has heightened connectivity. As mobile learning continues to expand worldwide, the demand to remain connected will be stronger than ever before, thus aiding in the further blurring of what constitutes appropriate use, the erosion of personal time, and the blending of working, playing, and learning. Trends indicate a continued increase of telecommuters; they will undoubtedly find themselves adjusting to a work schedule that mixes business not just with pleasure, but also with personal and educational demands. The blending of these realms affects everyone, and every facet of their life: personal, professional, and educational.

THE ART OF GETTING THINGS DONE

In a society that is interconnected by mobile technology and digital communication, it is often difficult to get things done due to the many opportunities for interruptions and distractions. The challenge is of equal importance when working, playing or learning. There are more demands placed on our time than ever before. Getting someone's undivided attention is becoming rare, "I hear you but I am not listening to you" is often a source of frustration. In the sections that follow the focus is shifted to exploring how members of a fast paced society are able to blend working, playing and learning and how it affects each of these facets of life. The term "pajama effect" is here introduced as a means of understanding this phenomenon.

The Pajama Effect

After following telecommuters for a number of years, researchers generally agree that there are many positive benefits to working remotely. Study after study suggests that aside from increasing profits for the company, telecommuters have a unique sense of what it means to balance personal and work life. In a study conducted by the Office of Information Resources Management in 2000, it was reported that 93% of participants had achieved a better balance between personal and professional lives as a direct result of telecommuting.

As stated in the introduction section of this chapter, the term "pajama effect" is being introduced in this chapter by the authors to help explain how telecommuters and online learners are able to get things done amidst the blending of different facets of life, and all the distractions that surround them in an environment that is isolating by nature. Although telecommuting has been around for many years, not much is known about the phenomenon of how telecommuters are able to blend work and play, yet be productive. The definition proposed for discussion is as follows:

The pajama effect is the ability of those connected via digitally mediated communications, such as telecommuters and online learners, to blend their private and public lives while remaining highly productive as they work, play and learn online, hence thriving in a flexible environment that is physically detached and where distractions and interruptions abound. Such individuals may work in a more relaxed environment yet they are vulnerable to isolation and other challenges that emerge from being detached from the physical work, play, or learning space.

The literature however, does point out to a number of outcomes that have consistently been identified by researchers. Telecommuters for example, learn to cope with distractions, both personal and professional and therefore maximize their time.

Table 1. The Pajama Effect

Cause: increased flexibility, less external direction, may experience lower stress levels, higher satisfaction with work and personal life, higher motivation, more comfort, informal work setting.
Effect: increased focus, more time-on-task, higher productivity

Because they spend more time working from home and they can create their own schedules, telecommuters report having a good balance between work and family life, are generally more satisfied with their work and experience lower levels of stress (Baruch, 2001; Manoochehri, & Pinkerton, 2003; Office of Information Resources Management, 2001; Tremblay, 2002).

In order for there to be an effect, a cause or agent of change is necessary. For the purpose of this discussion, all items listed under cause and effect in Table 1 are acknowledged to be outcomes of telecommuting (the primary change agent), however, it is because telecommuters have flexibility, less stress and higher satisfaction, their behavior is affected. Telecommuters are therefore able to focus, spend more time working and therefore be more productive. The latter are the effects of being able to create their own schedule, be around family more often, therefore blending work and play. Similarly, online learners have added flexibility that allows them to blend their roles and responsibilities while still keeping up with a training or educational program.

Why pajama? The words pajama or pajamas have been repeatedly used in the literature when discussing the obvious flexibility telecommuters have to work in pajamas and slippers. This reference is not just in the literal sense, but it is also an attempt to emphasize the lack of traditional structure around a telecommuter's workday and lifestyle. The pajama effect presents a broad range of research opportunities. For example, it could be applicable to online learning, not just working from a remote location. The sections that follow provide a sampling of issues that come about as a result of the blending work, play and study online for telecommuters and non-telecommuters alike.

Play and Work for the Sake of Learning

Many would contend that the distinction between play and work in the constructivist pedagogy is counter-productive. Many cases can be made for the blurring of lines between play and work to create an environment in support of playful learning and the co-construction of knowledge. Perceptions of play and work are usually presented in contrast (Cooney, Gupton, & McLaughlin, 2000). Online and blended learning environments however, are making it difficult to distinguish between what constitutes work versus play. Many are looking to play as a window to understanding how the learning process and how learners are able to grasp new knowledge. Spontaneity is generally described as a characteristic of play but both spontaneity and serendipity are elements that are surfacing online in social networks and with social software. Often this refers to the freedom felt during play as opposed to the restrictive feeling associated with work.

Traditionally learning was thought of as work, but more of the shared control between instructor, content and context is creating blurred lines between work and play. Work and play are often linked by spontaneity. Constructivism combines elements of play and work, thus encouraging the co-creation of knowledge, a pillar of constructivism. The ability to spontaneously shift directions and adapt to new situations and learning challenges enhances the ability to imagine possibilities. Creativity, critical thinking and problem solving are all traits considered necessary to sustainability and marketability in the 21st century. The ability to shift directions, compensate and readjust are all necessary skills for success in the global marketplace.

The number of online courses offered at colleges and universities is growing more rapidly than ever before. All sectors of the economy including, government, higher education, professional organizations, K-12 school districts, the health industry, and the business sector are developing and providing online learning and training. The days of using online learning only as a means to cut cost and enhance cash flow while providing education and training, is being replaced by the realization that good online programs have many more benefits. Some elements of online education are attractive to almost everyone.

For example, the flexibility in terms of location and time, physical access, social access, online resources and scheduling are inherently advantageous to most individuals. These same advantages can be disadvantages for some as well. The concept that learners and teachers are busy brings forth the reality that in an already full day it is impractical to ask a person for more hours. The reality of anywhere, any time is often incompatible with the reality that an adult learner still needs some time to do the coursework while working a job and likely caring for a family. Despite the challenges, the blending of these facets of life are almost necessary in the 21st century in order to get things done.

Synchronous technologies such as chats and virtual whiteboards offer the ability to meet online in real time and add the flavor of teleconferencing. These technologies attach the factor of spontaneity and remove the structures associated with traditional face-to-face lectures. For example, conducting meetings using synchronous technologies such as Voice Over Internet Protocol (VOIP) or Elluminate®, enhances the overall experience. Recording and archiving are simple enough, as instant electronic transcripts provide a history of meetings and classroom events, providing a detailed description of who attended, when they logged in and for how long.

Video and Web cams have also enhanced the real time feeling of being together and made participation in online communications even easier (Schneider, 2000). Most technical problems like unstable connections and bandwidth are becoming manageable although slow and shaky connections are still a part of the online experience.

These synchronous sessions work well and people can usually concentrate on the content and context to be covered, even as they blend working, playing and learning. The pajama effect becomes evident as participants get past distractions and interruptions to produce outcomes. Whether in a training or university course, if participants are held accountable for a product or milestone upon completing the synchronous session, then they will be more likely to focus and participate during the event. The flexibility of the online environment coupled with transparent expectations, is a powerful motivator for producing outcomes.

In the realm of teaching and learning in a virtual, asynchronous environment, there are also advantages and disadvantages to working and playing online. Whether it is a company online training or a university course, the learner must learn to manage their time in a new way. Anywhere, anytime can offer both teachers and learners the ability to conveniently attend class from anywhere on the globe, on their own time schedule, as long as there is an Internet connection.

Learners can attend class in their pajamas or workers can attend a conference in the same attire coffee cup in hand. Online courses and collaborative activities are successful because of the interactions of individuals and the valuable insights brought about by sharing. Individuals who use digitally mediated communications for working and learning may have more time to think through responses. This may be due to the removal of the formal structure and time constraints of most traditional work or learning environments. The informality and flexibility of the online environment provides a less restrictive environment, which encourages creativity.

Efforts to stay connected through online communities and establish identities are fueled by social software that supports the placement of personal pictures, videos and conversations online. Digital communities and identities are different that face-to-face and although they can stimulate the sharing of ideas, these ideas are often different than the thoughts that might develop otherwise (Brown & Green, 2003). Meaningful interactions among all participants are essential to quality online learning. Whether teaching or taking an online course, there are only twenty-four hours in a day for everyone and sleeping is essential. Although it is intriguing to be able to take the course in your pajamas, dazzling technologies neither makes the course effortless or less time consuming.

Technology aides in turning the act of learning into play instead of work. The blending of these tasks becomes prove prevalent as they are increasingly conducted via online environments. The flexibility of the online environment, when combined with clear expectations, removes the constraints of time and traditional structures, thus allowing participants to focus on the outcomes. Constructivist pedagogy encourages critical thinking, problem solving and the co-construction of knowledge that is made possible via online interactions. The many options of synchronous communications provide a more relaxed, yet accountable, environment for participants, where the pajama effect allows them to remain productive while learning or working online despite obvious challenges and distractions.

Professional Development and Networking Online

There is no question that ubiquitous learning removes the physical barriers to time, space and place. One strong motivation for professional continuing education online is when and where learning takes place. Discussions in the literature lack consensus over the intrinsic value of communication with other learners. This may be due to a number of reasons including the feeling of isolation sometimes experienced in online learning or the fact that some online courses might provide the participants who are already knowledgeable about course content with the opportunity to gain continuing education credits without spending time in a face-to-face classroom.

Cyber learning is an excellent medium for facilitating credentialing, mandatory compliance training and professional development. One of the challenges that face the development of successful online learning for this audience is the alignment of the goals of the participants with the professional agencies or course providers. Research shows that participants often want to gain a better understanding of the material while the goal of the provider is to present new information.

The main purpose of continuing professional education should be to improve the practice of the professional. Unfortunately too often training programs only satisfy the rules of governing body with evidence of training compliance and saves participants from being in a classroom for a specific amount of time (Nocente & Kanuka, 2002). By blending work, play and educational endeavors, individuals learn to prioritize and work through the challenges of having only 24 hours in the day to accomplish all responsibilities. Taking this into consideration and respecting the professional's time, professional development courses should provide four main things: updated information which is current and relevant to the field, facilitate professionals in developing higher order skills when considering knowledge such as critical thinking and analyses, enable practice using skills of judgment and support the construction of new knowledge based on practice.

Most professional continuing education follows the update paradigm. Online delivery of alternative methods of instruction makes them more accessible to professionals and more cost effective for institutions. A favorite instructional method was using case studies to promote analytical and critical thinking processes. Cyber education not only offers the removal of time and place barriers but also enhances the ability to deliver instruction using alternative pedagogies (Nocente & Kanuka, 2002). Certainly there should be an alignment of professional development goals and methods of online or face-to-face delivery.

Technology removes barriers and makes online learning less isolating and more engaging. These emerge as two important elements in constructing a continuing professional course for the online environment. Independent of gender or age, most professionals feel confident with their computer skills for work related tasks, but maybe not as comfortable with those same skills when used for learning activities. Some of this apprehension may be attributed to the lack of experience with emerging technologies and cyber education. It is possible that participants are not satisfied with online learning not because of the courses themselves, but because of the anxiety attributed to technical difficulties, lack of certain computer skills or feelings of isolation. Research has shown a relationship between level of education and success factors as well as completion rates of professional development courses (Nocente & Kanuka, 2002). Future research is needed to understand the relationship between education and the ability of someone to blend their different online roles and responsibilities as part of the pajama effect.

Since the inception of Web 2.0, networking has been the apparent purpose behind the interactions afforded by these technologies. Online networking has always been a social space for connecting with old contacts and making new ones. The shift to using technology for social purposes requires accepting a certain set of assumptions which include: networking for business and personal reasons is good, there is a need for people to become more and more connected and using a network of existing connections and expanding it is the best way to accomplish this task. Most users will agree that the applications are intuitive, fast and easy.

The first social networking site was called Sixdegrees.com and lasted for about four years. Although it was short-lived, it established a precedent in the minds of people; it caused them to think of the online world as a social rather than private space. Status, power and even privilege have begun to be associated with online activities, including learning. Ubiquitous and instant access to contacts and their information is the main element to social networking communities.

Working, playing and learning are so blended in our society that one hardly thinks about it. On the work side there is work from home, the day at the office or the plant, plus the work of parenting and serving the community. On the learning side, there are online courses and job specific training that are essential to prosperity. Play through technology adds a new dimension to working and learning and eases the transition from one activity to the other. Virtual reality games are used by medical schools to train surgeons, by the military to train troops and by NASA to train astronauts. Pilots train inside flight simulators and law enforcement agencies. The blending of roles and responsibilities is therefore not limited to those distractions afforded by digitally mediated communications; it also encompasses the literal shift to using play as a pedagogical approach.

Working and playing is becoming more and more a matter of being online. Reality is defined by the ability to communicate digitally or its "digitability" (Capurro & Pingel, 2002, p.189). Instead of casting reality as separate and independent from the digital world, it is defined online instead. This has vast implications for blending work and play, as well as learning. According to O'Conner (2008) part of the fun of learning in the digital world is the pretend element. Therefore the use of virtual reality games for the highly specialized training adds the dimension of fun, while having a sense of "being" connected to that digital world.

Communication and connectedness tools are multiplying at an alarming rate. There are many tools such as smart phones, softphones, iPads, notebooks, laptops and countless applications and networking sites such as instant messaging, texting, Facebook®, MySpace®, Twitter®, LinkedIn® among others. The sheer number of options makes it difficult to determine what is really an effective and useful tool for communication and what is instead an annoyance, which causes more disconnection than connection (Orenstein, 2009). The norms governing the human behaviors associated with using such tools and applications are also changing. Cell phones for example are discretionary and it is not imperative that they be answered in a crowed café during the dinner hour, but the expectation is that that it will be answered.

Although adoption of new technologies has always been greeted with some ambivalence, "picturephones" were around as early as 1964 World's Fair in New York. One of the reasons they never really became a household item was due to the cost, but also because many were skeptical about its benefits. Anonymity provides a refuge when the user does not want anyone know he is in pajamas and has not made the bed yet.

Many of the new technologies both support this idea and reinforce it by giving "too much access, too little control" (Orenstein, 2009, p.11). Skype is a modern example of a Web-based application that integrates the features of picturephones and teleconferencing. It offers users free features as well as more sophisticated options for a fee. The question as to whether or not applications such as Skype are breaking down the anonymity barrier is up to the user. The mere fact that the user can opt to use a Web cam or not, indicates that the choice to remain anonymous or be seen in pajamas is in his/her hands. This is an element of a privacy policy that is cognizant and respectful of the rights of the user.

To blend working, playing and learning is not only common, but also a necessity of post-modern life. For most individuals it happens unconsciously. Online learners, telecommuters, as well as non-telecommuters are equally plagued by the same challenges and demands brought about by connectivity and digitally mediated communications. The art of getting things done requires clear expectations, prioritizing and the blending of work, play and study. The term "pajama effect" may be helpful in understanding the phenomenon of getting things done amidst the distractions and interruptions caused by the very technologies we use. Furthermore, learning and working in a connected digital environment creates opportunities for the integration of play as a element of constructivist pedagogy used in professional development, online learning and virtual reality training. The blending of work, play and learning affects all members of the digitally connected society.

LOOKING AHEAD

The future of work, play, and learning will continue to be influenced by emerging technologies. In the next decade there will be the tendency to blend all three even further. Trends point toward the increase of telecommuters, online learning, virtual reality training, and faster, better tools to keep people connected. Where and how we work, play, and learn will be radically altered. The way in which we communicate over digitally mediated communications will change to a globally accepted form that facilitates cross-cultural understanding regardless of native language.

Now What?

1. Telecommuters must adjust to a work schedule that mixes business not just with pleasure, but also with personal and educational demands.
2. Business and institutions must realize it is possible for telecommuters to be more focused, spend more time working and therefore be more productive.
3. Organization must educate workers and learners on the skills necessary create their own schedule, be around family more often, and blend work and play
4. Organizations must embrace the way in which we communicate over digitally mediated communications and facilitate a globally accepted form that facilitates cross-cultural understanding regardless of native language.
5. Technology will also blending learning and playing and force the pedagogy pendulum to swing toward constructivism and connectivism.
6. Organizations must be oriented towards results and outcomes and learning and working environments must change drastically to incorporate the positive influences of technology.

There will be swift changes in pedagogical approaches, relying more on mLearning to deliver constructivist content anytime, anywhere. Faster 4G networks and mobile devices with increased capabilities for user control will deliver content. Augmented reality, changing perspectives on work, learning, and play, will all contribute to added flexibility to the worker or learner, but it will also further blur the lines between work, play, and learning. The demand for a person's time is likely to increase, as well as the expectations by employers and schools, thus adding pressures already experienced by individuals.

The Future of Work and Play

The future of work is already here. Just think in terms of globalization. The workplace continues to add flexibility in terms of location, but it is also becoming increasingly competitive. The types of jobs needed in ten years are non-existent today. What is required to compete in a global economy goes far beyond traditional skills, as workers will be expected to collaborate across the globe and think outside the box.

In the next decade it is quite possible that work will change significantly due to the influences of globalization, technology and economics. Pressed to reduce operational costs and increase profits, more companies will adopt telecommuting, as indicated by trends. Employers no longer need to pay employees to drive and sit in a building. Jobs that require process and repetition will be outsourced to countries where labor is cheaper. Digital communications have made global teamwork easier than ever before and the emphasis will be on finding the essential people to get the job done (Godin, 2009). Global collaboration means that communication skills will remain highly necessary to future workers adapting to a rapid changing environment.

Life in the cubicle will be reduced to a memory of how things were done, with only key positions reporting to a work location. Many cubicles and offices will be replaced because they are just not cost effective. The return on investment of maintaining a physical facility and losing countless hours to absenteeism and commuting does not compute to a beneficial number. Some industries are more likely than others to adopt telecommuting due to the nature of their business; however, all will be impacted in one way or another by this trend.

Futurists and researchers already claim all the good that would come out of increased telecommuting. Kate Lister, a researcher with the Telework Research Network, compiled figures to highlight and hypothesize the impact to the United States economy if 40% of the workforce telecommuted at least half the time (Chafkin, 2010):

- American companies would gain $200 billion due to increased productivity.
- There would be a $190 billion savings due to reduced electricity bills, real estate costs, increased employee retention and less absenteeism.
- Employees save 100 hours per person not commuting any more.
- The emission of green house gases is reduced by 50 million tons.
- Savings in oil due to less driving would equate to about 276 million barrels or about 32% of today's oil imports.

- Telecommuting would account for 1, 500 lives saved, which would other wise be lost in car accidents.
- American companies would save a total of $700 billion.

The jobs of the future, according to Godin (2009), will require new organizational and management skills, because the workforce is spread all over the globe. This however, adds to the flexibility of work far away from the cubicle. Accountability says Godin, will be high because the boss will use technology to measure and track all activities and the team will have access to everything the other teammates produce. The interconnectedness of the virtual team translates into a "three legged race" (p.1) according to Godin, because team members who cannot perform as well or as fast, will slow everyone else down.

The profile of the worker is also likely to change. According to Oravec (2001) the emergent "knowledge worker" will use games and play to decrease heightened stress levels as a means to be able to handle longer working hours. Oravec (p.129) defines a knowledge worker as a "highly skilled, well educated" individual who follows a highly irregular work schedule. Current models of transition to the labor market do not accommodate for the placement of knowledge workers or even traditional workers. Many experts believe that current models are outmoded.

The very nature of the labor market is changing as we approach the first part of the twenty-first century. The traditional linear model, although prevalent in legislative settings and policy circles, does not take into account the forces currently shaping the workforce. The globalization of the marketplace, outsourcing, telecommuting, technology, increased formal and informal training and increased blending of work, play and learning, are all forces that currently shape the labor market. The narrative of life as a linear journey from student to worker has been replaced with a more complex way of defining and redefining identities to fit with the positions that may be available in the workplace (Stokes & Wyn, 2007). A wide variety of educational and work arrangements, especially those that are virtual, are slowly replacing the traditional linear model to support current trends. This shift is necessary in order to successfully position today's youth for the future.

Changing where we work automatically changes how we work. There are changes in the way communication is exchanged and how people collaborate. Collaboration tools will get smarter, more flexible and easier to use. Virtual teams will feel less isolated when using collaboration tools and other technologies to make social connections. Examples of these tools are already available such as Basecamp, which helps with keeping track of shared tasks and managing an entire project; Yammer, which acts as a private virtual watercooler or breakroom; Google Wave™, which uses live transmission to create instantaneous edits as a virtual team collaborates synchronously; Google Docs™, which also allows to store and edit shared documents and presentations; and Dropbox™, which provides 2GB of storage space, allowing users to access it from anywhere and share it.

Companies will likely invest more on training employees on how to work in virtual teams, because the sustainability of the organization will depend on the ability of its employees to adapt to the changing work environment. Trust, communication and accountability will remain key underpinnings of successful virtual teams. The traditional manager is passé; the new manager gives the team flexibility and is willing to listen to what team members have to say. The new manager also builds trusting relationships within the team and allows play as an escape valve, as well as a training tool. Outcomes and output will be used as the main measure for productivity; therefore the new manager will always create virtual teams based on each individual's strengths. Success of the team will largely depend on the ability of the manager to know his employees and maximize their potential for the greater benefit of the organization.

Communication within virtual teams is likely to become lighter and playful due to the blending of work and play. Cyber talk or Internet slang will continue to evolve and permeate work and play. However, there will be more of a tendency to globalize business and Internet language into an accepted form, regardless of native language spoken. Also, augmented reality will likely become part of everyday digital interactions. Tools capable of augmenting perception and enhancing reality are becoming prevalent.

Changing the language in text messages or chats or taking the wrinkles out in a picture or a video cast can change what is projected online. Translation between multicultural and multinational business partners has typically been a challenge in a face-to-face world and it has become even more challenging online. Currently we can structure our thoughts and images without limitation as long as we can translate them into a common language. The perception of the intent is left up to the receiver.

Online language translators are adopting "common English," other dialects and jargons as well as translation between natural languages. The trend to use English as the Internet language is likely to continue, especially due to the impact of globalization. English is already a standard business language and its Web dominance is likely to cause discomfort and be resisted by speakers of other languages around the globe. Without the traditional body language and verbal cues of face-to-face interaction, interpretation of a translation is often altered intentionally or intentionally.

Augmented reality is likely to infiltrate digitally mediated communications, regardless of purpose and alter what is viewed or read. Today, techniques are available to alter the photographs and video streams and to adjust facial features and body images of the person on the screen. Advanced real-time video filters could remove wrinkles, those ten extra pounds and maybe even lighten your hair. The problem with enhanced or augmented reality is when it is out of our control.

In many of the 3D worlds this is an accepted practice because of the avatars we identify with, but it becomes a bit scarier when we are not aware it is being done. Augmented reality is not just about altering the physical image of a model to make her flawless; therefore women who desire to look like her run out to buy the clothes she advertises. The danger of augmented reality lies in other subliminal applications. Filtering that causes viewers to subconsciously focus on objects by amplifying or differentiating them intentionally or altering a message whether pictorial or written, for propaganda, are all dangers of augmented reality. The implementation of augmented reality has the potential to be abused by those willing to use manipulate for some kind of gain.

In looking ahead, the impact of global positioning systems (GPS) will also influence the way we work and play. As GPS systems track the planet, it is becoming more and more possible to locate a person's physical co-presence and incorporate this into the social software. Social software can enhance our physical social interactions, giving rise to a variety of virtual physical systems. For example by attendance at the same physical event, social networking systems could augment our network, based on common attendance. Although most social networking software has not yet integrated this component, it is beginning to take place.

Meet-up is an example of the integration of a physical co-presence and online social networking tool. Meet-up brings people of similar interests together and helps them organize events. As social software becomes more integrated with even more capable mobile devices, it has a greater possibility of augmenting our physical world (Counts & Geraci, 2005). The danger with this technology is the fact that it diminishes privacy and anonymity even further.

For example, Twitter plans on capitalizing on location-tracking technologies to show a person's location when they post a tweet. Aside from providing users with a geographical map of tweets, the data collected by this feature can be used by companies or any entity for any desired purpose. Although Twitter has said it would not turn on this feature by default, the potential to compromise privacy is nonetheless evident. Implications of this type of technology are not hard to imagine. Those who turn on their location tracking feature risk having an employer discover they are sampling beer at the local brewery instead of working on the pressing project or a teenager may inadvertently advertise to the world, including his parents and school officials, that it was a great day surfing. The blending of work and play through technology will become more prevalent than ever, with mobile devices catering to faster, more sophisticated social networking sites and applications.

The Future of Learning and Playing in Cyber Education

The future of learning and playing is up to the imagination. No one is even sure of what educational institutions will look like in ten years. Once thing is for sure, education must change rapidly in order to keep up with technological advancements. The risk of having outdated, stagnant education is that it will fail to prepare young people to compete in the global marketplace. Technology is shaping education in many ways. Trends point toward the rapid increase of mobile learning platforms especially designed to deliver content, thus pushing mLearning to the forefront of education. Technology is also further blending learning and playing and forcing the pedagogy pendulum to swing toward the application of constructivism and connectivism theories.

The continued inception of online learning initiatives on the part of K-12 education, higher education, government and corporate entities, means that the future of education and training involves using technologies to create learning communities and communities of practice where knowledge is co-created, shared and discussed. Connectivity via mobile devices will be paramount as more individuals become highly mobile and blend working, playing and learning. It also means that content must be conveniently pushed to the learner via such mobile devices.

Mobile devices are adapting to learning trends and will be used to increase the value and impact of learning experiences. Learning theories, according to Price (2007) offer rationale for using digital augmentation for learning. There will be further intermingling of other theories such as constructivism and connectivism. Constructivism offers the view that learners co-construct knowledge through interactions within the learning community, while connectivism (Siemens, 2005) recognizes how learners use technology and networks to research, create new connections and meaning. Pedagogical trends will be informed by the basic principles of these theories.

Service providers will continue catering to mLearning. Mobile devices will be faster, more wireless, will provide rich multimedia experiences and will consist of user centric services (Nix, 2008). A new generation of mobile devices will include television and video outputs, relying on wireless cable connections, according to Nix's report on behalf of Ericsson Corporation. The new devices will even include laser projectors, thus enabling on the spot presentations on the part of students, educators and business people alike. Perhaps the biggest impact to the learning community will be the combination of presence technology with the creation of virtual groups, as described by Nix. This combination will allow users to show themselves as "available" to communicate with the learning group for example and be able to collaborate with fewer distractions, while remaining "unavailable" to receive messages from co-workers. This feature is likely to give users more flexibility in determining how much they are willing to blend work, play and learning. It may also become a good strategy for prioritizing tasks and getting things done.

In the report, Nix (2008) also alludes to the use of Mobile Positioning Systems (MPS) to track where people are and when they leave a physical location. Although originally intended to locate family members, any person could be included. MPS will also add a new dimension to social networking applications, because the mobile device will deliver the position coordinates to any application requesting information about the user. Current trends indicate that mobile networks are racing to jump from 3G to 4G due to customer demands. Also called *IMT- Advanced* by the International Telecommunication Union, 4G is defined as a network with 100Mbps for wide area coverage and 1Gbps for hot spots, it is expected that 4G will be delivered via bands with 100 MHz channels (Nix).

The first 4G networks are already providing services to customers with an insatiable need for network speed. Ten times faster than the 3G networks, 4G is already offered in Sweden and Norway since December 2009 (International Tele-communication Union, 2009). As networks get faster and mobile devices smarter, mLearning will undoubtedly be on the rise. Mobile learning increases capacity while decreasing costs to deliver training or entire courses. Mobile learning will increase speed at which we connect, but also the speed at which we learn, work and play.

CONCLUSION

Technological advancements continue to shape the way in which individuals communicate for work, leisure and learning. Technology facilitates the blending of these three facets of life, therefore adding pressure to remain constantly connected with friends, co-workers and loved ones. The demands on personal time are greater than ever. The learning and working environments are changing drastically due to the influence of technology. With telecommuting on the rise, more workers will find themselves blending work, play and learning.

The current mobile revolution has made tracking information to the individual even more accessible. Workers are no longer tied to a work station, they can access work or personal email from anywhere and not have to wait until they get to the office, school or even home. They can check their information on the sidelines of the children's soccer game, in line for coffee or while riding the commuter train. This has added to expectations beyond an already crunched and demanding life style. The advent of smart phones and other mobile devices provide more than Internet connectivity; they provide new expectations that users will remain connected.

In this chapter the blending of work, play and learning was explored through the lens of the pajama effect. The term "pajama effect" is proposed by the authors of this chapter as a means of understanding the blending phenomenon. Blending has become necessary in our connected society because the time available to get everything accomplished is usually less than adequate. Blending of these facets of life is inevitable, but it should be managed. The blending phenomenon beckons further exploration, as it is a natural and inconspicuous result of using digitally mediated communications and mobile technologies to work, play and learn.

A new generation of telecommuters and online learners will find themselves using collaboration tools that allow them to remotely collaborate and manage entire projects with ease. Virtual games and mLearning technologies will facilitate connectedness but also a new way of learning using constructivist and connectivist theories. Globalization increases the speed at which the blending occurs and also creates a need for a globally accepted form of communication. Internet jargon and cyber talk will continue being used, but English is likely to emerge as the preferred language of the Internet. This is a cause of concern, because meaning can be lost in translation.

Technology has removed the time barrier from the concept of location. Instant access to contacts will show us their specific geographical location using Mobile Positioning Systems. Connectivity although desired by most individuals, comes with a setback. Connectivity is also the source of many distractions at work, play and while learning. Users gravitate toward their mobile device, even during the most inopportune moments. New norms for appropriate use continue to emerge, as the tendency is for everyone to expect an instant response. More people are working during play and playing during work. The same is to be said about learning.

The blending of work, play and learning are not limited to telecommuters and those who work, play or learn online. It is a phenomenon that affects everyone and every facet of their lives. Increased connectivity through faster networks and smarter gadgets will increase the demand to give up personal time, which is potentially dehumanizing. The art of getting done relies on blending and prioritizing work, play and learning, but without sacrificing one's ability to have down time to enjoy those things that matter most in life.

REFERENCES

Apgar, M. (1998). The alternative workplace: Changing where and how people work. *Harvard Business Review, 76*(3), 121–137.

Baron, N. (2005). Cybertalk at work and at play. *Visible Language, 39*(1), 64–84.

Baruch, Y. (2000). Teleworking: Benefits and pitfalls as perceived by professionals and managers. *New Technology, Work and Employment, 15*(1), 34–49. doi:10.1111/1468-005X.00063

Brown, A., & Green, T. (2003). Showing up to class in pajamas (or less!): The fantasies and realities of online-professional development. *Clearing House (Menasha, Wis.), 76*(3), 148–151. doi:10.1080/00098650309601992

Capurro, R., & Pingel, C. (2002). Ethical issues of online communication research. *Ethics and Information Technology, 4*(3), 189–194. doi:10.1023/A:1021372527024

Chafkin, M. (2010, April 1). Telecommuting by the numbers. What the U.S. could save if more people worked from home. *Inc.* Retrieved October 24, 2010, from http://www.inc.com/magazine/20100401/telecommuting-by-the-numbers.html

Cooney, M., Gupton, P., & Laughlin, M. (2000). Blurring the lines of play and work to create blended classroom learning experiences. *Early Childhood Education Journal, 27*(3), 165–171. doi:10.1007/BF02694230

Counts, S., & Geraci, J. (2005). *Incorporating physical co-presence at events into digital social networking.* Conference on Human Factors in Computing, Portland, Oregon, April 2-7, 2005, (pp.1308-1311). New York: ACM.

EyeMags.com. (2010). *Phone count.* Retrieved October 20, 2010, from http://phonecount.com/pc/count.jsp

Godin, S. (2009, May 14). The last days of the cubicle life. *Time.* Retrieved October 19, 2010, from http://www.time.com

Hall, B. (2009, January). Take five. Five learning trends for 2009. *Chief Learning Officer.* Retrieved October 20, 2010, from http://www.clomedia.com/take-five/brandon-hall/2009/January/2503/index.php

International Telecommunication Union. (2009, December 21). *4G mobile networks launched in Sweden, Norway.* News release. Retrieved October 24, 2010, from http://www.itu.int/ITU-D/ict/newslog/4G+Mobile+Networks+Launched+In+Sweden+Norway.aspx

JALA International. (2010). *Definitions.* Retrieved October 24, 2010, from http://www.jala.com/definitions.php

Kress, G., & Pachler, N. (2007). Thinking about the m in m-learning. In N. Pachler, (Ed.), *Mobile learning: Towards a research agenda.* (pp.7-32). London: WLE Centre, Institute of Education. Retrieved October 19, 2010, from http://www.wlecentre.ac.uk/cms/files/occasionalpapers/mobilelearning_pachler_2007.pdf

Manoochehri, G., & Pinkerton, T. (2003). Managing telecommuters: Opportunities and challenges. *American Business Review, 21*(1), 9–16.

Nilles, J. M. (1976). *The telecommunications-transportation tradeoff: Options for tomorrow.* New York: John Wiley & Sons.

Nix, J. (2008). *Trends in mobile learning 2008.* Report for Ericsson corporation. Retrieved October 24, 2010, from http://www.ericsson.com/ericsson/corpinfo/programs/resource_documents/judy_nix_july_2008.pdf

Nocente, N., & Heather, K. (2002). Professional development in the online classroom. *The Canadian Journal for the Study of Adult Education, 16*(1), 1–12.

O'Conner, A. (2008). Friends abroad: At home, part 1. *Library Journal.*

Office of Information Resources Management. (2001). Report on OIRM flexiplace and hoteling pilot. Washington, DC. Retrieved October 24, 2010, from http://www.iima.org

Oravec, J. A. (2001). Online recreation and play in organizational life. The Internet as virtual contested terrain. In Chidambaram, L., & Zigurs, I. (Eds.), *Our virtual world: The transformation of work, play and life via technology* (pp. 124–140). Hershey, PA: Idea Group Publishing. doi:10.4018/9781878289926.ch008

Orenstein, P. (2009, July 28). The overextended family. *The New York Times.*

Price, S. (2007). Ubiquitous computing: Digital augmentation and learning. In N. Pachler, (Ed.), *M-learning: Towards a research agenda.* (pp.33-54). London: Institute of Education. Retrieved October 27, 2010, from http://www.wlecentre.ac.uk/cms/files/occasionalpapers/mobilelearning_pachler_2007.pdf

Schneider, K. (2000). The committee wore pajamas: ALA debuts online chat. *American Libraries, 31*(11), 62–65.

Siemens, G. (2005). Connectivism: A learning theory for the digital age. *International Journal of Instructional Technology and Distance Learning.* Retrieved October 24, 2010, from http://www.itdl.org/Journal/Jan_05/article01.htm

Stokes, H., & Wyn, J. (2007). Constructing identities and making careers: Young people's perspectives on work and learning. *International Journal of Lifelong Education, 26*(5), 495–511. doi:10.1080/02601370701559573

Tremblay, D.-G. (2002). Balancing work and family with telework? Organizational issues and challenges for women and managers. *Women in Management Review, 17*(3/4), 157–170. doi:10.1108/09649420210425309

Woodill, G. (2010). *Worldwide mobile learning trends 2010. The state of mobile learning today*. Brandon Hall Research. Retrieved October, 2010, from http://www. brandon-hall.com/publications/worldwidemlearning/worldwidemlearning.shtml

WorldatWork. (2009). *Telework trendlines 2009: A survey brief from Worldat-Work*. Retrieved October 27, 2010, from http://www.worldatwork.org/waw/ adimLink?id=31115

Section 3

What are Some Approaches for the Future of Teaching and Learning Using Digitally Mediated Communications?

Chapter 9
What was Good for the Goose is No Longer Good for the Goslings

ABSTRACT

Traditional teaching methods are outmoded. The face-to-face environment cannot be transferred online. It can only be effective if the design is learner-centric, providing opportunities for different types of interaction, flexibility, choice, collaboration, real-world skills, and learner control. The role of cyber educators is changing from a facilitator to a partner in learning. Learning in the online environment is a reciprocal exchange of knowledge between members of the community, as well as between the instructor and the learner.

OBJECTIVES

- Recognize the role interactions play in learner success.
- Identify the elements necessary to create a learner centric environment.
- Be aware of the need for instructor preparedness for the online environment.
- Determine the influence of affordances when designing using technologies.
- Identify the necessity to shift control from teacher to learner in a constructivist learning environment.

DOI: 10.4018/978-1-60960-543-8.ch009

INTRODUCTION

The evolution of formal education over the centuries is a testament to mankind's quest for progress. Through it all, however, new tools and ideas were not always welcomed. From royal courts where only the elite had access to learning to Socrates' garden where free thinking was encouraged, naysayers resisted change to the old ways of thinking, learning and doing. It is no different today, at the dawn of the 21st century, when we find ourselves discussing old issues in education that need creative solutions. Modern technology has revolutionized the world, just as papyrus rolls and Gutenberg's printing press did centuries ago.

Digital technologies offer many options for learners, including online learning. Cyber education is in demand, yet many outdated practices are still espoused in adult training and higher education as well as K-12 education. This chapter discusses mindsets that hinder the progress of education and highlights the importance of interaction in the virtual learning environment. Many old ways of teaching may have been appropriate for students, but advancements in technology and research make it imperative that educators rethink what is appropriate for learners today.

BACKGROUND

In the last few hundred years, there have been innumerable changes to education, but unfortunately, some aspects remain the same. The first one-room schoolhouse in the United States, located in St. Augustine, Florida and built 200 years ago, very much resembles the few ones still operating in rural America and other corners of the world. While some may wish to discuss only the negative aspects of the one-room schoolhouse, this type of learning environment can provide insights into the principle of learner-centric pedagogy and andragogy. Likewise, the great thinkers of the old world applied learner-centric principles to encourage self-discovery and critical thinking. Technology, however, requires us to re-think what learner-centric means now and to identify which outdated practices from the industrial revolution still remain in the minds of educators today.

Over the years, educators stopped encouraging self-discovery and embarked on the quest to produce citizens who could function in the industrial age, working in factory lines and performing routine tasks. Critical thinking was not necessary for those jobs. Postmodern times have brought about the technology revolution, yet educators hardly modified their practices. In the era of technology, cyber education is replacing old systems and changing old mindsets. Cyber education is here to stay for a long while. Government agencies, corporations, higher education and, more recently, K-12 education have all embraced online learning. Online courses in the higher education sector are in greater demand than traditional courses according to a 2008 report published by Sloan-C (Allen & Seaman, 2008). The report indicates that from 2002 to 2007 enrollments for online courses jumped by 19.7 percent, compared to a 1.5 percent increase of face-to-face courses. According to Brooks (2009), seven reasons why higher education will continue to offer online learning include: (a) The active engagement of learners; (b) the ability to reach students with diverse learning styles; (c) the ability to offer a variety of experiences outside of the classroom; (d) emphasis on learners conducting independent research; (e) it makes college accessible to more students; (f) it makes attending college more affordable; and (g) it helps teach students values and ethics.

The demand for online learning in higher education continues to be a central focus for administrators and instructors, who must be prepared to meet the needs of students. The economic crisis has contributed to the surge of online learning programs, according to the 2008 Sloan-C report, especially undergraduate programs (Allen & Seaman, 2008), which make up the largest type of program offered online. During the fall of 2007, there was a 12 percent increase in students taking at least one online course, for a total of 3.9 million students (Allen & Seaman, 2008). It is expected that the overall percent of U.S. higher education students enrolled in at least one online course will surpass the 2007 figure of 20 percent. Interestingly, public institutions make up the largest sector of higher education institutions offering online courses, due in part to the fact that larger institutions started their programs earlier than their smaller counterparts.

Traditional brick-and-mortar K-12 schools have been slower to embrace technology for instructional purposes. A 2008 survey of U.S. public schools indicated that there was an average of three students for each Internet-enabled instructional computer in schools (Gray, Thomas, & Lewis, 2010). Technology in K-12 education is still not used to its full potential. If implemented correctly for instructional purposes, technology could very well force a new shift to learner-centered practices that resemble the old one-room schoolhouse. These practices include more learner control, flexibility, co-construction of knowledge within the learning community and facilitation on the part of the instructor.

Although strides were made in K-12 education to embrace technology, online learning is still not an option for every student. The Keeping Pace report for 2009 identified that in the U.S. 45 out of 50 states plus Washington D.C. now have either a state virtual school or a full-time online learning initiative, while some states have both types of programs (Watson, Ryan, & Wicks, 2009). While each of these programs continues to grow, a lack of research and funding for this sector exists, but most importantly there is a lack of understanding on the part of traditional educators.

Many traditional educators across all levels of education refute the idea that technology should play such a key role in education, mainly because they were educated under the old school of thought when technology was not part of the mainstream. With each new generation of technology literate educators, however, there is the expectation that technology will become a required instructional tool to reach every learner. Some K-12 teacher-training programs now include online teaching as part of the program, better preparing new educators to meet the needs of their students. Likewise, more colleges and universities are training faculty to design and teach online courses.

Much of the challenge holding back education reform for K-12, as well as higher education, is a lack of funding. Implementation of technology is gaining an edge over other concerns because technology is now accepted as a necessary tool for delivering instruction to the 21st century learner. Investing in information technology (IT) has been a focus of every industry and government institution. Education, although it is the smallest sector represented in IT growth, spent \$61.46 billion in 2009 and is expected to increase spending to an estimated \$63.99 billion in 2010 (Nagel, 2010). Higher education as well as K-12 school districts are investing heavily to update their infrastructure. Miami-Dade County Public Schools, the fourth largest school district in the U.S., has recently revamped its IT infrastructure to provide 24/7 portal access to parents, teachers and students. With a savings of \$5.18 million in hardware and \$1.5 million in energy savings, the district has virtualized 95% of its IT environment (VMware, 2010).

Cyber educators and face-to-face educators alike are compelled to learn new ways of teaching. The skills needed to present a traditional lesson are far different than those required to present it online. Educators must learn to use technology tools that most of their students already know how to use. Most educators are digital immigrants, while their students are digital natives. Prensky (2009) enlightens educators by further expanding his 2001 position on digital natives versus immigrants. He points out that digital technology is making humans wiser. Prenksy (2009) alludes to earlier technologies such as the pocket watch, which took away people's ability to tell the time by observing the sun, yet opened up the mind to other possibilities. He contends that digital technology including games, the Internet and television, are more cognitively demanding than older forms, thereby augmenting a person's cognitive capabilities. Digital wisdom, as defined by Prensky, is brought about when technology enhances the individual, thus allowing him to make wiser decisions.

Digital technologies bring about challenges as well as opportunities to rectify practices that are not in the best interests of learners. A major challenge of creating quality cyber education is integrating meaningful interactions between members of the learning community to promote and enhance the learning experience. The success of an online course hinges on its ability to connect the learner not just with the content, but also with the learning community. The next section explores the importance of interaction in the online learning environment.

Interaction as a Key to Success

One of the most important aspects of the online revolution is the change in position of pedagogy, as well as andragogy. The role of the instructor evolves from one of subject matter expert and provider of content to a facilitator and, eventually, a partner in learning (Beldarrain, 2006). This requires a commitment of excellence on the part of the organization or institution, thus recognizing the importance of designing for online learning and the time, effort and structure needed to create and implement alternative teaching practices.

A wide range of tools and techniques such as problem-based learning, online debates, role playing, storytelling, virtual teaming and collaborative projects are available to assist in the design of online courses; however, all of these require careful planning and support for activities (DeVries & Lim, 2003). These resources are often not tapped due to money or time constraints or simply lack of knowledge on the part of designers or online instructors.

Learner-centric environments promote choice, flexibility and personalize the learning experience based on interests, motivation, abilities and learning styles. The more customized the learning experience, the more engaged the learner will be and the more likely he is to succeed. Interaction with every aspect of the environment, whether technological or human, must be deliberately weaved through the course in a way that exposes the learner to many different types of learning opportunities and maximizes the learner's potential. Good course design is imperative.

A common problem for new online learning programs is design. Often, the individuals involved in the original design of the course and/or program lack appropriate knowledge and skills. The problem is also evident when traditional instructors are given the assignment to teach online without proper training. These efforts to create an online course with no prior knowledge of the virtual learning environment produce a course that is mediocre and ineffective. The end result is usually an interaction-void online version of the preferred textbook and digital versions of the instructor's traditional lectures. It simply does not work because it lacks strategies to deliver content and support the learning process.

The role of social interaction in the learning process has been expounded since the early part of the 20th century. Dewey (1916) argued that learning was an interactive and transactional process. It was later explained by Vygotsy in 1978 that language and thought are developed as a result of social practice. Even more evidence surfaced with Lave and Wenger (1991) in support of learning as a contextual and social practice.

Social theories of learning argue that knowledge can usually be measured by what is contributed and that knowledge is constructed by our participation in different activities. This focus on the social aspects of learning has presented special challenges for the evolution of learning in the online environment. Because of the increasing popularity and economics of online learning, more attention is now given to social interaction in higher education, K-12 virtual schools and corporate training. This has led to a need for an increased understanding of the constructs of socialization and building of knowledge online (Laffey, Lin, & Lin, 2006).

Nearly every social theory postulates that social activity is undertaken as a way to fulfill motives. One of the most popular motives for human interaction is thought to be the need to fit in or belong. According to Laffey, Lin and Lin (2006) social capital is often explained in terms of units of social benefit derived from interactivity within a group. Affiliation with a standpoint or group consensus is often times a reward in itself. This position does not mean that all social activity is rewarding but rather that motivation for human interaction is part of being human and that humans have a desire to obtain satisfaction and enjoyment from it. Levels of trust and social norms are often a strong influence for work and interaction. These are established through being a part of a group and sharing mutual experiences. This has been extrapolated to include interpersonal trust, mutual norms and reciprocity as well as networks of affiliation. The concept of embodiment also helps cyber educators understand interactions.

The concept of embodiment focuses on the way humans interact not only with technologies but through them. The affordances of the technology will establish how well it supports meaningful social interaction. Examples of this might be the ability of the technology to support conversation in the person's native language or the familiarity with the features of the technology such as clicking on buttons or selecting features. According to Laffey, Lin and Lin (2006) the important element here is that the social ability is supported neither by the tool itself, a set of features of the tool or the person, but rather through the relationship among them. Virtual communities rely on the technological features that support interaction and on how socially connected its members feel.

For social communities to be successful, they must support social ability. Communities with features such as a defined purpose, appropriate selection of members, defined roles and a balance of structure and flexibility are usually more supportive of social ability. Two determinants of successful online communities are social presence and social navigation. In networked virtual environments, social presence is the sense of actually being there and, more importantly, being there with others. Laffey, Lin and Lin (2006) describe social navigation as the sense of awareness of what others are doing and the impact that it has on one's own actions and contributions.

Social presence theory (Short, Williams, & Christie, 1976) is concerned with how successful technology tools are in conveying a sense of physical presence and uses face-to-face communications as a standard for that comparison. Social presence is important because it affects how learners can sense emotions, relationships and closeness. In the early days of the Internet, bandwidth for graphics and visuals was scarce thus text only systems were primarily used. This allowed for limited cues to establish social, emotional and contextual communication. Limited cues in turn inhibit relationship development and increase misunderstandings (Preece, 2000). The consequence of missing cues is not only poor communication, but also the lack of signals such as pauses, gazes and glances diminish physical presence and accentuate the differences such as time zone, cultural and language barriers.

Research of the effects of different kinds of computer mediated communication used for collaboration and socialization has shown that video conferencing for example, more closely resembles face-to-face communications and that textual systems are less effective in consensus building than the face-to-face environment (Preece, 2000). This could be in part because computer mediated communications supports socio-emotional communications poorly according to Preece (2000). Technological advancements now make it possible to mix different media in the same interaction, thus providing visual, audio and contextual clues to the users. Applications such as Skype combine these features, creating a stronger socio-emotional bond between participants while also supporting social ability.

The emerging theory of connectivism also attempts to address how learners make connections through technology. Siemens (2005) acknowledges that today's learners have different skills and use different tools that were not around before. Siemens proposes that learners use networks for different purposes, such as researching and connecting with peers, thus through the use of networks learners make connections and gain new knowledge. Modern technology promotes networking in ways never anticipated. Today's generation of learners is savvier and is exposed to more information daily than any other generation before.

Constructivism describes how learning should provide real-life experiences through interactive and collaborative interactions. In this way, learning becomes authentic (Jonassen, 1994). Through social negotiation and knowledge exchange, learners co-construct and gain more knowledge than it may be evident to the instructor. Online learners, especially adults, have more autonomy and are more self-directed. It is the role of the instructor to guide students toward the learning objectives and involve them in the educational process.

Online learning is not just about using technology, it is about creating an engaging and meaningful learning environment. To determine what is considered a best practice for today's learner, cyber educators must analyze and apply theories that keep the learner as the main focus, but that are also relevant to cyber education. Creating a learner-centric environment involves the infusion of meaningful interactions, preparing instructors for the virtual learning environment and shifting control from the instructor to the learner.

CREATING A LEARNER-CENTRIC ENVIRONMENT

Interaction is often cited as the most important component for success in online courses. The literature identifies five main types of interaction in the online learning environment: learner-to-learner, learner-to-content, learner-to-instructor, learner-to-interface interaction and vicarious interaction (Hillman, Willis, & Gunawardena, 1994; Moore, 1989; Sutton, 2001; Wagner, 1997). Today, in diametric opposition to the days when a good student sat dutifully and listened attentively, interaction is paramount in both the face-to-face and online learning environments.

Social interaction is of utmost importance in cyber education because the physical distance from peers and from the instructor adds to feelings of isolation. Isolation and limitations of the learning environment are minimized through the integration of the different types of interactions. The constraints of the online environment have led to new ways of communicating in the virtual classroom. The recognition and expression of emotions through nonverbal cues such as smiling, looking puzzled, raising one's hand, are replaced by new communication strategies. Whether the course is fully asynchronous or a blend of asynchronous/synchronous delivery, the use of digitally mediated communication enhances the experience.

Interaction can involve not only interaction between humans but also interaction between audio, visual, text and graphical components. The interplay of these interactive technologies can contribute to the perception of quality in distance learning. For example, a course that incorporates multimedia or video may be perceived as being better. An important distinction between interactivity and interaction must be established. Interaction is the establishment of mutual influence between reciprocal events requiring two objects and two actions (Wagner, 1997). Interactivity is the ability of the technology to establish a point-to-point connection either from one point to another or from one point to multiple points. Interactions are behaviorally based, while interactivities are attributes of the technologies used.

Online discussion boards are used in blended and in fully asynchronous online courses as a way to share thoughts and ideas and to collaborate. Both the quality and quantity of interaction between instructors and learners can be enhanced using digitally mediated communications; if these interactions are going to be productive for learning, they must be planned. In addition to the instructional benefits, online discussion boards also help to establish the rapport between learners. Online discussions can support both social and instructional goals (Martyn, 2005).

Discussion boards were adopted early in the implementation of distance education to promote communication and interaction between learners. However, it has become clear that a good course design should not solely rely on discussion boards to bring students together. Learner-learner interaction must be dynamic, not static. Many discussion boards are mere lists of prescribed topics for the students to discuss, while the instructor monitors participation and awards a numerical value toward the final grade. Effective discussion boards provide learners with the flexibility to discuss pertinent issues related to the course and to highlight the key points learned. Current events provide teachable moments for young as well as adult learners. Adding another human element to online learning according to Kaplan-Leirserson (2003) may help to increase retention and support collaboration.

Techniques like pair share and small groups can help to facilitate communications and build the learning community. Synchronous technology tools such as Elluminate®, Fuze Meeting®, GoToMeeting® and Genesys Conferencing® offer web conferencing options for different needs. Virtual trainings or virtual courses can easily integrate real-time communication opportunities to increase the sense of connection within the members of the learning community.

The success of online discussions and interactions hinges on the involvement, both cognitively and emotionally, of both instructor and students. The emergence of an online identity develops over time and is an integral part of learning online. The psychological aspects of the online environment augment certain traits in the individual while diminishing others. Some learners who would be too shy to raise their hands in the physical classroom, for example, may feel less inhibited in the online environment and participate more actively.

Another aspect of interaction through writing as opposed to speaking is that it may lead to deeper reflection and thought because learners must construct and write down their communication before delivering it. The asynchronous nature of the online environment also lends itself to reflection and considerable engagement, because the learner can read a post and then contemplate a response for days instead of being forced to provide an instantaneous response. Others may prefer to read what others have shared without necessarily responding. This is a form of vicarious interaction as proposed by Sutton (2001).

The flexibility to access content is part of learner-content interaction. Today's learners need flexibility of access, but also increased control over the content itself and control over the speed at which the learner can move through the course. Instructional strategies that focus on giving control to the learner are more likely to infuse 21st Century Skills and integrate Web 2.0 tools. Today's learners desire to create content. The advent of Web 2.0 tools has provided new ways to show mastery of concepts in engaging, meaningful ways for learners. The pencil and paper test, or even the computerized multiple-choice test, is no longer the only form of valid assessment available. Authentic, open-ended assessments allow learners to apply higher order thinking to solve real-world problems. The topic of designing for authenticity is covered in Chapter 10 of this book.

Learner-interface interaction occurs as the learner navigates the course, accessing or creating content and interacting with peers and the instructor. Just as a physical book has different parts designed to organize the contents for the reader, the course navigation must do the same for learners. The main difference is that digital learners do not navigate a Web page the same way they flip through the pages of a book. The linear, sequential way of reading a book does not apply online. Online learners move randomly from link to link searching for what they need. The element of time and ease of use are important for a good experience. The user needs quick and easy access to the information he needs so he can focus on the learning process.

The anonymity of the environment also supports equalization of position between instructor and learner thus altering the traditional mode of learner-instructor interaction. The lack of face-to-face and physical proximity disarms the instructor and challenges their traditional position of authority. This mind shift is crucial for developing positive learner-instructor relationships. The traditional position of power only creates mistrust and disconnect in the online learning environment. Without trust, modeled by the instructor, the online learning community cannot thrive.

Positive modeling on the part of the instructor cultivates trust and creates an environment where learners feel safe to debate intellectual issues and challenge traditional authority, not only because of the anonymity offered in the online environment, but ultimately because their input is valued in the co-construction of knowledge. The role of the instructor changes from lecturer to facilitator and from facilitator to a partner in learning (Beldarrain, 2006).

When learners are allowed to share knowledge and participate in the creation of content, they become true contributors of knowledge (Beldarrain, 2006). This departure from the traditional instructor and student role repositions the learner at the center of the learning process, thus encouraging contribution-oriented pedagogy. Collis and Moonen (2005) argue that student contributions should be collected and shared as part of the course content, thus learners can see what other students have learned in the course and build on their own experiences. The learner-created content becomes a permanent library of knowledge made available to future students as a valuable resource.

In the absence of interaction there exists a heightened sense of disconnect and isolation. There is also the potential for identity loss for some participants, while others display a new self. The initial loss of identity and anonymity of the learner and instructor is eventually replaced as the online course proceeds and recognizable personae emerge. The emerging personae are what classmates and the instructor will "see" online, thus each individual's online presence manifests itself in different ways. Over a period of time, consistencies of communication style, ideas, attitudes and writing style create a personality that becomes recognizable and known (DeVries & Lim, 2003). It is precisely these virtual cues that an effective online instructor uses to connect with learners and build trust within the learning community. It is up to the instructor to leverage the virtual cues to maximize and personalize the learning experience for each online learner.

One of the most pronounced differences between interactions of instructors and learners in the online environment compared to the traditional face-to-face environment is greater equality. The nature of digitally mediated communications requires the instructor to provide explicit instructions and feedback in a written format, greater workloads in designing and facilitating a course and provoking deeper thinking through online discussions and synchronous sessions. In turn, learners should be expected to do the same as part of participating in the learning community. According to Smith, Ferguson and Caris (2002), the learning community provides a sense of greater equality between instructor and learner, greater freedom of speech, emergence of an online identity, greater individual relations and helps to build relationships between learners and instructors, which in turn support learner success. It is the instructor, however, who models for the learners and creates a safe learning environment where academic discourse can flourish.

Instructor Preparedness

Regardless of their proficiency with technological applications, many instructors hesitate if asked to teach in the online environment because they may be afraid to embrace the redefined roles of both the instructor and the learner. Anonymity and the shifting of space and time in the asynchronous environment present a new frontier and a new way of viewing the complexities of physical, cognitive and virtual space (Meloncon, 2007). Instructors new to the online environment may be familiar with the nuances of technical communications but may not necessarily understand how they all fit together. It is crucial that organizations train instructors properly so they may comprehend the affordances of technology, their impact in the online learning environment and how to implement best practices to capitalize on those affordances.

The online learning landscape is a very different place than the traditional face-to-face classroom; it refers to more than the physical space and geographical constraints. A landscape includes the different types of interactions and the learning or social community and its spaces. Embedded are visual cues that reinforce the familiar and establish patterns for expected behaviors and for conducting interactions. Moreover, artifacts and visuals embedded in the virtual environment provide meaning, a sense of identity and steer participants toward accepted social norms for the group. A combination of processes and patterns form the foundation for interactions within the group and the space. For many instructors, this represents a huge shift because traditional views on instruction do not rely on technology tools to deliver instruction or to interact.

Different technology tools help bridge the physical distance and therefore promote interaction. Synchronous communications including video conferencing platforms initially gained popularity because the communication more closely resembled face-to-face communications (Preece, 2000). Consensus building and social presence using text-based systems is more difficult to achieve than in a face-to-face environment, but not impossible. Instructors must be prepared to use media and collaborative tools to enrich the learning experience but to also increase social presence and the feeling of connectedness. The online landscape of cyber education requires more effort in establishing commonalities and interactions. Every media and technology tool provides affordances and opportunities. Preece expanded on the idea that media afforded different benefits: co-presence, visibility, audibility, contemporality, simultaneity, sequentiality, reviewability and revisability (Clark and Brennan, 1991; Gaver, 1992). However, technological advancements and changes in best practices since these authors discussed the topic make it necessary to broaden the scope of the eight characteristics of media to also include newer digital technologies, keeping in mind that future technologies will continue modifying these affordances. Table 1 below explains the relationship between each characteristic and its impact on the online learning environment (Cyrs, 1997; Preece, 2000).

An effective online course integrates these characteristics to maximize their impact in the learning environment. Instructors must be prepared to be more deliberate with design of a virtual course because many of the obvious elements of face-to-face are missing online. Evidence supports the conclusion that the structure and design of asynchronous learning is crucial (Scalzo, Jennings, & Wilson, 1999). Lack of proper training on the part of instructors presents a hindrance; they must be trained in the techniques and methods of designing for online learning. Techniques of instructional design, learning cycles, multiple intelligences and distance learning must be combined for successful design. Two important elements to focus on are the humanization of the online experience and the establishment of a learning community. A clear introduction with stated objectives and prerequisites, concrete examples and reflective observations as well as abstract conceptualization followed by active experimentation, all need to be part of this experience.

A challenge for novice online instructors is how to align learning goals, learning activities, feedback and evaluation. Well-trained instructors recognize the importance of providing clear learning objectives and challenging activities that allow the learner to show mastery of concepts in open-ended assessments, rather than traditional tests. The online environment has the tendency to diminish linear thinking patterns because of the random navigation inherent in the technology. Instructors therefore must design activities that build on previous concepts in the course, but also provide enough stand-alone content that would enable the learner to complete the activity out of sequence. Traditionally, instructors want learners to complete

Table 1. Characteristics of digital technology tools and their impact on online learning

Characteristic	Definition	Impact on Online Learning
co-presence	Two parties share the same physical environment as in traditional communication	Co-presence is strived for in many online communities and includes the nuances of face-to-face communications. Co-presence refers to the physical and temporal proximity of two individuals. It may be enhanced through synchronous activities, especially those with audio and visual capabilities. Co-presence fosters collaboration and connectedness.
visibility	Two parties can see each other.	Emoticons are a development of early online efforts to compensate for these nuances. Visibility includes the ability to read body language, facial clues, visually communicate feelings. Literal visibility may be enhanced through the use of Web cams. Visibility in the online environment may also include one's level of participation and how "visible" the person makes themselves by replying to classmates in the discussion board, collaborating, etc.
audibility	Two parties can speak and hear each other.	The tone of a person's voice can communicate feelings and meaning. Synchronous Web conferencing tools include audio features that add audibility. In the online environment audibility can also be the tone of voice used for written communication.
simultaneity	Both parties can send and receive the exchanges of communication rapidly.	This includes the element of spontaneity and is present in online chats, instant messenger, whiteboards and other synchronous tools.
sequentiality	Two parties communicate one after another by taking turns.	This is experienced in asynchronous communications where exchanges and responses can span a period of hours, days weeks or even longer. A longer wait time may cause the learner to become disengaged, therefore minimizing learning. Using synchronous tools may enhance sequentiality.
contemporality	Two parties exchanges are sent and received immediately	Many forms of synchronous verbal online communications like VOIP (Voice Over Internet Provider) as well as Web conferencing tools enhance contemporality.

Table 1. Continued...

Characteristic	Definition	Impact on Online Learning
reviewability	One party can review or replay someone else's communication.	Provided by archiving synchronous sessions, emails, chat sessions and discussion postings.
revisability	Changes can be made to the original message between two parties	This can occur if the messages are allowed to be reviewed and edited by users.

page one before going to page two. In the online environment, this is not necessary because the technology provides flexibility of access and enables learners to move at their own pace and pursue their own interests. This point will be further explored in the next section about shifting control.

Instructors must also be cognizant of learner satisfaction. The questions of instructional effectiveness and learner satisfaction in Web-based courses have been well researched. One factor that is predominant is the effect of learner interaction. The interactive cycle between learner and instructor is perceived as important to all academic learning and includes task, action and feedback. Other research shows that learner perceptions of courses may impact satisfaction but may not be linked directly to learning outcomes. This may be a result of familiarity and expectations. Bruckman (2002) states forcefully that learner-to-learner interactions online may make a difference in learning because of the ability to create mutually supportive communities. Much research is still needed to establish a relationship between delivery and outcome (Glenn, Jones, & Hoyt, 2003) as well as to determine which types of interactions may have a stronger impact on learning outcomes.

Interactions provide the mechanism to establish expectations between instructor and learner. The satisfaction and persistence of distance learners has been linked to interactions, especially learner-instructor, because of the natural relationship that builds between the two individuals through continued communication. When an instructor provides timely, concise feedback on student work or quickly addresses concerns, the student will sense that the instructor cares about his success. As stated earlier, it is the responsibility of the instructor to model trust in the online learning environment. Likewise, the delivery system must be chosen carefully, always keeping the focus on learning and the learner and not on the convenience of the selection of a delivery system. The selection should be based on the benefits of medium, the course content and the needs of the learner (Berge, 2002).

Well-trained online instructors will make the most of the affordances of technology. They will model trust within the learning community, align learning goals, learning activities, feedback and evaluation to help learners achieve success. They will also ensure that visual cues are embedded throughout the course and that interaction is integrated in meaningful, deliberate ways that promote the co-construction of knowledge thus shifting control from the instructor to the learner.

Shifting Control through Technology

One of the most difficult shifts in paradigm is the shift of control from the instructor to the learner. This includes a shift in perception of the learner's time and position within the group. The constructivist environment is centered interactions and flourishes through shared responsibility for learning. The instructor is responsible for establishing appropriate learning outcomes within that environment, developing appropriate instructional strategies, developing assessment strategies to facilitate and measure learner achievement and selecting learning activities and technologies to support those learning activities. The instructor selects content, plans outcomes and establishes how success will be achieved, measured and assessed (Major & Levenburg, 1999). The learner on the other hand, is responsible for actively participating and contributing to the knowledge base as a way to show mastery of concepts.

At the root of andragogy is the idea that, for adults, learning is a two-way process because the instructor is learning as much as the student (Gessner, 1956). Shared authority gives value to the learner's experience through formal and informal activities and assessments. Adult learning happens best when it is under democratic conditions (Knowles, Holton, & Swanson, 2005).

Shifting control to the learner means the instructor will provide choice and flexibility.

Technology provides flexibility and speed of access. The mindset that students should complete work in sequential order and within a certain time undermines the need for choice and flexibility. Learners should be able to move at their own pace, but given time parameters to complete the course. Some learners, due to ability, motivation or time availability, may be able to progress faster through the course than other learners.

Choice over content and assessment is also influenced by technology. Learners become the creators of content through the use of Web 2.0 tools for reflective and collaborative learning. Instead of the instructor being the source of all content, learners share their experiences and their products, thus adding to the virtual repertoire of collective knowledge shared by the learning community. Product-based assessment allows learners to infuse all their newly acquired skills with prior knowledge therefore producing a tangible product that displays mastery of learning objectives.

With the controls of learning shifting from the instructor to the learner, the learner becomes the central and most important component in the learning process. A student's time becomes more valuable and individualized learning becomes critical. A learning environment should help learners make meaning out of what and why they are learning and context is very important in determining meaning. Context goes much further than just the setting or real world. An interactive learning environment is needed to engage learners and tap their prior knowledge.

Active learning encourages the building of social relationships and the completion of learning goals through verbal, visual, cognitive and affective participation. The interaction can be two-way with the instructor or classmates or it can be one-way communication between the learner and content. Freedom over content enables the student to learn based on interest or abilities while remaining engaged. This is true for learners of all ages. One-on-one interaction with the content can be done by studying, reviewing, rehearsing or reflecting to construct competencies and reach learning goals. Reflection is a way for the learner to look back, review and evaluate (Berge, 2002) what is learned. Interaction, action and reflection all support the learning process.

If the learner finds instruction meaningful and engaging, then he is actively learning. Learning environments should strive to facilitate involvement in authentic experiences and problem solving. Active learning places learners in situations that compel them to read, write, ask questions, imagine and generate ideas. Only the learner can generate what is learned and manage it within his own constraints. Learning environments should focus on establishing high order thinking, such as analysis, synthesis and evaluation skills.

Rather than the learner being engaged solely by the instructor, constructivist theory implies that the environment itself must be engaging. Early attempts at e-Learning traded the inclusion of technologies for human interaction. Technologies, however, have changed and continue to evolve. The continuing development of these new technologies will support the new pedagogies for learning. The days of shovel-ware are not yet gone, but they are numbered. Shovel-ware is the text heavy instructional content that was put online in the early days of e-Learning when little was known about how people learned using technologies. That was then and this is now. Over a decade has passed since individuals began using the Internet for learning. Technological innovation now successfully connects people across the globe to each other and to knowledge.

Instant messaging, blogs, wikis and other forms of synchronous online communications are being used to supplement online and blended courses. Traditional educational software grouped people and fostered a top down approach to communications. Social networks take a grassroots and bottom up approach. Some experts in online adaption attribute the surge of Internet connectivity to the adaption of social software. Others contend that it is the restructuring of corporations, because of a change in business climate that is making the difference in the way humans communicate. Still another adaption theory says that people are searching for a sense of belonging and community over the Internet. Social software is providing a way of making this connection. It is highly probably that each of these theories holds some truth regarding the high adaption rate and ever increasing popularity of social software. Social software undoubtedly adds another way to establish human connections in online learning and may help to increase retention and support collaboration (Kaplan-Leiserson, 2003).

In order for technology to be successfully integrated into learning environments the educational community must be open to making changes in the way teaching takes place and instruction is delivered. "Just go there and teach the way you have always taught. There isn't any difference between traditional classroom teaching and teaching at a distance" (Cyrs, 1997) is an erroneous statement. This approach may keep the costs down and support the pedagogy of traditional classrooms but it will not be successful with technological integration. Technology integration requires course planning and appropriate verbal and non-verbal presentation skills. These differ in an asynchronous and synchronous environment. Solid collaboration, teamwork and questioning strategies are essential in the online. Graphics and visual integration play an even more important role in learning than in a face-to-face environment. The idea that teaching using technologies is the same as teaching in a face-to-face classroom is flawed. Instructors need more time to plan, more instructional support and additional training. Traditional methods of delivery must be modified. Good online pedagogy includes continually upgrading the capabilities of the faculty to interact with new technologies. It also includes instructional planning to optimally integrate the affordances of these technologies.

Optimally technological integration is all about engagement and supporting the learner. The active engagement of learners for example might include the incorporation of group projects, presentations, debates, and videos but supports a constructivist pedagogical approach. Emerging technology tools facilitate the integration of student interaction in distance education and support the merger of different approaches. Meeting the needs of the 21st-century learner may require a multi-theory approach, integrating best practices from different theories. This paradigm shift frees distance educators to explore inquiry-based learning, apprenticeship, and other approaches to distance education.

Three common forms of instruction exist that are applicable to the face-to-face as well as online learning environments. Cooperative, individualistic and competitive instruction represent three different forms of social interdependence, which can be characterized as positive, neutral and potentially negative. Technology has the ability to emphasize each of these characteristics; therefore, it is the responsibility of the instructor to manage instruction in a way that nurtures learning. In cooperative instruction, learners work together, share resources and goals and rely on each other in an interdependent exchange to achieve common goals. Successes and failures are perceived as a group outcome. In individualistic instruction, the learner has the ability to work at his own pace and with his own content. The success or failure of others is irrelevant and ignored. In a competitive environment, learners work hard to do better than their classmates or slack off because they perceive the inability to compete. According to Ghaith (2003), inappropriate competition causes learners to internalize the view that goals are attainable by only one or a few of the learners.

Control is shifted best through informed choices. By allowing learners to use different technology tools for learning purposes, educators take on the responsibility of ensuring that instructors, as well as students, know how to use such technologies. Educators need to provide clear expectations for students in terms of use and also evaluation. In K-12 education, parents need to be informed about these issues as well. Traditional face-to-face K-12 schools in particular are experiencing unprecedented issues with regard to technology tools. School districts face difficult decisions when dealing with student privacy. A school district in Pennsylvania, for instance, was sued in 2010 for allegedly using Webcams to spy on students (Associated Press, 2010). Although the district maintained the only intention was to locate missing laptops, it invaded the privacy of students by capturing 56,000 screen shots and Webcam images.

All sectors of education are being shaped by technology. Technologies will continue to evolve and cause pedagogical shifts, alter mindsets and force educators to learn more about the conundrums of cyber education. The future of education depends largely on the ability of educators to adapt to the changing needs of learners who, as explained by Prensky (2009), are now digital natives seeking digital wisdom. The learner-centric environment is reminiscent of the one-room schoolhouse where students were likely to receive individualized attention, learning from older peers through collaboration and co-constructed knowledge within the small learning community.

LOOKING AHEAD

The needs of the digital native are different than the needs of previous generations; therefore, current practices in education must change. Modern technology has forced educators to rethink best practices for both online and face-to-face instruction. Creating a learner-centric environment is likely to be one of the main ideas behind education reform in the next decade.

Now What?

1.   Organizations must incorporate technologies and practices that include more learner control, flexibility, co-construction of knowledge within the learning community and facilitation on the part of the instructor.
2.   Organizations and institutions should make a commitment of excellence.
3.   Learner-centric online environments should be created that include meaningful interactions, preparing instructors for the virtual learning environment and shifting control from the instructor to the learner.
4.   It is crucial that organizations train instructors properly so they may comprehend the affordances of technology, their impact in the online learning environment and how to implement best practices to capitalize on those affordances.

A learner-centric environment must take into account the whole person. The physical, affective and cognitive domains must be given equal attention. In cyber education, the physical distance is minimized through interaction with peers, instructor, content and the interface, as well as vicariously observing others. The affective domain is addressed through timely, constructive feedback, building trusting relationships within the learning community and feeling less isolated. The cognitive domain is enhanced through engaging, collaborative activities that allow the learner to co-construct knowledge and show mastery of learning objectives.

The first roadblock to moving ahead is the attitude of educators who do not embrace the impact of technology. The mindset that technology only serves the purpose of keeping costs down is what supports the same old pedagogy of traditional classrooms, passive lecture and talking heads (Cyrs, 1997). In order for technology to be integrated into learning, changes must take place in the way instruction is delivered as well as how courses are designed. Most online courses do not take advantage of the potential of story telling, role-playing, virtual teaming, problem based learning, online debates and other collaborative activities that enrich the learner's experience and moves them toward learning.

Much has been explored about the need to individualize learning; however, the future of cyber education truly relies on the ability of educators to personalize the learning experience. Instructors must know their students as individuals who have different levels of preference for interactions, different interests, skills, abilities and background knowledge. In looking ahead, learning paths emerge as a much anticipated approach to cyber learning.

Learning paths as an approach to online learning will provide the learner with open choice based on ability, skill set, interest, preference and background knowledge. The content unfolds before the learner, based on his decisions. Fuzzy logic, the same approach used to create games, may be helpful in developing online courses that provide different learning paths for students. Chen, Liu, Liu and Hsiech (2005) propose using fuzzy logic to create a personalized online curriculum. Today's learners use fuzzy logic without realizing it: each time they play a video game they are making on the spot decisions about what to do in different situations. Each action has a consequence; therefore, the player learns quickly from his mistakes and adjusts his strategy as the game progresses. The "what if" plays a key role in fuzzy logic. Examples of this are the Sims2 and SimCity games where players create their own virtual world and must make decisions very much like in real life. Learning paths hold promise to creating an online learning environment that truly meets the needs of learners.

Gaming in education also holds promise of delivering engaging, interactive learning. Gaming and simulations are already used extensively to train the military, law enforcement officers, pilots and even surgeons. Cyber educators have been slow to use gaming because of the cost associated with producing a single course. However, integrating short scenarios through gaming or simulations will greatly enhance the content of the course and support learning. The active engagement of learners includes the integration of group projects, presentations, debates, videos and technologies that support a constructivist pedagogical approach.

The digital natives have grown up as part of the millennial generation and have had access to the Internet throughout their lives. The Millennials are equally comfortable communicating digitally and may even feel more comfortable doing so than listening in a face-to-face classroom. Instead of sitting in on a lecture, the online learner needs to be re-connected with the instructor. More one-on-one interaction with the instructor may be a byproduct of online learning, yet instructors must take into account the fact that some learners prefer higher interaction levels than others.

Activities for online courses that offer a variety of experiences to support learning should be purposefully integrated. Service projects, internships, directed studies and Webquests are only a few examples. Carefully mapping out learning objectives and aligning them with a range of possible activities will provide choice to the learner. All course participants should not be expected to have the same cookie cutter experience or create the same kind of product. Learner choice includes choice over content and activities, as well as over assessments.

Interaction and collaboration are pillars of constructivism. In looking ahead, more deliberate design is needed to incorporate the various types of interaction and to encourage collaborative activities that mirror real world problems, thus preparing learners for the workforce. Web 2.0 tools and other emerging technologies should be integrated more often to allow learners to create content and contribute to the group. Control of learning must be shifted from the instructor to the learner through contribution-oriented pedagogy and shared responsibility. Learners are to be held accountable for sharing their knowledge with others and adding to the collective repertoire of knowledge. The role of the instructor is more than a facilitator and manager of resources, but also a partner in learning (Beldarrain, 2006) because the instructor and learner participate in a reciprocal exchange of knowledge.

Increasingly, all research is being conducted using the Internet and related technologies. Libraries are often located online and brick-and-mortar buildings are becoming rare. In order for learners to function in the 21st century, it is essential for them to be technologically literate and proficient. It is the responsibility of cyber educators to model and promote research skills for students. Gone are the days of having to learn the Dewey decimal system to find resources in the physical library. These times require technical literacy skills and the ability to discern what is of value in a sea of information.

The future of education also hinges on disruptive innovations yet to come. Learning in the digital age requires out-of-the-box thinking and often calls for taking risks by doing what is not popular. According to Christensen and Horn (2008), a disruptive innovation is one that alters the trajectory of products or services that already have a strong hold in the market by offering a product or service of lesser quality and likely more affordable. The key, however, is that the disruptive innovation actually ends up offering something to those consumers who could not use the original product or service, thus opening up a new market which becomes stronger over time and disrupts the progress of the older one (Christensen & Horn, 2008; Christensen, Johnson, & Horn, 2008). In education, online learning is an example of how the new way of teaching is forcing changes upon the traditional methods. Online learning is disruptive because suddenly education is more accessible to those who would otherwise not be able to step into a classroom for a myriad of possible reasons. Likewise, K-12 online learning has opened up the doors to many students who would otherwise not be able to complete their education.

Learners also need the flexibility of time to create their own virtual space. Online learners are likely coming from nontraditional situations. In K-12 it may be the child who is homebound or the pregnant teenager, a young athlete, an actress or a dancer. There is also the student who did not do well in traditional school or the one who wants to get ahead by taking extra courses. All of them need the flexibility to work at their own pace in a learning environment that supports their needs. Adult learners have jobs and families to care for, hence the same need for flexibility applies. Many online instructors "close" discussion threads or assignments after a set date and those students who did not make the "deadline" are locked out. This practice mirrors teacher-centric practices of the traditional classroom where the student was penalized for turning in "late" assignments. If online environments are going to truly be designed around the needs of the learner, they must allow learners to move at their own speed. This is not to say that all time constraints should be removed. Learners should work within the timeframe provided for completing the course to help them stay focused, but within that time frame learners should be able to move ahead of their peers if ready or spend more time on more difficult concepts.

The characteristics of learners in both online and traditional educational settings are changing. Both younger learners and older learners are embracing technologies as part of the learning environment. The Millennial Generation has had access to the Internet throughout most of their lives. They are as comfortable communicating digitally as they are face to face. Many may feel more comfortable doing this than sitting back and listening in a face-to-face classroom. Connecting with an instructor through text messaging may not only be more natural for these learners it may also be a way of providing more one on one, instructor to learner interaction. Increasingly, the new adult learners are coming from nontraditional venues and often have jobs and families. The increasing cost of education is causing more students to work and take courses at the same time. These learners are often in diverse geographical locations, busy with families and work responsibilities, and paying for continuing education themselves. Whether these learners are younger or older, many of them recognize that learning in this day and age is not optional, it is a lifelong necessity for gainful employment and a satisfying life.

Integrating technologies into the education mix has given us both the opportunity and the means to explore the optimization of learning. It has forced us to reexamine a paradigm that was in desperate need of revision. This journey has only just begun. Educators, instructional professionals and learner s must work together to expand the limitations and boundaries of the past. New ideas, new theories and much research will emerge that support and transform what we currently call learning. Approaches to teaching and learning as well as the technologies that support them will continue to evolve. The pace of adaption of these changes will be hastened or restricted only by the readiness of all involved parties to be open and willing to do things differently. Fortunately, technologies continue to evolve and provide evidence and opportunities for continued research to support more accurate and appropriate theories of learning and instruction.

Certainly collaboration and an ever growing collective body of knowledge will point the way to more well suited principles and practices. Researcher-practitioners such as Collis and Moonen (2005) believe that students should contribute to the content of the course by adding their projects and ideas to a collection of student work that is then used as a repository of knowledge by new students. This contribution-oriented pedagogy (Collis & Moonen, 2005) allows students to use and reuse what others have produced as part of their learning process.

Students who collaborate in this type of learning community understand that their finished product will add to the knowledge base of the group, not just their own. Collaboration and contribution further prepare students to become part of a more expert community, a community of practice.

Collective contributions have also found their way into the world of workforce learning and training. Social software of all varieties have invaded the workplace. Web 2.0 has influenced everything including job titles like Web Master and Blog Master to virtual meetings in virtual worlds. Corporate learning is driving company culture and strategy. A global workforce is being connected by technology and an ever changing workplace. Aligning company needs and capitalizing on collective intelligence companies are solving problems and developing strategies to position themselves for the new century.

Unquestionably the new global network will require a workforce that is continuously learning both by formal and informal means. The rate of change in our world is increasing at an increasing rate. Ever since the Internet enabled and inspired connection, sharing and collaborating, human kind has embraced the inevitable. Our path forward seems to be driven by the distribution of content openly and with few restrictions. The Open Educational Resources (OER) began in 2001 with William and Flora Hewitt and Andrew W. Mellon joined forces with the Massachusetts Institute of Technology (MIT). The Open Courseware Initiative (OCW) provides undergraduate and graduate content to individuals, schools and universities around the globe. More importantly MIT has inspired many organizations to follow suit (Brown & Adler, 2008).

The open sources movement that was originally applicable to computer software code has spread to content and knowledge. The advent and continued use of Web 2.0 tools that support community and collaboration have contributed to an atmosphere of openness and sharing. Then distinction between provider and consumer are less pronounced. This new social learning epistemology stands in stark contrast to traditional Cartesian views of teaching and learning. The perspectives shift from content to human interactions and activities. From virtual apprentices to Second Life course rooms, institutions and organizations are embracing new ways of delivering and constructing knowledge. Some examples are: The University of Southern Queensland in Australia built a lecture style classroom in Second Life that attracts millions, also in Second Life, Harvard Law School constructed a court of public opinion, and the University of Michigan has opened up social networks to reach over 250,000 student (Brown & Adler, 2008).

The new goslings expect experiences with knowledge that permits them to chare, construct, vet, collaborate and try out new things. They have a strong desire for demand-pull learning rather than supply-push. According to Brown and Adler (2008) demand pull learning enables participation in a flow of action. The demand-pull approach provides rich communities of practice that encourage passion and participation. The new learners want the freedom, autonomy and the resource availability to learn to be part of a community of practice and acquire the collateral knowledge necessary to learn about, create or perform in that community. The new learners are aware that once and done knowledge is not enough. They want to learn what they want when they want and are not satisfied solely being directed by others.

Cyber education continues to push pedagogical boundaries, yet it is still in its infancy. The future of many industries will depend on the ability of cyber educators to prepare learners for the workplace. More research is needed to understand the influence of interaction on achievement and how the different technology tools influence learning. Innovative solutions are needed in order to achieve educational reform at all levels, including higher education. The use of gaming, learning paths to individualize instruction, collaborative projects and added learner control is likely to help create more learner-centric environments.

CONCLUSION

Cyber education has evolved over the years and may be considered a disruptive innovation that has made education more accessible to sectors of the population, but also changed the expectations of what education should look like in the 21st century. Some of the basic principles of learner-centric pedagogy were found in the simple life of the old schoolhouse where older students tutored younger ones and where learning often took place outside without many textbooks. While there were also many constraints with this environment, the idea is that over the years, education became industrialized, therefore learners became yet another product in a factory line.

In the 21st century those outdated practices that place the teacher in control are no longer appropriate. The world has changed and, with it, advances in technology connect learners from all facets of life. The cookie cutter approach to education is obsolete. The 21st century learner requires flexibility of time, place and space. The learning environment must be engaging, providing different opportunities for interaction with peers, instructor, the content and the interface of the course. Learners also need the space and freedom to vicariously observe the interactions of others, because this too is another way to learn and co-construct knowledge.

Educational institutions will likely continue to invest in IT infrastructures in order to prepare for the next decade. Corporate, government and educational institutions can no longer wait to implement effective online learning initiatives. Instructor preparedness is paramount. All sectors must ensure that those involved in online learning have the knowledge and skills necessary to create learner-centric environments that support learning; they must know how to utilize alternative teaching practices, emerging collaborative tools, instructional strategies and theories to create meaningful, engaging courses.

As technologies become more sophisticated, interactions will remain important and cyber educators will continue to adjust and create best practices that work in the online environment. Cyber educators are responsible for modeling the use of new technology tools for learners, so they are prepared to use those tools in the course. Pedagogical shifts are being caused by technology and emerging theories such as connectivism will help frame the construction of learner-centric environments that integrate connectivity and social networking to enhance learning. It is vital that cyber educators understand the affordances of technology tools and their impact on the online learning environment.

Today's learners are digital natives while most of the instructors are digital immigrants. Prensky (2005) exposed the difference between the two generations and proposed that digital natives are moving toward digital wisdom. Educators must take advantage of the affordances of digital technologies to deliver instruction and engage students while keeping the student at the center of all decisions. Learner-centric teaching methods have the potential of truly reforming education at all levels. Cyber educators must understand that digital technologies are vehicles through which good, solid instructional strategies are delivered. Digital technologies are not instructional strategies in and of themselves.

Digital technologies offer many options for learners, including online learning. Cyber education is in demand, yet many outdated practices are still espoused in adult training, higher education as well as K-12 education. One of the most important aspects of the online revolution is the change in the position of pedagogy as well as andragogy. The role of the instructor evolves from one of subject matter expert and provider of content, to a facilitator. This requires a commitment of excellence on the part of the organization or institution, thus recognizing the importance of designing for online learning and the time, effort, and structure needed to create and implement alternative teaching practices. These challenges bring about opportunities to rectify practices that are not in the best interest of learners. A major challenge of creating quality cyber education is integrating meaningful interactions amongst members of the learning community to promote and enhance the learning experience.

Interaction is often cited as the most important component for success in online courses. Today, in diametric opposition to the days when a good student sat dutifully and listened attentively, interaction is paramount in both the face-to-face, and in the online learning environment. One of the most pronounced differences between interactions of instructors and learners in the online environment is greater equality. The nature of digitally mediated communications requires the instructor to provide explicit instructions and feedback and provoke deeper thinking through online discussions and synchronous sessions. In turn, learners are expected to do participate in the learning community. The online learning landscape is a very different place than the traditional face-to-face classroom. It refers to more than the physical space and geographical constraints. A landscape includes the different types of interactions and the learning or social community. An effective online course integrates these affordances to maximize their impact in the learning environment. Instructors must be prepared to be more deliberate with design of a virtual course because many of the obvious elements of face-to-face are missing online.

One of the big shifts in paradigm is the shift of control from the instructor to the learner. This includes a shift in perception or value of the learner's time and position within the group. The constructivist environment is centered on interactions and flourishes through shared responsibility for learning. With the controls of learning shifting from the instructor to the learner, the learner becomes the central and most important component in the learning process. A student's time becomes more valuable and individualized learning becomes critical. With the controls of learning shifting from the instructor to the learner, the learner becomes the central and most important component in the learning process. A student's time becomes more valuable and individualized learning becomes critical. A learning environment should help learners make meaning out of what and why they are learning and context is very important in determining meaning. Context goes much further than just the setting or real world. An interactive learning environment is also being an active learning environment. Active learning encourages the building of social relationships and the completion of learning goals through participation, verbally, visually, cognitively, and affectively.

New technologies have given us both the opportunity and the means to explore the optimization of learning. It has forced us to reexamine a paradigm that was in desperate need of revision. Certainly collaboration and an ever growing collective body of knowledge will point the way to better suited principles and practices. New practices are already emerging, the development of social software, Web 2.0, online communities of practice, Personal Learning Environments, Virtual Worlds and innovations yet to come are causing us to reevaluate what we call teaching and learning, and how we deliver it to a human population globally dispersed but increasingly united by technologies that make us more inter connected and inter-dependent than ever before.

Traditional teaching methods are no longer effective. The face-to-face environment cannot be transferred online. The nature of the online environment requires the design of a learner-centric course that includes many opportunities for the different types of interaction, as well as flexibility, choice, collaboration, real world skills and more learner control. These new ways of teaching can only become a reality if cyber educators are well trained and focused on the learner's needs.

REFERENCES

Allen, E., & Seaman, J. (2008). *Staying the course, online education in the United States, 2008*. The Sloan Consortium. Retrieved June 2, 2010, from http://www.sloanconsortium.org/sites/ default/files/staying_the_course-2.pdf

Associated Press. (2010). Family won't seek class damages for webcam spying. *Education Week, 29*(32). Retrieved June 2, 2010, from http://www.edweek.org

Beldarrain, Y. (2006). Distance education trends: Integrating new technologies to foster student collaboration and interaction. *Distance Education, 27*(2), 139–153. doi:10.1080/01587910600789498

Berge, Z.L. (2002). Active, interactive and reflective elearning. *The Quarterly Review of Distance Education, 3*(2), 181-191. (EBSCO Host Database 7548973).

Brooks, M. (2009). The excellent inevitability of online courses. *The Chronicles of Higher Education, 55*(38), 64. Retrieved June 1, 2010, from http://chronicle.com/article/ The-Excellent-Inevitability-of/44251/

Brown, J. S., & Adler, R. P. (2008). *Minds on fire: Open education, the long tail, and learning 2.0*. Retrieved June 23, 2010, from http://net.educause.edu/ir/ library/pdf/ERM0811.pdf

Bruckman, A. (2002). The future of e-learning communities. *Communications of the ACM, 45*(4), 60–63. doi:10.1145/505248.505274

Chen, C.-M., Liu, M.-C., Liu, C.-Y., & Hsiech, Y.-L. (2005). Personalized curriculum sequencing approach utilizing modified item response theory for web-based instruction. In Y. Liu, G. Chen & M. Ying (Eds.), *Fuzzy logic, soft computing and computational intelligence, 2nd ed.* (pp. 1101-1106). Eleventh International Fuzzy Systems Association World Congress, July 28-31, 2005. Beijing, China: Tsinghua University Press.

Christensen, C. M., & Horn, M. B. (2008). How do we transform our schools? *Education Next, 8*(3). Retrieved June 2, 2010, from http://educationnext.org/how-do-we-transform-our-schools/

Christensen, C. M., Johnson, C. W., & Horn, M. B. (2008). *Disrupting class: How disruptive innovation will change the way the world learns*. New York: McGraw-Hill.

Clark, H. H., & Brennan, S. E. (1991). Grounding in communication. In Resnick, L. B., Levine, J. M., & Teasley, J. S. D. (Eds.), *Perspectives on socially shared cognition*. American Psychological Association. doi:10.1037/10096-006

Collis, B., & Moonen, J. (2005). Collaborative learning in a contribution-oriented pedagogy. In Howard, C., Boettecher, J. V., Justice, L., Schenk, K. D., Rogers, P. L., & Berg, G. A. (Eds.), *Encyclopedia of distance learning* (pp. 277–283). Hershey, PA: Idea Group.

Cyrs, T. E. (1997). Competence in teaching at a distance. *New Directions for Teaching and Learning, 71*(1), 15–18. doi:10.1002/tl.7102

DeVries, J., & Lim, G. (2003). *Significance of online teaching vs. face-to-face: Similarities and differences.* Paper presented at E-LEARN 2003, World Conference on E-Learning in Corporate, Government, Healthcare, and Higher Education, November 7-11. Phoenix, AZ.

Dewey, J. (1916). *Democracy and education: An introduction to the philosophy of education.* Project Gutenberg. Retrieved May 27, 2010, from http://www.gutenberg.org/etext/852

Gaver, W. W. (1992). The affordances of media spaces for collaboration. *Proceedings of the 1992 ACM Conference on Computer-supported Cooperative Work,* (pp. 17-24). Toronto, Canada.

Gessner, R. (1956). *The democratic man: Selected writings of Eduard C. Lindeman.* Boston: Beacon.

Ghaith, G. (2003). The relationship between forms of instruction, achievement and perceptions of classroom climate. *Educational Research, 45*(1), 83–93. doi:10.1080/0013188032000086145

Glenn, L., Jones, C., & Hoyt, J. (2003). The effect of interaction levels on student performance: A comparative analysis of Web-mediated versus traditional delivery. *Interactive Learning Journal, 14*(3), 285–299.

Gray, L., Thomas, N., & Lewis, L. (2010). *Educational technology in U.S. public schools: Fall 2008, first look.* Institute of Educational Sciences, U.S. Department of Education. Retrieved May 27, 2010, from http://nces.ed.gov/pubs2010/2010034.pdf

Hillman, D. C., Willis, D. J., & Gunawardena, C. N. (1994). Learner-interface interaction in distance education: An extension of contemporary models and strategies for practitioners. *American Journal of Distance Education, 8*(2), 30–41. doi:10.1080/08923649409526853

Jonassen, D. H. (1994). Thinking technology: Toward a constructivist design model. *Educational Technology,* (March/April): 34–37.

Kaplan-Leiserson, E. (2003). *We-learning: Social software and e-learning, part 1.* Learning Circuits, ASTD December 15, 2003. Retrieved June 1, 2010, from http://www.astd.org/LC/2003/1203_kaplan.htm

Knowles, M., Holton, E. F., & Swanson, R. A. (2005). *The adult learner* (6th ed.). Burlington, MA: Elsevier.

Laffey, J., Lin, G. Y., & Lin, Y. (2006). Assessing social ability in online learning environments. *Journal of Interactive Learning Research, 17*(2), 163–177.

Lave, J., & Wenger, E. (1991). *Situated learning: Legitimate peripheral participation.* Cambridge, MA: Cambridge University Press.

Major, H., & Levenburg, N. (1999). Learner success in distance education environments: A shared responsibility. Retrieved August 22, 2009, from http://www.eric.ed.gov:80/ERICDocs/data/ericdocs2sql/ content_storage_01/0000019b/80/19/b1/d2.pdf

Martyn, M. (2005). Using interaction in online discussion boards. *Education Quarterly, 4*(1), 61-62. Retrieved June 1, 2010, from http://net.educause.edu/ir/library/pdf/eqm05410.pdf

Meloncon, L. (2007). Exploring electronic landscapes: Technical communication, online elearning and instructor preparedness. *Technical Communication Quarterly, 16*(1), 31–53. doi:10.1207/s15427625tcq1601_3

Moore, M. G. (1989). Three types of interaction. *American Journal of Distance Education, 3*(2), 1–6. doi:10.1080/08923648909526659

Nagel, D. (2010). IT trends. Education IT to grow $2.5 billion this year. *T.H.E. Journal.* Retrieved May 31, 2010, from http://thejournal.com/articles/2010/05/19/education-it-to- grow-2.5-billion.aspx

Preece, J. (2000). *Online communities.* New York: Wiley & Sons.

Prensky, M. (2009). H. Sapiens digital: From digital immigrants and digital natives to digital wisdom. *Innovate, 5*(3). Retrieved June 2, 2010, from http://www.innovateonline.info/pdf/vol5_issue3/H._Sapiens_Digital-__From_Digital_Immigrants_and_Digital_Natives_to_Digital_Wisdom.pdf

Short, J., Williams, E., & Christie, B. (1976). *The social psychology of telecommunications.* London: John Wiley.

Siemens, G. (2005). Connectivism: A learning theory for the digital age. *International Journal of Instructional Technology and Distance Learning.* Retrieved May 24, 2010, from http://www.itdl.org/Journal/Jan_05/article01.htm

Smith, G., Ferguson, D., & Caris, M. (2002). Teaching over the Web versus in the classroom. [from http://www.umsl.edu/technology/frc/pdfs/ teaching_over_the_web_versus_in_the_classroom.pdf]. *International Journal of Instructional Media, 29*(1), 61–67. Retrieved June 1, 2010.

Sutton, L. A. (2001). The principle of vicarious interaction in computer-mediated communications. *International Journal of Educational Telecommunications, 7*(3), 223-242. Norfolk, VA: AACE. Retrieved May 31, 2010, from http://www.editlib.org/p/9534

VMware. (2010). *Miami-Dade public schools, a technology leader. WMware customer case study.* Retrieved June 2, 2010, from http://www.vmware.com/files/pdf/customers/09Q4_cs_vmw_MDCPS_english_01.pdf

Vygotsky, L. (1978). *Mind and society: The development of higher mental process.* Cambridge, MA: Harvard University Press.

Wagner, E. D. (1997). Interactivity: From agents to outcomes. *New Directions for Teaching and Learning, 71,* 19–26. doi:10.1002/tl.7103

Watson, J., Ryan, J., & Wicks, M. (2009). *Keeping pace with K-12 online learning. An annual review of state-level policy and practice.* Retrieved from http://www.kpk12.com/downloads/KeepingPace09-fullreport.pdf

Chapter 10
Designing for Authenticity

ABSTRACT

Designing for authenticity is supported by learner-centric theoretical and pedagogical approaches. Technological advancements in digitally mediated communications now make it more feasible than ever to ensure the authenticity of online learning environments. Activities and assessments must be authentic to the learner and should provide choice, engagement, and opportunity for reflection. Authentic activities and assessments require the learner to use higher order thinking skills, collaborate, and co-construct knowledge within the learning community. Departing from traditional assessment methods minimizes academic integrity issues because learners must be able to produce tangible evidence of learning and apply real-world skills in a variety of scenarios. Authentic assessment measures learning gains by assessing the thought process behind the product and not just the product itself.

OBJECTIVES

- Define authenticity versus authentication.
- Explore the different theoretical and pedagogical approaches that support authenticity in online learning environments.

DOI: 10.4018/978-1-60960-543-8.ch010

- Identify the distinctiveness of authentic assessments and activities.
- Discuss the dangers of pre-authenticating activities and assessments.
- Discuss strategies for embedding authenticity in the online learning environment.

INTRODUCTION

Online education continues to expand at a rapid rate with more teachers and learners joining online programs and companies conducting more web-based trainings than in years past. Online learning is now more established and widely recognized as a valid and reputable form of instruction. This expansion, however, exposes the issues of trust and authenticity in cyber education, issues that were always present in all forms of distance education. Trust is directly influenced by authenticity of learning in both synchronous and asynchronous digitally mediated communications. While it is appealing to think that technologies can provide a reliable means for delivering learning materials and assessing learning, some doubts remain in the minds of the most well-intentioned cyber educators. Many of these doubts are centered on the issue of assessment and the validity of results. Educators who transfer outdated methods of assessment, such as multiple-choice tests, to online learning programs are, in essence, designing a program that is deficient; they should, therefore, employ alternate methods of authentic assessments that are administered in a secure, trustworthy learning environment.

Traditional forms of face-to-face assessment do not work in the online environment and increase the risk of plagiarism and other forms of academic integrity breaches as discussed in Chapter 7 of this publication. Traditional types of assessments are part of an old paradigm of educating the masses that has proven inefficient over the decades. A lack of confidence in the results of assessments already plagues many face-to-face environments and is amplified in online learning. Assessing learners in a face-to-face environment typically requires proctors, which costs time and money. This form of assessment also requires control of materials and their administration. Though administration of assessments may be simplified in the online world (Rowe, 2004) through the use of digitally mediated communications, the challenge of cyber educators is compounded by the lack of consistent focus for authenticity of design and authentication concerns.

Authenticity and authentication are terms with different meanings. Authenticity involves using types of activities and assessments that require the learner to apply real-world skills, while authentication is the process of establishing the validity of a person's identity. Authenticity is not possible without authentication. Although much attention has been given to plagiarism in the online environment because of the anonymity inherent in the technology, little focus has been given to fact-based assessments such as multiple choice questions and calculation questions. These two types of assessments, while appropriate in some traditional face-to-face settings, raise concerns about security and trust in the virtual environment. The challenge of keeping information secure in cyber education goes hand-in-hand with concerns about security and trust (Rowe, 2004). The first safety measure is authentication because of the veil of anonymity makes the establishment of true identity more difficult with digitally mediated communications. Authentication is essential to both privacy and anonymity on the Internet; it is also crucial in establishing trust in the online learning environment.

Identity authentication, however, is a complex issue compounded by the fact that a person's offline and online identities are not simple concepts to understand. Most people have a compound identity that is multifaceted and complex. Verifying if an individual possesses certain untrustworthy properties relative to assessment can be dealt with in the context of technology and risk management principles. Experts also predicate that approaches for authentication in online learning can be built upon the foundations of computer and communication security to minimize unauthorized access to information and systems and to prevent hiding or misrepresenting one's identity (Committee on the Internet in the Evolving Information Infrastructure, 2001). Cyber educators are typically far removed from issues that concern authentication, as it is a topic likely reserved for the organization's information technology team. The topic of authentication and authenticity is introduced here in the context of looking at the big picture of designing authentic learning opportunities for online learners. The emphasis of the chapter will not be on authentication but on authenticity.

Authentication systems for online education are still in their infancy. In most cases, there exists no single affordable solution to authentication in online learning. Generally, authentication revolves around something memorized, such as a password. All current authentication methods have shortcomings. Simple authentication challenges the other party with a question about the secret password, while public cryptography keys are commonly used to provide authentication and non-repudiation services for businesses by matching a private profile key with the public profile key of the user. Public key infrastructure (PKI) refers to the technology policies and procedure that underlie the use of key. These are not currently as prevalent in education as in the world of business and commerce. Biometrics is another method of identification and is based on physical characteristics such as fingerprints or iris shape. This is equally rare in cyber education. Any selection of an authentication mechanism requires trade-offs between expense, management and practicality. The efficacy of security software is often undermined by the lack of security on the computer on which it runs. Personal computer operating systems are subject to well known security improprieties and limitations.

It is important for cyber educators to realize the importance of authentication and authenticity. If the institution has a weak authentication method, the chances of security breaches increase. Increased security breaches include those intended to cause damage or steal information, but they also compromise academic integrity. The process of authentication can be seen as the first level of security to confirm the identity of the learner and establish trust. Once the learner is in the course submitting work, it is the instructor's responsibility to ensure the work submitted matches the learner's ability, hence further confirming the identity of the learner and establishing authenticity of the work and of the learning experience. Authentic learning involves activities and assessments that require the use of real-world skills to show mastery of the learning objectives (Harrington & Harrington, 2006). Assessment is essential to cyber education because it validates learners' knowledge and measures learning gains. It also provides necessary data to evaluate online learning programs. Academic integrity concerns and confirming the learner's identity present a real challenge for cyber educators. This chapter will explore the steps and processes cyber educators may use to design for authenticity in online learning environments. In this way, learning gains may be measured properly, while also establishing learner identity.

Theories in Support of Authentic Learning

A learning environment is not credible if it there is no proof of learning. Cyber education has the unique challenge of having to prove that learning has occurred, though the instructor cannot physically see the learner. In order for formalized learning to be credible, it must have authenticity (Miller & King, 2003). In the online environment, authenticity is achieved through the implementation of activities and assessment strategies which require the learner to apply the knowledge learned by using higher order thinking skills and not just simply using traditional memorization and recall. Authentic learning begins with engaging, yet challenging, lessons and activities that move the learner toward achieving learning goals. Such activities and assessments place the learner in real-world situations to make decisions.

Contemporary learning theorists have recognized the need to focus on the processes that lead to learning, thus a constructivist approach to designing instruction is favored. Constructivism is a multitude of ideas combining educational psychology, instructional technologies and sciences. Constructivists assert that knowledge comes through an individual's internalization of events and is influenced by the real world. Knowledge construction comes about when the learner attempts to make sense out of the world by interacting with it. Learners are not "empty vessels to be filled" (Driscoll, 2000, p.376), but are active and responsible for learning. This proposal is generally accepted as a fundamental part of constructivism.

Views of learning by both Piaget and Vygotsky are strong influences on the theory of constructivism. These influences, the "cognitive and developmental perspectives of Piaget and the interactional and cultural emphasis of Bruner and Vygotsky and the contextual nature of learning..." (Driscoll, 2000, p. 377) form the foundations for this movement. Piaget (1972) focuses on the learner's role in the acquisition of new knowledge and Vygotsky (1978) on the way in which knowledge is transmitted. Certainly, Piaget's developmental learning theory, Vygotsky's social developmental theory, Bruner's (1961) discovery learning theory and Lave's (1988) situated learning are all significant contributions to the movement. In a constructivist environment, the learner takes on an active role. Active engagement is necessary in order to build, comprehend and make sense of the outside world (Eggen & Kauchak, 1999). This is a revolutionary theory to traditionalists who systemize instruction depriving the learner of autonomy over his own learning.

Taxonomies, curricula, courses and programs all exist independent of the learner (Hein, 1991). The methods from the agrarian era that supported industrialization were centered on transmittal and recall of information but did not sustain critical cognitive processes as the demand for higher order thinking became more preeminent (Mayer & Reigeluth, 1999). Traditional methods have long been deemed ineffective because of the exposure to increasing amounts of information available to learners in post-modern times.

Activity theory is yet another approach that supports authentic learning. At the center of activity theory is the idea that consciousness and activity are one. Activities are the human interactions of which both the objective world and the conscious mind are parts. Not only is activity a prerequisite for learning, but the learner is the central character defining learning activity. Activity and consciousness are mutually supportive and exist together. Consciousness is the unifying agent bringing attention, intention, memory, reasoning and speech together. Vygotsky, as quoted in Jonassen and Rohrer-Murphy (1999, p. 65) claim "you are what you do."

Jonassen and Rohrer-Murphy (1999) provide a different way of looking at the construction of authentic learning environments. They advocate engaging learners through the tools used, the social and contextual relationships and the goals and intentions of the activities. The richer the context and the more embedded in the conscious thought processes of the learners, the more meaning the learners will construct. Jonassen and Rohrer-Murphy intertwine the issues of learner consciousness, intention and prior knowledge into a comprehensive theory of activity-based learning that sets forth the foundations for authentic learning environments.

Activity theory stipulates that learners adjust and prepare activities and interactions. Goal orientation is inherent in the proposed activity, thus the learner has clear expectations. Activity theory claims that knowing and doing are indivisible and initiated by intention. The basis for this intention is the object of activity itself.

By adapting to the object of activity, the learner moves closer to their goal. In this way, a transformed object may become the motive for new activity. According to Jonassen and Rohrer-Murphy (1999), a dynamic relationship exists between the object and the activity. In cyber education, digitally mediated technologies and delivery systems have affordances for activity and interactions.

As explored in other chapters, interaction in the online environment manifests itself in five main forms: learner-learner, learner-instructor, learner-content, learner-interface and vicarious interaction. Each type of interaction supports activity within the online learning community. Trust impacts the interactions and activities of individuals as part of a community or group. The social identity model of deindividuation theory (Postmes, Spears, & Lea, 1998) suggests that distributed collaboration within virtual communities or groups promotes a group identity. Individuals as part of a group with strong group identity may make judgments based on the faith they have developed in the group, which could potentially impair their ability to make judgments about veracity. It could also lead to manipulation or performance impairment because the ability to detect dishonesty becomes somewhat impaired (Burgoon, Stoner, Bonito, & Dunbar, 2003).

The potential for deception and dishonesty is inherent in digitally mediated communications because of the anonymity afforded by these technologies. One way to understand deception and how it can be minimized in the online environment is to use interpersonal deception theory as a lens through which to observe virtual interactions. Interpersonal deception theory was developed as a framework to account for the nature and success of deception by applying interpersonal communications principles to the domain of deception. At the heart of this theory is the position that interaction processes and outcomes can be influenced by the degree and affordance of the interactivity. For example, being involved in an interaction is fundamentally different that just observing it. This difference may influence the levels of trust and accuracy in detecting deception.

Meaningful learning, however, can only take place if it is embedded in the social and physical content where it is used, as postulated by situated learning and situated cognitive theories (Brown, Collins, & Duguid, 1989; Lave, 1988). Some of the strategies for embedding authenticity in learning include but are not limited to:

- Authentic context that reflects how the acquired knowledge will be used.
- Authentic activities that reflect real life.
- Expert performances and modeling processes.
- Multiple roles and perspectives.
- Co-construction of knowledge through collaboration.
- Coaching and scaffolding at critical times.
- Reflection to enable abstraction to form.

- Articulation to enable tacit knowledge to be made explicit.
- Assessments integrated within the learning.

Brown, Collins and Duguid (1989, p.32) explain that situated cognition occurs when "knowledge is situated, being in part a product of activity, context and culture in which it is developed and used." Activity and context are regarded as an integral part of learning. There exists no separation between what is learned and how and where it is learned. This is an enormous departure from traditional didactic education that treats knowledge as a separate substance. Situated cognition integrates the activity and the situation with the learning with no separation between the two. Psychological research supports this principle, which requires further research, also becomes a very important consideration in designing online learning opportunities. Situated cognition wrestles with the implications of explicit knowledge and implicit understanding, thus creating dilemmas for designers (Brown et al., 1989). The focus shifts to activity and perception.

Jonassen (1999) warns against misinterpreting the concept of authentic tasks or problems that is so central to constructivist pedagogy. By insisting that authentic equates to the real world, designers are very narrowly interpreting what is authentic. Problems of authenticity can involve the community of learners, the physical setting, goals, constraints, affordances and tools through which activities are mediated, including technologies.

Research conducted by Harrington and Oliver (2000) substantiate the validity of authentic learning environments. Conducting qualitative research in a multimedia environment, they offer nine criteria for an authentic learning environment: (a) a situated learning model, (b) authentic context, (c) authentic activity, (d) multiple perspectives, (e) expert performances, (f) collaboration, (g) reflection articulation, (h) coaching, and (i) scaffolding and authentic assessment. The results of the research appear to be successful and provide support to Jonassen's claim (1991) that a situated learning framework as an alternative to support advanced knowledge acquisition is a viable option. Courses and curricula can be built using complex and realistic scenarios resembling the context in which the knowledge they are constructing can be realistically applied. Authenticity has been successfully incorporated into a wide variety of subject matter and across many disciplines according to Herrington, Oliver, and Reeves (2002). Ten characteristics of authentic activities were proposed by Herrington, Oliver, and Reeves (2006) after reviewing the literature (Herrington, Reeves, Oliver & Woo, 2004) on authentic learning, situated learning, anchored instruction, and problem-based learning.

According to the authors, authentic activities:

1.   Must be relevant to the real world and be applicable to each profession.
2.   The problems to be solved are multi-dimensional and open to multiple inter-pretations, therefore requiring the student to define tasks and sub-tasks needed to accomplish the end goal.
3.   Are comprised of complex tasks to be investigated by students over a sustained period of time, instead of quick responses that do not explore the subject in depth.
4.   Provide the opportunity for students to examine the task from different perspectives, discerning information from a variety of resources, therefore allowing the learner to examine the problem from various theoretical and practical perspectives.
5.   Are collaborative.
6.   Are reflective.
7.   Are integrated and applied across different subject areas, thus encouraging interdisciplinary perspectives.
8.   Are seamlessly integrated with assessment in a manner that mirrors the real world.
9.   Lead to culminating products.
10. Allow for multiple correct answers, instead of one definitive right answer.

Theories such as constructivism, activity theory, social model of individuation, situated learning and situated cognition provide a combined framework for designing online learning environments that promote authenticity. Authentic learning involves using real-world skills in an educational context and demonstrating knowledge in alternate forms of assessment. It also means that lessons are personally relevant and meaningful to the learner. For instructional designers and cyber educators, authenticity means activities that engage the learner, help instructors confirm the academic integrity of the assessment and measure learning outcomes.

AUTHENTICITY ISSUES IN ONLINE LEARNING ENVIRONMENTS

Digitally mediated communications utilized in the online learning environment make it more feasible to integrate theories that support authenticity. There are also certain types of learning methodologies such as performance and immersion learning that integrate features and approaches with authenticity. Authenticity is always learner-centric and it is through interaction and engagement that authentic learning nurtures the co-construction of knowledge.

Providing authentic content that mirrors the real world is essential in the design of online learning environments. There is also a need to integrate authentic activities and assessments that allow the learner to take on multiple roles and perspectives. Self-assessment adds the dimension of reflection, thus augmenting the benefits of the authentic learning experiences. Assessment should be varied and purposeful and carefully aligned with learning objectives. Learners should be asked to evaluate situations and make decisions based on the problem at hand, thus preparing them to make decisions in the real world.

Most constructivist pedagogy also implies that learners have some prior knowledge that is incorporated into the knowledge acquisition process. Instructors can pose situational questions but learners create the connections and internalize the content to be able to solve them. The emphasis shifts from the instructor to the learner for instructional activities as well as assessments. The active part of the instruction can take place within collaborative or team-based learning activities. This also indicates the social and communal aspects of learning. Knowledge is no longer dispensed through the instructor. The role of the instructor changes from a facilitator or coach to a partner in the learning process where reciprocal learning takes place (Beldarrain, 2006). The focus is always on the learner thereby promoting motivation, autonomy and discovery on the part of the learner.

Interactions can then be judged as to whether the interaction is engaging or passive, solicits patterns of behavior and perceptions of mutuality and entails exchanges of individuating information. The degree of interdependence, participation, synchronicity and contingencies will affect the out come of the communications. Deceptive interchanges may result from higher levels of interactivity but higher truth biases and failure to detect deception (Burgoon, Stoner, Bonito, & Dunbar, 2003). This includes social judgments such as honesty, trust and credibility. Higher trust and credibility may be associated with higher levels of interactivity and truthful interchanges.

Success can further be obtained through the design of a learning environment that uses technologies effectively to promote the connection of learners in meaningful ways. The most important attribute of these types of learning models tends to be the focus on the learner. An important inference of this explanation is the need for learners to assume a high level of accountability for learning. The next most important component of creating these environments is to encourage learning activities that are relevant and authentic to the participants (Herrington et al, 2006).

Authentic activities and assessments, combined with student choice, increase the level of control surrendered to the learner, thus making the environment more learner-centric. Authentic activities have a new place in the virtual course room mainly because of the acceptance of the constructivist movement in education, the impact of new technologies and the flow of research showing its effectiveness.

Activities are now used to affirm learning and to take learners beyond reading and listening. Most importantly they affirm and encourage the learner to respond in an active way rather than remain passive. In authentic learning activities are place at the heart of the curriculum and support the learning process. Placing the learner at the heart of the instruction facilitates authentic learning whether the approach used is case-based, problem-based, immersion settings, scenarios or role-playing.

Feedback and practice are important in every learning environment, yet a more constructivist approach focuses on the learner, not the instruction. Therefore, practice is designed to give the learner confidence in his new skills and feedback is not used in strictly negative ways, but to coach the learner in encouraging ways so he may be able to learn from his mistakes. Learning from mistakes is crucial to authentic learning because in the real world humans learn best through trial-and-error. It is the responsibility of the instructor to encourage, model and activate prior knowledge. In authentic instruction, there is no attempt by the instructor or instruction to break up content into areas and teach in a systematic form with practice and feedback. Activities for authentic learning give purpose and meaning to the learning and do not limit or decide the scope and sequence of the inquiry (Reeves, Herrington, & Oliver, 2002). Instructional scaffolding is necessary to activate prior knowledge and provide the learner with enough upfront information to pique their interest and tap their motivation source. Authenticity in the learning environment engages the learner from the very beginning.

As discussed in Chapter 9 of this publication, it is necessary to make the change from instructor and instruction-dominated learning to learner-centric knowledge construction. Resistance to change has been evident over the years because traditional instruction is easiest to prepare, it is widespread, and is familiar to instructors. Instructors rely on their own educational experiences to create courses and do not understand active learning (Clark, 2003). Learning environments are regarded as authentic when similarity exists between learning activity and some meaningful context for that activity. Authenticity is a relative term and varies according to the learner because evaluating authenticity must include the learner's personal and professional realities.

By nature, what is meaningful to one person is not necessarily meaningful to another. Instructors must get to know their students in order to personalize the learning experience as much as possible. Overall, current events and scenarios should be integrated as part of the learning experience if they are directly applicable to the learning objectives of the course. There will be a range of options that tap into the interest of the larger audience while still meeting objectives.

Authenticity is not something that can be mandated by instructional designers, communities of practice or the desires of the learner. The "buy-in" of the learner is critical to authenticity (Barab, Squire, & Dueber, 2000) as is the type of assessment.

A product-based assessment, for example, allows the instructor to know if the learner missed a concept because it will be evident in the final product. It also helps the instructor match the product with the learner's ability. If the learner submits a product that is inconsistent with previous work, academic integrity becomes a concern.

Interactivity and interaction play a distinctive role in the design of authentic online learning environments. Interactivity occurs through the features and affordances of the digital communications used, while interaction focuses on the actual exchange or contact, whether human-to-human or human-to-technology. Interactivity is a way to engage the learner with the instructional materials. According to Allen (2003), learners to act on what they find motivating and therefore choose to interact. However, not all interactivity is created equal. The complexity of the content, the structure and sequencing of the instruction or the instructional objective can increase the element interactivity. The level of integration and mental processes necessary to interact with the content can be compounded, thus increasing cognitive load. Combining auditory and visual channels when presenting materials can accelerate learning by taking full advantage of available capacity in working memory (Clark et al, 2005).

Interaction takes on a broader meaning in instructional design, especially considering the different types of interactions possible: learner-learner, learner-instructor, learner-content, learner-interface and vicarious interaction. The abundance of cues in the face-to-face environment influences the immediacy and exchange of information. The flow of information and rate of exchange is also influenced by the proximity of participants to each other during the exchange. Participants develop strategies in the online environment to make up for the verbal cues that are missing.

The spatial, temporal and contextual limitations online have led learners to develop strategies such as the use of emoticons and capital letters to compensate for the lack of visual and spatial cues. A particularly unique experience online is how learners have the opportunity to reflect on their postings without being intimidated by the physical presence of others. For those students who are not as outgoing or assertive, this provides opportunities to flourish. This may be true due to personality traits, cultural or other personal characteristics. Although some online interactions may be slower and more disjointed in some ways than face-to-face interactions, they can be just as authentic. Integrating activities and assessments such as case studies, scenarios or projects that require the learner to apply real-world skills will enhance the learning experience.

Bill Clancey, a pioneer in constructivist application in the artificial intelligence (AI). community, proposed the concept that what people do is oriented in their interactions. He contends that the ways in which content is interpreted is itself an unpredictable interaction. Learners do not interact in a linear fashion; they continually adjust and reinvent patterns. This undoubtedly has implications for instructional designers, who must consider how users access and interact with the content and interface of the course. Clancey advocates that instructional designers become participant observers in the community of practice and use ethnographic methods to observe and reflect on the situation. Instructional designers can also use the feedback from learners through participatory design where the learners actually participate in the redesign process (Wilson 2004). The ideal situation is one in which stakeholders are active participants and contribute to the improvement of the course. More research is needed to understand how to make this happen in an effective, democratic manner that promotes learning.

Performance learning is another way to promote authenticity in the online learning environment. Performance learning especially promotes excellence by complementing other learning with specific transferable job related skills that can be subject-specific (Quin, Hunt, & Sparrow, 2005). Learners are encouraged to reflect on their learning needs and naturally link learning needs to future employment options. By enhancing opportunities with professional associations and networking, performance learning may also facilitate employment prospects for the learner.

Along with performance learning, technology affords the opportunity to create realistic or immersive environments that simulate the real world. Virtual reality, simulations and advanced computer applications are used with considerable success for medical, military and aviation training. Immersion training is experiential by nature. Some would argue that in order to be authentic, these types of environments must replicate the real world. Others have determined that physical realism is less important to authentic learning than cognitive realism. According to Herrington, Reeves & Oliver (2007) cognitive realism is created by emerging learners in complex, yet engaging, tasks and projects and contend that cognitive realism is more important than physical realism because the task itself is the key element for immersion and engagement. Higher order thinking skills such as analysis, synthesis and evaluation should be embedded in the task in order to obtain maximum the benefits of the experience.

Although immersion learning has been widely used in high-stakes settings such as flying an airplane or medical training, these types of authentic environments in the form of simulations are usually expensive. It is not readily available in other areas of education. Simulations also tend to focus on linear tasks, which require repetition and practice. Even the best of these simulations have a finite number of possible outcomes; therefore, it may not be the best option when the goal is an open-ended task.

Authentic tasks may increase the complexity of designing online learning environments, yet they are the keys to ensuring authenticity and minimizing academic integrity breaches. For instance, learners must demonstrate they are able to discern information and make decisions when working with problems in scenario-based tasks. By promoting a deeper level of knowledge construction and avoiding traditional forms of assessments such as multiple choice tests that can easily be used for cheating, the instructor gets to know the learners on a more individual level.

Dangers of Pre-Authenticating the Online Learning Environment

The temptation for cyber educators and instructional designers to pre-authenticate the online learning environment places real world learning at risk, thus defeating the purpose of authentic activities and assessment. Pre-authentication involves designing instruction based on what the designer or educator believes will be a positive and authentic experience for the learner. Educating the masses through Web-based technology is the opposite of learner-centric online instruction. The ultimate question in the epistemological debate is: Who is constructing these tasks and for whom are they authentic? Attempts to reduce the individual to a list of traits and group norms are pretentious and do not mirror individual perception or take into consideration individual needs. Furthermore, it undermines the need to shift control from the instructor to the learner.

In constructivist learning environments, authenticity is more a judgment than an objective state. It is the imminent responsibility of cyber educators and instructional designers to provide a structure for learning. This may involve integrating a combination of instructional and assessment strategies that are student driven, yet meet the objectives set forth by the course. In every course or training there exists a pre-determined scope of content from which learning objectives are derived. What may be an authentic experience for the designer or instructor is not necessarily authentic for the learner. The interplay of activity and assessment choice guarantees the learner will find a connection between the content and the real world in a manner which is authentic to him.

Pre-authentication reduces the learner to the same uncomplicated, passive and inexperienced being that constructivism claims to reject. Barab, Squire and Dueber (2000) agree that to push authenticity out to the learner by instructor or instruction is to deny authenticity.

In the design of learning environments for children, authenticity may not play such a high-stakes role as it does for adult learners. The fact that adult learners bring a plethora of prior knowledge, skill sets and a certain level of expertise, makes it nearly impossible to pre-authenticate learning (Petraglia, 1998). The knowledge construction process also moves the instructor from the center of instruction to the sidelines and places the learner in control of learning.

Another element that challenges pre-authentication of learning environments is content domains. Too often, authenticity is the aspiration of designers and instructors, yet little consideration is given to the problem itself. First, math is an example of a variation in content domain that may not lend itself to authenticity, particularly at the higher levels. In fact, attempts to authenticate abstract concepts may actually hinder or bog down the learning process. Secondly, ethics and law, for example, are fields in which the instructor may need to provide specific instructor-led support until the learner can become more independent. In such situations, the instructor reverts from a partner in learning to the facilitator or coach, adjusting instruction as the learner increases in skill and confidence.

Authenticity in learning is not confined to real world locations or activities, but is comprised of critical characteristics that are incorporated in Web or face-to-face situations, which create the learning environment. This is substantially more comprehensive than the notion of learning by doing. The challenge has come in the translation to effective online teaching methods. Only by observing and analyzing learner needs can best practices be set forth that allow for the application of authentic activities and assessments in cyber education.

Attempting to make learning environments authentic to the real world prior to the learner's interaction in the course is counterproductive for learning and for design purposes. In order for a problem to be authentic, it must be perceived as authentic by the learner. When learners interpret an activity or environment as being unrealistic, learning can be reduced and narrowly focused, according to Petraglia (1998). The thought process cannot be perceived as being independent of situational variables, which are unique to the individual and influenced by the dynamics of the group.

Authentic activities also have to be rich with information to be constructivist in nature. Collaboration and apprenticeship are often linked to the goal of authenticity. Multimedia is used to impart reality and anchor the learning in a realistic context. The concept of authentic tasks, problems and investigations being an integral part of meaningful learning is not new. The real innovation is the contention that these activities and assessments are not academic exercises in practice, but are building blocks in the learning process that promote motivation, collaboration and higher order thinking skills through meaningful, engaging and relevant content. Activities that require the use of team work, the application of multiple perspectives, interpersonal communication skills, problem solving and decision making skills, add complexity of a real-world situation to the learning experience, thus achieving authentic learning.

The American educational system has largely departed from the concept of hands-on apprenticeship by accentuating the differences between applied practices and abstract intellectualizing. Simulation ushered introduced the concept that learning activities should be made similar to the real world in which they are applied. This brought forth the notion of the classroom as practice field. Participation, rehearsal, repetition and redundancies, as well as the concept of creating learning communities or communities of practice, increased the tendency to pre-authenticate meaning for learners. In this way, the emphasis was still on the instructor or the instruction itself, instead of finding a means for the learner to take ownership of the learning (Barab, Squire, & Dueber, 2000). Similarly, simplified attempts at apprenticeship deny the most important construct: the social environment in which the learning is taking place (Petraglia, 1998). It is imperative that a combined approach be used, building best practices that not only bring the real world into the virtual course room, but also take the learner out of the course room and into the real world.

A learner may often not be ready or willing to engage himself or herself in an authentic task such as a scenario or role-playing activities because it is a new approach for learning that they have never experienced. The approach may be so radically different from many prior experiences in academic venues, students sometimes are reluctant to participate and enter into the learning situation with a predetermined disbelief (Herrington, Oliver, & Reeves, 2002). The learner may need to defer disbelief before taking on the task. The suspension of disbelief may be one of the essential components of engagement in authentic learning environments because participation becomes impossible unless the learner commits to the task. Instructors must therefore monitor the level of engagement of learners and proactively encourage those who may be experiencing disbelief and disconnect. Authenticity can only be established through the dynamic interaction of a variety of components, both human and technological. Authenticity is not always an objective feature that can be obtained but is rather a quality of the overall environment that evolves through the emergence of learning within the community.

Because global trends point to a continued increase in the number of online learning programs, it is necessary to explore ways instructional design can address the challenges for ensuring authenticity in online learning. Instructional designers, cyber educators, learners and administrators need to understand the impact authenticity has on the learning process and should continue exploring the constraints, affordances and implications associated with it. The current shift in pedagogy toward a constructivist environment, coupled with a movement away from a teacher-centered setting towards a learner-centered setting, presents challenges for instructional designers creating activities and assessments in an online course. Many online courses use traditional assessment procedures that compare the learner to other learners, but authentic assessments measure what learners can do with what they have learned (Wiggens, 1998) but not necessarily to measure one student against the other. The ultimate purpose of instruction is for the learner to walk away from the experience with new knowledge that broadens his views and can be applied in the real world. Assessments must be authentic and effective in measuring learning (Drummond, 2003). Traditional types of assessment are not designed as a proactive tool to aid in learning.

Assessment should be integrated into the learning experience, engage the learner and promote future learning. Authentic assessments support a constructivist approach that takes into consideration learner satisfaction. One of the factors for success in online learning is learner satisfaction with the learning environment. The Sloan Consortium (2010) has recognized student satisfaction with the learning experience as one of the five pillars of a quality online learning program. Environments that engage learners and maximize learning should incorporate assessment as part of the learning experience. Assessment should be part of the pedagogy and should support learning theories that are learner-centric. Environments where learners are given the opportunity to demonstrate mastery through authentic activities and assessments that enhance learning should be viewed favorably.

Traditional assessment methodologies used in the face-to-face classroom do not provide the necessary methodologies of achieving authenticity in online learning. Authentic assessment not only is effective in measuring learning achievement but also enhances and causes new learning to occur. Likewise, authentic learning activities should provide the learner with enough practice to learn new skills and gain confidence. Consideration must be given to learner needs, motivations and interests. Shifting control to the learner through activity and assessment choice ensures that pre-authentication does not occur. In looking forward, there are many possible strategies related to authenticity, all of which need to be further explored in the context of learner-centric pedagogy.

LOOKING AHEAD

The advent of technology and its applications in online learning has brought the concept of authenticity to the forefront of education. The early beginnings of distance education had limitations and raised concerns about the ability of digitally enhanced learning environments to be built around constructivist principles. Technological advancements now make it more feasible to incorporate learner-centric pedagogy that uses authentic activities and assessments to achieve learning goals. More than ever, cyber educators have the opportunity to make a much needed impact on online learning and teaching practices.

Now What?

1.   The design of instruction must place the learner at the heart of the instruction and facilitate authentic learning whether the approach used is case-based, problem-based, immersion settings, scenarios or role-playing.

2. Traditional educators must change their approach and realize the role of the instructor is more than a facilitator and manager of resources, but also a partner in learning because the instructor and learner participate in a reciprocal exchange of knowledge.
3. More research is needed to understand how to have stakeholders participate as active participants in the design, evaluation and redesign and contribute to the improvement of the course.
4. New approaches to assessments must be authentic and effective in measuring learning because traditional types of assessment are not designed as a proactive tool.
5. Activities in the online learning environment should be designed to activate prior knowledge, allow the learner to co-create knowledge and provide sufficient practice of new skills.
6. The educational Community should embrace the inclusion of new options to deliver education, including mobile learning technologies.

In a constructivist environment, learners and instructors do not exist independent of each other but are reliant upon each other. Knowledge is constructed by interactions with others and with the learning environment. An end of unit exam may measure some knowledge transfer but it cannot measure true learning performance. Each learner brings a host of experiences that, if activated, serve as the building blocks for further learning. Activities in the online learning environment should be designed to activate prior knowledge, allow the learner to co-create knowledge within the learning community and provide sufficient practice of new skills.

In the discussion presented here, the point was made that learning activities and assessments must be authentic to the learner, not just the instructional designer or instructor. If activities and assessments are not authentic to the learner, the design has failed. The only way to know what is authentic to the learner is to get to know him in a more personal way, a concept that may make some traditional instructors uncomfortable. The role of the instructor must shift to facilitator, and eventually partner, in learning. Otherwise, the instructor will never make the connection with the learner and get to know his needs, motivations, prior knowledge and preferences.

Specific ways to get to know the individual learner will vary depending on the comfort level of the instructor and his/her own personality. Each instructor must develop his own method of reaching out to students through trial-and-error. Some instructors may prefer to informally survey students through virtual icebreakers, "getting to know you" type of threaded discussions or even synchronous virtual meetings on the whiteboard reserved only for social purposes. Others may prefer scheduling a "virtual coffee break" on a regular basis or hosting a "water cooler" corner in a class wiki or blog. The idea is for the instructor to get to know the learners, as well as to build trust and a sense of community. Other methods may include instructor-created surveys with direct questions. These are easily created using a myriad of free survey generators that provide a link for participants and the collected responses for the instructor.

More personal methods may involve a quick personal phone call to the student to see how they are feeling about the course or a personalized email. Staying in touch with learners through out their learning experience also provides the opportunity to implement participatory design. The instructor should be able to redesign those parts of the course, whether it is an activity, an assessment or modifying content, based on ongoing student feedback. The purpose is to make continuous improvements with the course for the benefit of all learners.

Constructivist pedagogy asserts that the learner, through meaningful interactions, constructs knowledge and this can lead to substantial learning gains. Activities that are collaborative should be incorporated. Such activities are likely to be completed over a period of time due to the collaborative process, but also because they should cause the learner to probe problems in detail and offer alterative solutions. Incorporating activities that are interdisciplinary in nature will add the dimension of reality and, thus, authenticity. In the real world, situations are multi-dimensional and they should be in the online learning environment, as well.

Activities should be designed to provide the learner with enough practice so he may feel confident with the new skills learned. Scaffolding and modeling difficult concepts and skills is critical for learning. Tasks that require repetition and memorization, as in the case of technical training, should be presented in various contexts. Diversity of context provides the learner the opportunity to practice skills while analyzing each new situation and adapting his strategies to solve the problem at hand. Additionally, giving the learner choices of activities and assessments potentially enhances authenticity. Choice frees the learner to pick those tasks that are meaningful and authentic. The learner may also choose how to complete a certain product or how to demonstrate mastery.

Authenticity in online learning environments must include authentic assessments that truly gauge learning. Instructors should expect that final products would vary in responses and outcomes because they elicit open-ended responses with no wrong answer. The culminating project used to assess learning should aim at evaluating the thought process behind the product, not just the product itself. Digitally mediated communications and Web 2.0 tools facilitate collaboration but also promote engagement, creativity, relevance and technology literacy that is cross-cultural and interdisciplinary in nature.

Current trends indicate that online learning will be more likely to incorporate avatars, gaming, virtual worlds and other types of digitally mediated environments where the learner can take on a new persona. Given the number of learners who participate, socialize and communicate in online learning environments, an examination of self identity as it relates to anonymity may provide instructional designers with ways to improve the learning environment and facilitate authentic interactions, activities and assessment. Research and educational pedagogy support that the construction of knowledge is linked to identification of self. This identification is usually defined in social sciences as a relationship to others, whether in individual settings, dyads or groups.

The expansion of online learning demands that cyber educators inquire about factors that will ensure continued success of their programs. The United States Distance Learning Association (USDLA) is already gathering data for its 2012 report on these factors. Not only do cyber educators need to know how to expand their programs, they need to know how future advancements in technology will shape education and create new options for learning (USDLA, 2010). The question of authentication will continue to puzzle IT departments due to the increased connectivity that mobile learning applications will bring to the forefront and issues yet unforeseen. Authentication, as discussed in the introduction above, is a precursor to designing authentic learning environments because the learner's identity must first be established.

Future options will undoubtedly include more collaborative and engaging tools that facilitate learning any time, anywhere, especially using mobile devices. New capabilities will also bring new challenges. Cyber educators and instructional designers will have to continuously adapt to emergent technologies to ensure the authenticity of instructional strategies, activities and assessments.

CONCLUSION

Meaningful learning only takes place if it is embedded in the social and physical constructs in which it is used, thus making it authentic. Context then becomes an integral part of the learning experience. It becomes critical to design learning environments that implicitly support knowledge transfer. Learner-centric design involves integrating activities and assessments that are authentic to the learner. Several pedagogical and theoretical approaches such as constructivism, activity theory, social identity model of deindividuation theory and situated cognition aid cyber educators and instructional designers in framing the learning experience around authenticity.

Authentic designs situate the task in real-world scenarios, thus causing the learner to pause for inquiry, analysis, evaluation and to engage in decision-making. Too often, cyber educators and instructional designers revert to teacher-centered practices and attempt to pre-authenticate learning environments, thus compromising the critical epistemological foundations of constructivism. Instructors must get to know the learners in order to personalize the experience as much as possible and understand what is authentic to the learner. The subject matter and content may also play a role in authenticity, as some content may require more instructor-led support, especially with abstract concepts, until the learner becomes more confident with his new skills.

Authentic activities and assessments help minimize academic integrity issues because learners are asked to discern information, co-construct knowledge through collaborative and reflective practices and be able to apply real-world skills to solve situational problems. Tasks are designed to provide ample practice of new skills and assessments are seamlessly integrated into the learning process. Culminating projects may take longer to complete than traditional assessments, but rather than evaluating the product itself, the thought process behind the product may provide the instructor with a better measure of learning gains.

There is no question that interactions are different through digitally mediated communications versus face-to-face interaction. Appropriate technologies can be selected and implemented to place the responsibility of learning back in the hands of the learner, thereby encouraging interactions within the learning community to promote the co-construction of knowledge. The learning activities and assessments are more authentic and reflective if the learner is empowered to choose how to show mastery of concepts and skills learned and how to interact.

Designing for authenticity is supported by theoretical and pedagogical approaches that place the learner at the center of instruction. Technological advancements in digitally mediated communications now make it more feasible than ever to ensure the authenticity of online learning environments. This can only be made possible, however, by relinquishing instructor control and incorporating activities and assessments that are meaningful, engaging, challenging, collaborative, reflective and require the learner to apply real-world skills in a variety of contexts.

REFERENCES

Allen, M. W. (2003). *Guide to e-learning: Building interactive, fun and effective learning programs for any company*. Hoboken, NJ: John Wiley & Sons.

Barab, S., Squire, K., & Dueber, W. (2000). A co-evolutionary model for supporting the emergence of authenticity. *Educational Technology Research and Development*, *48*(2), 37–62. doi:10.1007/BF02313400

Beldarrain, Y. (2006). Distance education trends: Integrating new technologies to foster student collaboration and interaction. *Distance Education*, *27*(2), 139–153. doi:10.1080/01587910600789498

Brown, J. S., Collins, A., & Duguid, S. (1989). Situated cognition and the culture of learning. *Educational Researcher*, *18*(1), 32–42.

Bruner, J. S. (1961). The act of discovery. *Harvard Educational Review*, *31*(1), 21–32.

Burgoon, J., Stoner, G., Bonito, J., & Dunbar, N. (2003). Trust and deception in mediated communication. *Proceedings of the 36th Hawaii Intl. Conf. on System Sciences*, Honolulu, HI, (pp. 44-54).

Clark, R. C. (2003). *Building expertise: Cognitive methods for training and performance improvement* (2nd ed.). Silver Springs, MD: International Society for Performance Improvement.

Clark, R. C., Nguyen, F., & Sweller, J. (2006). *Efficiency in learning evidence-based guidelines to manage cognitive load*. San Francisco: John Wiley & Sons.

Committee on the Internet in the Evolving Information Infrastructure, Computer Science and Telecommunications Board on Physical Sciences, Mathematics and Applications National Research Council. (2001). *The Internet's coming of age*. Washington, DC: National Academy of the Sciences Press.

Driscoll, M. P. (2000). *Psychology of learning for instruction* (2nd ed.). Needham, MA: Allyn & Bacon.

Drummond, C. M. (2003). *Authentic learner assessment in an online environment: Using instructional design techniques to create an assessment model for an introductory computer science course.* (Doctoral dissertation). Retrieved October 28, 2010, from Dissertations & Theses: Full Text. (Publication No. AAT 3112977).

Eggen, P., & Kauchak, D. (1999). *Educational psychology* (4th ed.). Upper Saddle River, NJ: Prentice Hall.

Hein, G. E. (1991). *Constructivist learning theory*. Retrieved October 29, 2010, from http://www.exploratorium.edu/ifi/resources/constructivistlearning.html

Herrington, A., & Herrington, J. (2006). What is an authentic learning environment? In Herrington, A., & Herrington, J. (Eds.), *Authentic learning environments in higher education* (pp. 1–14). Hershey, PA: Idea Group. doi:10.4018/9781591405948.ch001

Herrington, J., & Oliver, R. (1995). Critical characteristics of situated learning: Implications for the instructional design of multimedia for higher education. In J. Pearce & A. Ellis (Eds.), *Learning with technology, ASCILITE'95 Conference proceedings*, (pp. 253-262). Melbourne: ASCILITE.

Herrington, J., & Oliver, R. (2000). An instructional design framework for authentic learning environments. *Educational Technology Research and Development, 48*(3), 23–48. doi:10.1007/BF02319856

Herrington, J., Oliver, R., & Reeves, T. (2002). Patterns of engagement in authentic online learning environments. Retrieved October 31, 2010, from http://www.ascilite. org.au/conferences/auckland02/proceedings/papers/085.pdf

Herrington, J., Oliver, R., & Reeves, T. (2006). Authentic tasks online: A synergy among learner, task and technology. *Distance Education, 27*(2), 233–248. doi:10.1080/01587910600789639

Herrington, J., Reeves, T., & Oliver, O. (2007). Immersive learning technologies: Realism and online authentic learning. *Journal of Computing in Higher Education, 19*(1), 65–84. doi:10.1007/BF03033421

Herrington, J., Reeves, T., Oliver, R., & Woo, Y. (2004). Designing authentic activities in Web-based courses. *Journal of Computing in Higher Education, 16*(1), 3–29. doi:10.1007/BF02960280

Jonassen, D. H. (1991). Evaluating constructivist learning. *Educational Technology, 31*(9), 28–33.

Jonassen, D. H. (1999). Designing constructivist learning environments. In Reigeluth, C. (Ed.), *Instructional design theories and models: A new paradigm of instructional theory* (Vol. 2, pp. 215–239). Mahwah, NJ: Lawrence Erlbaum Associates.

Jonassen, D. H., & Rohrer-Murphy, L. (1999). Activity theory a framework for designing constructivist learning environments. *Educational Technology Research and Development, 47*(1), 61–79. doi:10.1007/BF02299477

Lave, J. (1988). *Cognition in practice: Mind, mathematics and culture in everyday life*. Cambridge, UK: Cambridge University Press. doi:10.1017/CBO9780511609268

Mayer, R. E., & Reigeluth, C. (1999). Designing instruction for constructivist learning. In Reigeluth, C. M. (Ed.), *Instructional design theories and models* (Vol. 2, pp. 141–159). Mahwah, NJ: Lawrence Erlbaum Associates.

Miller, T., & King, F. (2003). Distance education: Pedagogy and best practices in the new millennium. *International Journal of Leadership in Education, 6*(3), 283–297. doi:10.1080/1360312032000118225

Petraglia, J. (1998). The real world on a short leash: The (mis)application of constructivism to the design of educational technology. *Educational Technology Research and Development, 46*(3), 53–65. doi:10.1007/BF02299761

Piaget, J. (1972). *Psychology and epistemology: Towards a theory of knowledge.* Harmondsworth, UK: Penguin.

Postmes, T., Spears, R., & Lea, M. (1998). Breaching or building social boundaries? SIDE-effects of computer-mediated communication. *Communication Research, 25,* 689–715. doi:10.1177/009365098025006006

Reeves, T., Herrington, J., & Oliver, R. (2002). Authentic activities and online learning. Retrieved October 31, 2010, from http://www.herdsa.org.au/wp-content/uploads/conference/2002/papers/Reeves.pdf

Rowe, N. C. (2004). Cheating in online student assessment: Beyond plagiarism. *Online Journal of Distance Learning Administration, 7*(2), 1-8. Retrieved October 29, 2010, from http://www.westga.edu/~distance/ojdla/summer72/rowe72.html

Sloan Consortium. (2010). *The five pillars.* Retrieved October 29, 2010, from http://www.sloan-c.org/5pillars

United States Distance Learning Association. (2010). Distance learning 2012: Factors for continued success. Retrieved October 29, 2010, from http://www.halegroup.com/distancelearning2012/index.html

Vrasidas, C., & Zembylas, M. (2003). The nature of technology-mediated interaction in global distance education. *International Journal of Training and Development, 7*(4), 217–286. doi:10.1046/j.1360-3736.2003.00186.x

Vygotsky, L. (1978). *Mind and society: The development of higher mental process.* Cambridge, MA: Harvard University Press.

Wiggens, G. (1998). *Educative assessment: Designing assessments to inform and improve student performance.* San Francisco: Jossey-Bass.

Wilson, B. G. (2004). Designing e-learning environments for flexible activity and instruction. *Educational Technology Research and Development, 52*(4), 77–84. doi:10.1007/BF02504720

Chapter 11

The Use of Avatars and Virtual Worlds for Learning

ABSTRACT

Virtual environments (VEs) can be immersive (IVE) or collaborative (CVE). Networked collaborative virtual environments (NCVEs) connect participants in real time via a network. Each type of VE presents opportunities to use different combinations of technologies to design engaging learning experiences, especially using avatars. Avatars are used as forms of self-representation for students as well as instructors. Anonymity enables users to alter their identities and interact in new ways through transformed social interactions. Advancements in technology continue to humanize avatars, thus changing their role in the VE and also changing the role of the instructor.

OBJECTIVES

- Define virtual environments, immersive virtual environments, collaborative virtual environments and networked virtual environments.
- Define transformed social interaction and explore its implications in cyber education.
- Identify the challenges of networked individualism.

DOI: 10.4018/978-1-60960-543-8.ch011

- Define and discuss the Proteus Effect.
- Explore how social awareness impacts learning in virtual worlds.
- Discuss the possible implications of the changing role of the avatar and how this new role will also impact the role of the instructor.

INTRODUCTION

Virtual environments and avatars are transforming social interactions within learning communities and have the potential of radically changing what is known about online learning. The unique features of these digital technologies impact human behavior and alter current methods of delivering content. Although avatars and some types of virtual environments are recent developments, their ability to deliver learning in context is already recognized by cyber educators and researchers. The benefits of recent technologies such as avatars remain largely unexplored and untapped. The question is how to develop learning applications with the limited technical knowledge currently available.

A virtual environment (VE) can be immersive (IVE) or collaborative (CVE). New technologies have also allowed for the emergence of sophisticated networked collaborative virtual environments (NCVEs) that connect participants in real time via a network. A virtual environment can be as simple as a Web-based conference using a webcam or as sophisticated as a simulator. Blascovich, Loomis, Beall, Swinth, Hoyt and Bailenson (2002) further define a VE as the type of environment that provides synthetic sensory information about the surroundings and the content, yet it is perceived as if it was not synthetic and thus realistic. The term virtual reality (VR) is derived from this concept because the user experiences sensory immersion in a virtual world that mimics the real world.

Every VE can enable transformed social interactions (TSI) because interpersonal communication can be either enhanced or degraded depending of the methods used by designers (Bailenson, Beall, Loomis, Blascovich, & Turk, 2004). Immersive virtual environments use the senses to immerse the user in the digital environment, thus removing him from the actual physical world; they include simulators and games that allow the user to become the character and to control that character with body movements and gestures.

The collaborative virtual environment involves multiple users that interact via avatars. Avatars are also used in IVEs, but are yet to provide a truly realistic representation of humans. Recent research demonstrates how VEs impact learning and how changes in technology may bring cyber educators one step closer to using virtual immersion and collaboration for learning. This chapter will explore some of the possible implications of VEs as they relate to the learner's behavior and learning. The terms VE and virtual worlds may be used interchangeably throughout the discussion because virtual worlds are themselves virtual environments.

BACKGROUND

Virtual environments may improve the way knowledge is transferred through digitally mediated communications. Collaborative and immersive virtual environments that use current and future technologies provide new delivery methods which frame concepts in real world scenarios. VEs have the natural propensity of transforming interactions. As the social dynamics within the VE change, the traditional learning experience evolves into a more engaging one.

Like any new technology, those applications used in virtual environments come with a host of benefits as well as challenges. VEs are digital representations of content, learners, and instructors for learning purposes. According to Bailenson, Yee, Blascovich, Beall, Lundblad and Jin (2008), a TSI is the ability to alter one's identity and context or representation using digital technology in order to improve learning. VEs are unique in that they are not real, yet the learner perceives the environment as being real and is able to interact with it and react to the surroundings. Learners can interact with VEs in different ways than other types of multimedia environments by using the perceptual channels such as auditory or visual.

CVEs are collaborative virtual environments. In these environments, multiple virtual users interact via their avatars. Avatars are models driven by human beings and are not to be confused with embodied agents that are models driven by computer algorithms (Bailenson, Yee, Blascovich, et al., 2008). Several examples of popular CVEs are available, each with a different degree of collaboration or avatar features. Some have social objectives, while others are mainly for gaming. Second Life®, launched in 2003, has recently added Teen Second Life® to cater to the social needs of 13-17 year olds. Likewise, *Cybertown* takes on a futuristic theme to connect members but is not as sophisticated as Second Life® because it lacks the multiple features that allow users to build their own virtual world and "live" in it. Multi-player gaming CVEs continue to be popular, such as *Final Fantasy 14* and *Everquest* by Sony©, both of which offer plenty of role-playing. Gaming CVEs and IVEs have yet to truly make their mark in online learning, partially due to the cost of the equipment necessary to experience true perceptual immersion in the game and partly due to their ability to give the user more flexibility in creating their character. The educational applications of gaming CVEs and IVEs will be explored in the *Looking Forward* section of this chapter.

IVEs are immersive virtual environments that increase the user's sense of actually being part of the environment. The user is perceptually immersed in the sounds, visuals and even smells of the virtual environment. In IVEs, Tracking technology follows and records the user's movements with head, arm, leg and facial expressions. The IVE is then instantaneously changed according to the user's position or orientation. Designers have a tremendous amount of control over what the user experiences and can create and change the appearance of the environment to meet goals and adjust to user actions. The goal is to mentally remove the user from the physical world so he is truly engrossed in the virtual world (Bailenson et al, 2008). An authentic VR experience envelops the user in multi-sensory stimuli. Bailenson et al (2008) point out that although technologies to support the perceptual channel for audio and visuals are improving, methods for using channels to the other senses remain relatively undeveloped, thus hindering the advancement of the photographic and behavioral realism of avatars.

TSI stresses the importance of social interactions in the digital environment. Transformed social interactions occur as the user interacts with the ever changing environment and the environment itself changes in respond to user needs. Social interactions can be transformed in essentially three ways through self-representations, social-sensory abilities and the social environment (Bailenson et al, 2008). According to these authors, self-representation is the "strategic decoupling" of the behavior of the avatars from the humans driving their behaviors. A user may choose to design its avatar to resemble himself physically and to behave similarly. Others may choose to do the opposite. Researchers believe that users view avatars that look like themselves more favorably and intimately than those who look or behave differently.

This poses an opportunity for cyber educators to adapt the avatar to match the learner's preferences. For example, in CVEs, some learners may learn better with a teacher that smiles often and uses a more personable approach, while other students may learn best with a teacher who is more serious. According to Bailenson et al (2008), the physical appearance and facial expressions of the teacher avatar can be modified to gain the student's attention and promote learning. The second way of transforming interactions is through the social-sensory abilities inherent in the technology. Bailenson et al (2008) discuss how the creation of invisible consultants, whether they are actual humans represented by a digital presence or algorithms, can promote learning by providing information only to a particular learner who needs it. The flow and amount of information transmitted to each individual can be manipulated and personalized using real-time data about the user or his avatar. The instructor may choose to use automatic registers to track how he is addressing student needs and decide how to provide equal attention to all learners.

Finally, the social environment or virtual meeting space can be configured optimally in a different way for each learner to enhance his or her learning experience. This includes altering the flow of rendered time by allowing pausing, fast forwarding and rewinding as strategies for learning or changing the expressions of other avatars that are distracting to the user (Bailenson et al, 2008). Likewise, an instructor may decide to change the expressions of his own avatar to be more similar to the learner, thus exploiting the similarities to have a stronger impact and develop a deeper connection with the learner. "The strongest case for VEs as learning modules stems from their ability to implement contexts and relationships not possible in a traditional learning setting" (Bailenson et al, 2008, p. 106).

Virtual environments are driven by the premise that additional stimuli in the form of visual and audio input should increase not only the interactions between avatars, but also between avatar and environment. By comparing avatars to audio and video baseline communications, researchers have examined the differences between interactions that use complete visual information, such as video from the head and shoulders, with those that lack visual information and rely only on audio. The purpose of much of this research is to understand how facial expressions and expressive behaviors in avatars can enrich the learning environment.

An overall analysis by Garau, Slater, Bee and Sasse (2001) suggests that head and eye movements must correspond to the conversational flow to be meaningful. There is some evidence that an avatar with a random gaze is worse than just audio in a situation where there is a co-presence. In the research conducted by Garau et al, participants paid more attention when the gaze was active and engaging than when it was not. Another surprising finding was that avatars with meaningful expressions were not significantly different from the video, which was a representation of face-to-face communications. They concluded that for avatars to meaningfully contribute to communications, they must be more than just lively; they must reflect some aspect that integrates the conversation taking place and that avatars that are engaging can make an important contribution to learning.

Likewise, Bailenson et al, (2008) conducted three experiments to understand the role of gaze, social perception and transformational interactions in VEs. In one experiment, they found that gaze augmented the teacher's social perception and enabled the teacher to distribute their attention more evenly among learners. Those students who were in the teacher's periphery received more gaze. In a CVE, virtual eye contact can be maintained simultaneously with multiple students, which is impossible in the real world. The authors explain that it is possible to render multiple, yet separate versions, of the teacher because each participant sees his own rendition of the shared virtual space.

In the second and third experiments, Bailenson et al, (2008) explored how proximity to the teacher in the CVE influenced learning; they concluded that students learned better if they were at the center of the teacher's field of view instead of the periphery and that overall, those students who were closest to the teacher had higher learning gains. This is particularly valuable to learning VEs because it helps designers create embodied agents that keep the learner within the instructor's field of vision.

The study of the effects of gaze in learning is of great value to cyber educators. Gaze can be manipulated in IVEs to assess the individual contributions of conversational partners (Bailenson, Beall, & Blascovich, 2002). This is achieved by "locking" an individual's gaze so the conversational partners do not see where the other person is looking (via head or eye movements) even though the partner's face can be seen. This helps cyber educators understand this phenomenon and determine what causes attentive or inattentive behaviors in the learning IVE.

Earlier designs of VEs were more concerned with visualizing and simulating physical places, but have since evolved into synthetic places that take into account the virtual presence of people as well as desired behaviors and outcomes. Embodied agents are systems that operate independently and rationally, seeking to achieve goals in the virtual environment. An agent executes actions based on behaviors and goals. Cognitively-based agent models for virtual worlds are developed using sensors to collect data and analyze the interactions between the agent, the user and the VE. Agents are able to display reflexive, reactive, reflective/proactive and social behaviors (Maher & Gero, 2002). Interactions in virtual worlds are a major focus of most design platforms today. Agents take virtual worlds beyond 3D visualization.

The literature exposes different features of VEs and their accompanying learning options. Understanding what they are may help cyber educators to maximize the impact of these features in the learning environment. Each learning option offers differing degrees of immersion and collaboration. Table 1 below lists the key features of VEs and several learning options that are available to cyber educators and instructional designers. Aside from the use of embodied agents to cause the learner to behave or interact in particular ways, the co-learner's behaviors can also be modified and adapted in response to the user's own behaviors. VEs with enhanced visualizations provide insight into difficult concepts because the learner is able to see problems from different perspectives. This is particularly beneficial if the concept would be too expensive or too dangerous to demonstrate in the physical space. Cyber educators are able to analyze student behavior by synthesizing their behavior patters and therefore better personalize instruction. Through immersion in the VE, the learner's sense of presence is heightened and he is more likely to interact with peers and co-construct knowledge in the virtual world. The features and benefits of the different types of VEs are promising to cyber educators who seek to create learner-centric learning environments.

Social Awareness and Individualized Networking

Social awareness in VEs creates reciprocal opportunities for knowledge sharing. Lack of social awareness can break down the flow of knowledge because it interferes with the natural interactions that typically take place between learners, instructor

Table 1. VE features and learning options

VE Term	Learning Options
Embodied Agents	Intelligent agents teach a learner about a specific domain.
Co-learners	Virtual co-learners modify their behaviors in response to the user and enhance the learning experience.
Visualizations	Enhanced visualizations provide perspectives into complex scenarios; provide information and better understanding of abstract concepts. Visualizations allow for the manipulation of the environment, creating, altering and rotating structures in a three dimensional view.
Synthesis of Archived Behaviors	The micro and macro behaviors of teachers and learners are recorded, stored and analyzed to create behavioral profiles and summaries over time.
Presence, Immersion and Learning	The degree to which a learner actually feels he or she is present in a virtual environment.
Simulation of Dangerous or Expensive Lessons	Teaching lessons that are either to expensive or too dangerous to conduct in a physical space are easily simulated in IVEs.

From Bailenson, Beall, Loomis, et al. (2004) and Bailenson, Yee, Blascovich, et al. (2008).

and content. The VE becomes the learning community, which evolves as members interact with their surroundings. The adaptive technologies inherent in the VE make these changes more rapid.

The changing needs of the learner and the learning community should be incorporated in the VE so that it can serve both, as a learning environment and a repository for community resources that enhance future experiences (Prasolova-Forland & Divitini, 2003). Cyber educators continue to learn about the advantages of community-based approaches to learning. According to Barab, Kling, & Gray (2004), the best method to determine which practices or processes are needed to design Web supported communities is to look through an interdisciplinary lens that includes educational psychology, sociology, anthropology and computer science, among others.

The different types of VEs are networked reality environments that immerse the user in a synthetic world. In this world, presence and proximity become telepresence and teleproximity due to the technologies that are used to enhance the senses. The technology removes the physical constraints to make the interaction more familiar and the perception of being physically close. The interactions of users with each other and with their surroundings help to establish forms of identity.

Telepresence and teleproximity help members of the VE to connect with each other. Users may take on a new identity for themselves or choose an alter ego identity for their avatar while maintaining their true self protected. The phenomena of presence, proximity and identity have been explored in the context of online learning as the deindividuation and anti-normative patterns (Postmes & Spears, 1998) that emerge as a result of the virtual experience. Research is needed to gain insight into why VE participants may choose to change their identity or not when using an avatar for self-representation.

Anonymity is still a concern in VEs, especially as learners can change their self-representation through avatars and portray any desired personality. Anonymity is necessary to protect the privacy of the learner, which in some cases is what causes shy individuals to exhibit social behaviors they would otherwise not display. In other cases, anonymity and lack of cues in the virtual environment cause deindividuation. Yee and Bailenson (2007) suggest that the behavior of avatars may cause deindividuated people to taken on a new identity inferred from their avatars. Postmes and Spear's (1998) social identity model of deindividuation (SIDE) proposes that the individual may choose to accept group norms through the process of deinviduation; however, Yee and Bailenson expose the influence of the avatar on the individual through what they have termed the Proteus Effect.

The Proteus Effect, like SIDE, explores acceptance and conformity of behavior, but each theoretical approach focuses on a different aspect. SIDE deals with the conformity of the individual to group norms and behaviors, which cause him to accept the group's identity as his own. The Proteus Effect on the other hand, is rooted in perception theory and indicates that individuals will behave as other expect them to behave (Yee & Bailenson, 2007). This effect is paramount in designing CVEs as well as IVEs because of the implications it has on interactions. Yee and Bailenson (2007) insist however, that the Proteus Effect is not a prerequisite for interaction, but it is a phenomenon that manifests itself even if the user is alone because the individual evaluates himself from a third-person perspective as stipulated by self-perception theory.

The idea of collaboration in the different types of VEs is challenged by the concept of networked individualism (Barney, 2004; Wellman, 2001), which emerges as a result of digitally mediated communications. The very nature of online learning is based on the premise that learners do not have to be co present to participate because the place and time barriers are removed. Cyber educators go to great lengths to create a constructivist environment that facilitates the co-creation of knowledge. The sharing of knowledge has long been established as a relatively strong connection in the online learning environment that is supported by constructivist approaches to learning that are learner-centric. Emotions are considered a much weaker connection because they take longer to develop and be nurtured in the right environment. In the case of avatars, early researchers such as Olveres, Billinghurst, Savage, and Holden (1998) recognized the importance of emotional expressions of avatars and their ability to build relationships.

Relationships established in the online learning environment or VE often imply closeness due to unity of purpose, shared interests or goals and are usually human-to-human even in digitally mediated environments. The different degrees of perceived emotional ties could be influenced by many factors such as personality traits, personal preferences, learning style, cultural background and gender among others. The possibilities exist for weaker and looser ties if the tendency is for less focused grouping. The concept of networked individualism (Barney, 2004; Jones, Ferreday, & Hodgson, 2008) suggests that goals of community-based consensus and collaboration might be challenged when networked individualism is the dominant form of sociability because the newly established social patterns are based on individualism and not collectivism. Weak ties may also operate between primary groups in the learning community and influence the social activity outside of the main groups. The weak ties however, are necessary in order for groups to co-exist. Both strong and weak ties play an important role in digitally mediated communications.

Grounded in the principles of constructivism, including active and experiential learning, VEs are committed to discourse, sharing knowledge and community building. Founded on the basis of constructivist ideas, they can combine both networking technologies and virtual reality. Until the late 1990s, the virtual reality that was used in education was restricted to researchers with the financial means to develop fully immersive environments. Early pioneering in virtual reality worlds included *Active World, Blaxxun and Community Place* (Chee & Hooi, 2002). The rise of the Internet gave way to environments for chatting and socializing that included virtual reality and allowed users to share virtual space.

Research published by the Human Interface Technology (HIT) lab at the University of Washington indicates that learners found virtual realities both fascinating and enjoyable, especially if the field of vision (FOV) is enlarged. Jeng-Weei, Duh, Abi-Rached, Parker, and Furness (2002) also contend that participants "…may develop more spatial awareness as well as higher sense of presence and consequently they may exhibit better memory structure of that VE…" (p. 1). The pedagogical basis of using virtual worlds has been fairly consistent from the beginning. Rooted firmly in activity theory and determined to use technology to support knowledge construction, these worlds have followed four primary epistemological tenets. Doolittle (1999, p.1) expanded on von Glasersfeld's (1984) constructivist views to incorporate the interdisciplinary origins of knowledge and knowing:

1. Knowledge is not passively accumulated; it is constructed through the active cognitive processing of the individual.
2. Active cognition is a process that helps individuals adapt their behavior in different situations.

3.   Cognition does not render an accurate view reality but helps individuals organize and make sense out of their experiences.
4.   Knowing has roots in biology, neurology, social, cultural and language based interactions.

From their infancy, virtual reality worlds were created to provide the learner with an environment where they could ask "what if…" questions and explore problems from different perspectives.

VEs leveraged activities and experiences to directly support the individual learner. Focusing on a context that motivates learners to ask questions and experiment, it also fostered peer assisted-learning and reciprocal tutoring. By creating a context where learners were encouraged to interact and articulate their ideas and understanding to each other, it fostered the building of community and group consensus. As these environments evolved, they incorporated the transitions from first-person experiential learning to third-person symbolic learning. Kolb's (1984) experiential learning cycle involves active experimentation that leads to concrete experiences. Through a recursive cycle, the active experiences in turn provide the basis for reflective observation, which eventually leads to abstract conceptualization. Kolb's model offers yet another learning theory for framing VEs.

Cognition by definition involves more than just brain structures and processes; it is also dependent on social relationships, symbolic content, learning resources and any other interaction experienced by the learner. Learning then is more than an individual's construction of knowledge; it is a projection along paths of participation and growth within a given community (Steinkuechler, 2004). Most virtual environments include avatars and are created around actionable knowledge instead of knowledge its own sake. VEs are also used most effectively when supporting group work that is learner-centered and can provide resources and context that support a discovery approach to learning (Chee & Hooi, 2002). According to Chee & Choi three-dimensional worlds and virtual realities can support learning both as a mechanism for distance education and as an extension to the traditional classroom.

Aside from the well-known learning styles postulated by Kolb (1984), emerging learning styles are based on immersion in virtual learning communities. Dede (2004) identifies five learning styles predominant among the Millennial generation, which grew up surrounded by educational technologies. These learning styles include:

•   Fluency in multimedia and virtual worlds.
•   Learning as a community and distributed knowledge across a community and context not just with in an individual.
•   Balanced learning including collective reflection, experiential learning and mentoring.

- Non-linear expression through web representations.
- Learner involvement in the design of the learning experience.

Dede (2004) points out that many traditional educators find it difficult to adapt to these shifts in learning styles and that in order to do so they must cultivate and develop the same set of learning styles through immersive experiences or they risk not being effective in their teaching role. Likewise, instructional designers and cyber educators who have transferred outdated methods of instruction to the online classroom may find it difficult to understand how avatars and virtual environments can be used to enhance learning.

Immersive learning has been a widely accepted approach to education for many years, but it was mainly through role playing and scenario-based learning. Technology has changed the structure and delivery of instruction. VEs add elements that make learning engaging and transform interactions in ways not possible face-to-face. Learners have the ability to interact with the environment, other individuals, objects and places and influence the behavior of others as a result. Embodied agents that are there to keep the student's attention and maximize learning can also modify an individual's behavior. In new multi user environments communities, societies and entire cultures can emerge. These new experiences can be analogous to the real world or they could simulate experiences that would be very difficult to achieve in real life. The different types of VEs take learning into the 21st century. Virtual reality worlds have much to contribute to learning.

LEARNING IN VIRTUAL WORLDS

Virtual reality focuses on constructing VEs that are centered on computational tools or representations of the real world that learners can manipulate. These applications and representations influence the interactions between the learners and their VR environment as well as the social interactions between learner-to-learner, learner-to-instructor and how the learner interacts with the interface or content. As the VEs have evolved over the years, avatars began to represent learners who could collaborate openly or vicariously interact and use virtual objects to learn through experience. This immersion has shifted the way learners interact with the external world from one that is peripheral to one that fundamentally shapes the experience in both the physical and social context. The terms *virtual worlds* and *virtual environments* will be used interchangeably in this section. The term *virtual reality* will be used to describe types of VEs that simulate the real world or create imaginary worlds, some of which could be immersive (IVE) or collaborative (CVE) as defined in the introduction.

Behind the mask of an avatar, a student has not only some autonomy but also a certain amount of anonymity. VR simulations as a learning tool evolved from the United States Department of Defense in the late 1980s. The objective was to provide authentic and virtual contexts similar to the real world scenario where the skills would be used. In education and entertainment, the goal of VRs is similar. Cyber educators need alternative methods of delivering instruction that is learner-centric and engaging. VR worlds provide engaging features but also promote the use of critical thinking, very much like VR worlds created for entertainment that force the user to make decisions and learn from mistakes.

For-profit virtual worlds, such as Second Life®, offer a combined environment of social, cultural and economic dimensions, mimicking real life. Participants of virtual worlds that use avatars tend to treat each other as imaginary beings and collectively form virtual communities where they construct new lifestyles and Utopian societies (Dede, 2004). The possible applications in education are exciting because the interpersonal dynamics in VR environments allow for interactions that provide the learner with different experiences and perspectives not available in traditional face-to-face education.

Virtual worlds are now being used as a medium for synchronous and asynchronous e-learning. These VR learning environments are helping to close the gap between learning focused on information and experiential learning (Dickey, 2005). The learning communities developed in VEs provide a supportive structure where knowledge is shared and where learners are provided with role models and opportunities for role playing and a safe environment for honing new skills. Virtual worlds are not always based on games. Current practices in online learning include the use of video gaming principles to immerse the learner in the synthetic world. Virtual worlds are open-ended and can be applied to any context. Games, on the other hand, tend to be goal-oriented and have a fixed purpose. A game is often in the form of a simulation and is driven by software programming. VR environments designed for learning provide open-ended activities and interactions that lead toward instructional goals but are driven by the learner's behavior.

In virtual worlds, basic skills must be learned and mastered in order for the participant to thrive. Resources must be made readily available to the learner, either in the form of embodied agents or instructor feedback. The use of reward is a powerful element in virtual worlds. Appropriate behaviors and achievement can be instantly rewarded in the VR to enhance the learner's motivation, self-esteem and satisfaction. Learning milestones can be celebrated within the learning community thus leveraging interaction and promoting a sense of community.

Many of the virtual worlds currently in existence have in excess of five million residents, with any number of them connected synchronously at any given time. Interpreting the behaviors of new residents of the VR can be difficult. Likewise, new residents may find themselves feeling insecure in the new environment, especially as they take on a new identity. Through familiarity and social interactions their security and place in the virtual culture is established (Johnson & Levine, 2008). Common concerns are centered on whom to trust as well as how to represent one's self using a new identity. After the basic rules are mastered, the participants' self-esteem and security are likely to increase. The same concerns apply in VR worlds for educational purposes. Particular attention should be given to welcoming learners to the new space and providing tutorials so they learn key rules and functions of the environment. Providing clear expectations and information about the environment will likely diminish the initial sense of insecurity perceived by new residents of the VR learning community.

The features of a virtual word can impact pedagogical applications that help learners explore perspectives and co-construct knowledge. Virtual worlds can provide support for creating community with geographically dispersed learners (Dickey, 2003a). VR environments are an ideal place to foster creativity, collaboration and critical thinking. Learners assimilate new knowledge by building on prior knowledge of the real world. Self-directed learning activities aide in the exploration and the construction of knowledge. The creation, manipulation and exploration of objects, systems and ideas are an integral part of the VR learning environment.

Learning takes place when the learner is engaged in constructing a personally meaningful object. Equally important to the construction of knowledge is the experience gained by participation in a group. Collaboration can occur across virtual communities and sometimes even physical communities that create a shared experience that enhances the learning. Interactions can take place between the learners and the other avatars or embodied agents that populate the virtual environment. Much research must be done in this area for it is currently in its infancy (Roussos et al, 1997). Despite the perceived benefits to the VR, it is critical to use evaluation methods that establish the effectiveness of instructional practices in VEs and to determine how much learning is actually taking place.

VR technology has developed more intensively over the last few years. The more interactive features suggest that interactive and collaborative VEs not only support constructivist pedagogy but may also help to bridge the gap between experiential and informational learning. All virtual worlds have strengths and weaknesses in design, yet VR learning environments promise to deliver information in context, immersing the learner in situations that require adaptability, flexibility, decision-making skills and enable the learner to learn from mistakes. Other situations may be open-ended with no wrong or right outcome, but that require the learner to apply the new skills and concepts learned in order to achieve the next level or step in the VR world. Many of the worlds available today support avatars which serve as visual representations of learners and as communication agents and forms of interactive chat or audio environment (Dickey, 2003b). Design must be maximized to leverage the benefits of the technology.

Other immersive VR environments include massively multiplayer online games (MMOGs) which are highly graphical, avatar driven and are becoming not only a form of entertainment, but also a form of socialization for young adults. Avatars interact not only with the gaming software, but with each other; they provide persistent social and material worlds, although often structured around fantasy, they still provide social realism. These games can be addictive in nature and continue to grow in popularity among young and old alike. They may hold a key to cultural cognitive analysis of the social and material practices they represent. "From a Learning Sciences perspective, cognition is (inter) action in the social and material world" (Steinkuehler, 2004, p. 521). They may help define social literacy in the new social space, how to become a member of the community and what it is like to be an individual in the larger virtual community. Learning itself is not embedded in the game, but in the community of practice of those that play it.

In most online learning environments, formal instruction is still predominant. Much attention lately has been directed toward the importance of informal or incidental learning because educators acknowledge that learning is frequently unintentional. When Tamagotchis became an unexpected overnight success in the late 1990s, experts began to wonder why they were so successful. According to Holzinger, Pichler, and Almer (2001), the most important lesson from the Tamagotchis was the importance of motivation and the ability to learn with the character. This lesson can be applied to VR worlds that use special characters to engage the learner and deliver instruction without the learner even realizing he is learning.

Another dynamic that offers opportunities for learning in virtual realities is the fluidity of a person's identity. Just as telephones and television dissolved social boundaries related to time and space, virtual environments using avatars remove identity boundaries by enabling communications about personal thoughts through very impersonal media. This opens the learner to the possibility of new ideas and minimizes conflict with the real self. A corollary of this openness is that the identity of avatars is always questionable and unreliable. Magical media using avatars can be very seductive and addictive. Underlying this behavior might be a need for control and mastery if the environment is used for escapism (Dede, 2004). The intellectual, emotional and normative archetypes generated in the different types of VEs can lead learners toward a complex experience associated with mental models according to Dede (2004).

Social awareness in any context of the VR world can encompass an undetermined time span. It may increase or decrease depending on the perception of the learner. Social awareness is a vital part of any learning scenario and should not be ignored. It will require much research if it is to be effective in enhancing the learning experience. The interplay of personalities and sense of presence affect the interactions of learners using an avatar. The feeling of presence can be enhanced if members of the VE display closer proximity, which can be encouraged by the instructor on an individual basis or by the software itself. The usability of virtual worlds is also paramount in improving VR worlds for learning. Flexibility and better awareness mapping can provide a solid structure for building interactions and creating opportunities for delivering content.

VR environments that support learning must be flexible, adaptive and structured for collaboration. Many newer VEs for learning offer not only hypermedia, but also a variety of tools for conferencing, planning, meeting, videoconferencing, role playing and scenario-based learning. One of the most interesting attributes of VEs is the ability of these environments to offer multiple modalities in support of knowledge construction (Dufresne & Paquette, 2000). Each technology feature and tool embedded in the VR will require supportive interfaces designed to unfold gradually as the learner acquires more knowledge and expertise.

Supportive and Adaptive Interface Using Avatars

The interface is the first and last interaction the learner experiences in an e-learning application. Avatars are becoming more useful and capable of providing support as part of that interface. From info bots that disseminate timely information to newsreaders, avatars are used more now than ever before. An avatar in the broadest definition is one side of an interactive exchange. Avatars can represent human beings or be part of the e-learning application that operates as an agent and simulates human activities. Often, the avatar is the missing link between the learner and the knowledge the learner is seeking.

The balance between usability and user control of the avatar is key to a successful application. *Clippy* from Microsoft© is an example of an earlier avatar that was highly recognized but unsuccessful. *Clippy*, the smiling paper clip was unsuccessful because although it functioned well, it was not part of the user's experience and was deemed annoying. The character was too intrusive and distracting, it tried to force help on users who naturally responded with negative feedback (Sheth, 2003). Learning VEs can make use of avatars in many different ways including on-demand tutorials, quick help finding additional resources and definitions, but also to prompt the learner to take action, check for understanding or extend teachable moments. The interface of each application must be easy to use and must provide learner control to bypass the avatar, make it repeat the information or simply pursue the avatar's prompt and engage the learner in a re-teaching or enrichment activity concurrent with the learner's mastery level at that particular moment in time.

The advantage of avatars is the multi-dimensional interactions they provide. Text-to-speech software has increased the number and kind of interactivity options of the avatar, while voice recognition applications are also becoming increasingly powerful. The attributes and capabilities of avatars continue to increase with technological advancements and make it possible to construct ideal worlds for learning. Although their capabilities are constantly increasing, cyber educators are still learning how to use avatars in online learning.

At first, avatars were mainly used as a fun way to get the user's attention. Their role was limited and they were considered a marketing gimmick, rather than an actual conversational agent. After much evolution in concept and in application, avatars are now poised to become an aid in self-learning. Capable of two-way conversations in multiple languages, the development of avatar capabilities has been driven largely by text to speech and speech synthesis technologies. Eventually avatars will be able to provide information, teach a lesson, correct responses and remediate learners without criticism (Sheth, 2003). The ultimate goal according to leading experts is to achieve one-on-one learning. This personalized approach to learning will have a desirable impact on distance learning.

Adaptive interfaces have been limited by the ability of the system to obtain information about the learner and his activities. Adaptive interfaces play an important role in reducing confusion for the learner and navigation disorientation. In virtual environments for learning, it is important that the system not be the center of interaction, reserving this focus for the instructors and the learners because the system serves only as a tool to facilitate those interactions (Dufresne & Paquette, 2000). Ease of navigation is a requirement for constructivist approaches to learning environment design that aims to create an active, situated and collaborative setting. Navigation and interface must be as transparent as possible, especially if it includes different types of adaptive support, graphical highlights, annotations, animation and audiovisuals to guide the learner.

The role of avatars in virtual worlds of learning will continue to evolve. They were originally introduced as an interface tool that provided basic information. Mixed adaptive environments provide the learner with more support of the long term learning (Dufresne & Paquette, 2000), this includes using avatars to enhance the learning environment and also facilitate learning. Avatars are likely to become role models for the student because they are easily adaptable and can manipulate any given scenario to obtain desired learner behaviors. Their ability to use gaze to gain the user's attention can be used to optimize learning.

When humans communicate in a face-to-face environment, there are many cues that are both voluntary and involuntary. These cues interplay with each interaction and help establish or augment meaning. Glances, stares, body position, gaze and gestures, both subtle and overt, make extensive use of the visual channel. Simple things like eye blinking and head turning make a difference in responding to human conversations (Viljalmsson & Cassell, 1998). In virtual environments, the avatars must model and emulate such fundamental behaviors to establish credibility and effectiveness in virtual communications. Even when communication is text-based, it is important that avatars provide attention, respond with salutations, facial expressions and back channel feedback that let the learner know that he was heard.

The role of the avatar has to expand beyond the role of just a presence that provides information and actually contribute to the interactions within the learning environment. Multimodal communications among humans are enhanced by subtle body language and visual cues. Avatars must be improved to reflect the natural cues that are part of conversation and must be able to interact with humans to both initiate and sustain communications (Viljalmsson & Cassell, 1998). Avatar mediated interactions must enhance the overall experience.

The eyes of the avatar are especially important in communicating in VR environments. The eyes express emotions and intentions and help direct attention toward a particular objective. The eyes are critical in creating better user interface to facilitate communications and interaction between humans and between avatar representations of users. Culture, gender, age and distance can influence eye gaze patterns. For avatars to be effective learning and communication agents, eye gaze must be natural and help direct attention from avatar to avatar (Colburn, Cohen & Drucker, 2000). Eyes help to regulate the flow of conversation and create breaks in a conversation to allow for taking turns when speaking.

VR environments must provide adaptive and supportive interface design through the use of avatars; they must be easy to understand and should provide the learner with control over their usability. Highly interactive avatars that can quickly respond to the user's behavior are likely to enhance the sense of presence for learners and improve the learning experience.

Second Life® Reality

Second Life© is one of the more popular virtual worlds on the Internet and is unique in the way that its residents are able to develop it and participate, much like a real community. The possibilities are exceptionally rich and adaptable to education. Second Life® has become an example of a virtual environment that is ripe for educational applications because it has an already well-established community. Much of this virtual world can be maneuvered and changed to create entirely new learning experiences, including the manipulation of identity and form of both the avatar and the physical space.

Residents build and recreate their surroundings in Second Life® giving it form and substance (Wagner, 2008). Although it has received a great deal of attention, the impact of Second Life® on education is debatable. This is due partly to a lack of research and fear of involvement on the part of many educational institutions that undermine the educational potential of this virtual world. Pathfinders in the field of online learning include government agencies and educational institutions. The Teacher's College at Columbia University uses its virtual island called TC Educator to conduct classes in a virtual amphitheatre or on a platform in the sky (Columbia University, 2010). The Open University in the United Kingdom opened its Second Life® campus in 2006 (Open University, 2010). They created Cetlment Island as a collaborative space with whiteboards, chat tools, blogs and other features.

According to a United States government report, several government agencies continue exploring the potential of Second Life® for education, virtual collaboration and outreach programs (Pellerin, 2007). The report points out that some agencies such as the National Oceanic and Atmospheric Administration (NOAA), the National Air and Space Administration (NASA), the National Institutes of Health (NIH), the Centers for Disease Control and Prevention (CDCP), the National Science Foundation (NSF) and the United States House of Representatives have virtual facilities in Second Life® that vary in level of interaction as well as complexity of the environment. The agency least expected to create a virtual format is the Department of Homeland Security, which, according to the report, holds regular virtual meetings within Second Life® to explore its options, features and benefits.

Virtual worlds can provide insight into human interactions, individual and group behavior, as well as establishing connections that are not constrained by geography (Johnson & Levine, 2008). It is difficult to predict the durability or sustainability of Second Life® itself, especially as high membership does not necessarily equate high participation. One of the reasons might be the learning curve for using and being productive in this virtual world. Second Life® has a high learning curve for new users entering this virtual world. Nearly 90% of individuals who create an account in Second Life® do not return (Sanchez, 2009). The interface in Second Life® is not intuitive and is difficult to learn. Another reason might be that the software to run Second Life® is very computer processor intense and requires a fast Internet connection. Second Life® is also time consuming and the expectations of the user may be higher than the virtual world delivers (Sanchez, 2009).

There are some important considerations when adapting multi user virtual world such as Second Life® to education and training. Despite all the inherent features in the VE, there is often a mismatch between the perceived depth and breadth of a conversation or idea and what is actually captured in the virtual world (Rappa, Yip, & Baey, 2009). It is more difficult to build on abstract ideas and hypothetico-deductive reasoning using traditional media. In the VR world, almost anything is possible. There are four strategies to push the interactions from a mere exchange to higher levels (Rappa, Yip, & Baey, 2009). Facilitating collaboration based on the necessity to negotiate and form a collective alliance initiates the interaction process. The replication of real-world task in the virtual environment, followed by scaffolding, helps in the negotiation process. Finally, learners should have the opportunity to reflect and reevaluate learning in terms of a broader context that goes beyond the course.

An important aspect of using virtual worlds is applying pedagogy to take advantage of the benefits. Several approaches seem to have merit: digital storytelling, role playing, community involvement and peer-to-peer tutoring. With digital storytelling, participants use the environment to tell a story; they work in groups and create stories using avatars, renditions of physical objects and spaces. Role playing frees the learner to view a situation from different perspectives. The options for creating content, scenarios and discussions are endless. There are also many opportunities for learners in virtual worlds to connect with others that are geographically dispersed but may have common interests or concerns.

The combination of reflection, creativity, active learning and a variety of pedagogical approaches can be transferred and work well in Second Life® (Sanchez, 2009). For example, encouraging learners to take on projects that may benefit the non-profit or targeted communities easily promulgates civic responsibility. Virtual worlds can become a platform for real-life community engagement. A large number of non-profit organizations can be located at the Commonwealth Island and Non-profit Commons. Another venue created by Second Life® developers was Teen Grid, a special platform for teens ages 13 through 17. The developers however, announced in August 2010 that Teen Grid would be closed due to lack of profits. Those ages 16 and above would be moved to the main Second Life® grid, but accounts of younger members would be closed. Teenagers engaged socially as well as educationally on Teen Grid. One example is a group of students that created and built in a project designed to examine gender and equity in computer science (Sanchez, 2009). A concern arising from the closing of Teen Grid is that educators who had developed educational applications for the younger audience now have no platform for experimentation.

The features of virtual worlds may also enhance learning because the user has extended options. Learning in constructivism environment entails learning from peers and through experiences that simulate real life as much as possible. The process of knowledge construction should be reciprocal among members of a learning community. Used for both formal and informal learning, these virtual worlds hold innovation and potential for collaborative distance learning (Dickey, 2005). Activities that facilitate creativity, problem solving, reflecting and decision-making will prepare the learner to move from abstract concepts to concrete representations. Learner-centric VEs allow the learner to have control over how the world will be built and modified.

LOOKING AHEAD

Enhanced technological capabilities have made VEs, including forms of CVEs and IVEs, available to typical end-users, including students. While some applications may be currently cost-prohibitive for educators, cyber education is likely to see an increase in the use of all types of VEs. The future of VEs for education will also see an increase in gaming approaches and other experiential methods of instruction. Each approach, especially those involving avatars, is likely to influence and change not just the role of the avatar, but also the role of the instructor.

Now What?

1. Three-dimensional worlds and virtual realities should be used to support learning both as a mechanism for cyber education and as an extension to the traditional classroom.
2. The many possible applications in education for the use of virtual worlds should be explored because the interpersonal dynamics in the different types of VEs allow for interactions that provide the learner with different experiences and perspectives not available in traditional face-to-face education.
3. Teaching and learning in all forms of VEs must include evaluation methods that establish the effectiveness of instructional practices and determine how much learning is actually taking place.
4. Much research is needed to assess the different combinations of technologies and approaches needed to create highly engaging learning using CVS and IVEs and further determine their pedagogical value.

The educational applications of gaming CVEs and IVEs have been tapped but not yet maximized by educators. Collaborative and immersive online courses using gaming concepts have been developed by cyber educators, but more as pilots and not as a way to re-design their programs. One example is Florida Virtual School's Conspiracy Code course, which teaches American History through a game-based approach (Florida Virtual School, 2010). The course was intended to be an experimental project that would inform future practices (this writer participated in the early beta testing of this course) because though trends indicated that students liked a gaming approach, there was not enough research available in the field to determine what was indeed a best practice using CVEs and IVEs.

The costs associated with creating a gaming environment for an online course are very high. Costs are driven by the intricacies of the course and the type of technology used, as well as the labored needed for each stage of production and implementation. Actual games played on consoles rely on sales to make their profits, but in education funding is always elusive. Unlike computer or Web-based games that are solely moderated by the technology, education gaming CVEs and IVEs involve the instructor. More research needs to be conducted on existing gaming online courses and new courses need to be created using newer technologies. Each new course represents an opportunity to discover benefits and determine best practices. If a gaming environment is to be created, designers must ensure that the role of the instructor does not become a system administrator, but a facilitator. This implies that the design must be flexible enough to personalize instruction as much as possible, both through the technology and through the instructor's feedback and interactions.

In any VE including gaming options and VR, the system should capture relevant data that can be used for longitudinal purposes but also for immediate use. The instructor should have real-time access to data that can be used for determining learning outcomes and for modifying instruction based on learner needs. This should not be limited to data from formative and summative assessments but should also include data about the interactions within the learning environment.

Communication, visualization and organization are vital prerequisites to offering environments that will support learning. Learners desire and should have flexible environments that provide options. Although ongoing research explores the constraints and benefits of VEs, commercial products have tended to focus around the available technology instead of the needs of the learner. Collaborative e-learning using virtual environments should include various synchronous and asynchronous technologies such as real-time audio, on-line translation and intelligent agents in flexible and efficient ways that are easy for the learner to use and support various models of leaning and training.

Avatars are sure to play an important role in the evolution of "just-in-time learning" (Sheth, 2003, p. 8). With mobile and wireless technologies developing at a rapid rate, avatars will be developed to communicate through mobile applications. Avatars will be able to explain and illustrate difficult concepts or provide feedback in real time. Avatars will also be used to supplement content and to follow up on training and learning sessions. The intelligent avatar, rather than the instructor, can initiate learner remediation as well as enrichment activities.

Avatars offer the learner personal attention and privacy, but they are likely to also change the role of the cyber educator.

As the avatar becomes more humanized, it may replace some roles and responsibilities currently assigned to the instructor. The avatar becomes a role model, facilitator, content provider and possibly an evaluator of learning. The intelligent avatar will not likely replace the instructor as the main facilitator, but it is likely to drastically change the role of the instructor who is no longer a facilitator or even a partner in learning, but could dangerously change the instructor's role to system administrator. To avoid this, designers must keep in mind that the learner should remain at the center of the learning experience and that the ultimate resource for learning is other human beings. In an ideal VR world, some avatars can behave like tutors, while others model concepts for the student. The avatar would then be another source of support for learning, yet not the only support.

An area of improvement in VEs will be human communications. The fact that learners share the same virtual environment with others enhances their ability to communicate. More systems are supporting nonverbal communications such as facial expressions, gestures and emotions as well as enhanced text and speech systems. Lip movements, body posture, gestures and expressions are tracked and synthesized (Pandzic, Joslin, & Thalman, 2003) by the system. Multi-modal and multi-media interfaces will make analogous communications in computer interactions a reality.

Communications between humans and computer may become more sophisticated and more beneficial because human indicators may be used as real-time biometrical measures and output devices such as avatars can change behavior according to those measures. Kempter, Weidmann, and Roux (2003) indicate that analogous communications include the typical symbolic communications, speech and signs of conventional semantics, as well as the mental processes that are non-conscious or verbalized. The great benefits form this type of communication with computers will be the maintenance of the processes of interaction which support collaboration and problem solving (Kempter, Weidemann, & Roux, 2003). Analogous communications will give the advantage of fast, spontaneous, reliable and real-time evaluation of what learners have mastered or key areas of improvement.

Networked Collaborative Virtual Environments (NCVEs) emerged in the late 1990s and are now receiving renewed interest on the part of cyber educators. The main difference between a CVE and a NCVE is the ability of participants to be connected real time via the network, which updates the shared environment instantly based on the actions of users. In looking ahead, the benefits of current NCVEs will continue to increase as faster and more intelligent capabilities are added to the networks. Both academic and industrial institutions are conducting research that may yet shed light on these for learning powerful tools. Virtual worlds such as Second Life© offer synchronous and asynchronous capabilities that can be harnessed for learning. The benefits will be augmented if the focus is on using the virtual world as a delivery mechanism for instructional strategies and not just as a place to meet.

Current designs of NCVEs are likely to be used more in education than its predecessors because of the flexibility offered by new technology that can facilitate networking, simulations, human-computer interactions and artificial intelligence applications. Scalability of the network to expand and contract depending on the number of users is also improving. The transmission of events between hosting servers is becoming transparent and more sophisticated. Global trends indicate that reputable higher education institutions as well as global agencies are using forms of VEs, including NCVEs, to teach, train and conduct business. Harvard University has held conferences on immersive education while Boston College, Amherst College, Columbia University, Massachusetts Institute of Technology, Sweden's Royal Institute of Technology, Japan's University of Aizu, the Israeli Association of Grid Technologies, NASA, Sun Micro Systems, the City of Boston and the New Media Consortium are supporting various forms of VEs (Foster, 2007).

The future of cyber education will undoubtedly include forms of VEs and virtual worlds, probably in ways we have not yet envisioned. The different combinations of technologies and approaches have led cyber educators and information technology experts to use acronyms such as CVEs, IVEs and NCVEs. Each of these has the potential of creating highly engaging learning environments that include avatars with humanized capabilities. The interactions of the avatar with the learner will likely resemble those interactions for which the instructor is currently responsible for, such as tutoring, providing feedback and assessing learning. The changing role of the avatar may indeed change the role of the instructor and the way that learners represent themselves in the virtual environment.

CONCLUSION

Virtual environments such as IVEs, CVEs and NCVEs provide cyber educators with a myriad of options for creating virtual worlds for learning. Each type of VE has unique characteristics influenced by the combination of technology tools used in the environment. VEs enable transformed social interactions through the technology itself. Both, collaborative and immersive virtual environments can use avatars that can change the social dynamics of the virtual world through because learners are free to use a new identity for their avatars.

Immersive virtual environments rely on the senses to immerse the learner in the digital world and remove him from the physical realm. These environments include simulators and games that allow the user to become the character and to control it with his own body movements and gestures. The collaborative virtual environment involves multiple users that can interact via avatars. The benefits of IVEs and CVEs are largely unexplored but it is known that constructivism, social awareness, self-representation theory and the social identity model of deindividuation are all frameworks for designing virtual worlds of all types.

Networked collaborative environments are likely to provide yet another option for cyber educators wishing to make the most of the combination of technologies thus immersing the learner in a collaborative environment that is updated instantaneously with each learner's actions.

Using avatars to represent the learner as well as the instructor will likely continue as a best practice, especially as the capabilities and applications of avatars continue to expand. Although avatars are not yet able to provide a truly realistic representation of humans, they will evolve into more humanized digital representations. Avatars will be an aid in self-learning acting as a tutor, providing feedback, remediating or enriching the learning experience and taking on some of the current responsibilities of the instructor. Text-to-speech and speech synthesis technologies will eventually enable avatars to provide information, teach a lesson and achieve one-on-one learning.

The changing role of the avatar will also change the role of the instructor. Caution is necessary, however, because the role of the instructor could be reduced to that of a systems administrator who is removed from the learning process. Technology advancements make it possible to record and manipulate the actions of participants. Data about user interactions, gaze direction and preferences can be tracked and analyzed to improve instruction. Specific affordances for creating invisible agents are present in VEs, embodied agents can prompt users to change their behavior based on interactions or learning outcomes.

While some applications may be currently cost-prohibitive for educators, cyber education is likely to see an increase in the use of all types of VEs, including gaming and other experiential forms of education. Each approach presents benefits and challenges that should not be overlooked because they take education into the 21st century. The potential of using virtual worlds for learning remains largely unexplored. Each attempt is a step closer to discovering new best practices that promote learning through the use of technology.

REFERENCES

Bailenson, J. N., Beall, A. C., & Blascovich, J. (2002). Gaze and task-performance in shared virtual environments. *The Journal of Visualization and Computer Animation*, *13*, 313–320. doi:10.1002/vis.297

Bailenson, J. N., Beall, A. C., Loomis, J., Blascovich, J., & Turk, M. (2004). Transformed social interaction: Decoupling representation from behavior and form in collaborative virtual environments. *Presence (Cambridge, Mass.)*, *13*(4), 428–440. doi:10.1162/1054746041944803

Bailenson, J. N., Yee, N., Blascovich, J., Beall, A. C., Lundblad, N., & Jin, M. (2008). The use of immersive virtual reality in the learning sciences: Digital transformations of teachers, students and social context. *Journal of the Learning Sciences*, *17*(1), 102–141. doi:10.1080/10508400701793141

Barab, S., Kling, R., & Gray, J. (2004). *Designing for virtual communities in the service of learning*. New York: Cambridge University Press.

Barney, D. (2004). *The network society*. Cambridge, UK: Publicity Press.

Blascovich, J., Loomis, J. M., Beall, A. C., Swinth, K., Hoyt, C., & Bailenson, J. (2002). Immersive virtual environment technology as a methodological tool for social psychology. *Psychological Inquiry, 13*(2), 103–124. doi:10.1207/S15327965PLI1302_01

Chee, Y. S., & Hooi, C. M. (2002). C-VISions: Socialized learning through collaborative, virtual, interactive simulations. *Proceedings of the Conference on Computer Support for Collaborative Learning: Foundations for a CSCL Community*, Boulder, CO, (pp. 687-696).

Colburn, R., Cohen, M., & Drucker, S. M. (2000). *The role of eye gaze in avatar mediated conversational interfaces*. (MSR-TR-2000-81). Microsoft Research. Retrieved October 16, 2010, from http://research.microsoft.com/pubs/69800/tr-2000-81.pdf

Columbia University. (2010). *Second Life information*. Retrieved June 21, 2010, from http://www.tc.columbia.edu/computing/techinit.asp? Id=Technology+Initiatives+%40+TC&Info=Second+Life

Dede, C. (2004). *Planning for neomillennial learning styles: Implications for investments in technology and faculty*. Retrieved October 24, 2010, from http://www.gse.harvard.edu/ ~dedech/DedeNeoMillennial.pdf

Dickey, M. D. (2003A). Teaching in 3D: Pedagogical affordances and constraints of 3D virtual worlds for synchronous distance learning. *Distance Education, 24*(1), 105–121. doi:10.1080/01587910303047

Dickey, M. D. (2003B). *3D virtual worlds: An emerging technology for traditional and distance learning*. Retrieved October 24, 2010, from http://72.3.228.162/conferences/OLN2003/ papers/Dickey3DVirtualWorlds.pdf

Dickey, M. D. (2005). Three-dimensional virtual worlds and distance learning: Two case studies of active worlds as a medium for distance learning. *British Journal of Educational Technology, 36*(3), 439–451. doi:10.1111/j.1467-8535.2005.00477.x

Doolittle, P. (1999). *Constructivism and online education*. Paper presented at the Online Conference on Teaching Online in Higher Education, Fort Wayne, Indiana.

Dufresne, A., & Paquette, G. (2000). *ExploraGraph: A flexible and adaptive interface to support distance learning*. Research for TeleLearning Network of Centres of Excellence, Canada. Retrieved October 24, 2010, from http://lrcm.com.umontreal. ca/dufresne/ Publications/DufresneEdMedia2000.pdf

Florida Virtual School. (2010). *Conspiracy code*. Retrieved June 22, 2010, from http://flvs.net

Foster, A. (2007). Immersive education submerges students in online worlds made for learning. [from http://chronicle.com]. *The Chronicle of Higher Education, 54*(17), 22. Retrieved October 17, 2010.

Garau, M., Slater, M., Bee, S., & Sasse, M. A. (2001). The impact of eye gaze on communication using humanoid avatars. *Proceedings of the SIGCHI Conference on Human Factors in Computing Systems*, CHI '01, (pp. 309-316).

Holzinger, A., Pichler, A., & Almer, W. (2001). Triangle: A multi-media test-bed for examining incidental learning, motivation and the Tamagotchi-effect within a games-show like computer based learning module. [from http://www.iicm.edu/ iicm_papers/triangle.pdf]. *Proceedings of ED-MEDIA, 2001*, 766–771. Retrieved October 24, 2010.

Jeng-Weei, L. J., Duh, H. B. L., Abi-Rached, H., Parker, D. E., & Furness, T. A. (2002). Effects of field of view on presence, enjoyment, memory and simulator sickness in a virtual environment. *IEEE Virtual Reality Conference Proceedings*, (p. 164). Retrieved October 26, 2010, from http://ieeexplore.ieee.org

Johnson, L., & Levine, A. (2008). Virtual worlds: Inherently immersive, highly social learning spaces. *Theory into Practice, 47*(2), 161–170. doi:10.1080/00405840801992397

Jones, C. R., Ferreday, D., & Hodgson, V. (2008). Networked learning a relational approach: Weak and strong ties. *Journal of Computer Assisted Learning, 24*(2), 90–102. doi:10.1111/j.1365-2729.2007.00271.x

Kempter, G., Weidmann, K., & Roux, P. (2003). What are the benefits of analogous communication in human computer interaction? In Stephanidis, C. (Ed.), *Universal access in hci: Inclusive design in the information society* (pp. 1427–1431). Mahaw, NJ: Lawrence Erlbaum.

Kolb, D. A. (1984). *Experiential learning: Experience as the source of learning and development*. Englewood Cliffs, NJ: Prentice-Hall.

Maher, M.L. & Gero, J.S. (2002). *Agent models of 3D virtual worlds*.

Olveres, J., Billinghurst, J., Savage, J., & Holden, A. (1998). Intelligent, expressive avatars. In *Proceedings of the First Workshop on Embodied Conversational Characters* (WECC '98), October 12-15, 1998, Lake Tahoe, California. Retrieved October 17, 2010, from http://www.hitl.washington.edu/pubs/hitlpub.php

Open University. (2010). *Activities*. Retrieved October 21, 2010, from http://www.open.ac.uk/colmsct/activities/details/ projectpage.php?itemId=478b5caf2c3f7&pageId=478b69e14c14c

Pandzic, I., Joslin, C., & Thalman, N. (2003). Trends in networked collaborative environments. *Computer Communications, 26*(5), 430–437. doi:10.1016/S0140-3664(02)00163-9

Pellerin, C. (2007). *U.S. government presence grows in Second Life online world.* Retrieved October 31, 2010, from http://www.america.gov/st/washfile-english/2007/May/ 20070508163536lcnirellep0.2645075.html

Postmes, T., & Spears, R. (1998). Deindividuation and anti-normative behavior: A meta-analysis. *Psychological Bulletin, 123*(3), 238–259. doi:10.1037/0033-2909.123.3.238

Prasolova-Førland, E., & Divitini, M. (2003). Collaborative virtual environments for supporting learning communities: an experience of use. *Proceedings of the 2003 International ACM SIGGROUP Conference on Supporting Group Work* - GROUP '03, Sanibel, Florida. (pp. 58-67). New York: ACM.

Rappa, N., Yip, D., & Baey, S. (2009). The role of teacher, student and ICT in enhancing student engagement in multiuser virtual environments. *British Journal of Educational Technology, 40*(1), 61–69. doi:10.1111/j.1467-8535.2007.00798.x

Roussos, M., Johnson, A., Leigh, J., Barnes, C., Vasilakis, C., & Moher, T. (1997). The NICE project: Narrative, immersive, constructionist/collaborative environments for learning in virtual reality. Retrieved October 24, 2010, from http://ice.eecs.uic.edu/~nice

Sanchez, J. (2009). Implementing second life. Ideas, challenges and innovations. *Library Technology Reports, 45*(2).

Sheth, R. (2003). Avatar technology: Giving a face to the e-learning interface. *The eLearning Developers Journal.* Retrieved October 22, 2010, from http://www.elearningguild.com/ pdf/2/082503DES-H.pdf

Steinkuehler, C. (2004). Learning in massively multiplayer online games. *Proceedings of the 6th International Conference on Learning Sciences*, Santa Monica, CA, (pp. 521-528). Retrieved October 27, 2010, from http://portal.acm.org

Vilhjálmsson, H. H., & Cassell, J. (1998). BodyChat: Autonomous communicative behaviors in avatars. *Proceedings of the Second International Conference on Autonomous Agents, Minneapolis, Minnesota*, (pp. 269-276). New York: ACM.

von Glaserfeld, E. (1984). An introduction to radical constructivism. In Watzlawick, P. (Ed.), *The invented reality* (pp. 17–40). New York: Norton.

Wagner, J. (2008). *The making of Second Life: Notes from the new world*. New York: Harper Collins.

Wellman, B. (2001). Physical place and cyber place: The rise of personalized networking. *International Journal of Urban and Regional Research, 25*(2), 227–252. doi:10.1111/1468-2427.00309

Yee, N., & Bailenson, J. (2007). The Proteus effect: The effect of transformed self-representation on behavior. *Human Communication Research, 33*(3), 271–290. doi:10.1111/j.1468-2958.2007.00299.x

Chapter 12
Groups, Games
& Community

ABSTRACT

Games are being used to develop environments that promote learning. The tremendous strides made in game design and gaming technology over the last decade have caused an increased interest in using them for learning. Gaming is becoming more complex and the algorithms used are more advanced. Simulations and strategy games are framed in constructivist principles that rely on co-construction of knowledge and higher level thinking, but can also include drill and practice. Research suggests the benefits of games can impact both the educational and training environments. When engaged in games, players are using complex and multi modal capabilities that are much more challenging than what is traditionally required in formal education.

OBJECTIVES

- Define "game" as applied to digitally mediated communications.
- Identify a variety of digitally mediated gaming environments.
- Discuss cognitive development, disequilibrium and social identity.

DOI: 10.4018/978-1-60960-543-8.ch012

- Discuss the attributes and challenges of games as applied to learning environments.
- Analyze the learning option such as multi-agent learning, Q-Learning and Hyper Q- Learning and the instructional strategies need to promote learning.

INTRODUCTION

The use of games to foster learning has been a common practice among educators for a long time. Many educators are already using new technologies to create virtual environments to foster learning through simulations and virtual games. Simulations and games have been used extensively by the military for drill and practice activities, but also for developing skills that require hand-eye coordination for teaching pilots and tank operators. Medical schools also rely on simulations to train surgeons how to perform delicate procedures. Games like World War II and Gettysburg among others have infiltrated the schools.

Individuals of all ages across the globe are talking about and playing video games. An entire generation has now grown up immersed in gaming. Definitions of exactly what games really are vary depending on who is doing the defining: educators, business people, anthropologists or social scientists. For the purposes of this chapter a game will be defined as a digital application that can be controlled by individuals using a personal computer, mobile device or a console (Stanford & Williamson, 2005). The expectation is that technology will continue to evolve and redefine gaming both, in definition and in application. The topic of games must be included when discussing cyber education. A new generation of mobile devices makes it possible for learners to access educational games regardless of location. As new and more sophisticated digitally mediated communication tools are developed, cyber educators must remain aware of how the issues of anonymity, authenticity and trust continue to impact learning as discussed in the previous chapters of this manuscript.

The tremendous strides made in game design and gaming technology over the last decade have caused an increased interest in using them for learning. Most obvious are the advances in the technologies that support games and the creation of rich digital worlds with improved 3D sounds and visuals even more significant are the improvement that have been made in the design of games. Interactivity, rich visuals, and audio have continuously enhanced the environment of games since the days of Pac-Man. Games today make use of strategies, simulations, role playing, sports, puzzles, inquiry, problem solving, and adventures. They have gone from single player games to Massively Multi-player Online Games (MMOGs) and Massively Multi-player Online Role Playing Games (MMORPGs) where as many as 100,000 people can be connected at once. These technologies present a great opportunity for cyber educators, yet much research and empirical studies needs to be conducted to how games are and can be used to promote learning (Squire, 2003).

The learning process itself, which is very difficult to define, is often thought of as a combination of skills and cognitive learning outcomes that include procedural, declarative and strategic knowledge as well as attitudes. Procedural knowledge also known as imperative knowledge is knowing how to perform certain tasks. Declarative or descriptive knowledge is knowledge of facts, definitions, rules and procedures. Strategic knowledge is the ability to plan or devise a course of action and carry it out to reach a goal (Eggen & Kauchak, 1999). While there are many other labels applied to identify different types of knowledge, these three are particularly applicable to educational gaming.

Digital Game Based Learning (DGBL) is in essence the term used for the application of digitally mediated gaming environments for learning (Prensky, 2003). Throughout this chapter the word "game" will be used to discuss games in general, including MMOGs, MMORPGs and DGBL environments that promote learning. An important question facing cyber educators is how to effectively use virtual games and simulations in education. In the last decade an explosion of conferences, journal articles, books and software have focused on games and education. The challenges appear to be related to game design and acceptable pedagogy, but cyber educators must also remain cognizant that anonymity is a natural feature of DGBLs.

The newness of virtual games in education causes educators to debate over what pedagogical or ontological stance should be taken in the design of virtual educational games and simulations. Educators generally also debate over the place and the role of virtual gaming in education because much of the phenomenon remains unknown. Gaming and simulations are not a one size fits all solution to education, but another delivery method. The real challenge is not bringing gaming technologies into a traditional learning environment, but rather changing the culture and the mentality of educators to one that is learner-centric.

BACKGROUND

The influx of educational software or "edutainment" for the past several decades paved the way for more sophisticated forms of gaming today. Basic computer games found their way into formal and informal learning settings because of their wide appeal to different sectors of society most of which are based on the entertainment culture, and because the ability of games to simulate the real world (Kirriemuir & McFarlane, 2003). Games that were not originally designed for learning purposes yet engage the participant through specific strategies may offer clues to cyber educators on how to capitalize on virtual games for training and learning.

Games usually have a set of conditions, rules, goals, and some level of competition between participants. One or more players are involved in a set of activities that have constraints, payoffs, goals and consequences. Guided by rules and algorithms, games are artificial environments where the individual competes with something, someone, or himself (Asgari & Kaufman, 2004). Games can be an effective way to transfer many different types of knowledge, especially the transfer of declarative, concept, and rule based knowledge. Although it is sometimes difficult to get organizations to see the benefits, the intelligent application of games can be used constructively in the corporate environment as well as in education and training. Games can actually save companies money if used wisely.

An example of the misunderstanding of knowledge transfer and games is the removal of the game Solitaire from Microsoft's desktop package in the late 1980's. After complaints by companies that employees were spending too much time playing games, Microsoft pulled the Solitaire game from their software package. Companies then proceeded to spend countless dollars, time, and effort teaching employees how to drag and drop, double click, and right click, all which are simple tasks that employees could have learned in a few minutes playing Solitaire. Although the perception of the game was one of frivolity and time wasting, what was really transpiring was the transfer of simple rules and concepts necessary for successful interaction with the software. Perhaps because of the generation gap between digital natives and digital immigrants, games that are fun and interesting are often overlooked as simple approaches to the transfer of declarative, conceptual, and rule based knowledge. This oversight can cost companies and educators significantly.

Games are also well suited for the transfer of higher level knowledge including procedures, principles, and problem solving. One of the drawbacks to the development of more sophisticated games has been cost. Unlike lower levels of knowledge the transfer of higher levels of knowledge is not necessarily hierarchical. Because of a complex interrelationship between prior knowledge and application of knowledge, transfer at the higher levels is not always easy. Solving problems and applying principles can be strengthened by rehearsal and reinforcement. Practice using simulations is one way that educators and trainers can accomplish this goal. Simulations must be well-constructed and engaging in order to attract and hold the learner's interest if they are to be effective. Table 1 provides definitions and examples of the different levels of knowledge transfer according to Kapp (2007).

At the heart of the debate in the use of games for both formal and informal learning is the simple belief that young people find games motivating and fun, hence they should somehow be integrated into the educational environment. Most experts suggest that games are meant to encourage learning and therefore function as good

Table 1. Levels of knowledge transfer and correlation to types of games

Knowledge Level	Definition	Types of Games	Structure
Declarative	Question and answer, matching, labeling fact based.	Word search, drag and drop, fill in the blank.	Hierarchical, first level of basic knowledge.
Concept	Application of concepts in limited situations.	Road races, isolation exercises.	Hierarchical, builds on previous declarative knowledge
Rules	Answer questions and follow rules to move a piece of gain position in some way.	Board, trivia, crossword and wheel based.	Hierarchical, builds on previous declarative knowledge and concepts.
Procedures	Sequential order of rules or tasks to complete a task.	Simulations	Builds on the first three levels of knowledge, then following a structured sequence of events.
Principles	Non sequential events or guidelines for behaviors or actions.	Simulations	Differentiating between the application of multiple values and choosing an approach.
Problem Solving	Application of prior knowledge to determine a solution to a problem.	Simulations	Determining a best practices type of approach by analyzing a situation and applying prior knowledge.

representations of real world experiences, whether it be for young or older learners. Games with a specific educational content in mind as well as those commercially available for edutainment can both be used in educational contexts.

Much discussion has emerged concerning generational differences and gaming. It is estimated the today's young people will spend on average 10,000 hours playing digital games by the time they are 21(Prensky, 2003). Often these games are played for hours at a time, which is in opposition to the theory that children have short attention spans. The audience has also expanded from adolescent boys to include girls and all ages of adults. Originally it was thought that it was the violence or content of a game that was able to attract and keep the player's attention, but more of the emphasis has reversed to the learning process. All humans innately love to learn, particularly when content is not being forced upon them and it is enjoyable. Gaming provides opportunities for learning with each interaction, decision, or move made by the user. These games provide for complex interactions, thus creating strategies to overcome obstacles, collaborating, making use of deduction, and creating a self-identity.

Three main factors have influenced the widespread interest in gaming and learning. The first factor is research. Ongoing research has substantiated the powerful engagement that games provide. For the last several decades the literature has captured how games can be an effective method to help individuals to learn. The second factor is the coming of age of the digital natives, who have been surrounded by technology and gaming since birth. They are more noted than previous generations for their multi-tasking skills, inductive reasoning, and frequent, quick interactions. Digital natives have developed visual literacy skills, and interact with content and each other in quick and short bursts. Lastly, the popularity of games has impacted every facet of life.

Gaming is becoming more complex and the algorithms used are more advanced. The concept known as the "Nash equilibrium" is one of the features that makes DG-BLs so powerful. The Nash equilibrium is when a game participant makes decisions based on the other participant's behavior (Nash, 1950) therefore constantly strategizing and examining the equilibrium of others in order to make the best decisions. In MMOGs or MMORPGs often the player does not have full information about the other agents, their counter parts, and the environment constantly changes and adapts as agents learn about each other and make decisions. DGBLs can use technology to purposely track, monitor, and change the behavior of participants through special agents. The use of multi-agent systems challenges traditional gaming theory, which identified the Nash equilibrium as being limited because of the imperfect state of the information. Multi-agents are likely to influence this sense of equilibrium, but research on using multi-agents is limited and therefore it is not clear how effective they would be in causing learners to make the best decisions based on the concept of Nash equilibrium. Nonetheless, learning by trial and error can develop good strategies and is highly effective for a single learner in a stationary environment.

Unique to multi agent environments are the interplay of other agents that are similarly adapting to and influencing an ever changing environment. In single agent systems, the concept of maximizing one's position in terms of expected payoffs is predominant. In multi agent systems, these payoffs are contingent on the other agent's strategies. The goal of learning is to find optimization of these values through repeated play and in terms of the Nash equilibrium. Nash (1950) indicated that each player holds an effective and correct expectation about the behavior of the other agents and then acts rationally with respect to that expectation. This means the agent responds rationally to the best of his/her ability to the other's strategies.

Research indicates that agents in thee multi agent environments converge on a mutually optimum path and the performance of both agents is generally better than anyone agent in a single agent environment (Hu & Wellman, 2003). When multiple Nash equilibrium exists in a game, optimal strategies are obtained by combining other learning techniques. Reinforcement learning is well suited when agents know little about other agents and the environment changes during learning. Stochastic learning is more suited for non-competitive games where agents pursue self-interests and make independent choices (Hu & Wellman, 1998).

The process by which equilibrium arises in a game has been explored by many including Nash, but Camerer, Ho, and Chong (2002) explain the process in terms of experience based attraction, given the premise that humans learn faster in games than the biological models predict. By studying learning dynamics including how choices arise from a participant's previous behavior and experience, they explain learning in terms of reinforcement and belief in learning. In doing so, they have conducted studies that empirically suggest a connection. The intricacies of this phenomenon however, make it necessary to continue exploring how reinforcement and belief in learning may influence learning outcomes, but independently of each other. Emerging theories may help guide future research endeavors, especially those related to agent learning. Agents in the virtual world can be software agents such as avatars, or robots that interact with each other and with the humans using the environment (Panait & Luke, 2005). Agents are a vital component of MMOGs and MMPRPGs because they can collaborate with other agents and the humans to achieve desired outcomes. Advancements in the field of artificial intelligence enhance the interactive capabilities of intelligent agents.

Many new theories including Q-Learning and Hyper Q-Learning provide versatile options for multi-agent learning. More advanced options allow the establishment of model based estimators where a player can model the other players' dynamic behavior (Tesauro, 2003). For example, emerging learning models are identified using time series analysis and data mining (Tesauro). Q-Learning is an algorithm that reinforces learning by delaying rewards and encouraging exploration (Sandholm & Crites, 1996). According to Tesauro, Hyper Q-Learning is an approach rather different than Q-Learning because the values of mixed strategies are learned, instead of the base actions, and the strategies of other agents are observed via Bayesian inference. Bayesian inference, based on Thomas Bayes' theorem published in the late 1700's, occurs when individuals or agents use evidence from observations to make inferences that help them identify new strategies based on the probability that the newly formed hypothesis is true (Winkler, 2003).

The formation of hypothesis through Q-Learning and Hyper Q-Learning demands higher levels of cognition. Cognition is the "interaction in the social and material world" as defined by a body of research that follows the Learning Sciences perspective (Steinkuehler, 2008). Examples of this body of research and theory include work in activity theory, distributed cognition, ecological psychology, mediated action, situational learning and social cultural theory according to Steinkuehler. Cognition from this perspective is greater than what goes on in the mind and must include the complex social interactions, mind-body processes and culturally organized activities.

Individual come to understanding of the world by participation in communities of practice and the perspective of that community, concepts which are in alignment with constructivist paradigms. Learning from this perspective is a combination of participation and identity established within a given community of practice. The individual is transformed overtime from an outsider to an apprentice, and then to an integral contributing member of the community. Through the growth of shared knowledge and the reorganization of the individual's patterns, new identities emerge.

Van Eck (2006) attributes the success of games to cognitive disequilibrium. Piaget explored this topic with his children's learning theories and included concepts of assimilation of knowledge and accommodation. With assimilation, new information is thought to fit into existing slots or categories, while accommodation requires us to modify our existing thoughts or structures to create new ones if the new information does not fit into any existing paradigm. Cognitive disequilibrium is the process of holding conflicting beliefs at the same time and is dependent upon the cycle of assimilation and accommodation. The extent to which the learner can play the game and resolve the conditions of disequilibrium directly depends on the level of engagement he experiences. Games require a continuous pattern of hypothesis formation, testing, and revision (Van Eck) thus making them an excellent medium for the process of disequilibrium and resolution.

The pedagogy of learning and the connection to games design is encouraging. Two learning theories supported seem to be Gagne's (1985) Conditions for Learning and Howard Gardner's (1993) Multiple Intelligences. While there is overlap between the two, there are also recognizable differences. Gagne focuses on cognitive constructs, where as Gardner uses a more accessible classification based on social interactions and culture. Most well designed games already possess the major components of both theories necessary to meet the needs for sound instruction.

Gagne's theory stipulates levels of learning and implies that each type requires a different approach to instruction. According to Gagne (1985) an instructional plan can bring about change in the cognitive structures and operations of the learner because it causes environmental stimuli and instructional interactions. In most well constructed games verbal information is provided both in text and in audio. Game design promotes intellectual skills such as interpreting rules and applying concepts to seek solutions. When the player finds innovative ways to problem solve, he is employing cognitive strategies and acquiring new skills through practice and reinforcement. The cognitive reward is getting through each gaming level or winning the game. While it is clear how games make use of cognition, the use of the psychomotor domain is not always evident in games. Not all games promote improved gross motor skills, but many incorporate fine motor skills. Gaming consoles such as the Wii now make use of the psychomotor domain to give the player a more realistic experience. Attitudes, Gagne's final type of learning, are central to game playing because it attitudes are applied when dealing with ethical and often moral dilemmas where consequence can drastically alter the outcomes.

Many give Howard Gardner (1993) credit with one of the most important learning theories to come out of the last part of the 20th century. The theory of Multiple Intelligences is that each learner employs different strategies for learning. Garner's theory originally encompassed eight categories but this has expanded over time. The implication of this theory is that learning can become more effective if we can target instruction to focus on each of the intelligences. Cultural differences are also believed to play a part in the intelligences because the value placed upon them by each culture may differ. Although not every game addresses each of the intelligences, the majority of games embody most of the intelligences, although it is possible to find games that favor one over another (Becker, 2005).

There are different types of games that lend themselves to particular outcomes. Drill and practice games for example, have been around for years and used by educators and trainers as a recognized strategy. Drill and practice games in the digital era became popular because they provide repetition and can be worked into the curriculum at off hours as independent study time, and it can be modified from a group to an individual activity and vice versa. Behavioral in nature, drill and practice games are not necessarily grounded on constructivist pedagogy but serve a purpose when the goal is to teach procedural tasks that require preciseness. These types of games provide a way to integrate rehearsal into a traditionally didactic curriculum that relied heavily on rote memorization.

Simulations and strategy games are framed in constructivist principles that rely on co-construction of knowledge and higher level thinking, but can also include drill and practice. Simulations tend to model reality by either attempting to re-create physical environments, social systems, or situations through the computer interface. Some simulations are very life-like while others simplify the system and highlight only key components. Either way, simulations are very expensive to produce and are used primarily when the actual activity is either too dangerous or too expensive to undertake. As explored in other chapters of this book, examples include the military, where simulations have been used to replicate piloting jets and engagement on the battlefield.

Used to engage the learner in situations that they are then expected to participate in real life or to develop a conceptual understanding of complex systems, many simulations are then remarketed as entertainment software. Critical to the learning process are the ability of learners to reflect on the understanding and the instructors' role in fostering collaboration, encouraging reflection, creating feedback, and providing follow up activities (Squire, 2003). These simulations allow the learner to manipulate variables, develop new perspectives and observe behaviors. They also provide the opportunity to pose "what if" questions, visualize in 3D, and develop and understanding of the dynamics of a system.

Debriefing is an important aspect of playing games and can link knowledge to the real world through reflective learning (Pivec, Dziabenko, & Schinnerl, 2003). One of the main characteristics of a virtual game is that instructional content is intermixed with gaming features and is delivered using strategies that support decision-making and problem solving skills. This is accomplished by encouraging the learner to perform in iterative cycles of the game and by providing instant feedback. Feedback is crucial in simulations and games because it elicits particular behavioral or cognitive reactions through the interaction of the learner with the game, and causes the learner to readjust such behaviors or reactions in order to achieve the desired objectives.

One of the aspects that has aided the development of computer games is departure from most paradigms for developing computer software. Following a less restrictive set of ideas for development, a more open minded and creative approach has produced innovations that make gaming interfaces highly usable. The hope is that games can bring to the learning environment the same features they have incorporated for entertainment: effortless community, learning by observation, deep customizability, and a fluid system of human interactions (Dyck, Pinelle, Brown, & Gutwin, 2003). Ease and openness in developing games and educational applications continues to offer possibilities for teaching and learning (Kirriemuir, 2002). The global expansion of online education creates a wide range of possibilities for developing educational games.

LEARNING WITH GAMES

Research suggests the benefits of games can impact both the educational and training environments. When engaged in games, players are using complex and multi modal capabilities that are much more challenging than what is traditionally required in formal education. This line of reasoning suggests that games can be complex learning environments if challenging skills and social interactions are integrated to contribute to cognitive development. It is generally accepted that based on the structure and way the games are built, they are by their very nature effective learning environments (Stanford & Williamson, 2005). Learning takes place through constant practice and interaction with the environment and other players. As players progress through the games, they are challenged with increasingly difficult and complex tasks and underlying sets of rules.

Games also offer the player the opportunity to take on new identities. The individual has the opportunity to play a character outside of himself and construct a new identity based on role playing. In some cases the learner must not only construct an identity but also hypothesize and justify the identity they are assuming. By constructing these identities the game environment is merged with the player's own wishes and fantasies. There is no question that the knowledge and skills learned from playing games is very different in terms pedagogy and level of knowledge applied than what is generally taught in formal educational settings.

Games can be highly interactive and demand interpretive competence. Games are often multimodal and require concentration and attention. One of the complaints about games is that participants are learning to play the game instead of focusing on knowledge acquisition. While this may be true in the early stages of playing a new game that is unfamiliar to the learner, with sufficient time the learner will learn the rules and be able to focus on the concepts taught through the game. Designers are therefore responsible for creating games that are intuitive.

Many educators realize nonetheless, that the pedagogical approach used in games does provide ample opportunities for the participants to engage in lessons that are multidimensional, immersive, and support learning by allowing the learners to probe the rules of a system. Games can also promote higher order thinking skills. From a learning theory standpoint games bring people in contact with the complexities of the 21st century workplace. By dealing with dynamic information, multiple modes and media, learners are efficiently interacting with dynamic sources, just as they would in the real world. Recent success of thousands of people interacting simultaneously in MMOGs and MMORPGs combines the opportunity to change one's identity through avatars that take on specific roles, and the concept of apprenticeship which prepares learners for the actual workplace (Stanford & Williamson, 2005). The integration of social and collaborative technology tools make gaming practices even more appealing to cyber educators.

Social interactions in virtual places such as MMOGs and MMORPGs seem particularly well suited for building social capital and creating social ties that expose the individual to a diversity of worldviews, even if these ties do not supply deep emotional support (Steinkuehler & Williams, 2006). Current MMOGs/MMORPGs also provide spaces for interactions and social relationships beyond the home or the office, but the ones created for educational purposes require deeper personal connections that will be discussed in the Looking Ahead section of this chapter. Informal sociability is possible in a third space, a place where everybody knows your name or at least your screen name. There is no doubt that a "cyber culture" is established in MMOGs/MMORGs. The culture evolves based not only on styles of play and implicit tension from within a community of players but also on people's expectations of a pre-specified story line and what emerges as interactive play.

Educators, business leaders, and entertainment executives are interested in the design and evolution of these MMOGs because the design principles may be applicable in designing better learning environments, customer help sites, and entertainment options. Players in these games invent languages, identities, power structures, relationships, and engage in complex arguments according to Squire & Steinkuehler, (2006). Being literate in an MMOG/MMORG cyber culture means understanding the actions and languages used in the virtual space.

A thirty billion dollar industry, gaming is popular worldwide (Prensky, 2003) and continues to grow. Virtual and video games are effective at integrating the concept of motivation, the holy grail of learning. The infiltration of digital games on all levels has been on the rise partly because they seem to foster the exact attitudes that are intrinsic to learning: collaboration, competition, result orientation, actively seeking information, engagement, peaked interest, cooperative and solution orientation (Prensky, 2003). The merging of games and education therefore seem to be a natural fit.

Although online learning has been adopted by many organizations, there remains a discrepancy between what learners do outside the classroom with digital technology, and the experiences that educational institutions are providing. Outside the classroom learners connect with blogs, social networking sites, and are media consumers as well as producers. They participate in online gaming, and increasingly use collaboration tools and conduct online research. Most of these connections are goal driven, complex, and engaging. The capacity of technology to furnish cognitive connections is being demonstrated everyday outside the current educational settings are providing. MMOGs/MMORGs and games are an excellent starting point to examine these connections and plan for educational programs.

It is not only the games themselves that are causing cognitive connections, the communities that emerge around games also supply the opportunities for individuals to create identities, values, and intellectual as well as social practices. These gaming environments are capable of extracting considerable cognitive investment from those that play them (Steinkuehler, 2004). Beneath the facade of fun and fantasy, there is the development of cognition, complex problem solving, emergent identities, multimodal spaces, and collaboration.

MMOGs/MMORGs have also provided insight into the connections between identity and social discourse. These environments are mirrors for examining the effect the individual has on culture and the effect that culture has on the identity of the individual. Steinkuehler (2004) proposes that by looking at games through the dual lens of both, the individual as the creator and developer in the virtual environment, insight can be gained about the way the surroundings framed the identities created by users. Steinkuehler also proposes to incorporate discourse theory in order to focus on individual identity creation as well as the ways in which a much broader context may influence, shape, and constrain our individual pursuits. Discourse theory deals with the interpretation of natural language, which may be influenced by the anonymity inherent in MMOGs/MMORGs.

While for years educators have pointed out the potential of MMOGs/MMORGs and highlighted the important questions of identity, community, and the influence on learning and life, the ability of these environments to facilitate networked learning that transcends the game itself has come to the forefront in recent years. Other educators yet stipulate that the safety of game environments coupled with the playful mood of intellectual freedom makes it easier for the learner to immerse in the learning (Delwiche, 2006). Learning environments and games share characteristics such as interactivity, physicality, persistence, and safety. Safety is crucial to learning environments because when learners feel threatened they experience a fight of flight response, which is a lower brain cell response. Safe environments however, support the upper most levels of human brain function.

Lessons learned from video gaming show that games used for learning are most powerful when they are "personally meaningful, experiential, social and epistemological all at the same time" (Shaffer, Squire, Halverson, & Gee, 2004, p.2). Video games may make their mark on learning because they can provide simulated or virtual environments that can support both informational and social knowledge. Video games can encourage the participation of in a community of practice while simultaneously supporting and developing thinking that supports the community.

There is no doubt that technologies can and have already changed the way we learn. Video games give us a glimpse of how we can create powerful new ways for people to learn in schools, communities and the workplace. Games not only create social and cultural worlds they also help people integrate thinking, social interactions, and technology. MMOGs/MMORGs can deliver content-rich virtual worlds that place experiences in context. Games provide a more concrete opportunity for learners to experience things than mere words or symbols. Technology makes is possible to immerse the learner using a multisensory approach. Through such experiences, and in multiple contexts, learners can experience the complexities of real life situations without losing connection to abstract ideas and real problems.

Situated learning has been around for a good number of years, but virtual gaming has made it possible to create the situation around the learner. Games have the quality of bringing learners together; whether it is a MMOG/MMORG or an alternative on the desktop computer, games unite learners competitively and cooperatively. Unlike classroom social interaction where there is relatively little impact beyond the school walls, virtual games force learners to develop effective social practices. By developing and participating in these practices, players also have the opportunity to develop new identities and use anonymity to their advantage. These identities can be an experiment with new roles and power structures.

Roles and identities may influence how much learning takes place, however more research is needed in this area. It could be stipulated that based on motivation, participants who take on a more passive role may not be actively learning as much as those who display higher levels of engagement. Gaming supports the exchange of knowledge through a community of individuals who share common goals. According to Shaffer, Squire, Halverson, and Gee (2004) this in turn supports the epistemology for organizing knowledge, skills, identities, and values based on a particular way of thinking in a coherent epistemic frame. The immersive experience provides connections to shared values, effective social practices, situated understanding, meaning and common values.

Motivation and learning go hand in hand. Young and old alike are capable of spending hours playing computer games and not on traditional studies or tasks. Increasing research suggests that games impact thinking in ways that can in turn affect learning. Facer (2003) summarizes Prensky's (2001) ten characteristics that might explain the cognitive differences and a new set of cognitive abilities that are developed through virtual games:

1. Twitch speed vs. conventional speed
2. Parallel processing vs. linear processing
3. Graphics first vs. text first
4. Random access vs. step by step
5. Connected vs. stand-alone
6. Active vs. passive
7. Play vs. work
8. Pay-off vs. patience
9. Fantasy vs. reality
10. Technology as friend vs. technology as foe

The tools and technology that young people are growing up with may actually cause them to think differently. Digital media and gaming holds the potential to motivate and encourage diverse ways of engaging the learner (Facer, 2003). It is risky however to assume that one size fits all. It is more likely that the development of digital games is best suited for creating new environments that support learning by providing simple drill and practice to complex acquisitions of processes and skills. Most games go through an input process output type of model that elaborates on key features of the game, the game cycle of learner decisions, judgments, feedback, and types of learning outcomes to be achieved (Garris, Ahlers, & Driskell, 2002). Implicit in the literature is the notion that pairing instructional content with particular game features can engage learners and achieve instructional goals.

Fantasy, Imagination and Learning

Another relationship between learning and virtual games is brought about by the elements of curiosity and fantasy. Games provide a way for learners to explore the imaginary world as well as their own imaginations comfortably and safely. By creating games that present content in either an imaginary context that is familiar or a fantasy context that is emotionally appealing, games can stimulate learner motivation (Asgari & Kaufman, 2004). Creating engaging environments is therefore paramount.

The implication that computer games give learners the opportunity to explore their imagination is one reason why games are believed to be intrinsically motivational for learning. Virtual games are classified under different categories such as adventure, simulations, competition, cooperation, programming, puzzles, and business management games (Asgari & Kaufman, 2004). Situating the game scenario in a fantasy or in an imaginary context that is perceived to be real to the learner is likely to be more engaging because of the curiosity factor. One effective strategy for learning may be to situate the game in an imaginary or fantasy context that requires the participant to learn and apply real world skills relevant to his field of study. According to a literature review by Asgari and Kaufman (2004), well-designed games that are fun and intrinsically motivating are also challenging, provide appropriate goals, uncertain outcomes that depend on the participant, constructive and encouraging feedback that is clearly presented, and offer an element of curiosity and fantasy. In order to enhance learning some aspect of the game must be activated in an instructional content, games themselves are not enough to enhance learning.

Fantasy may be the element that activates learning by providing the emotional hook and by meeting needs for the learner that are not being met in real life (Asgari & Kaufman, 2004). These might include power, control success and or fame. A way to maximize the learning experience is to provide the learner with a goal that can be personalized and made relevant to his interests. Over embellishing games with too many features though may is thought to be distracting for the leaner and therefore decrease learning. Fantasy in gaming and learning can be studies from two aspects as discussed by Asgari and Kaufman (2004): the cognitive aspects and the emotional aspects. By relating to prior knowledge, fantasy can stimulate learner to a better understanding of information. It is important however to realize that goals in games must reinforce instructional goals, otherwise the game itself does not promote relevant learning.

In game design, it is important that the consequences of failure are not made to be more interesting than the consequences of success. The emphasis must always be on the instructional goals not the fantasy activities themselves. The emotional aspects of fantasy incorporate the personalization of learner interest and prior interests. Personalizing fantasy might be important to intrinsic motivation and learning and by incorporating prior interests and positioning the instructional problem in relationship to those interests engagement may be increased. Asgari and Kaufman (2004, p.6) admonish that although creating fantasy context can be emotionally appealing, it is important to remember that in order for games to be effective for learning, five basic rules should be followed:

1. Use fantasy to reinforce instructional goals, instead of competing with them.
2. Provide appropriate metaphors and analogies for learning.
3. Provide imaginary characters that are familiar to the learner.
4. Accommodate for gender differences in fantasies.
5. Relate the fantasy to the content to be learned.

Van Eck (2006) discusses the difference between endogenous and exogenous fantasy elements. Endogenous elements are those that are seemingly integrated within the game, while exogenous are those elements that are present in the game but do not seem to have much relationship to the story line. Endogenous fantasy elements make games more interesting and help promote flow, but exogenous elements may aide the participant in transferring knowledge from previous a situation to another. Both elements should be considered when deciding if a particular game is truly a good investment of time and effort to achieve certain learning outcomes. If it is not, the game should be abandoned because it is not a good fit (Van Eck, 2006).

Challenges

Games should provide learner control because the learners are the ones making the decisions and directly experiencing the feedback (Pivec, Dziabenko, & Schinnerl, 2003). Opinions differ about what characteristics of games are more important to learning; interactivity, dynamic visuals, goals, rules, challenge, and risk are all essential features that augment engagement and learning. Many arguments have surfaced surrounding games and young people however. Critics contend that virtual and video games erode the social lives and social skills of youngsters. Negative aspects of the games also include obesity, strain injuries, and actual aggression toward others (Stanford & Williamson, 2005).

The debate around gaming and the impact on learning has been going long before the Internet came into play. While some educators indicate that games can be intrinsically motivating and increase enjoyment, attention, and learner satisfaction, others argue that such activities can distract learners from educational content and weaken learning (Asgari & Kaufman, 2004). It is often perceived that those against using games for learning purposes are generally digital immigrants who do not necessarily feel comfortable with technology or understand the pedagogical applications of gaming.

There are currently computer and virtual games for just about any theme. In 2004 there were 248 million games sold. Major companies continue to reinvent their gaming consoles and produce more intricate games. The majority of cyber educators today believe that games can be fun, engaging, and have a place in the learning environment (Van Eck, 2006). There are generally two classifications of games for learning: those that have been developed specifically for learning, and those that are available commercially off the shelf (COTS) brought into the traditional classroom.

One of the challenges of COTS is to align an engaging game with content. How the game is used in instruction, either pre-instructional, or as a post-instructional strategy, depends on the curriculum and on the game itself. According to Van Eck (2006) what is included in the game is important but what is not included in the game can be even more important. Some criticism revolves around the way games are used to maximize student responsibility. A disconnect occurs when the learner has to go out of the game environment back into the traditional classroom (Van Eck). If games are to be a more significant part of the learning experience, instructional ideas that require little preparation and virtually instant execution are essential. Educators must also feel confident in the use of the game and confident as a facilitator (Becker & Jacobsen, 2005).

Games have the potential to change the way we look at learning. Virtual games and simulations become part of the larger topic of online learning because they are ubiquitous to the Internet culture, and create opportunities for social and communication practices that develop identity and promote learning. The capacities for recreating real world scenarios as well as creating imaginary or fantasy worlds without the barriers of time and space provide endless possibilities to engage learners. Further investigations of MMOGs/MMORGs will help educators understand the impact these environments have on issues such as culture, community, participation, social interaction, identity and of course learning.

LOOKING AHEAD

Gaming technology has improved dramatically. Educators have learned to design and develop learner-centered environments using games, but have yet to maximize the potential benefits. The use of virtual gaming or gaming concepts in educational settings remains elusive. More research needs to be conducted to determine how improvements in technology might be incorporated into games for education. Current MMOGs/MMORGs also provide spaces for interactions and social relationships beyond the home or the office, but educational MMOGs/MMORGs require deeper personal connections grounded on research.

Now What?

1. The educational community must realize gaming and simulations are not a one size fits all solution to education, but just another delivery method.
2. The educational community must accept that the real challenge is not bringing gaming technologies into a traditional learning environment, but rather changing the culture and the mentality of educators to one that is learner-centric.
3. Educators should realize that the pedagogical approach used in games can provide ample opportunities for the participants to engage in lessons that are multidimensional, immersive, and support learning by allowing the learners to probe the rules of a system.
4. Games for learning must be designed as instructional content that is fun and intrinsically motivating yet challenging.
5. By including elements of curiosity and fantasy, games for learning promote critical thinking and authenticity as learners are immersed in learning paths with multiple possible outcomes that depend on the participant's actions. Constructive and encouraging feedback is clearly provided by the instructor.
6. The future of gaming and simulations for learning is promising; however, it will entail further exploration of effective application and evaluation practices.

Educators have begun to incorporate commercially available products into the classroom but this is not enough. Design experiments and the incorporation of instructional design theory have given some insight into learning using games. What has been missing is the development and implementation of a coherent research approach. The greatest benefit from research on games may not be to develop more theory on learning but to inspire more sophisticated design and guidelines for creating new instructional designs (Squire, 2003). Interactive games have the potential to produce insight into the understanding of online environments and communities, and the development of character in individuals engaged in the gaming experience. They also pose the potential to provide a wealth of knowledge about learner interfaces, aesthetics and interactivity. Cutting edge technology in video games and simulations has given us a peek at what can be accomplished for learning purposes.

Many lessons can be learned from MMOGs/MMORGs simulations, and video games. Although on the surface it would appear that these games are just about killing witches and dragons, it is really much more complex than that. Designers should focus on the brain processes that occur with each interaction, decision, and interplay made by players. The use of intelligent agents can facilitate collaboration and problem solving. Pedagogically speaking, there is undeniable value in providing instant feedback, which participants can use to rethink their strategies. Learning from mistakes then becomes a natural step in the learning cycle, moving the learner from the initial interaction to the creation of knowledge, followed by application of this new knowledge and finding out by trial and error if they were correct.

The instant feedback continuously shapes the learner's perceptions, strategies, and reinforces learning. In digitally mediated games this happens very quickly, as players are immersed in the environment and are challenged to form quick hypothesis and act upon them. Experts such as Prensky (2001; 2003) and others have discussed that digital natives learn differently. The speed at which the gaming generation makes inferences and predictions based on the immediate feedback provided by the technology, is possibly altering the way information is processed by the brain. Although much brain research has been conducted in the last decade, this possible influence should not be ignored and grants further exploration.

Games offer the opportunity to present knowledge in a variety of situations and then for the learner to apply that knowledge. The learner then receives immediate feedback by the technology, hence reinforcing desired concepts. By creating a complex environment where interactivity can altered to be immersive or non immersive, object or linear, and stimulate the learner in ways that traditional methods of study might not be able to achieve. Games support the combination or synthesis of knowledge, decision-making, teamwork, negotiation, and improved social skills. According to Squire (2005), current learning environments can achieve high levels of engagement to promote learning if certain changes are made. Changes would include:

- Organizing curriculum around driving questions of personal relevance and open ended intellectual curiosity.
- Providing opportunities for different learners based on individual interests, abilities and learning capabilities.
- Reorganization of school days and curriculum based on the learners life and needs.
- Expanding the learning experience beyond the classrooms to media, simulations and other activities and integrating formal and informal learning.
- Treating assessments and evaluations as opportunities to improve and support the learning.

Current MMOGs/MMORGs also provide opportunities for interactions and relationships that transcend the social realm but most of these relationships are likely to be superficial. Educational MMOGs/MMORGs however, can only be truly effective if deeper personal connections are created. At the heart of learning are positive relationships and interactions with peers as well as the instructor. The emotional bond from human to human is not likely to be replaced by intelligent agents, even with sophisticated artificial intelligence capabilities. In looking ahead, there will be more humanization of these agents, however, the affective domain will likely remain an innately human attribute.

As more programs go online, the opportunity exists to rethink and restructure the culture of the traditional classroom or training setting. Games provide opportunities to examine learning environments that have proved to be motivation and stimulating (Squire, 2005). In looking ahead, designers and cyber educators should understand the difference between traditional instructivist and constructivist learning theories. While instructivists focus on using games for learning, constructivists may be inclined to focus on designing games for learning purposes only (Kafai, 2006). Instead of creating lessons in the games, the constructivists may choose to provide learners with greater opportunities to construct their own games, which facilitate the construction of new relationships in the process. In instructional games a great deal of time and effort is spent on content, graphics, and instructional practices. In constructivist games the learner is involved in the different stages of development and may begin to acquire technological know-how (Kafai, 2006). This may reserve the greatest learning benefits for those that are engaged in the design process.

The evaluation of games and simulations for learning is another important aspect for cyber educators. Measuring learning outcomes of games and simulations can be challenging at best. While commercial success can be documented and so can intensity and longevity of engagement, solid information about the effectiveness of games to train individuals of teams in acquiring knowledge or skills is less forthcoming. Part of the challenge is the evaluation models for measuring training and learning. Another challenge is the terminology and definition of games, simulations and simulation games. The applications in education are not wide spread; therefore the challenge is greater in cyber education.

It is generally agreed that there is a lack of empirical research on the effectiveness of games for adult learners. It is also hypothesized that it is instructional design that is responsible for learning and not the game itself. Some evidence seems to suggest that it is the elements in the game and not the game as a whole that activates the learning process through sound instructional strategies (O'Neil, Wainess, & Baker, 2005). The same can be stated for simulations. Instructional support in the form of scaffolding and modeling, coupled with good instructional design will help achieve learning objectives. In order to measure the effectiveness of a game or simulation must take into account as many variables as possible.

The future of gaming and simulations for learning is promising, however, it will entail further exploration of effective application and evaluation practices. Although they should not be considered a one size fits all solution for learning, gaming strategies have much to offer. Engagement is key to motivation, which in turn influences learning. Cyber educators should capitalize on the inherent ability of MMOGs and other gaming environments and simulations to capture the learner's attention.

CONCLUSION

Games and simulations challenge players to explore and overcome increasingly complex problems. MMOGs/MMORGs and other types of gaming and simulations can be highly engaging and collaborative environments. Educators continue to learn about the possible applications of these environments for learning, but have yet to harness their benefits. Gaming habits and preferences involve individuals of all ages, genders, and cultural backgrounds thus the ability to reach a wide range of learners is evident.

Much research has been conducted on the use of games, yet there is not enough information on how to create them for educational purposes, especially MMOGs and MMORPGs. These types of environments can attract and hold the learner's attention through engaging interactions and experiences that are multi media and content rich. Well-constructed environments can move the learner through the different knowledge levels, from declarative knowledge to problem solving. Gaming provides opportunities for learning each time the learner interacts, forms a hypothesis, or makes a decision. These games provide for complex interactions, problem solving strategies to overcome obstacles, collaboration, making use of deduction, and creating a self-identity.

Participants are constantly seeking equilibrium between themselves and other agents or players in the environment. They dynamics of behavior reinforcement and interactions provide a cycle of constant feedback that helps the participant constantly readjust his strategies, thus learn from his mistakes. In some environments, the use of fantasy, curiosity, challenge, and control provide heightened levels of engagement. Fantasy can free the participant to take on alternate identities in scenarios that could be far from the real world yet allows the practice of real world skills that the learner will need. Curiosity is sustained by the continuous change of information and new undetermined events and outcomes, thus allowing the participant's imagination to shape goals and desires. Challenge is provided by including levels of difficulty and feedback, including multiple goals and activities. Control is established by giving the learner the opportunity to make choices that have consequences associated with them, and in some cases by involving the learner in the design process.

Learning options using multi-agent learning and newer theories such as Q-Learning and Hyper Q-Learning will demand higher levels of cognition for game and simulation participants. In designing such environments, designers and cyber educators must scaffold the instructional strategies and the content in ways that prevent cognitive overload. Cognitive overload would be counter productive. Simulations and strategy games created with constructivist principles will likely promote higher thinking skills but can also include drill and practice opportunities depending on the subject matter.

Current MMOGs/MMORGs designed for entertainment build social connections that have low levels of emotional ties. Games created for educational purposes however, should support interactions that promote social connections that use the affective domain to build deeper relationships between the community of learners, and the instructor. Even with the humanization of intelligent agents, the relationship between humans and role of such relationship in learning is undeniably powerful. Cyber educators and designers must also develop evaluation methods to not just measure learning outcomes, but also the effectiveness of the game itself.

Games and simulations for learning will continue to evolve and likely become more readily available in traditional classrooms as well as cyber education. The scope of current research is wide but not conclusive. A deeper understanding of the use of intelligent agents, community building, interaction, engagement, the role of fantasy and motivation, are all necessary in order to create effective MMOGs and simulations for learning purposes.

REFERENCES

Asgari, M., & Kaufman, D. (2004). Relationships among computer games, fantasy, and learning. *Proceedings from the Second International Conference on Imagination and Education, July 14-17, 2004*, Vancouver, British Columbia, Canada. Retrieved October 5, 2010, from http://www.ierg.net/confs/2004/Proceedings/Asgari_Kaufman.pdf

Becker, K. (2005). How are games educational? Learning theories embodied in games. *Proceedings from DiGRA 2005 Conference: Changing Views-Worlds in Play*. Vancouver, British Columbia, Canada. Retrieved October 5, 2010, from http://www.digra.org/dl/db/06278.23299.pdf

Becker, K., & Jacobsen, D. M. (2005). Games for learning: Are schools ready for what's to come? *Proceedings from DiGRA 2005 Conference: Changing Views-Worlds in Play*. Vancouver, British Columbia, Canada Retrieved October 27, 2010, from http://dspace.ucalgar.ca/bitstream/1880/46705/1/Games_for_Learning_2005.pdf

Camerer, C. F., Ho, T., & Chong, J. (2002). Sophisticated experience-weighted attraction learning and strategic teaching in repeated games. [from http://jet.arts.cornell.edu/Main.html]. *Journal of Economic Theory, 104*(1), 137–188. Retrieved October 23, 2010. doi:10.1006/jeth.2002.2927

Delwiche, A. (2006). Massively multiplayer online games (MMOs) in the new media classroom. *Educational Technology & Society, 9*(3), 160-172. Retrieved October 5, 2010, from http://www.ifets.info/journals/9_3/14.pdf

Dyck, J., Pinelle, D., Brown, B., & Gutwin, C. (2003). Learning from games: HCI design innovations in entertainment software. *Proceedings from the Graphics Interface Conference*, February 2003.

Facer, K. (2003). *Computer games and learning*. Retrieved October 5, 2010, from http://www.futurelab.org.uk/resources/dcouments/discussion_papers/Computer_Games_and_Learning_discpaper.pdf

Gagne, R. (1985). *The conditions of learning* (4th ed.). New York: Holt, Rinehart & Winston.

Gardner, H. (1993). *Frames of mind: The theory of multiple intelligences* (2nd ed.). New York: Basic Books.

Garris, R., Ahlers, R., & Driskell, J. E. (2002). Games, motivation and learning: A research and practice model. *Simulation & Gaming, 33*(4), 441–467. doi:10.1177/1046878102238607

Hu, J., & Wellman, M. P. (1998). Multiagent reinforcement learning: Theoretical framework and an algorithm. *Proceedings from the 15th International Conference on Machine Learning, Madison, WI*, Morgan Kaufmann, San Francisco, CA. (pp. 242–250).

Hu, J., & Wellman, M. P. (2003). Nash q-learning for general-sum stochastic games. *Journal of Machine Learning Research, 4*(6), 1039–1069. doi:10.1162/jmlr.2003.4.6.1039

Kafai, Y. B. (2006). Playing and making games for learning: Instructionist and constructivist perspectives for game studies. *Games and Culture, 1*(1), 36–40. doi:10.1177/1555412005281767

Kapp, K. (2007). *Gadgets, games and gizmos for learning*. San Francisco: Pfeiffer.

Kirriemuir, J. (2002). The relevance of video games and gaming consoles to higher and further education learning experience. Paper presented at JISC. Retrieved October 12, 2010, from http://www.jisc.ac.uk/uploaded_documents/tsw_02-01.rt

Kirriemuir, J., & McFarlane, A. (2003). *Use of computer and video games in the classroom.* Paper presented at Level Up: The Digital games research Conference, 4-6 November 2003 at the Utrecht University, The Netherlands. Retrieved October 5, 2010, from http://www.digra.org/dl/db/05150.28025.pdf

Nash, J. (1950). Equilibrium points in n-person games. *Proceedings of the National Academy of Sciences of the United States of America, 36*(1), 48–49. doi:10.1073/pnas.36.1.48

O'Neil, H., Wainess, R., & Baker, E. (2005). Classification of learning outcomes: Evidence from the computer games literature. *Circulation Journal, 16*(4), 455–474.

Panait, L., & Luke, S. (2005). Cooperative multi-agent learning: The state of the art. *Autonomous Agents and Multi-Agent Systems, 11*(3), 387–434. doi:10.1007/s10458-005-2631-2

Pivec, M., Dziabenko, O., & Schinnerl, I. (2003). Aspects of game-based learning. *Proceedings of I-Know '03.* Retrieved October 5, 2010, from http://ww.unigame.net/html/ I-Know_GBL-2704.pdf

Prensky, M. (2001). *Digital game-based learning.* New York: McGraw-Hill.

Prensky, M. (2003). Digital game-based learning. *ACM Computers in Entertainment, 1*(1), 2.

Sandholm, T. W., & Crites, R. H. (1996). On multi-agent Q-learning in a semi-competitive domain. In *Adaption and Learning in Multi-Agent Systems* (pp. 191–205). Berlin, Heidelberg: Springer.

Shaffer, D. W., Squire, K. R., Halverson, R., & Gee, J. P. (2004). *Video games and the future of learning.* White Paper written for University of Wisconsin-Madison and Academic Advanced Distributed Learning Co-Laboratory. Retrieved October 25, 2010, from http://www.academiccolab.org/resources/gappspaper1/pdf

Squire, K. (2003). Video games in education. *International Journal of Intelligent Simulations and Gaming, 2*(1). Retrieved July 21, 2010, from http://ijigs.scit.wlv.ac.uk/ijigs41.htm

Squire, K. (2005). Changing the game: What happens when video games enter the classroom? *Innovate Journal of Online Education, 6*(1). Retrieved October 5, 2010, from http://www.innovateonline.info/index.php?view=article&id=82

Squire, K. D., & Steinkuehler, C. A. (2006). Generating CyberCultures: The case of Star Wars galaxies. In Gibbs, D., & Krause, K. L. (Eds.), *Cyberlines 2.0 languages and cultures of the Internet.* Albert Park, Australia: James Nicholas Publishers.

Stanford, R., & Williamson, B. (2005). *Games and learning.* A Handbook from NESTA Futurelab. Retrieved October 5, 2010, from http://ict.aps.nl/ictatelier/leraren/artikelen/games_and_learning.pdf

Steinkuehler, C. A. (2004). Learning in massively multiplayer online games. In Y.B. Kafai, W.A. Sandoval, N. Enyedy, A.S. Nixon, & F. Herrera (Eds.), *Proceedings of the 6th International Conference of the Learning Sciences.* (pp.521-528). Mahwah, NJ: Erlbaum.

Steinkuehler, C. A. (2008). Cognition and literacy in massively multiplayer online games. In Coiro, J., Knobel, K., Lankshear, C., & Leu, D. (Eds.), *Handbook of research on new literacies* (pp. 611–634). Mahwah, NJ: Erlbaum.

Steinkuehler, C. A., & Williams, D. (2006). Where everybody knows your (screen) name: Online games as third places. *Journal of Computer-Mediated Communication, 11*(4). Retrieved October 25, 2010, from http://jcmc.indiana.edu/vol11/issue4/steinkuehler/html

Tesauro, G. (2003). Extending Q-learning to general adaptive multi-agent systems. *Advances in Neural Information Processing Systems,* 16. Retrieved October 31, 2010, from http://books.nips.cc/nips16.html

Van Eck, R. (2006, March/April). Digital game-based learning: It's not just the digital natives who are restless. [from http://www.educause.edu]. *EDUCAUSE Review, 41*(2), 16–30. Retrieved October 12, 2010.

Winkler, R. L. (2003). *Introduction to Bayesian inference and decision* (2nd ed.). Sugarland, TX: Probabilistic Publishing.

About the Contributors

Bobbe Baggio is an accomplished author, speaker and educator. Her specific expertise is in how people learn and how to use technologies to help them learn. Her company, Advantage Learning Technologies, Inc. (ALT), has provided ID services and implemented projects for clients in finance, healthcare, gasses and chemicals, manufacturing, distribution, construction, government, and higher education. A more detailed list of clients can be found on her Web site at http://www.bobbebaggio.com. Bobbe provides programs and products so that people who are trying to use technology for teaching and learning can do so effectively. She is currently the Director of the Graduate Program in Instructional Technology Management at La Salle University in Philadelphia, PA and speaks regularly to organizations and companies around the globe. Her latest books include *The Visual Connection: You Listen with Your Eyes* and *The Pajama Effect*. Bobbe's prior experience includes being a Senior Scientist, Management Consultant, Director of IT, and Director of Software Development. Her education includes a BA from Waynesburg College, MA from West Virginia University, MS from Lehigh University and PhD from Capella University.

Yoany Beldarrain is an international speaker, accomplished author, consultant, and cyber educator with over 18 years of experience in K-12 and adult curriculum and instruction, instructional design, online teaching, as well as administrative educational leadership and faculty training. Her experiences include instructional design and evaluation of online learning initiatives, evaluation and assessment of staff, evaluation and assessment of educational and training programs, and integrating multicultural approaches in the decision-making process. Dr. Beldarrain is multi-cultural and multi-lingual, and believes in the power of cross-cultural collaboration through digitally mediated communications to meet the needs of the global marketplace. She is particularly interested in using technology tools to enhance interaction in online courses and deliver instructional strategies in engaging ways. Manuscripts by Dr. Beldarrain include *The Pajama Effect*, with co-author Dr. Bobbe Baggio. She continues to teach graduate level courses, present regularly at international distance learning conferences, conduct research, and provide international consulting services to educational institutions as well as the corporate sector. Dr. Beldarrain completed a PhD in Instructional Design for Online Learning from Capella University, MS in Educational Leadership from Nova Southeastern University, and a BS in Elementary Education from Florida International University.

Index